LANCHESTER LIBRARY
D0480467

A NORTON PROFESSIONAL BOOK

Principles of

Three-Dimensional Computer Animation

Principles of Three-Dimensional Computer Animation

Modeling, Rendering, and Animating with 3D Computer Graphics

REVISED EDITION

Michael O'Rourke

W. W. Norton & Company
New York • London

This book is dedicated to my students at Pratt Institute. Their talent, energy, and good spirits have been an inspiration.

Printed in the United States of America

For information about permission to reproduce selections from this book, write to Permissions, W. W. Norton & Company, Inc., 500 Fifth Avenue, New York, NY 10110.

The text of this book is composed in Berkeley Book
with the display set in Gill Sans.
Manufacturing by Edwards Brothers Inc.
Four-color insert printed by Brady Palmer Printing Co.
Book design and composition by Ken Gross
Jacket illustration by Marcus Meyer and Michael O'Rourke

Library of Congress Cataloging-in-Publication Data

O'Rourke, Michael.
Principles of three-dimensional computer animation : modeling, rendering, and animating with 3D computer graphics / Michael O'Rourke. — Rev. ed.
p. c.m.
"A Norton professional book."
Includes index.
ISBN 0-393-73024-7
1. Computer animation. 2. Three-dimensional display systems. 3. Computer graphics. I. Title.
TR897.7.076 1998 98-4553
006.6'96—dc21 CIP

ISBN 0-393-73024-7

W. W. Norton & Company, Inc., 500 Fifth Avenue, New York, NY 10110
http://www.wwnorton.com
W. W. Norton & Company Ltd., 10 Coptic Street, London WC1A 1PU

0 9 8 7 6 5 4 3 2 1

Preface

This book is intended for people who work with, or who wish to work with, 3D computer animation. It does not assume any prior knowledge of 3D computer graphics. It does not assume, nor does it present, any of the mathematics or program code that underlie computer graphics. And finally, it does not assume a prior knowledge of animation itself.

Since the book assumes no prior knowledge of the field, it is suitable for students in the process of learning 3D computer modeling, rendering, or animation. At the same time, since the book is very thorough and covers a wide range of topics, including many advanced topics, it is suitable for students who have acquired substantial experience and wish to enhance their understanding of the field.

In addition to students, the book is appropriate for working professionals who want to gain a more thorough and systematic understanding of the underlying principles of 3D computer animation. Animators who have worked with traditional animation techniques, art directors who need to understand their animators, industrial and interior designers and architects who may be involved in projects that entail 3D computer animation—any professional with an interest in or a need to understand how this technology works—will find the book valuable.

The book is not, however, a software guide. It makes no attempt to deal with specific software packages. Its subject matter is the general principles common to all 3D computer animation systems, not the implementation of those principles by one software vendor.

It is, nonetheless, a technical book, in that it deals with the *technical* principles of 3D computer animation. These are substantial, and they are also constantly expanding. It is always the case in 3D computer graphics that researchers in laboratories around the world are developing interesting experimental techniques well before these innovations are available in off-the-shelf software packages. This book does not attempt to deal with experimental techniques in early stages of development, but is limited to those techniques found in commercially available software packages.

Finally, I should emphasize that I have made every attempt to illustrate the topics being discussed with numerous drawings, diagrams, and renderings. Animation is a visual art, and I imagine that the readers of this book are visual people, for whom pictures will be worth even more words than usual.

Acknowledgments

I would like to thank first all the people from Pratt Institute who helped me while I was working on this book. Some of them helped directly; some helped simply by being friends and keeping me sane. Without their and Pratt's support, this book would not have come into being. Thank you, Rick Barry, Jeremy Gardiner, Sheba Grossman, Maureen Jones, Isaac Kerlow, Lynn Pocock, Sonya Shannon, and others too numerous to name. Thanks also to the following people, who provided invaluable help with the production of the illustrations: Iris Benado, Chuen Choi, Galen Chu, Jia-Ming Day, Sunmi Kang, Claude Policart, and Chris Shafer.

I also would like to thank all the tremendously talented people at the former New York Institute of Technology Computer Graphics Lab. It was they who taught me computer graphics. Special thanks to Ned Greene, Pat Hanrahan, Peter Oppenheimer, Robert McDermott, Fred Parke, John Schlag, Louis Schure, Jacques Stroweis, David Sturman, Steve Uzzo, Susan Van Baerle, and Lance Williams.

And finally, I would like to thank the people at the University of Pennsylvania who, years ago, helped me so much in my first fumbling attempts to learn this new technology. Thank you, especially, Norm Badler, Dave Bourne, Stan Cohen, and my brother, Joe O'Rourke.

Contents

Introduction

Animation has been around since before the turn of the century, and since then has undergone a tremendous evolution, both technically and artistically. The most recent upheaval in the world of animation has been the development of computer-generated animation. The impact of computer animation, however, goes well beyond what you normally think of as animation, since computer animation techniques also are used to produce special effects that fit seamlessly into live-action films. Computer-generated animation is changing the face of animation and of cinema in general, and 3D computer animation is among the most sophisticated and stunning of the computer techniques being used to do this.

All moving imagery, whether on film or on video, involves a sequence of still images played back quickly enough for your eye to see them as continuous. When these still images are produced individually, one by one, the process is known as **animation**. The word "animate" means "to give life to." The animator "gives life to" still images.

Animation first appeared in a rudimentary form in the mid-nineteenth century. On one of the first devices for animating still images, the Zoetrope, individual images were placed around the perimeter of a wheel. When the wheel was spun, the viewer looked through a fixed slot at the front of the wheel and saw, in quick succession, each image pass by. If the wheel was spun fast enough, the viewer's eye fused the still images together and saw the sequence as a moving image.

With the advent of film at the turn of the century, animation took a great leap forward. Now individual images, or frames, could be produced and played back with the sophisticated technology being used so successfully for live-action cinema. The wonder of this new technology, which made pictures move, was not lost on people. Whether involving live-action frames or animated frames, the cinema became known by the magical term "the movies."

Animators developed a number of techniques for generating individual frames. The most basic technique, of course, was to draw, and then photograph, each frame one by one. The early animations of Winsor McKay's Gertie the Dinosaur were done in this way and remain, in spite of their relative technical simplicity, delightful.

Walt Disney and the people he gathered around him in the 1930s and 40s took this hand-drawn approach and developed it into a stunningly sophisticated art form. One of the major technical advances made in this period was the use of transparent sheets, called **cels**, onto which were painted different layers of a scene. One cel might contain a stationary background, for example. A second cel might contain only the character intended to move in front of that background. The entire frame was composed by placing the two transparent cels on top of each other and photographing them. This technique became known as **cel animation**. The economies of labor that cel animation permitted were an important factor in making full-length animated films possible.

Other animation techniques developed as well. **Stop-action animation** involves using physical models, positioning them for each frame of the film, photographing them, and then repeating the whole process for the next frame. One of the early geniuses of this technique was Willis O'Brien. One of his earliest successes, *King Kong*, with its unforgettable image of Kong swinging from the Empire State Building and swiping at airplanes, made stop-action animation a standard of the monster-movie genre.

These and other techniques were used by animators with increasing effectiveness over the years to produce films that were purely animations as well as animated segments that were combined with live-action footage. They were used to produce endearing films for children and (most notably outside of the United States) serious films for adults.

In the early 1970s, the first efforts were made to use computers to help produce animation. Much of this initial experimentation was done at the New York Institute of Technology. The first program developed there focused on two-dimensional animation and enabled the animator to produce automatically what are called the "in-between" frames. In traditional animation, it is common for a more experienced, or master, animator to draw the most critical frames of the animation. These are called the "key" frames. The frames that fall between keyframes are called "in-betweens" and normally are drawn by less experienced assistants. The first computer animation programs mimicked this process, substituting the computer for the assistants.

The next step in the development of computer animation entailed applying this same principle—the automatic production of in-between frames—to three-dimensional animation. Once again, the pioneering groundwork was done at the New York Institute of Technology. Programs were developed that allowed the animator to position a three-dimensionally defined computer model in a series of key positions. The computer then automatically generated the in-between positions and rendered each position as a frame of animation.

The last ten years have seen an explosive growth in the sophistication of computer animation techniques, and especially of three-dimensional computer animation techniques. Today, three-dimensional computer animation is no longer limited to mimicking the techniques of traditional cel animation. Exciting techniques have been developed that move far away from the keyframe/in-between frame concept of traditional animation, and many software packages include techniques that only the computer could have produced, such as procedural animation, motion dynamics, and motion capture.

The increasing sophistication of computer animation also recently has made it possible to integrate animated three-dimensional imagery with live-action imagery in a seamless way. Herds of computer-generated dinosaurs run with human actors. Contemporary actors talk to and interact with historical figures who exist only on old film footage. Spaceships pass through computer-animated wormholes into other sectors of the universe.

The applications of 3D computer animation are not limited to big-budget films, however. An increasing number of commercial spots on television are produced with 3D computer animation. Almost all station-ID and company-logo spots on television are produced with 3D computer animation. Architects, designers, medical doctors, and sculptors all make use of 3D computer animation in their professions.

The techniques and principles of this technology are the subject of this book, and all of the material here is relevant for anyone interested in 3D computer animation, regardless of the specific software package and specific hardware you may be using. Whether you are working (or expecting to work) with a UNIX-based system on a high-end workstation, for example, or with the less expensive DOS- and Macintosh-based systems, the same principles of 3D computer animation apply.

I have organized the material in this book in such a way as to make it easily accessible, even if you consider yourself nontechnical. When a technical term is used for the first time, it is printed in boldface. Alternate terms are frequently provided, since different software packages may use different terminology to refer to the same concept. The principles of 3D computer animation are presented in a step-by-step fashion, with each section building on previous sections. Because of this organization, if you have experience in an area you may find that you can comfortably skip or skim certain sections. If you are a novice, you probably will want to read, in the order presented, each section in detail.

Even though the word "animation" occurs in only two of the chapter titles, the entire book deals with animation. In actual practice, it is impossible to separate "modeling" from "rendering," or either of those procedures from "animation." The process of producing 3D computer animation involves all of these activities, and separating them into individual chapters is a matter of conceptual convenience.

The first chapter, "Modeling," is devoted to the process of "building" the forms that will be animated. I have kept as separate as possible from this material any discussion of how the forms are colored or textured or how they move. In some situations, however, these issues can have a very direct and obvious impact on the modeling process, and I have pointed out those cases.

The second chapter, "Rendering," deals with the process of defining how the final picture of the model will look. This involves the surface properties of the model, the lighting of the scene, and the use of the virtual "camera" that is part of 3D computer graphics.

The third and fourth chapters deal with animation techniques directly. I have divided these discussions into "Animation" and "Advanced Animation Techniques." The former consists of those techniques found in all 3D computer animation systems. The "advanced" techniques are more recent and therefore found (currently) only in higher-end, more expensive software packages.

The next chapter is devoted to "Compositing and Special Effects" techniques. This vast topic easily could take up an entire book. What I have included here is a very brief introduction to some techniques as they apply specifically to 3D animation. Used for combining elements of an image or sequences of images, these techniques, when developed to a very high level of sophistication, permit the fusion of computer-generated imagery and live-action imagery seen in so many films today.

The sixth chapter, "Recording," is devoted to the principles and techniques involved in putting animation frames onto either film or video. Once again, this is a complicated topic, and what I have presented here is of an introductory nature. Most of this chapter is devoted to video recording, since most computer animation is recorded directly to video.

The final chapter deals with some production-related issues, including storyboarding, sound design and production planning. It is my hope that this organization makes the material clear and a pleasure to follow. The approach presented here should allow you to understand the complexities and subtleties of 3D animation easily, to delight in them, and quickly to use them to produce your own 3D computer animations.

CHAPTER 1

Modeling

Introduction

As soon as you start to think about animating in a three-dimensional space, you by necessity also are thinking about three-dimensional objects in that space. Even if you think simply of rotating a perfectly flat disk in space, that disk has a back side. In other words, it is three-dimensional. In short, if you want to animate things three-dimensionally, you must create, or "model," them three-dimensionally as well.

The very concept of "modeling" something within a computer may be confusing. You usually think of a model as something real, physical and tangible. In working with the computer, however, the models you develop have no physicality. You model an object in the computer in the sense that you *define* it. If you define the object thoroughly enough that the computer can display it on the screen from any number of points of view, then you have developed a workable **model** of the object. In this sense, you use the word "model" in computer graphics in the same way scientists use it when they speak of developing a "model" for the interaction of weather fronts, or a "model" of the behavior of a particle in a magnetic field. Their model is a description of a situation. The computer graphics model of a three-dimensional object is also a description, or a definition, of that object. In most computer graphics animation, you define an object in terms of its shape, or form, using either of two approaches.

Imagine that you are holding a brass sphere in your hand. One possibility (Figure 1-1a) is that the sphere is hollow—that it consists of a thin brass surface with empty space inside. If you were to cut such a sphere in half, you would get two brass bowls, into which you could place things. This approach to modeling is called **surface modeling.** In surface modeling, the surfaces that enclose an object define the shape of that object.

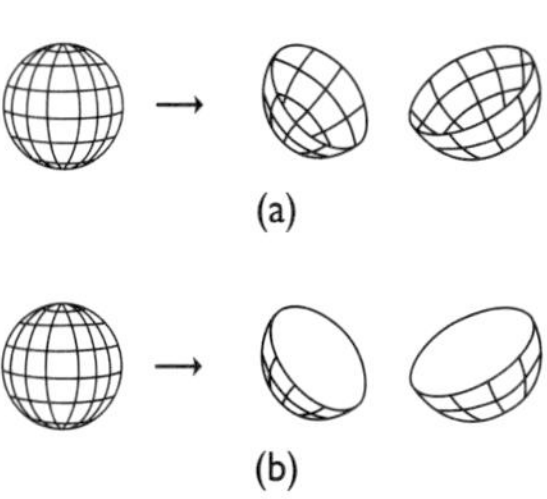

Figure 1-1. A sphere modeled with a surface modeler (a), and with a solid modeler (b).

On the other hand, the brass sphere could have been fabricated as a solid lump of brass (Figure 1-1b). If you cut this version of the sphere in half, there would be no hollows into which you could place anything. You would have two hemispherical solids. This approach to modeling is called **solid modeling**. In solid modeling, an object is defined as a solid mass—often with density, weight, and other attributes of a solid defined as well.

The distinction between surface modeling and solid modeling is important because the two approaches demand very different things of the animator and produce very different kinds of information. Depending on what you want to accomplish, one or the other might be more appropriate for your application. In many engineering applications, for example, solid modelers are used, because that approach makes certain sorts of information about the physical properties (density, mass, inertia, etc.) more readily available to the engineer.

In the great majority of animation applications, however, this kind of information is not needed and the computationally simpler approach of surface modeling is more appropriate. For this reason, in this book you will encounter surface-modeling techniques, with only an occasional reference to solid-modeling techniques when a comparison between the two approaches is helpful.

In addition, in chapter 4 you will encounter another approach, called **particle-system modeling**. This approach attempts to deal with such ephemeral phenomena as fire, clouds, and mist, which are composed of neither surfaces nor solid volumes and which do not have a stable "shape" in the same way that a chair has a stable shape. Such phenomena cannot be modeled readily with either a surface modeler or a solid modeler.

Before beginning the discussion of modeling techniques, however, bear in mind the following caveat about the order in which material will be presented here. Sometimes people working with three-dimensional computer animation think of the production process in a "first the modeling, then the animation" way. This seems to make sense from a conceptual point of view, since, as mentioned at the outset, you cannot animate three-dimensionally without some sort of three-dimensional model to animate. While this makes sense conceptually, however, it does not make good sense in practice. Many bad pieces of computer animation have been produced by adhering to a "first the modeling, then the animation" approach. The essence of animation is *movement*, and the person who relegates the animation to a secondary position "after the modeling is finished" risks ending up with a clumsy piece of animation.

In producing animation, the animation and the modeling must develop simultaneously. When you start working on an animation, there is no way of knowing with 100 percent certainty what the animation is going to look like. Consequently, there is no way of knowing exactly what the models should look like. The animation will be influenced by the way the objects are modeled, and the modeling of the objects will be influenced by the demands of the animation.

Nonetheless, I begin with modeling because conceptually it *is* a convenient place to start. Be aware, however, that when you actually make animation, you will not be able to proceed in the conveniently logical order in which material appears in this book.

Polygonal Modeling

When you use any modeling system, it is important to understand the concepts underlying the techniques. When you work with surface-modeling techniques, as you will in this book, understanding the basic concepts means understanding the geometric orientation of all 3D computer graphics systems. Computers are very good at manipulating numbers and quantifiable entities but very bad at dealing with subjective concepts. A computer would have a very difficult time, for example, following your instructions if you told it to make a shape "voluptuous," or to make it "more petal-like." It could easily follow your instructions, however, if you told it to make the shape "twice as long." Because of this, 3D modeling programs are based on numerically quantifiable and manipulable concepts of shape. They are based, in other words, on **geometry**, the mathematical study of shapes.

Telling the computer to make an object "twice as long" is, of course, an extremely simple example. If all you could do to models was make them twice as long, or other equally simple operations, computer graphics modeling would not be of much use. In fact, the techniques of 3D computer modeling are extremely numerous and extremely powerful. All of these techniques remain grounded on geometric principles and concepts.

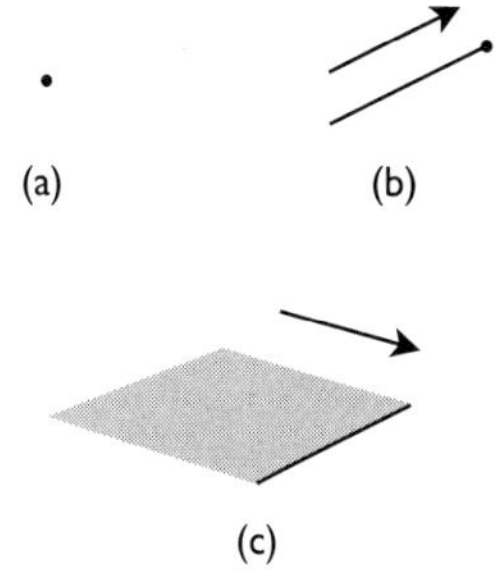

Figure 1-2. A zero-dimensional point, a one-dimensional line, and a two-dimensional plane.

One basic concept that is involved in all computer graphics modeling is that of a **point**, which is a location in space (Figure 1-2a). Imagine pointing with your finger to indicate that you want something placed "right there." The "right there" that you have indicated ("pointed" to) is a location, or point, in space. It is not a *thing*. It has no size or dimension. In fact, you can say that it is zero-dimensional—it has no width, no height, and no depth.

If you now move that point in exactly one direction (Figure 1-2b), the trace that you produce is a simple straight **line**. Depending on how far you move your original point, the line will be longer or shorter. A line, in other words, does have dimension. It has length. Notice, however, that it has only one dimension. It has no thickness at all (that is, no width or depth), since you produced it by starting with a dimensionless point and moving that point some distance.

Just as you moved a point to produce a line, you can produce the next basic geometric entity in a similar way. Given that you now have a straight, one-dimensional line, you can move that line in any one direction (Figure 1-2c). The trace produced by doing this is called a **plane**, which is simply a flat surface. (Strictly speaking, a plane is not a "surface" in the finite, measurable sense of that term, since a plane continues infinitely in two directions. Nonetheless, this definition is consistent with common usage.) Notice that a

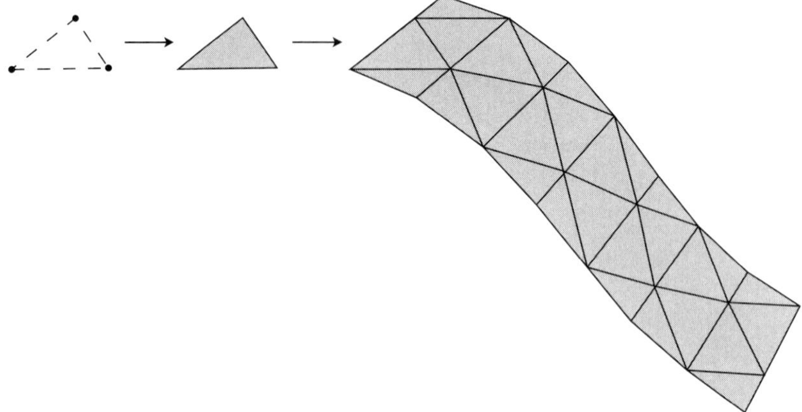

Figure 1-3. Three points define the corners of a triangular plane. Such planes can be combined to form a surface.

plane has two dimensions: the length of the original line, and now the width, or the amount you moved that line in the new direction.

Now imagine that you locate three points in space and consider them to be the endpoints of three straight lines, each of which touches the other. These lines define a triangle (Figure 1-3). When points in space define a figure such as this, each point is also called a **vertex**, while several of them are called **vertices**. If, instead of thinking of the lines you just defined as infinitely thin lines hanging in space, you think of them as the edges of a triangular surface, you have defined a flat triangular plane in three-dimensional space.

Using the same approach and the same three basic elements, you can form many other triangles, each connected to the other, and all at various angles in space. Where you decide to place your points, or vertices, in space determines where the lines are formed and consequently where the planes derived from those lines are formed. Using this approach, you can form any number of differently shaped surfaces (see Figure 1-3). You can then combine surfaces constructed in this way to form "objects."

In the example just given, all the planes defined were triangular planes. There is no reason, however, why a planar surface must be triangular, though there is an advantage to using triangles as your planes. That is, any number of points can define a flat planar surface, but three points in space always define a plane. More than three points may or may not, since one or more of them might not lie in the same plane. For example, if you place three points on the surface of a table, and a fourth point suspended above the table, these four points do not describe a perfectly flat surface.

The two objects in Figure 1-4 are composed of planar surfaces defined by different numbers of vertices. Any flat planar surface composed in this way can also be called a **polygon**. (The word comes from the Greek and means "many-sided.") The type of three-dimensional modeling that defines surfaces as consisting of flat polygons is therefore called **polygonal modeling**.

The two examples of polygonal modeling in Figure 1-4 have obviously and deliberately flat surfaces. Many objects, however, have surfaces that are curved—for example, the branch of a tree or an automobile tire. In spite of the fact that the individual polygons of polygonal modeling are flat, polygonal modeling can be used effectively for modeling curved surfaces such as these. The technique, called **polygonal approximation**, that accomplishes this uses large numbers of very small polygons to approximate the curvature of the surface (Figure 1-5).

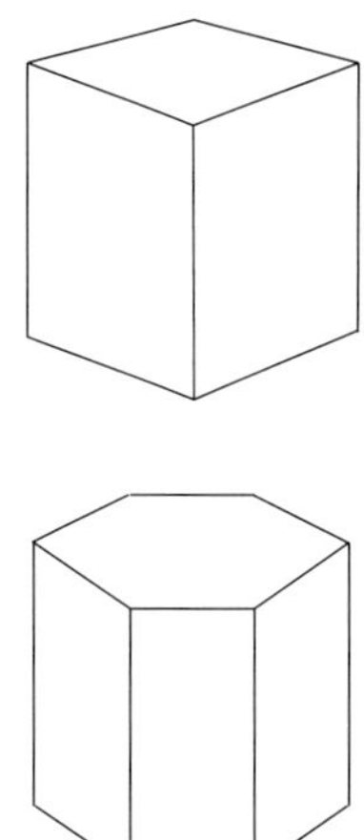

Figure 1-4. Two objects defined by flat planar surfaces composed of varying numbers of points.

Here the polygonal approximation technique has been used to model three different versions of a cylinder. In Figure 1-5a, where only six polygons approximate the curvature of the cylinder, you get a very rough approximation of a cylinder. This, in fact, looks more like the crystalline structure in Figure 1-4 than like a true cylinder. If you double the number of flat, planar polygons going around the side of the cylinder, as in Figure 1-5b, however, the cylinder begins to look more reasonable. And if you double them yet again, as in Figure 1-5c, the cylinder looks quite smooth.

You must understand, however, that polygonally approximating a curved surface will never yield a *truly* curved surface. No matter how many polygons you use and no matter how close the approximation, the surface is really and always a faceted surface composed of flat polygons. In many applications, this is not a problem, especially if you view the object from far enough away that the edges of the polygons are not discernible. If you move in close enough, however, any polygonally approximated curved surface, no matter how close the approximation, will reveal the flat polygons of which it is composed.

For complex objects, it is sometimes necessary to use a great many polygons to achieve a good approximation of the curved surfaces. Models with a lot of polygons are said to have a high **polygon count**. Since the polygon count, or total number of polygons, directly affects the speed with which a computer can process a model, it is usually desirable to keep the polygon count as low as possible. This is especially true in the game industry, where **real-time interaction**—that is, the ability to manipulate the screen image without any visible time delay—is critical. One way of achieving a low polygon count is through **polygon reduction**. This technique, also known sometimes as **polygon thinning** or **polygon culling**, reduces the total number of polygons of a model while retaining as closely as possible the model's original shape. One way to accomplish this is to specify the maximum polygon count of the new, thinned, model. For example, a model that originally had 3,460 polygons might be reduced to only 1,000 polygons, or perhaps to 500 polygons.

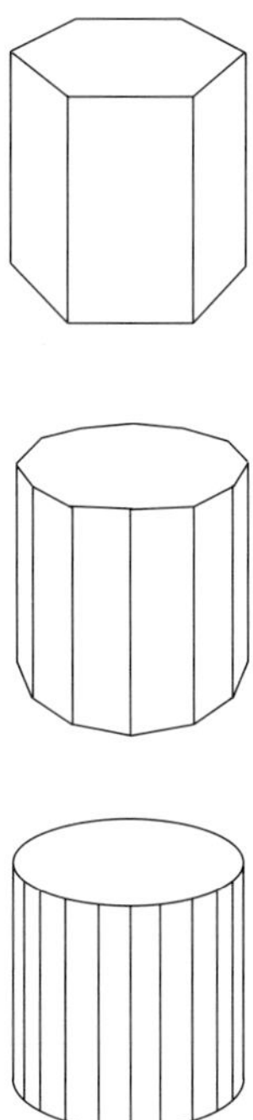

Figure 1-5. A cylinder modeled with three different resolutions of polygonal approximation.

Another way to reduce the polygon count is to specify the minimum angle allowed between polygons. If adjacent polygons have nearly the same orientation, they can be reduced to a single polygon without significantly altering

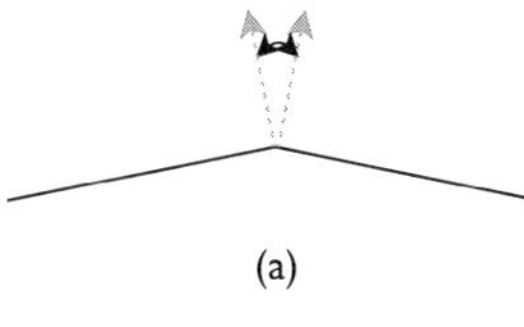

(a)

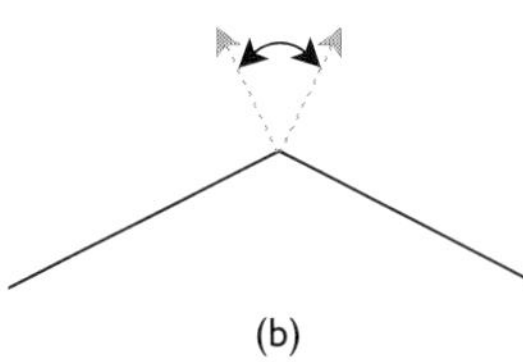

(b)

Figure 1-6. If adjacent polygons have a small dihedral angle, they can be reduced to a single polygon without significantly changing the shape of the model.

the shape of the model. If their orientation differs greatly, however, reducing them to a single polygon will not preserve the essential shape of the model (Figure 1-6). The relative orientations of the adjacent polygons is measured by the **dihedral angle**, which is the angle between lines coming perpendicularly off each polygon at the shared vertex. In Figure 1-6a, the two polygons (seen here from the side) have a very small dihedral angle between them, and can be reduced to a single polygon without significantly changing the shape of the model. In Figure 1-6b, however, the two polygons have a larger dihedral angle. Reducing them to a single polygon would substantially change the shape of the model.

Figure 1-7 shows an example of polygon reduction. Here, the original model, Figure 1-7a, has 8,000 polygons. Specifying a minimum dihedral angle of 5 degrees results in reducing the total number of polygons to 2,755 (Figure 1-7b).

The opposite of polygon reduction is **polygon expansion**, which retains the shape of the model while increasing the total number of polygons. Related to polygon expansion is **polygon rounding**, which smooths, or rounds, the sharpest angles of a polygonal model by adding polygons in those areas. Applying successive polygon rounding operations to a cube, for example, gradually changes the cube into a spherelike object (Figure 1-8a, b, c). Like polygon reduction, polygon expansion and polygon rounding usually require that you specify either some maximum total number of polygons for the new model or a minimum dihedral angle between adjacent polygons.

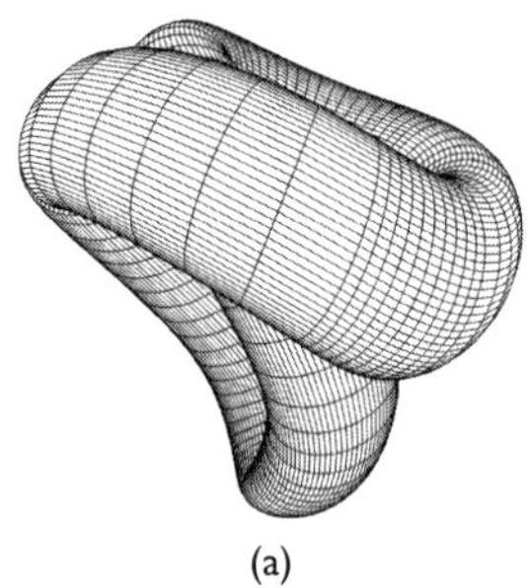

(a)

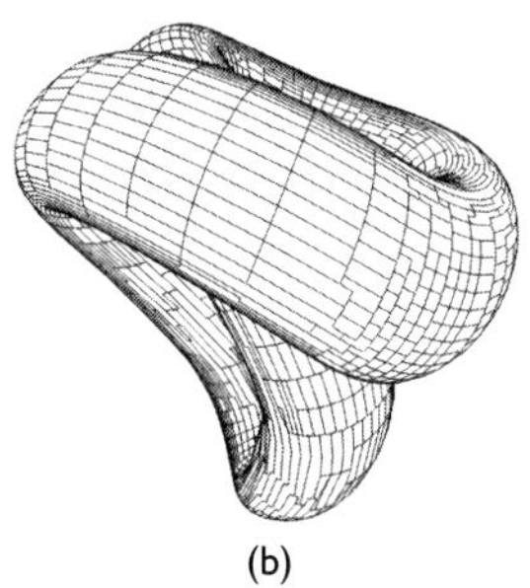

(b)

Figure 1-7. Polygon reduction decreases the total number of polygons while trying to retain the model's original shape.

The polygon reduction, expansion and rounding techniques all operate **globally** on the model. That is, whatever they do, they do to the entire surface of the model. Frequently, however, it is preferable to operate **locally**, restricting polygon expansion or reduction only to specific areas of the model. For example, in the human face model in Figure 1-9 a great deal of polygon data is needed in the areas of the eyes and mouth in order to create the facial expressions of the model. The additional polygons in these areas were created by **vertex** and **edge insertion**—adding vertices by clicking with the mouse to indicate where each new vertex should be. Once new vertices have been created, edges between them are created by clicking on the vertices that are to serve as the endpoints of the new edge. Since polygons are defined by their edges, creating new edges creates new polygons. All of the additional polygons in Figure 1-9 were created in this way. In fact, the model in this illustration began as a simple polygonal sphere! The artist created a very sophisticated head model by carefully adding vertices and edges and repositioning them. The holes for the eyes and mouth were created with the analogous techniques of **vertex** and **edge deletion**, by clicking and deleting vertices and edges one by one. Several shaded renderings

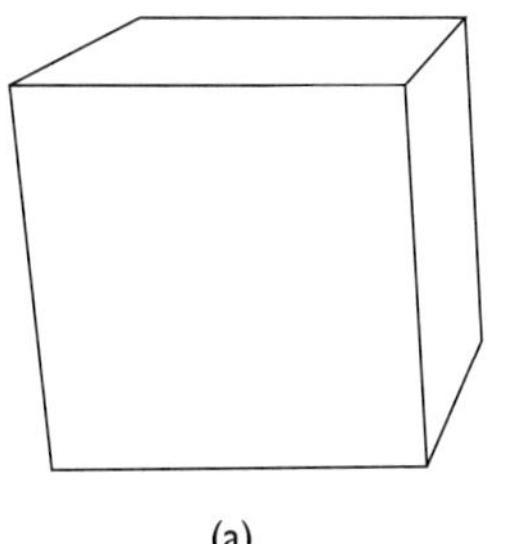

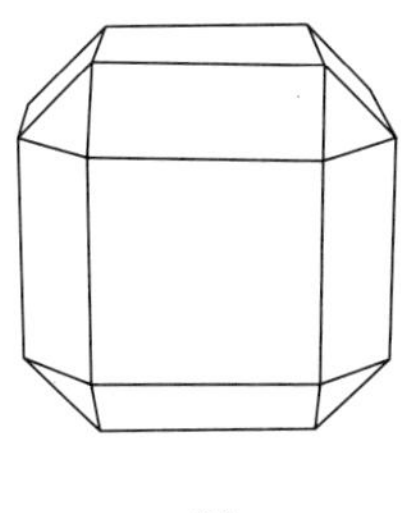

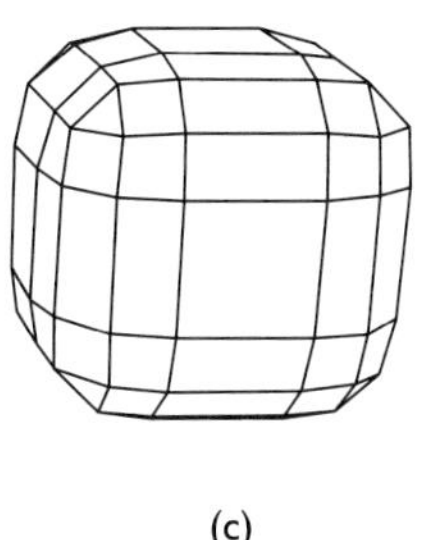

Figure 1-8. Polygon rounding collapses the sharp corners of a model to produce a smoother, rounder version.

of this head model, animated to produce different facial expressions, can be seen in color plate 12.

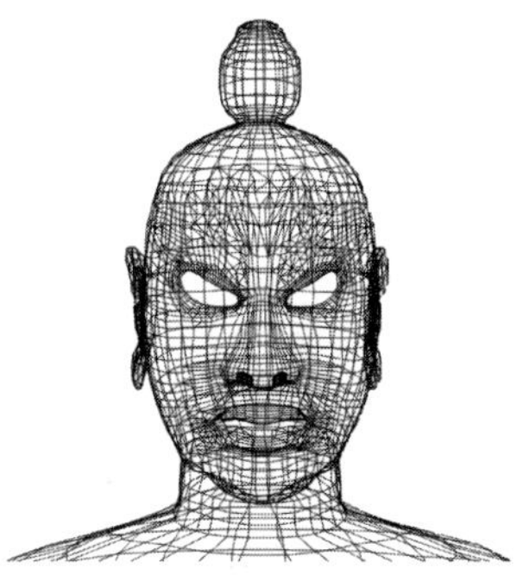

Figure 1-9. Polygons can be added or deleted locally by inserting or deleting individual vertices and edges. (Courtesy, Yukito Kurita)

The polygon modeling techniques just described are very powerful, but can produce large quantities of vertex data. Various data structures are commonly used to organize this data; knowing the strengths and limitations of these data structures can be very helpful to the artist who works with them. One approach to organizing the data of a polygonal model is to define the model as a **mesh**, or grid, of polygons. A sheet of graph paper is a good example of a mesh. The entire sheet of paper would correspond to a modeled surface. Each square of the sheet would correspond to a square polygon on that surface, and each corner of each square would correspond to a polygon vertex.

In computer modeling, however, the concept of a polygon mesh is more flexible than this. The polygons need not be square. The vertices of polygons can be moved in any direction to produce differently shaped and sized polygons. The crucial characteristic of a polygon mesh, however, is that all of the polygons must remain connected. Since all of the polygons are connected, you can think of mesh as consisting of **rows** and **columns** of polygons. This proves very convenient organizationally. Describing a mesh as, for example, a 100 × 200 mesh, immediately gives you a sense of how much data is involved. (From a computer programmer's point of view, the row-and-column organization of meshes is also extremely important. Two simple loop structures, one within the other, permit a computer program to access all the vertices of the mesh, no matter how large the mesh may be.)

The neat organization of vertices into rows and columns within the mesh structure, however, can be limiting. In order to maintain the structure, all rows must have the same number of points. The same is true of the columns. This organization restricts the **topology** of the surface. Think of topology as the structure of a surface, rather than the shape. If you pull the vertices of a mesh this way and that way, you change the shape of the surface, but not the structure. In this case, you change the geometry of the object, but not the topology. If, however, you delete a vertex from this structure, you change the topology of the surface. Deleting a vertex from a mesh changes the row/column topology, and the structure is no longer a mesh, properly speaking.

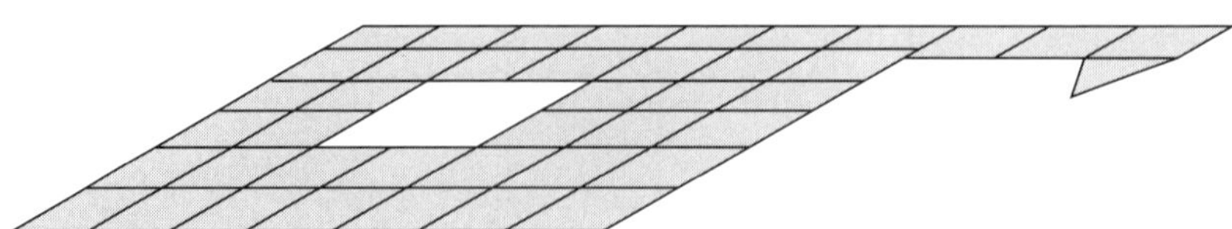

Figure 1-10. A polygonal surface with an irregular structure (topology) of vertices.

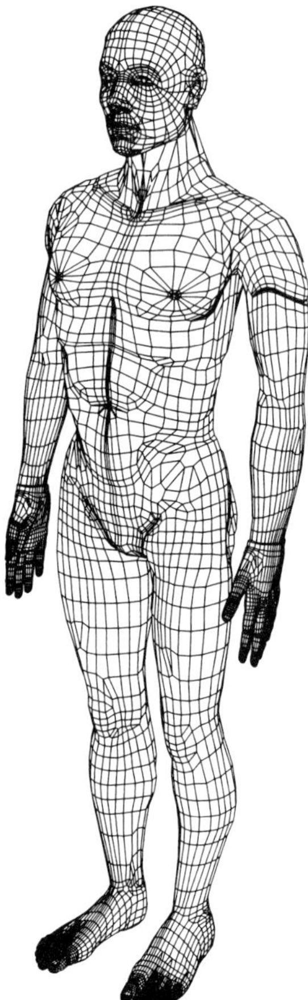

Figure 1-11. A complex model illustrating the subtlety possible with polygonal modeling. (Courtesy, Viewpoint DataLabs.)

One of the great strengths of polygonal modeling, however, is that you can build models with very irregular topologies. The mesh is very convenient, but it is not the only way to organize polygonal data. It is also possible simply to have a list of points, with information about which points connect to which other points. This is sometimes referred to as a **point list**. Using this organization, you can create any number of topologies. It is very easy, for example, to create a surface with a hole in it, as well as an extension branching off from one part of it (Figure 1-10). This structure would not lend itself to a mesh organization, but it easily could be defined as a point list. Deleting a vertex from the surface in Figure 1-10 would still change the topology of the surface, but doing so would be acceptable for this sort of polygonal model. This flexibility is one of the great strengths of polygonal modeling.

Fortunately, questions of how best to organize the data of a polygonal model are handled transparently by any good 3D software package. However, knowing what the implications of these organizational techniques are can be very helpful. With an understanding of the underlying techniques and either a skilled eye or a 3D digitizing device (see the section on *Digitizing Techniques* later in this chapter), you can produce models of great sophistication and subtlety (Figure 1-11).

In addition to the accuracy of the modeling, note the following two technical issues in Figure 1-11. First, the topology of this model is extremely irregular. The topological flexibility of polygonal modeling is crucial in this respect. Second, in those areas of the model where the curvature of the surface changes rapidly—for example, in the area around the eyes—the polygons both decrease in size and increase in number. This permits a more accurate approximation of the surface in those areas where it is needed. By contrast, in those areas of the model where the curvature changes only gradually (for example, the thighs), fewer and larger polygons are used without sacrificing any accuracy in the approximation.

Splines and Patches

In the previous section, you saw how the polygonal approach to modeling uses straight lines and flat planes as basic building blocks. In the real world, of course—especially in the world of nature—curved lines and curved surfaces are much more common than are straight lines and surfaces. Think of a tree branch, the curve of a beautiful neck, a muscular thigh, the hull of a ship, and so on. Polygonal modeling can *approximate* these curves, but it never represents them with perfect accuracy.

Because of this, a second, and very powerful, approach to modeling is common in 3D modeling systems. In these systems, the smoothly curved line, or more simply, the **curve**, is considered another basic geometric building block.

A curve can be two-dimensional or three-dimensional. When you draw a curve on a piece of paper, you draw a two-dimensional curve. When you wave a sparkler about at night, you trace a three-dimensional curve in space with the tip of the sparkler.

Computer graphics uses several approaches to representing curves. One is similar in concept to the polygonal approximation technique you saw in the previous section. When applied to a curve, this technique approximates a curve through a series of straight lines and is consequently known as **linear approximation**. It is also sometimes referred to as a **polyline** technique, because it makes use of many ("poly") lines to represent the curve.

Figure 1-12a shows a crude linear approximation of a curve. Figure 1-12b uses a greater number of line segments, and the approximation of the curve is somewhat less crude as a consequence. In Figure 1-12c, the number of line segments has been increased to give a smoother, more accurate representation of the curve.

The linear-approximation technique has the advantage of being extremely simple conceptually. A curve is represented simply as a series of points, which are connected in a dot-to-dot fashion.

The technique has several disadvantages, however. One is that it can be very awkward to edit the shape of a curve. Changing the shape of a linearly approximated curve can involve laboriously selecting each of many points and moving each point individually. A second disadvantage of the linear-approximation technique is that the number of points required to produce a good approximation of a curve may produce very large quantities of data, which may in turn slow down your interaction with the program. A final disadvantage of the polyline technique is that the "curve" is never truly smooth. It is, in fact, not a curve at all, but only an approximation of a curve. All three of these disadvantages apply equally to the polygonal modeling technique discussed in the previous section.

Most high-end computer modeling systems, therefore, provide a different technique to represent curves. This technique makes use of **splines**. The word derives from the era when ships were built of wood. In order to bend a plank

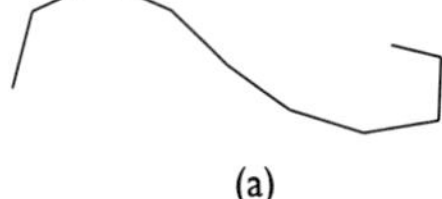

(a)

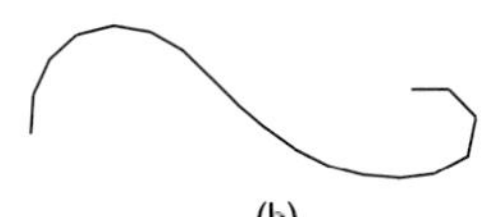

(b)

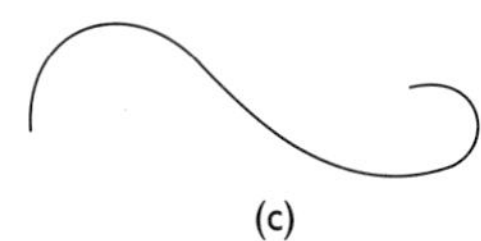

(c)

Figure 1-12. A curve can be represented as a series of straight line segments, yielding a linear approximation of the curve.

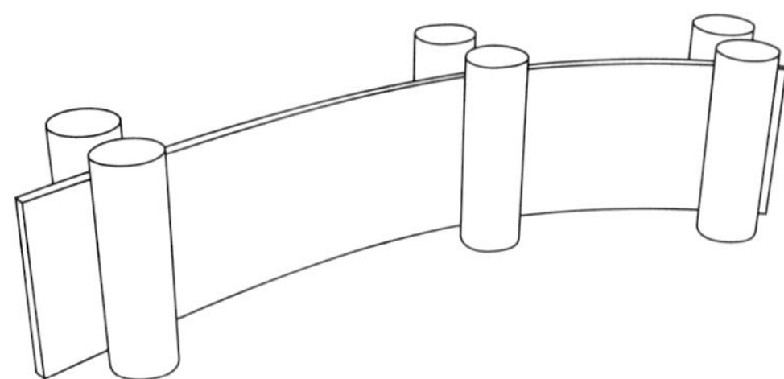

Figure 1-13. A shipbuilder's "spline."

of wood to fit the shape of the hull, shipbuilders would force the wooden plank to bend between several fixed posts, called "ducks." The resulting curved plank was called a "spline" (Figure 1-13). Notice that the placement of the posts determines how much curvature will be given to the plank.

As adapted by mathematicians for computer graphics, the wooden plank of the shipbuilders corresponds to a curve, and the ducks correspond to points in space that control the shape of the curve. Two typical spline curves that might occur in computer graphics appear in Figure 1-14. In both drawings, the solid curved line is the spline curve itself. The points that lie near each curve are the **control points**, which determine the shape of that curve. These points are sometimes called **control vertices**; a single point, a **control vertex**. The dotted straight line connecting each set of points often is known as the **hull** for that curve. The hull is simply the network of straight lines that connects the control points.

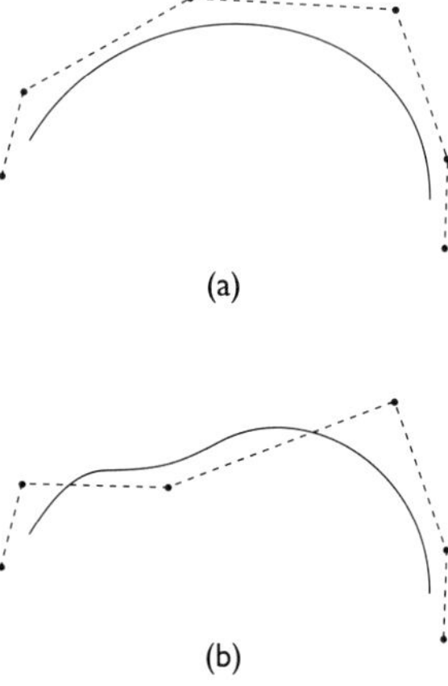

Figure 1-14. Two spline curves, each showing the network of control vertices that controls its shape.

As in the original shipbuilding situation, the placement of the control points determines the shape of the spline curve. Moving one of the control points changes the shape of the curve. In Figure 1-14a and Figure 1-14b, the control points are identical, except for the third control point from the left. In Figure 1-14b this control point has been pulled down, changing the shape of the curve. Notice, however, that only a portion of the curve changes. The right end of the curve is unchanged. Each control point affects only a certain region of the curve. Farther away from that point, the curve is unaffected. This example also illustrates another characteristic of spline curves, which may not be obvious. The hull of a spline curve does not necessarily have to stay on only one side of the curve. It may cross over to the other side of the curve, and will do so if one control point is pulled far enough, as it is in this example.

Notice that the spline approach to representing a curve answers the three objections raised above about the linear-approximation approach. First, a spline is very easy to reshape. Pulling a single control point can modify an entire section of the curve and do so in a smooth manner. Second, the spline is truly, mathematically curved. No matter how much you magnify a section of a spline, it remains truly curved. And finally, from the programmer's point of view, the spline representation of a curve is very compact and efficient in terms of the amount of data it requires. A handful of control points suffices to define an entire curve.

From a programming point of view, a spline is actually a mathematical formulation of a curve. (The splines of computer graphics are almost always what are called "cubic" splines. The term refers to the fact that the mathematical formulae that define these splines involve a variable raised to the third, or cubic, power.) Depending on what the programmer wants to accomplish, this formulation may differ from one program to the next. One programmer's approach might cause the "control" of the control points to be exerted in one way; another's approach might use the control points to shape the curve in a slightly different way. The exact effect of the control points depends on how the mathematical formulae are written, which in turn depends on what kinds of results the programmer wants to achieve. Over the years, however, a handful of formulations have emerged as the most useful, and these are the varieties of splines most commonly found in computer graphics systems.

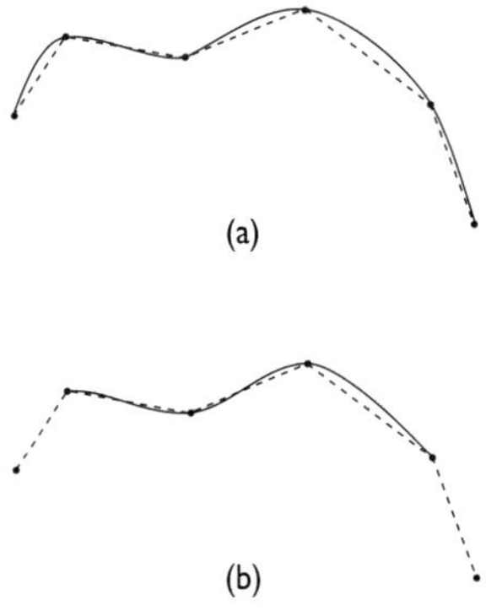

Figure 1-15. Two varieties of interpolating splines, in which the curve passes directly through the control points.

One of two broad categories of splines is the **interpolating spline**. In this form, the spline curve passes directly through each of the control points (Figure 1-15a). A specific type of interpolating spline sometimes found in computer graphics systems is the **Cardinal spline**, in which the curve goes directly through all but the first and last of the control points (Figure 1-15b).

An advantage of all interpolating splines is the direct relationship between the placement of the control points and the final curve they generate. If you want your curve to go "here," you simply place a control point "here." A disadvantage of this direct relationship, however, is that this approach can make it difficult to generate curves having a very smooth and gradual curvature. If a control point is misplaced even slightly, the curvature will not be smooth in that area of the curve, since the spline curve is required to pass exactly through the misplaced control point. The result may be an undesirable little bump in the curve. Imagine, for example, trying to draw a smooth circular arc with an interpolating spline. Unless you precisely and mathematically calculate the location of each control point, you are likely to get some undesirable irregularities in the curvature of your arc (Figure 1-16).

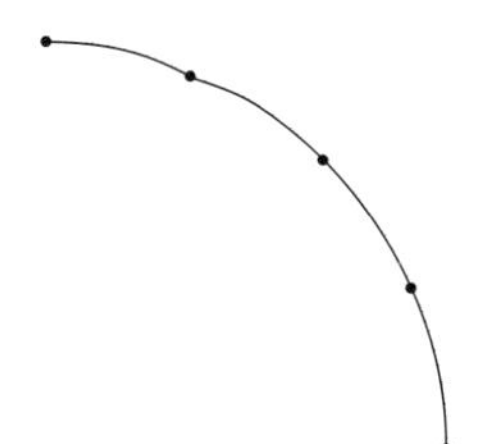

Figure 1-16. Any irregularity in the placement of the control points of an interpolating spline causes a visible irregularity in the curve itself.

The second basic category of spline, the **approximating spline**, addresses this problem of control-point placement by calculating the curve such that it goes *near*, but not directly through, any of the control points. This offers a wider margin of error in the placement of the control points and tends to yield a smoother curve.

One of the most commonly used types of approximating spline is the **B-spline** (Figure 1-17). (The B in the phrase B-spline stands for the word

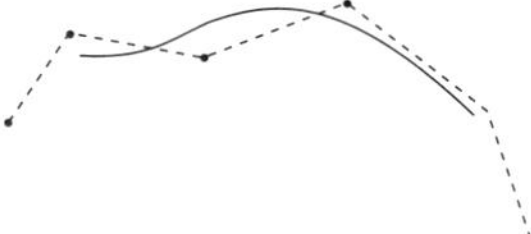

Figure 1-17. A B-spline curve.

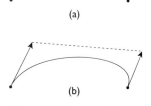

"basis," a mathematical term.) Notice that the B-spline curve does not actually touch any of the control points. This is the nature of the approximating spline. It goes near but not through the control points. Notice also that the curvature of an approximating B-spline is more gradual than the curvature of an interpolating spline that uses the same control points: the control points used for this B-spline are the same points used for the interpolating splines in Figure 1-15. And finally, notice that, like the Cardinal spline, the B-spline curve does not extend all the way to the far ends of the hull. It begins at approximately the second control point and ends at approximately the next-to-last control point.

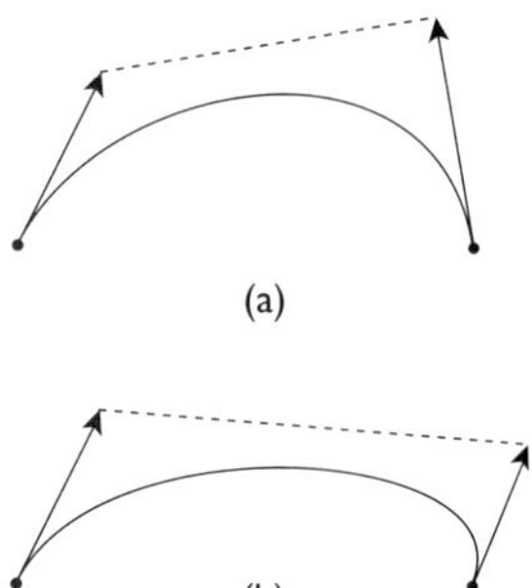

Figure 1-18. Two basic Bézier spline curves, showing tangent vectors at the ends. The length and direction of tangent vectors control the shape of a curve.

The **Bézier** spline, named after the man who invented it, is another very popular variety of approximating spline. A basic Bézier spline segment is defined by four control points (Figures 1-18a, 1-18b). As with the other splines, a dotted line connecting the control points makes the hull of the spline visible.

The Bézier curve introduces a very useful concept in computer graphics. Notice that an arrow appears at each of the two end points of each Bézier curve. Each of these arrows is called a **tangent vector**. A **tangent** is a line that just grazes a curve at one point, while a **vector** is a line that has both direction and length. Each of the arrows is tangent to the curve at the location of an end point and has both direction and length.

The significance of these tangent vectors is that the directions and lengths of each vector determine the curvature of the Bézier spline. Changing the direction of a vector changes the direction in which the spline curves, while changing the length of a vector changes the amount of area affected by that vector. In Figure 1-18b, for instance, the second tangent vector has been rotated to the right and shortened, causing the right end of the curve to change shape.

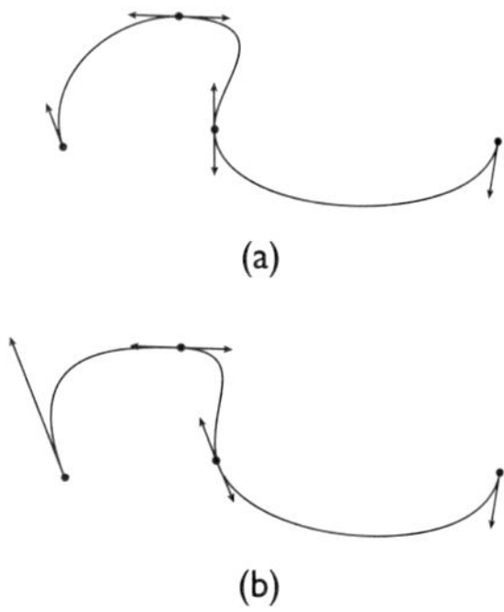

Figure 1-19. Two Bézier curves consisting of several curve segments attached. The tangent vectors serve as "handles" for changing the shape of the curve.

In everyday usage, more than four control points normally define a Bézier spline. In fact, complex Bézier curves consist of many connected simple four-control-point segments (Figure 1-19). In each of these two curves, the total curve consists of three segments, each of which has a tangent vector at the beginning control point and another at the ending control point. (Because the tangent vectors of a Bézier curve make the structure of control points so clear, the hull of a Bézier curve usually is not explicitly drawn.)

Figure 1-19 also illustrates how you can edit the shape of a Bézier curve. In both of these curves, the locations of all the control points are identical. In Figure 1-19b, however, two of the tangent vectors, or **handles**, as they are often called, have been adjusted. Notice that the length of the handle on the far left has been increased. This causes a larger area of the curve to be affected, and the curve therefore bows outward on the far left. Also notice that the third handle from the left (that is, the pair of arrows at the third control point) has been rotated, causing a change in the direction of the curve in the area of the third control point.

Normally, when two tangent vectors, or arrows, share a control point, they operate as a unit. When the third handle of Figure 1-19b rotated, for instance, the two tangent vectors at that point rotated together. This usually is desirable in a Bézier curve, because it assures that the curvature of the spline at that control point will remain smooth, that there will not be a "kink" in the curve.

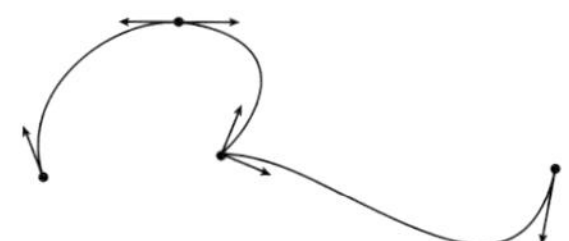

Figure-20. "Breaking"the pair of tangent vectors at a control point creates a discontinuity in the curve.

Sometimes, however, you specifically want a kink (Figure 1-20). In that case you can create a kink, more formally called a **discontinuity** or a **cusp**, by manipulating a pair of tangent vectors so that they do *not* operate as a unit (and do not appear as a continuous straight line). This has been done at the third control point of Figure 1-20. The locations of all of the control points for this curve are exactly the same as they were in Figure 1-19. Now, however, the handles at the third control point, broken apart, do not form a straight line. The curve is no longer continuous, or smooth, at that point. Instead, it has a cusp at the third control point.

Figure 1-21. The control points and the edit points of a NURBS curve.

A last type of approximating spline used in 3D computer systems is the **NURBS** curve, or Non-Uniform Rational B-Spline (Figure 1-21). (The terms *non-uniform* and *rational* both refer to specific mathematical properties of this type of B-spline.) A NURBS curve shares many of the best features of a number of spline types. Like an interpolating spline, it goes through the first and last control points. Like an approximating spline, however, it does not go through the intermediate control points. In addition, a set of **edit points**, sometimes called **knots** (represented by the series of small crosses in Figure 1-21), lie exactly on the curve, just as the control points do on an interpolating curve. Thus, you can adjust a NURBS curve by working either with the control points if you are more interested in smoothness, or with the edit points, if you are more interested in precision. This gives you enormous flexibility, effectively combining the best features of both interpolating splines and approximating splines.

These different varieties of spline curve share a critical feature deriving from their mathematical definitions; that is, each curve is defined as having a specific direction. A given curve starts here and ends there, with the first control point you specify being the starting point of the curve. Many software packages allow you to reverse the direction of the curve if necessary, but the curve always has a direction.

The direction of the curve is significant because it allows you to locate specific points on a spline curve. You do this by indicating that you want to move a certain distance along the curve away from the beginning. Thinking of the curve in these terms is known as **parameterization**, because you use certain parameters—direction and distance—to locate your point. Consequently, spline curves are also known as **parameterized curves**.

For example, many 3D modeling packages make it possible to learn the location of a point that lies 55 percent of the way along a given curve. Usually you specify the distance along a curve as a number between 0.0 and 1.0, and so the distance parameter is 0.55. Either by typing in this number or by interactively moving a cursor along the curve, you position yourself at the location of the point. Having positioned yourself there, you then either inquire as to the precise coordinates of that point, or add a control point, or cut the curve at that point, or perform any number of other operations that the software provides. You will see in later sections of this book that the parameterization of curves is important for a number of other reasons as well.

Because of the ease with which you can generate and edit them, spline curves are extremely powerful tools in any computer graphics package. But the real power of splines for a 3D modeling package lies in their ability to generate curved surfaces. Remember that a straight line, if pushed through space in some direction other than the direction of the line itself, defines a plane, or flat surface. Similarly, a curve moved through space, either along a straight line or along another curved line, defines a **curved surface** (Figure 1-22).

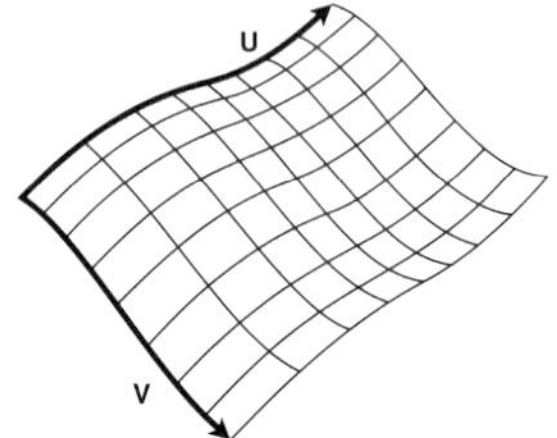

Figure 1-22. A patch generated from two spline curves. The directions of the two curves are the U and V directions.

The original curve is a heavy line running from left to right. This direction, the direction of the original curve, is by convention called the **U direction.** A second curve, the heavy line extending from top to bottom, runs in a different direction. The direction of this second curve is known as the **V direction**. If you push the original, U curve along the second, V curve, you define a curved surface. A curved surface generated from two spline curves in this way is often referred to as a **patch**. (More technically, since it is formed of two cubic splines, it is called a **bicubic patch**, "bi" meaning "two" and "cubic" referring to the fact that the mathematics of a spline curve involve powers of three.)

Because a patch is generated from two spline curves, different kinds of patches correspond to the different kind of splines. If the original curves are Bézier splines, for example, they generate a Bézier patch. If the original curves are B-splines, they generate a B-spline patch. In most 3D software systems, the two curves used to generate a patch must be of the same type. In a few high-end systems, the two curves may be of different types.

Although Figure 1-22 shows only the two spline curves and the resulting surface, in reality, of course, each spline curve is defined by a set of control points and these control points are connected by a hull. Consequently, when you generate a patch from two splines, you generate a whole network of control points with it, and this network of points is connected by its own hull (Figure 1-23). The number and the direction of the control points in the original

U-direction curve determine the number and the direction of control points in the U direction of the patch. In the same way, the number and the direction of control points in the V-direction curve determine the number and direction of control points in the V direction. The type of spline used for the original curves also carries over to the patch. Since the original curves in Figure 1-23 were NURBS curves, the patch generated from them is a NURBS patch.

Figure 1-23. The control points of the generating curves create a network of control points, which in turn define the patch.

The network of control points that defines a curved surface is extremely important. Just as you can change the shape of an individual spline curve by moving one of the control points, so you can change the shape of a surface by moving one or more of the control points. In Figure 1-24, several of the control points for the patch, pulled upward, have the effect of bowing the surface upward in the area of those control points.

The exact effect of moving control points for a patch depends on what type of patch it is. If the original, generating U and V curves were B-splines and the patch is therefore a B-spline patch, then the control points behave as B-spline control points. If the generating curves were NURBS splines, the patch will be a NURBS patch and behave accordingly, and so on.

Figure 1-24. Moving the control points of a patch changes the shape of the patch.

Notice also that the amount of control you have in deforming a curved surface depends on how many control points you have in the region you want to deform. If you have only a few control points, as in the previous examples, moving one control point causes a large area of the surface to be deformed. This is very effective for making broad, smooth changes in the shape of the surface, but it is not so effective for small, detailed changes in that shape. In order to make changes to the shape of the surface on a smaller scale, you need to insert additional control points. Most systems allow you to do this. However, because a rectangular grid of control points defines the surface, inserting a single control point in any direction generates an entire row of control points in that direction. In order to model the small spoutlike form at the bottom of the patch in Figure 1-25, you add several additional control points in the U direction. Doing so necessarily creates several new rows of control points, running all the way across the hull in that direction. With these control points in place, however, you pull the appropriate points to adjust the shape as desired.

Figure 1-25. For fine detail, additional control points may be necessary. Adding one control point creates a whole new row of control points.

Manipulating the control points of a surface can yield tremendously complex and subtle modeling. In Figure 1-26, the animator has modeled a strange, sculptural, almost mystical splash of water by manipulating the control points of B-spline patches. This image has been superimposed on a background image that was scanned—that is, digitally copied—into the computer from a photograph.

Most 3D computer graphics packages offer a great variety of modeling techniques for generating surfaces, and for editing them once they have been

Figure 1-26. An evocative example of modeling patches by manipulating control points. (Courtesy, Yoshiki Hagihara.)

generated. These techniques are discussed in detail in the remainder of this chapter. In the section *Shape Changes*, in chapter 3, additional techniques for editing the shape of a surface are discussed.

Coordinate Systems

In the previous two sections you saw that you can define surfaces either as polygonal approximations or as spline-based patches. You then can combine these surfaces to form objects.

No matter how you define your surfaces and your objects, however, somehow you have to know how to locate these things in space. If you say to yourself, holding your hand up in the air, that you want something located "right there," this is not a very precise form of location. The odds are that tomorrow you won't be able to find that exact spot, or point, in the air. In order to be able to define points in space and to place things accurately in space, you need some clear, precise, and repeatable method of describing where something is.

The method used in nearly all computer graphics systems is analogous to the method you probably used in your high school math classes when you made graphs. If you draw two lines perpendicular to each other, and then mark off little "tick" marks at certain distances along each line, you have drawn a system that allows you accurately to locate points within the space of those two lines (Figure 1-27). You can say, for example, "Start where the lines cross each other, go over to the right five tick marks, then go straight up three tick marks. That's the point I'm talking about."

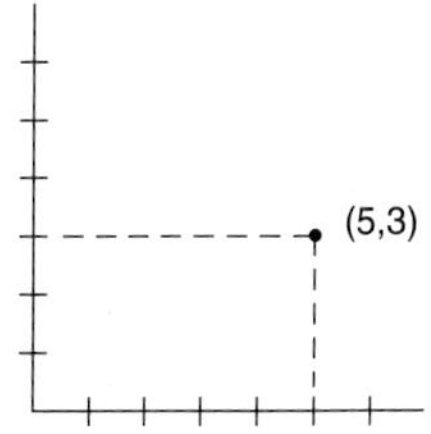

Figure 1-27. A simple two-axis coordinate system.

In the simple two-dimensional system just described, there is no ambiguity about where your point is located. If you come back tomorrow, you can relocate it exactly within the same system because you can still go over exactly five and up exactly three to define the location of the point.

This sort of numerical location system is called a **coordinate system**, and the numbers that identify where a point is (in this case, five and three) are called the **coordinates** of the point. The coordinates of a point usually are written as a pair of numerals separated by a comma—for example, (5,3). The two lines drawn perpendicular to each other are called the **axes** of the coordinate system; each one is an **axis**. The horizontal axis usually is called the X axis and the vertical axis usually is called the Y axis. The point at which the axes cross and from which you start counting when you move is called the **origin** of the coordinate system. The coordinates of the origin are (0,0).

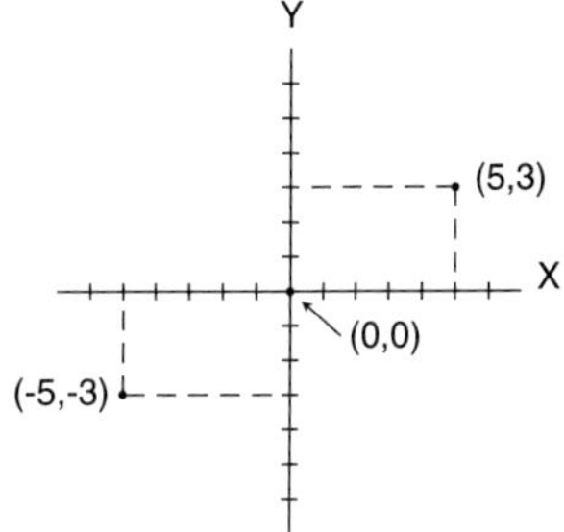

Figure 1-28. An XY coordinate system with both positive and negative directions.

A more flexible and powerful way of setting up this sort of coordinate system is to draw the two lines so that they continue past each other, forming a cross (Figure 1-28). This gives you the flexibility of moving in either direction away from the origin. In the horizontal direction, for example, you could move either to the right or to the left of the origin. To simplify things, the distances along an axis usually are thought of as being either positive or negative numbers, relative to the origin of the system.

In Figure 1-28, the coordinates (5,3) locate a point in the upper right section, or **quadrant**, of the coordinate system. To locate this point, you move along X (i.e., to the right) positive five and then along Y (i.e., up) positive three. The coordinates (–5,–3), on the other hand, are in the lower left quadrant, because you move along X (i.e., to the left) negative five and along Y (i.e., down) negative 3.

It is very easy to extend this two-dimensional coordinate system into a three-dimensional coordinate system, which allows you to locate points in three-dimensional space. Take a pencil and place the eraser end of the pencil at the origin point of the coordinate system in Figure 1-28. Make sure that the pencil is perpendicular to the paper—in other words, perpendicular to the X and Y axes drawn on the page. In doing this, you have just created a three-dimensional coordinate system (represented, by necessity, as a two-dimensional drawing in Figure 1-29). The pencil you placed on the page is your third axis, for the third dimension. This new, third axis normally is called the Z axis. Like the other two axes, it has positive and negative directions that

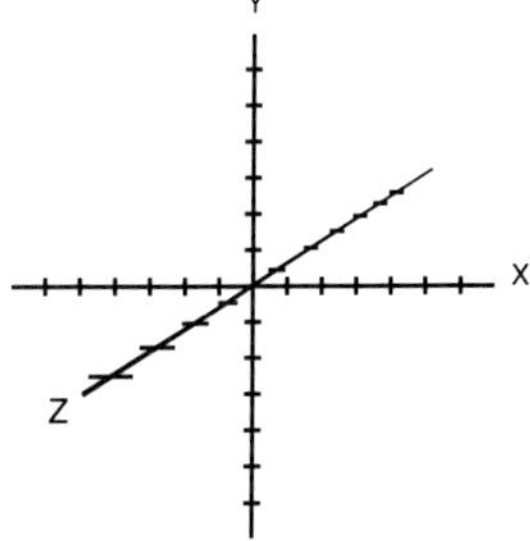

Figure 1-29. A three-dimensional Cartesian coordinate system.

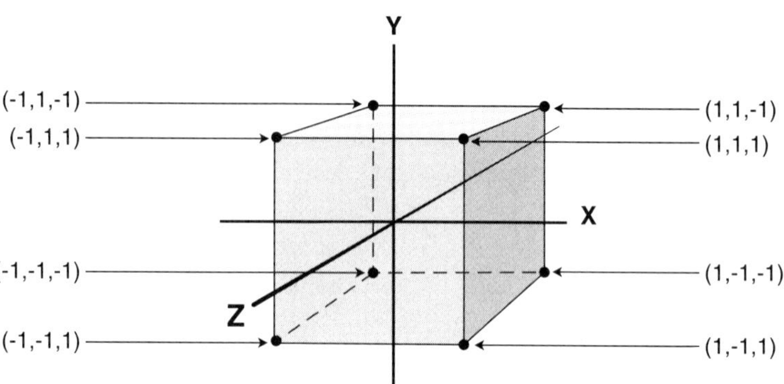

Figure 1-30. The coordinate system permits the precise location of points in space.

allow you to move either forward or backward in space. A point in this coordinate system has three coordinate values to define its location. For example, (5,3,1) means "move five units to the right along X, three units up along Y, and one unit closer in Z."

Suppose you want to define a cube in three-dimensional space. If the center of the cube is at (0,0,0), you can define a cube with the following set of eight vertices:

(1, 1, 1)
(1, 1, –1)
(–1, 1, –1)
(–1, 1, 1)
(1, –1, 1)
(1, –1, –1)
(–1, –1, –1)
(–1, –1, 1)

The result is the cube in Figure 1-30.

In addition to thinking about the space of a coordinate system in terms of its three axes, we also sometimes think of it in terms of the three planes defined by those axes. Recall from the section on *Polygonal Modeling* that any three points define a plane. Extending this approach, you can see that any two axes of a coordinate system also define a plane. Thus, the three fundamental planes of a coordinate system are the XZ plane, the XY plane and the YZ plane (Figure 1-31).

Whether two-dimensional or three-dimensional, whether we refer to its axes or its planes, coordinate systems of this type, in which the coordinate system is defined by a set of mutually perpendicular axes, are called **Cartesian coordinate systems**, after the French mathematician René Descartes, who first devised them. These sorts of coordinate systems go a long way

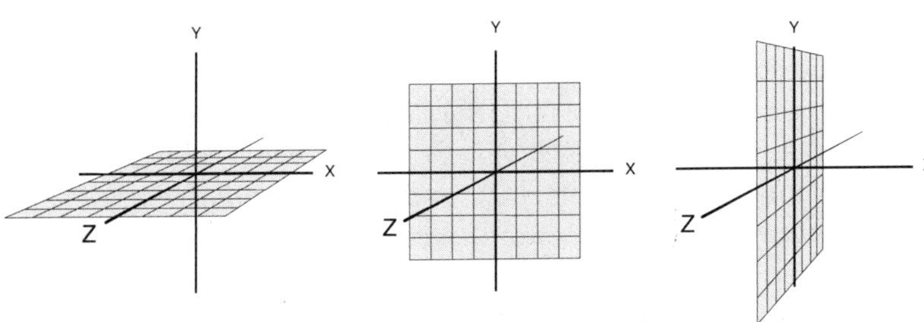

Figure 1-31. The XZ, XY, and YZ planes of a coordinate system.

toward solving the problem of how to accurately and predictably locate a point in space.

Suppose, however, I tell you that I want a point located at (–4,2,7). You start moving to the left along X for a distance of four units. But I start shouting at you, "No, no! Go the other way! Go to the *right* along X. For me, in my system, positive X is to the left and negative X is to the right." When you try to move in the Y direction, the same thing happens. You think you know which direction I mean by "positively in Y," but in my system negative Y is up and positive Y is down. The Z axis presents the same problem: which way is positive and which way is negative?

You may think such reversals are ridiculous. That is, you may be so used to seeing positive X to the right and positive Y up that it seems ludicrous to imagine them any other way. But think of the Z axis, which is not so familiar. Is there any reason positive Z must come "out" of the page, as in Figure 1-29, rather than go "into" the page?

In short, you must decide which direction is positive and which direction is negative, for all three axes, before you start. For three-dimensional Cartesian coordinate systems, there are two standards. And, in spite of the sophistication of the science of computer graphics, these two standards are defined with your fingers.

First take a pen and draw a little X on the tip of the thumb of your right hand. This is the positive X direction of the coordinate system. Now draw a Y on the tip of the forefinger of your right hand. This is the positive Y direction. Finally, draw a Z on the tip of the middle finger of your right hand. This is the positive Z direction. When you hold your right hand in such a way that those three fingers are extended perpendicular to one another, your hand represents a coordinate system with right-handed directionality, or a **right-handed coordinate system** (Figure 1-32b; see also Figure 1-29).

Now go through the same procedure with your left hand: X on the thumb, Y on the forefinger, Z on the middle finger. When you extend your fingers, they describe a **left-handed coordinate system** (Figure 1-32a).

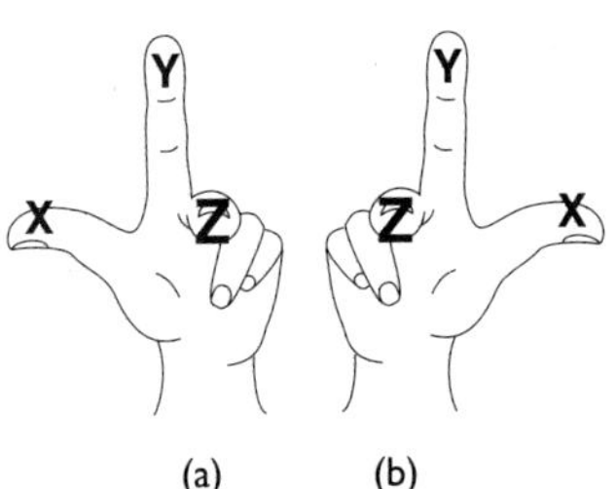

Figure 1-32. A left-handed coordinate system, and a right-handed coordinate system.

It is possible to rotate a given coordinate system without changing the definition of its directionality. Hold both of your hands/coordinate systems in front of you, with fingers extended as described above, and with the palms facing towards you. In this orientation, the directionality of the two systems is the same except for the X axes. On your right hand, positive X is to the right, while on the left hand, positive X is to the left. Keep your right hand in this position but rotate your left hand so that you are looking at the back of that hand. Now the X and Y of both systems are going in the same direction, but the Z is reversed.

Notice, however, that while things have changed for the left hand relative to the right hand, *relative to itself* nothing has changed. The middle finger of your left hand didn't suddenly start growing out the other side of your hand. Relative to the rest of your fingers on that hand, it is in exactly the same position as before. The whole system rotated, but within the system nothing has changed. A left-handed coordinate system, whether it is facing toward you or away from you, is still a left-handed coordinate system.

In fact, different industries (and sometimes even different companies within an industry) have different preferences for the way they like to orient a given coordinate system. For example, the aerospace industry likes to orient coordinate systems so that the Z axis is up. This makes the ground plane—that is, what you see from an airplane—correspond to the XY plane. In other words, the ground plane can be plotted using the standard XY axes that you are familiar with. Architects tend to use the same orientation, for the same reason. By contrast, the animation industry usually orients coordinate systems so that the XY plane corresponds to the picture plane. This makes the Z axis serve as the axis that extends back into space.

Figure 1-33a is a left-handed coordinate system, oriented so that positive Z extends back into space. Figure 1-33b is a right-handed system, with positive Z coming out of space toward you. Figure 1-33c is likewise a right-handed coordinate system, but this system is oriented so that positive Y goes back into space and positive Z goes up. All of these different possibilities

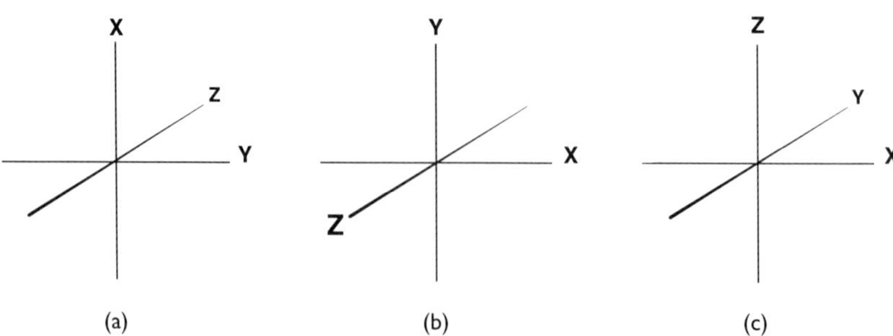

Figure 1-33. Three combinations of coordinate system handedness and orientation.

accomplish the same purpose—to make the location of points and objects in three-dimensional space convenient and unambiguous. None is inherently better than the others. It is important, however, for you to understand very clearly from the outset which coordinate system and which orientation is employed by the software package you use.

Viewing Windows

Whichever coordinate system and whichever orientation you use, the purpose is the same—to define the three-dimensional space in which you will be working. Three-dimensional computer modeling systems view this space by means of a set of **windows**, with each window being a particular view into the three-dimensional space (Figure 1-34).

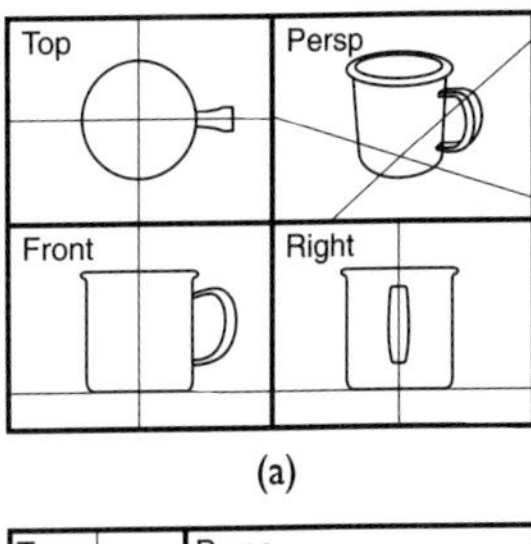

(a)

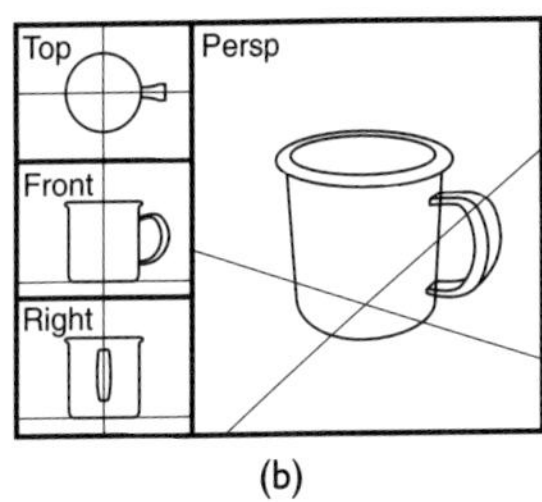

(b)

Figure 1-34. A typical window configuration consists of several orthographic windows and one perspective window.

One type of window found on all systems is the **perspective window**. (The concepts of perspective and cameras are discussed in detail in the section on *The Camera*, in chapter 2.) A perspective window, also sometimes called a **camera window**, is one through which you see a scene with the same sort of perspective distortions that you experience with your natural eyes. That is, objects in the distance appear smaller than objects that are close to the viewer, and lines that are parallel converge in the distance. In Figure 1-34a, the perspective window is the window in the upper right. In Figure 1-34b it is the large window on the right.

In addition to a perspective window, most programs also provide several **orthographic windows**. An orthographic rendering of the world does not include perspective. (The root word "ortho" comes from the Greek and means "straight.") In orthographic projection parallel lines do not converge; they remain forever parallel—that is, "straight." And objects in the distance do not get smaller; they remain the same size as they are when seen up close. In Figure 1-34 the windows labeled *Front*, *Top*, and *Right* are orthographic windows showing the model from directly in front, above, and to the right.

Although our eyes do not see the world in this orthographic way, an orthographic representation can be extremely useful because it sometimes allows us to perceive the dimensions of an object more easily. In a perspective rendering such as the one in Figure 1-35a, the lines that represent the rear edges of a cube are not as long as those that represent the front edges of the cube. Figure 1-35b shows the same cube seen from the same angle, but represented orthographically, without any perspective distortion. In this orthographic rendering, all the edges of the cube are represented as being of exactly the same length, as they are in reality.

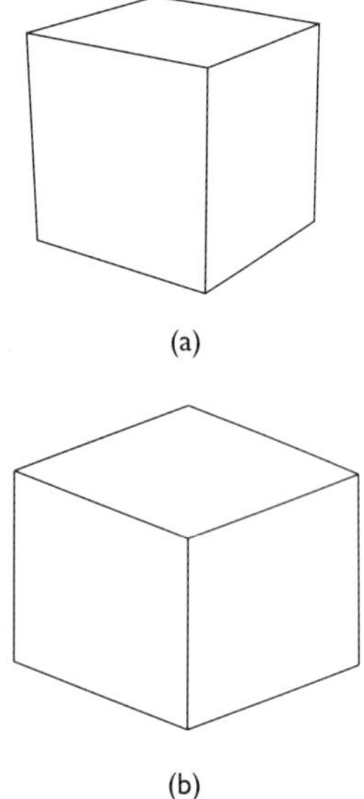

Figure 1-35. A perspective rendering and an orthographic rendering of a cube.

All 3D software packages provide a default configuration of windows, usually consisting of several orthographic windows and one perspective window. The standard configuration was illustrated in Figure 1-34a. Typically, you can select other combinations and configurations of windows, such as the one illustrated in Figure 1-34b. Most packages also allow you to move and resize any of these windows.

When developing a model or scene, you usually need to work in several of the available windows, using now one and now another depending on what you are trying to accomplish. Be aware, however, that moving objects by dragging in the perspective window can be extremely confusing because the mouse cursor always moves in the plane of the computer screen. Depending on how your perspective camera has been rotated, however, this screen plane will correspond to some arbitrary plane in the three-dimensional space of your coordinate system. For example, if you are looking at the scene from a 45-degree angle in your perspective view, then your screen plane corresponds to a plane running through the space at a 45-degree angle. In this case, when you drag the mouse cursor from left to right in the two-dimensional world of the computer screen, the object will actually move at a 45-degree angle through the three-dimensional space. This problem does not arise when you work in the standard orthographic windows, since the planes of their space are perfectly aligned with the plane of the screen.

Geometric Primitives

Certain basic geometric shapes are so easily defined mathematically and so widely used in 3D computer graphics that software packages handle them separately, as a set of special entities. These shapes are called **geometric primitives** (Figure 1-36). They include familiar shapes such as the sphere, the cube, the cone, and the cylinder, all of which are so familiar because they are so common, and so common because they are so useful.

A great many man-made objects are composed of some combination of these primitives. A table, for example, might have as the top a very wide and flat cylinder and as the legs, long tapered cylinders. A lamp might consist of a cube-shaped base, a cylinder-shaped column, and a cone-shaped shade. Because so many man-made shapes can be modeled with the geometric primitives, industrial designers and architects make particularly heavy use of them.

When you want to generate a geometric primitive using a computer modeling system, you follow a fairly standard procedure. First, you tell the system which primitive you want to use. Then you provide a few pieces of information to help define the primitive. And finally, you tell the system where in space

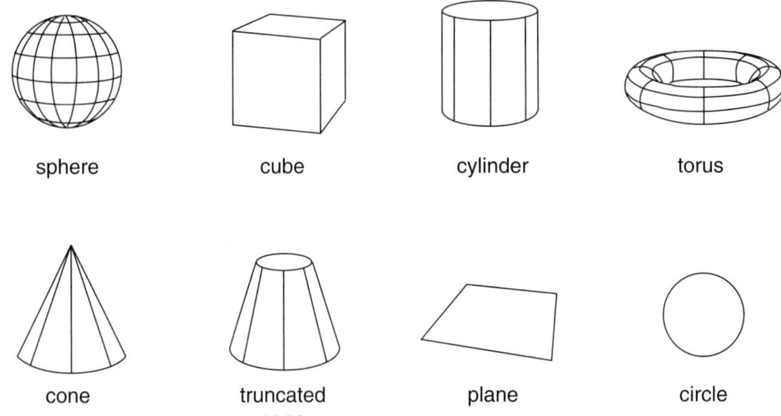

Figure 1-36. Some of the common geometric primitives.

you want to place the primitive. You may "tell the system," or provide the information, by moving a mouse device to make menu selections, by typing at the keyboard, or by using some other input device, such as a joystick or pen.

In order to generate a **sphere**, for example, which is defined as all the points at a given distance from a central point, you must tell the system where the center of the sphere is and what the radius of the sphere is. Many modeling systems, when you request a sphere, ask you to give them these two pieces of information. Informational selections such as these, which affect the outcome of a given procedure, are called **parameters**, as in "defining the parameters of a problem." If you tell the computer, for example, that the center of the sphere is at (10,0,2) and the radius is fourteen, you will get a very different result than if you say that the center is at (0,0,0) and the radius is one.

Some 3D modeling packages do not ask for these parameters. Instead, they provide the necessary values automatically. For example, a software package might generate all spheres at (0,0,0) with a radius of one. If the computer provides its own values for the parameters, those values are called **default** values.

Whether the computer provides default values or whether it asks you to provide at least some of the values, certain predictable parameters are involved for each of the geometric primitives. To create a **cylinder** primitive, the computer needs to know (from you or by default) the center point, the radius, and the height of the cylinder. To generate a **cone**, the computer needs to know the center of the cone, the radius of the circular base, and the height of the cone.

Some software packages condense the cone and cylinder procedures into one by asking you for a total of four parameters: the center, the height, the radius at the bottom, and the radius at the top. If the two radii are the same,

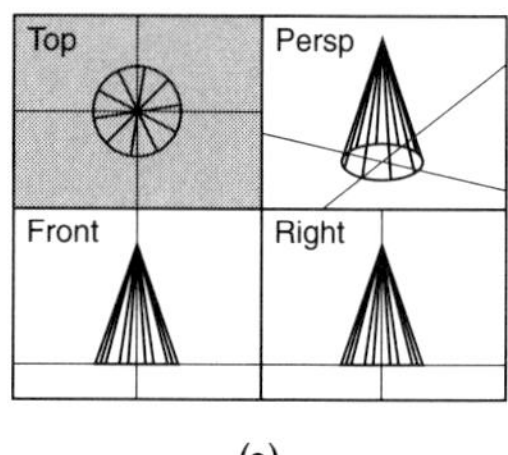

(a)

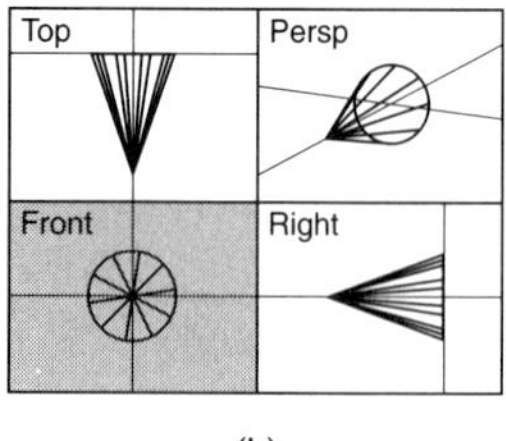

(b)

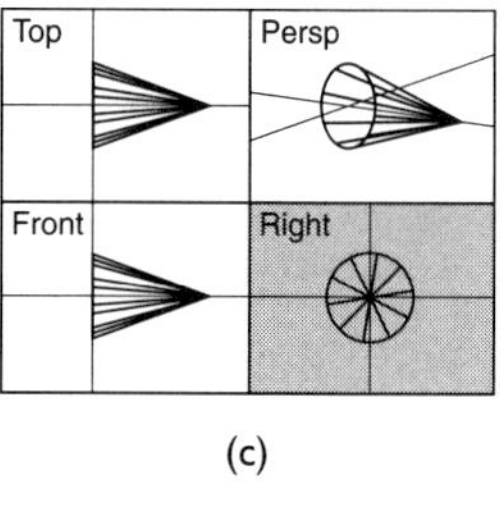

(c)

Figure 1-37. The initial orientation of an object depends on which construction plane was used to generate it.

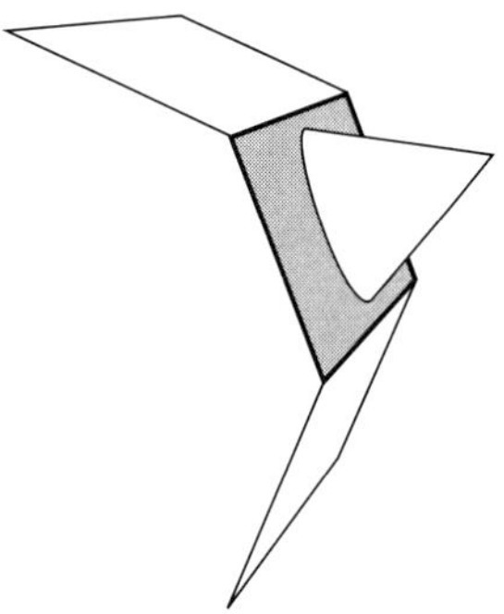

Figure 1-38. A construction plane may be defined to align with the face of an existing object.

you get a standard cylinder. If one of them equals zero, you get a cone, the point of which is at the end where the radius is zero. If the two radii are different, you get a tapered cylinder, also known as a **truncated cone**.

Some systems provide another geometric primitive called the **torus**. For this doughnut-shaped object the parameters usually are the center of the torus, the radius of the circular cross section, and the radius of the whole doughnut from the center to the edge.

Many systems also provide menu selections for two geometric primitives that actually are two-dimensional rather than three-dimensional: the **plane** and the **circle**. When generating a plane as a geometric primitive, you normally are asked to specify the two lengths of the rectangular plane. You also may be asked to specify the orientation of the plane—that is, whether it lies flush with the XY plane, XZ plane, or YZ plane of the coordinate system. When generating a circle, as when generating a sphere, you are asked to provide the center and the radius.

Software systems differ in exactly which set of geometric primitives they provide and which parameters they request. But all systems provide some primitives and request some parameters.

When the software creates, or constructs, a primitive, it initially appears on your screen in a certain orientation. A cone, for example, might appear pointing upward. The initial orientation of any object results from the construction of the object by the software relative to a specific, invisible plane in space. This plane is called the **construction plane**.

Some software packages always create their primitives in the same orientation, so the animator has no control over which construction plane is used. If you want the object to be in a different orientation, you rotate it after it has been constructed. Other software packages, however, give you control over which construction plane to use when generating a geometric primitive. This is done most simply by selecting one of the orthographic windows. (See the section on *Coordinate Systems.*) The plane of that window then becomes the construction plane for the next primitive. For example, in creating a cone primitive, selecting the Top window will activate the XZ plane as the construction plane, giving you the result shown in Figure 1-37a. Selecting the Front window will activate the XY construction plane, producing a cone in the orientation shown in Figure 1-37b. And selecting the Right window will cause the YZ plane to be used as the construction plane for the cone, with the result shown in Figure 1-37c.

Some systems provide additional control over the choice of construction plane by allowing you to use any flat surface, or **face**, in your scene as the current construction plane. In Figure 1-38, the animator has selected the face that is shaded, causing the software to create the cone on a construction plane aligned with that face. As a result the cone exactly coincides with the face. In many animation applications, this kind of accuracy is not necessary, and "eyeballing" an object's rotations after its creation is satisfactory. But in those applications where a more industrial level of accuracy is required, a wise use of construction planes can greatly facilitate modeling.

Transformations

If every object you defined in your computer graphics modeling system had to be in exactly the same location and of exactly the same size and oriented in exactly the same way, your modeling capabilities would be very limited and your modeling system of little use. You need at least the same sort of flexibility in modeling that you have in the real world. That is, you need to be able to move an object about in space, rotate it into other orientations, and scale it to change the size. These three operations collectively are called **transformations**.

When you relocate an object in space, you **move**, or **translate**, the object. In computer graphics modeling systems, whenever you translate an object in space, you make use of the same three-dimensional Cartesian coordinate system used for locating points in space. That is, you move the object either positively or negatively along any one of the three axes of the coordinate system.

Normally, in order to move an object to its final position, you move it some amount in all three of the axes—X, Y, and Z. Consequently, a translation is written as a set of three numerical values—translation in X, translation in Y, and translation in Z. Typical ways of writing this are *translate x,y,z*, or *translate (x,y,z)*, or *move x,y,z*, or *move (x,y,z)*, where *x,y,z* refer to the three numerical amounts by which the object is being moved. For example, *translate (5,3,–2)* indicates that you want to move in the X direction positive five, in the Y direction positive three, and in the Z direction negative two. The cube in figure 1-39, originally located at (0,0,0), has been translated to the right positive five, up positive three, and back in space negative two.

When you tilt an object or change the direction in which it is facing, you **rotate** the object. This is the second of the basic transformations. In rotating an object, you again make use of the three-dimensional Cartesian coordinate system, which allows you to specify precisely what kind of rotation you have in mind. As an example, imagine a wax statuette of a standing human figure (Figure 1-40a). Now imagine that the Y axis is a skewer going into the top of the head of the statuette and coming out at the bottom of the feet (Figure 1-40b). If you twirl the skewer between your fingers, the statuette rotates around that skewer—that is, around the Y axis; it "rotates about Y."

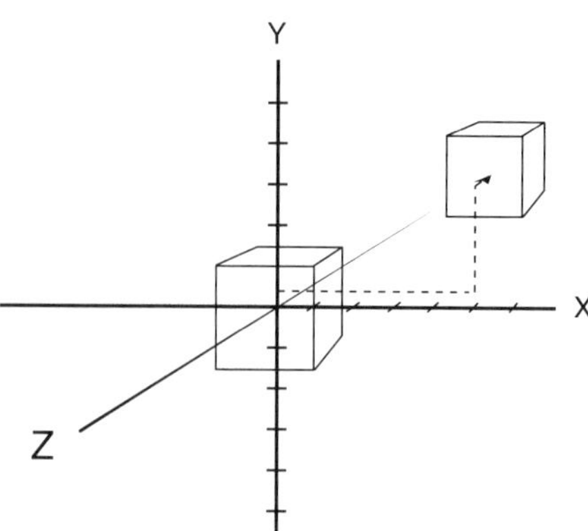

Figure 1-39. A simple translation of a cube.

If the skewer instead goes into the back of the statuette and comes out the stomach, the skewer corresponds to the Z axis of the coordinate system. You then can rotate the figure about the Z axis (Figure 1-40c). If you stick the skewer into one side and out the other side of the statuette, the skewer corresponds to the X axis. A rotation around X tilts the figure forward, almost as if it were bowing (Figure 1-40d).

You usually specify the amount of a rotation in degrees, 360 degrees being a complete rotation—from a given starting point, all the way around and back to the starting point. (Some systems, designed for more scientific purposes, use radians rather than degrees. One radian equals 57.29578 degrees [360/2π].) Changing the amount of rotation changes the final orientation of the object. For example, changing the rotation of the statuette to 90 degrees about X rotates the figurine so that it lies flat on its face.

Rotations, like translations, are usually written as a set of three values, one each for the X rotation, the Y rotation, and the Z rotation. *Rotate (90,0,0),* for example, means "rotate 90 degrees around X, nothing around Y, and nothing around Z."

Saying "rotate 90 degrees around X," however, is somewhat ambiguous. Does a 90-degree rotation about X mean rotate "this way" around X, or does it mean rotate "that way" around X? How do you indicate whether the statuette should rotate so that it ends up on its face (a forward rotation) or on its back (a backward rotation)?

As with the directionality of a coordinate system, a standard has to be agreed upon for the directionality of rotations. You need to know whether a 90-degree rotation is 90 degrees in this direction or in that direction. And again, in spite of the high-tech sophistication of computer graphics, your fingers provide the standard.

The accepted way of determining rotational direction is as follows. Using your right hand, consider the tip of your thumb the positive end of some axis.

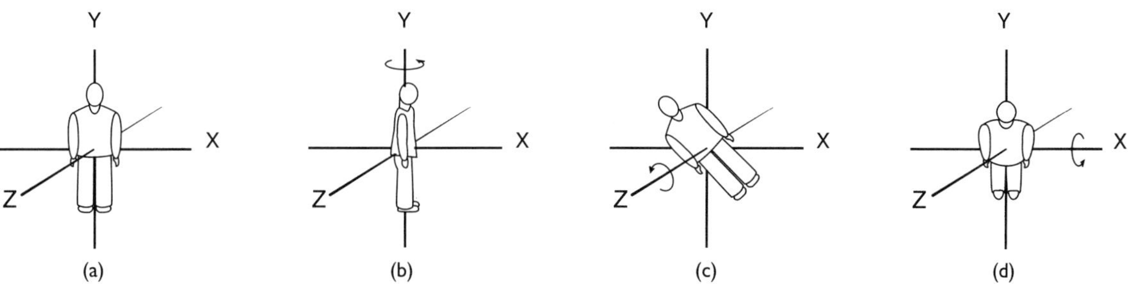

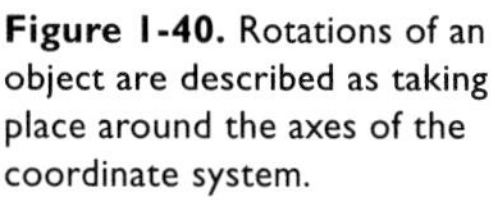
Figure 1-40. Rotations of an object are described as taking place around the axes of the coordinate system.

Hold your hand up with the thumb extended and your fingers straight up. Now slowly close the four fingers of your hand. The direction in which your fingers are closing is a positive rotation around the axis described by your thumb. Since you used your right hand, this is a **right-handed rotation**.

Apply this idea to an actual coordinate system. Imagine a right-handed coordinate system—that is, positive X to the right, positive Y up, positive Z coming out of the page. Place your right hand so that the thumb is along the line of the X axis, with the tip of the thumb at the positive X end. Keeping your thumb extended, close the fingers of your right hand. The direction in which your fingers close defines the positive rotation about X (Figure 1-41a). Now place your right hand so that the thumb aligns with the Y axis, with the tip of the thumb at positive Y. Close the fingers of your right hand to see the positive direction of rotation (Figure 1-41b). Finally, place your right hand on the Z axis, with the tip of the thumb at positive Z. Closing your hand shows you the positive rotation about Z (Figure 1-41c). Notice that, for all three axes, if you place your eye at the positive end of the axis and look down the length of the axis, the positive rotation around that axis is in a counterclockwise direction.

It is also possible to apply the right-handed rotation rule to a left-handed coordinate system. The handedness of a coordinate system and the handedness of rotations are completely independent of each other. Try applying the same right-handed rotations you just used to a left-handed coordinate system.

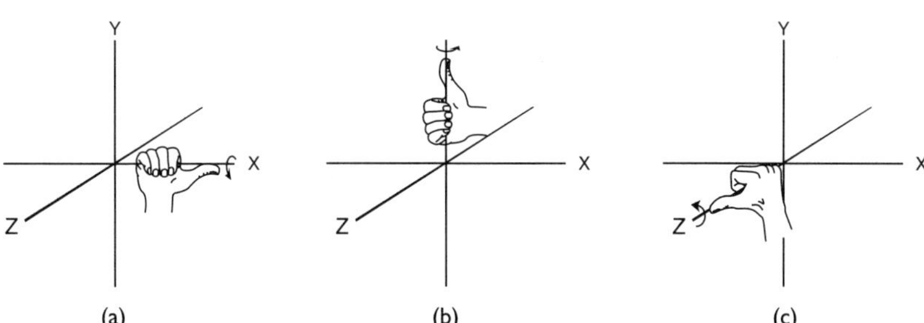

Figure 1-41. The right-handed rule for determining the directionality of rotations.

If you orient your left-handed coordinate system such that positive X is to the right, positive Y is up, and positive Z is going into the page, you see that the right-handed rotations are the same as they were in the right-handed coordinate system, except for the Z axis. This is because the difference between a left-handed and a right-handed coordinate system is simply a reversal of the Z axis.

Just as it is possible to have a right-handed rule for determining the positive direction of rotation, it is also possible to have a left-handed rule, producing **left-handed rotations**. You can visualize these rotations by placing the thumb of your left hand at the positive tip of each axis and closing your fingers. Again, the direction in which your fingers close indicates the direction of a positive rotation about that axis. Notice that left-handed rotations are in the reverse direction of right-handed rotations. That is, if you look down the length of a given axis, with your thumb near your eyes, each rotation is clockwise about that axis.

There is nothing sacred about these rules for rotational directionality. They are simply convenient ways of setting up a standard that the computer graphics industry can agree upon. Without some standard, there would be confusion about which direction to rotate. It is important, therefore, when you start using a particular three-dimensional software package, to determine which standard is in effect. Are positive rotations in the right-handed direction or in the left-handed direction? And furthermore, is the software using a right-handed coordinate system or a left-handed coordinate system? The most commonly found combination in animation packages is a right-handed coordinate system with right-handed rotations (see Figure 1-41). Because this combination is the most common, it appears throughout this book.

The third type of transformation involves changes of size. When you change the size or the proportions of an object, you **scale** the object, and you can scale an object along any one of the three axes.

If you scale an object along only one axis, you change the size in only one direction. In Figure 1-42a a cube is at the original size. In Figure 1-42b, the cube has been scaled along the X axis, making it longer horizontally. In Figure 1-42c the cube has been scaled along the Y axis, making it taller. In Figure 1-42d it has been scaled along the Z axis, making it longer as it goes back in space.

It is also very common, however, for an object to be scaled along more than one axis at a time. In Figure 1-42e the cube has been scaled along the Y axis by three and at the same time along the Z axis by two.

Since the sort of scaling operation just described does not retain the original proportions of the object, it is often called a **nonproportional scale**, or sometimes a **nonuniform scale**. If the scaling factor is the same for all three

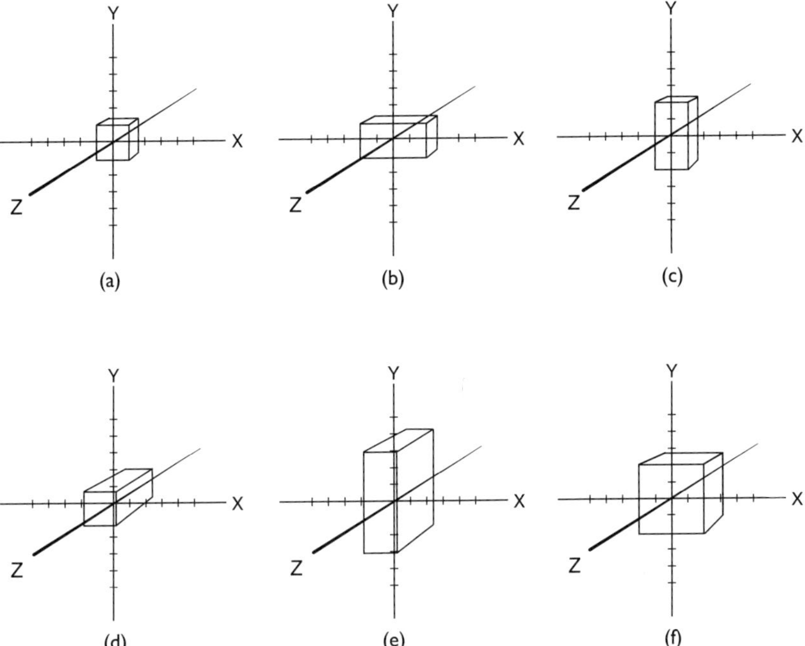

Figure 1-42. Different scaling operations applied to a cube. Scales may be either non-proportional or proportional.

axes, however, the overall size changes, but the original proportions of the object remain the same. This is called a **proportional scale** or a **uniform scale**. For example, simultaneously scaling the original cube by two in all three axes produces the cube in Figure 1-42f, which is twice as big in each dimension as it was before.

Scale transformations, like the other transformations, are usually written as a series of three numbers, one for each axis. To scale something uniformly by two in all directions, as in Figure 1-42f, you could write *scale (2,2,2)*. To bring about a nonproportional scale of two in the X direction, three in the Y direction and seven in the Z direction, you could write *scale (2,3,7)*.

From a mathematical point of view, scaling is an act of multiplication. Our language reflects this. When you make something twice as big, you make it two "times" as big—that is, you multiply all the numbers that define the object by two. For example, if all the vertices of a cube are at positive/negative one, as they are in Figure 1-42a, then after scaling by two they would all be at positive/negative two, as they are in Figure 1-42f. If you then rescaled the cube by three, all of the new, scaled vertices are at positive/negative six.

This multiplicative aspect of scaling has some interesting consequences. If you scale an object by one in all directions, for instance, the object does not change at all. This is because any number multiplied by one remains the same number. When you scaled the cube by two only in one direction, you effec-

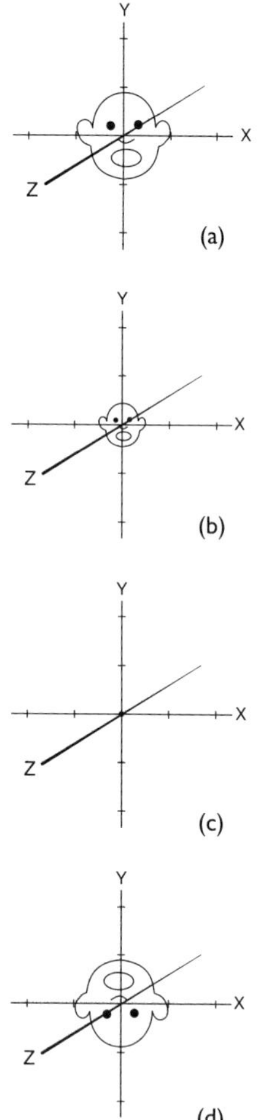

Figure 1-43. The multiplicative nature of scaling can produce some unusual results.

tively scaled it by one in the other directions; the scale operation performed in Figure 1-42b, therefore, is written *scale (2,1,1)*.

If you scale an object by a number less than one (Figure 1-43a), you decrease the size of the object. For example, scaling by 0.5 makes an object half as big (Figure 1-43b), because multiplying those numbers that define the surface of the object by a factor of 0.5 makes all those numbers half of what they were. If a vertex of a cube is located at (6,6,6), scaling the cube by 0.5 causes the vertex to be located at (3,3,3).

If you scale an object by zero, you reduce that object to an infinitesimally small, indeed invisible, point, because any number times zero equals zero. When multiplied by zero, all the points that define an object, no matter the original values, collapse to zero. The effect of this is to make the object disappear (Figure 1-43c).

Finally, if you scale by a negative number, you flip, or invert, the object. Left becomes right, up becomes down, and so on, because multiplication by a negative number reverses the sign of the original number. For example, if one of the points that defines an object is (2,5,8), and you scale (i.e., multiply) it by negative one in the Y direction, the new, scaled point is (2,–5,8). In Figure 1-43d the original head has been scaled negatively along the Y axis, but left unchanged along the other two axes. In other words, *scale (1,–1,1)*. Negating the numbers along the Y axis has the effect of making what was "up" become down and what was "down" become up.

Now that you understand the three basic transformations, you want to use them. Immediately, however, you encounter an ambiguity. Imagine the following situation: you are standing at (0,0,0) and I tell you to "move (3,0,0)." You do so. Then I say "move (3,0,0)" a second time. How do you interpret this command? Does it mean "move *to* (3,0,0)"? If it does, you are already there, so you should not move at all. Or does it mean "move *an additional* 3,0,0)"? If so, you should move to the right three more paces.

Often in the real world you want to move *to* a given location, regardless of where you start from. "Go to the corner of Fifty-third Street and Lexington Avenue," for example, means "no matter where you're starting from, go to the corner of Fifty-third and Lexington." This is called an **absolute transformation**. The specific transformation values refer to an absolute location in the three-dimensional coordinate system. Wherever the object begins, it moves to that absolute location. If it begins at that location, it stays there. So if I say "move absolutely (3,0,0)," there is no ambiguity. You move *to* (3,0,0).

In other situations it is more convenient to think in terms of transforming an object relative to the present location of that object, rather than to some absolute location in space. This kind of transformation is called a **relative transformation**. A real-world example would be "go north two blocks and east one block," which means "starting from wherever you are now, go north two

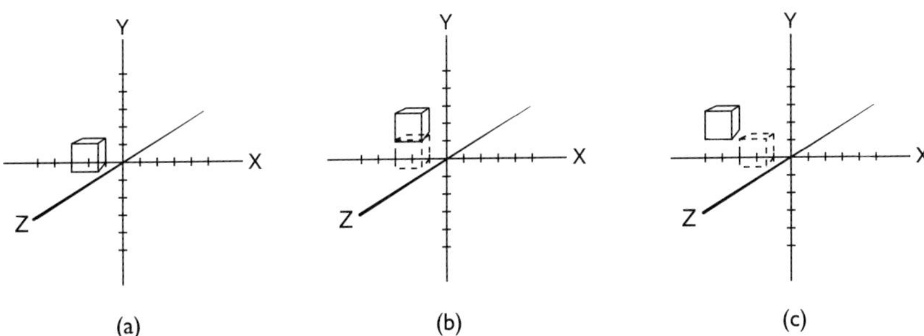

Figure 1-44. Absolute translations and relative translations.

blocks and east one block." Thus, if I tell you to "move relatively (3,0,0)," you know that no matter where you are now you must move an additional (3,0,0).

Imagine another example. Start with a cube located at (–2,0,0) (Figure 1-44a). If you request an *absolute* move of (–2,1,0), the cube does not move at all in X, because it is already at x = –2; it moves up one in Y, since it was at y = 0 and must end up at y = 1; and it does not move at all in Z, because it is already at z = 0 (Figure 1-44b). If, however, you return the cube to the original position of (–2,0,0) and request a *relative* move of (–2,1,0), the cube moves an additional (–2,1,0), causing it to end up at (–4,1,0) (Figure 1-44c).

Although the examples given so far involved only translations, the distinction between absolute and relative transformations holds true for the other two basic transformations—rotations and scales. Let's look at the other two transformations. When you say "rotate forty-five degrees about X," for instance, you may intend either an absolute rotation or a relative rotation. If you request an absolute rotation, the object ends up rotated exactly forty-five degrees about X, no matter what the original X rotation was. If you request a relative rotation, the object rotates an additional forty-five degrees around X. In Figure 1-45a a "board," rotated ninety degrees around X, lies flat. In Figure 1-45b this same board has been rotated absolutely forty-five degrees around X, and this causes it to pop up. In Figure 1-45c the original board has been rotated relatively forty-five degrees around X, causing it to rotate farther down around the X axis.

A similar thing happens when you apply absolute and relative scaling transformations. If you already have scaled an object by a factor of two in all three axes (Figure 1-46a), and you scale again by a factor of two, there are two possibilities. If the second scaling operation is an absolute scale, the object does not change size (Figure 1-46b). If the second scale is relative, the object doubles in size as a result of the operation (Figure 1-46c).

When working with a 3D computer graphics system, you must know whether you are applying absolute or relative transformations. Most software packages provide you with both alternatives and give you some way of indicating which you want to use. Depending on the individual modeling situation, it may be more convenient to work sometimes with absolute and sometimes with relative transformations.

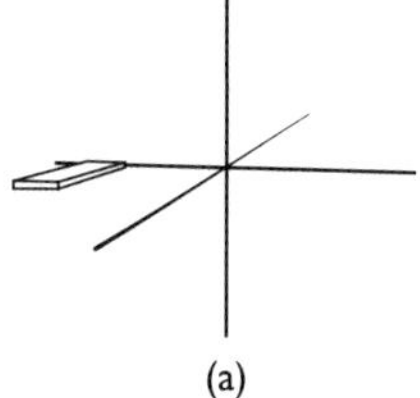

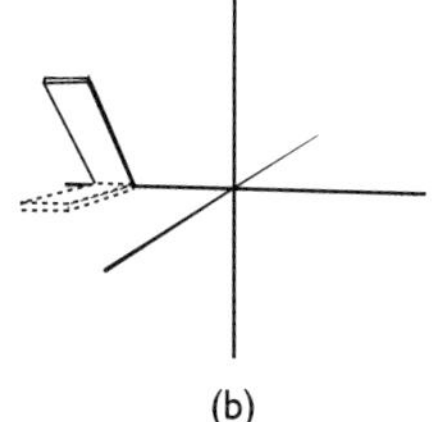

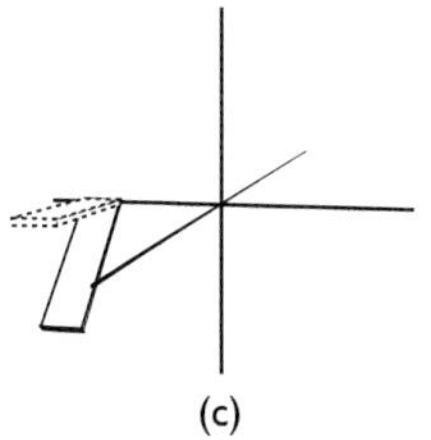

Figure 1-45. Absolute rotations and relative rotations.

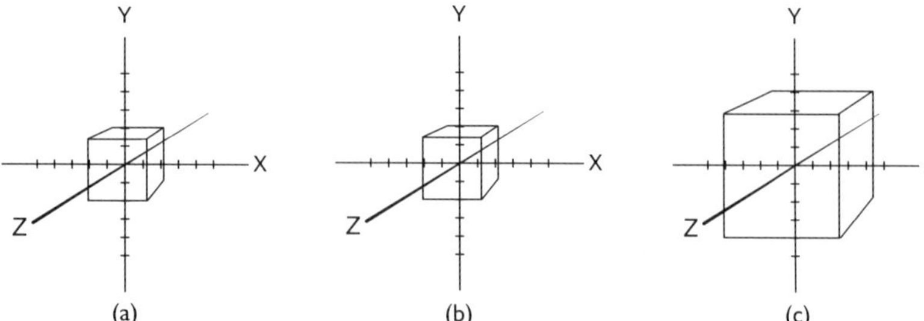

Figure 1-46. Absolute and relative scaling operations on a cube.

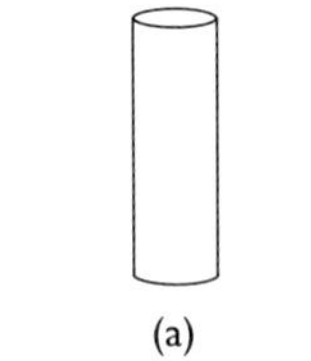

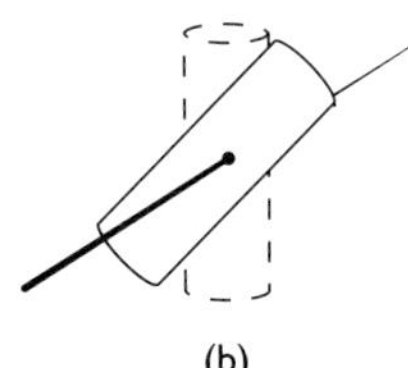

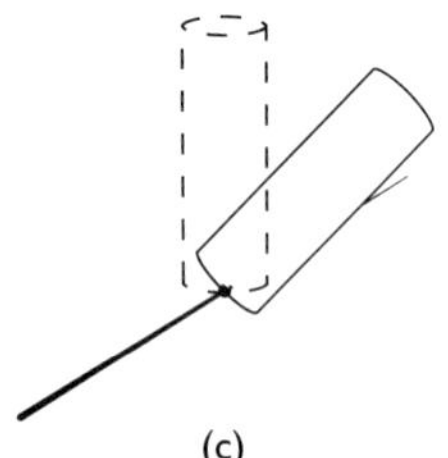

Figure 1-47. The result of the rotation depends on where the "axis" touches the cylinder.

Having resolved the possible confusion between absolute and relative transformations, you must resolve one last ambiguity. Imagine a cylinder standing vertically (Figure 1-47a). Suppose you rotate this cylinder negative forty-five degrees around the Z axis by sticking a pin in the front of the cylinder and twirling the cylinder about that pin. The final position of the cylinder depends on where your imaginary pin touches the cylinder; that is, if you insert the pin exactly into the center of the cylinder (Figure 1-47b), or if you insert the pin into the bottom of the cylinder (Figure 1-47c).

The point about which the cylinder rotates is called the **pivot point** or, more accurately, the **local origin** of that object. This second term introduces an idea crucial to the understanding of transformations: every object has a private coordinate system, which resides within the larger coordinate system of the whole world (Figure 1-48a). The **world coordinate system**, or **global coordinate system**, is the one used so far in this book. The "local origin" of an object, in contrast, is the center of the **local coordinate system** of that object.

Transformations of an object take place within the space defined by the local coordinate system of the object. If you define the local origin of a cylinder to be in the center of the cylinder (see Figure 1-48a), then the Z axis of the local coordinate system runs through the center of the cylinder. If, however, you define the local origin of the cylinder to be at the bottom of the cylinder, the local Z axis runs through the bottom of the cylinder (Figure 1-48b).

The importance of the local origin and the local coordinate system of an object is not limited to the rotation transformation, since all three of the transformations can be thought of in terms of a local origin and local coordinate system. When you translate an object, you are moving the object and the local coordinate system together, as a unit. The final numerical location of the object is, in fact, the location within the world coordinate system of the origin of the local coordinate system of the object. Thus, when you say that a cone (Figure 1-49a) is located at (5,3,0), you really are saying that the origin of the local coordinate system of the cone is located at (5,3,0). Suppose, however, that you shift the cone itself so that the local origin is at the *tip* of the cone, rather than in its center (Figure 1-49b). The local coordinate system and the local origin of this cone remain in the same numerical locations—that is, at (5,3,0). Even though you once again have translated the cone to (5,3,0),

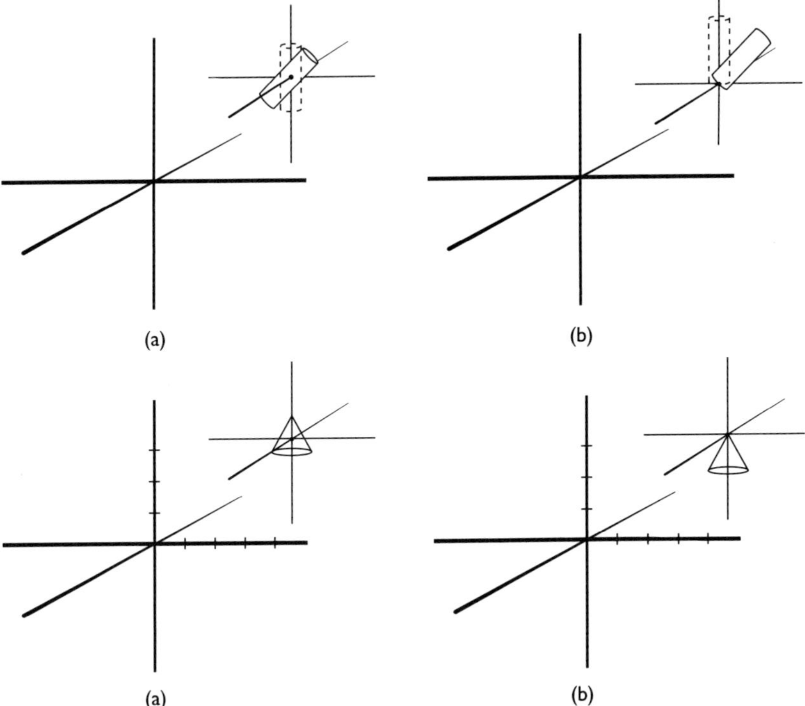

Figure 1-48. Each object exists within its own local coordinate system. Here, the local coordinate systems of the two cylinders differ, causing their rotations to differ.

Figure 1-49. The definition of the local coordinate system of an object affects translations applied to that object.

it ends up looking different because the placement of the cone relative to the local origin is different.

The effect of local origin on scaling can be even more dramatic. Remember that scaling is a multiplicative function. When you scale an object, you multiply the numbers that define the surface of that object. This multiplication takes place within the local coordinate system of the object. Therefore, the placement of the object within that system affects the final visual result of any scaling operation. Depending on where you place the object with respect to the local origin, you get different results from the same scaling operation.

As an example, imagine that you want to scale a cube by 0.5 in all three axes—in other words, make it half as big. If the local origin of the cube is in the center of the cube, scaling the cube by 0.5 makes the cube shrink equally in all directions (Figure 1-50a). This happens because you have multiplied by 0.5 all of the numbers that define the surface of the cube, making them approach by fifty percent the (0,0,0) point, or local origin, which is at the center of the cube.

In Figure 1-50b, however, the local origin of the cube is located at the lower left corner of the cube. A multiplication/scale by 0.5 causes all the numbers that define the surface of the cube to approach *this* (0,0,0) point. As a result, the cube slides down and to the left as it shrinks, approaching the local origin in the corner of the cube.

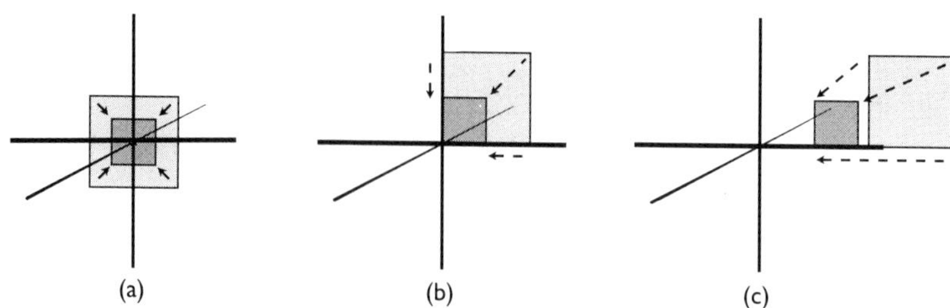

Figure 1-50. Scaling transformations are dramatically affected by the location of the origin of the local coordinate system. (The original cube is represented here in simplified form as the larger and lightly shaded square.)

In Figure 1-50c, the local origin of the cube has been moved even farther to the left. A scale of 0.5 again causes the cube to slide towards its origin, this time actually shifting the new, smaller cube substantially to the left.

Although you have been looking at such transformations in isolation from one another, in practice it is more common to apply several transformations to a single object in order to make the object do what you want. For example, if you were going to use a cone to model a lamp shade, you might want to scale the cone to the correct size, move it to the top of the lamp, and then perhaps tilt it a bit off center. Even more realistically, you might translate the cone, translate it again, rotate it, rotate it again, scale it, translate it once more, scale it again, and finally rotate it one last time. All of these transformations end up being compressed by the software of the 3D modeling system into one set of the three basic transformations—that is, into a single translation, a single rotation, and a single scale. This compression of multiple transformations into a single set of transformations is known as the **concatenation of transformations**.

The result of the concatenation of a series of transformations is nine transformation values: the three concatenated translation values (translation in X, translation in Y, and translation in Z); the three concatenated rotation values (rotation in X, rotation in Y, and rotation in Z); and the three concatenated scale values (scale in X, scale in Y, and scale in Z). These nine values are often represented by writing them in a three-by-three rectangular grid. Since a grid is also called a "matrix" (the plural of "matrix" is "matrices"), this representation is known as a **transformation matrix**. (The transformation matrix representation is especially significant from a mathematical point of view, because it permits software developers to easily manipulate transformation values using "matrix arithmetic.") In Figure 1-51a, which is a generic representation of a transformation matrix, the horizontal row at the top contains the three translation values, abbreviated as *tx*, *ty*, and *tz*; the middle row contains the three rotation values; and the bottom row contains the three scale values. In Figure 1-51b, a specific set of transformation values is arranged into a transformation matrix.

Whenever you create an object, the object automatically has a set of transformation values applied to it, even before you deliberately transform it. This

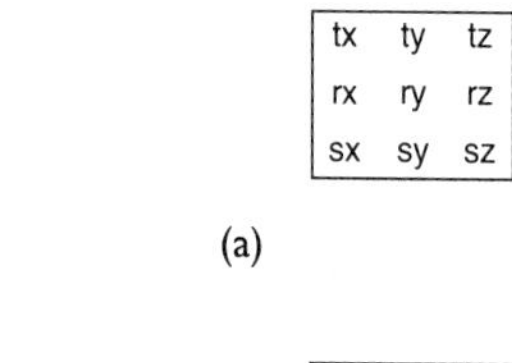

tx	ty	tz
rx	ry	rz
sx	sy	sz

(a)

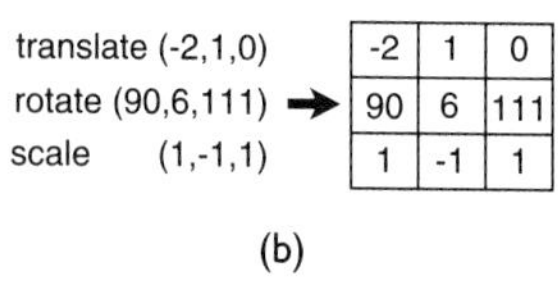

	-2	1	0
translate (-2,1,0)	-2	1	0
rotate (90,6,111) →	90	6	111
scale (1,-1,1)	1	-1	1

(b)

Figure 1-51. The nine transformation values can be organized into a transformation matrix.

default set of transformation values is effectively transparent, in that it doesn't move the object, doesn't rotate the object, and keeps the object at the original scale. This default transformation, in other words, consists of the following transformations: *move (0,0,0); rotate (0,0,0); scale (1,1,1)*. This particular set of transformation values, since it does not alter the object at all, is called the **identity transformation** (Figure 1-52). The identity transformation is also the set of values you return to if ever you want to "remove" all the transformations from an object.

0	0	0
0	0	0
1	1	1

Figure 1-52. The identity transformation.

The concept of the transformation matrix is central to 3D computer graphics, and one particular technique extends this concept. The technique involves situations in which you find yourself handling a large number of the same object in a scene. Chairs in a large office, for example, might all be of the same style and design—or, to phrase it more technically, the geometry of all the chairs is identical (Figure 1-53). Only the placement and orientation—that is, the transformations—of the chairs vary.

The technique in computer graphics developed to handle this sort of modeling situation is called **instantiation**. With this technique, it is possible to model a single chair and then to create **instances** of that model. An instance is not a "copy" of the model. A copy replicates the geometry of a model. With an instance, the geometry of the model is not duplicated but merely "pointed to," as if the software system were saying, "Give me seven more of those things over there."

You saw earlier that whenever you create a model a transformation matrix is automatically associated with it. When you create an instance, a new transformation matrix is created just for that instance, but again, no new geometry is created. Thus, if you model an original chair and then create an instance of it, there will be one geometry definition with two transformation matrices—the original plus that of the instance—pointing to it (Figure 1-54). Because each instance has its own transformation matrix, you can move the instances around and transform them independently of one another.

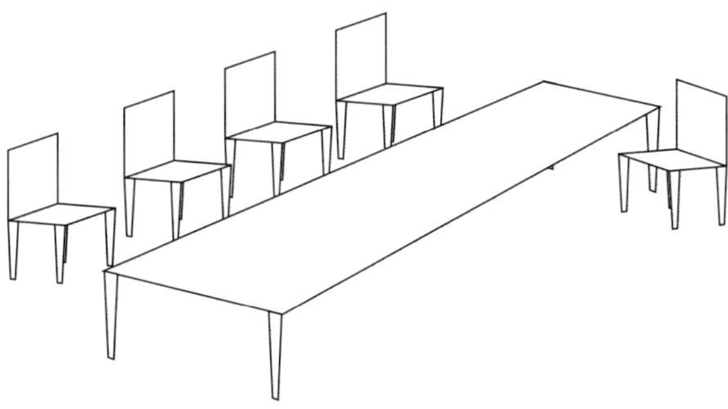

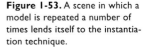

Figure 1-53. A scene in which a model is repeated a number of times lends itself to the instantiation technique.

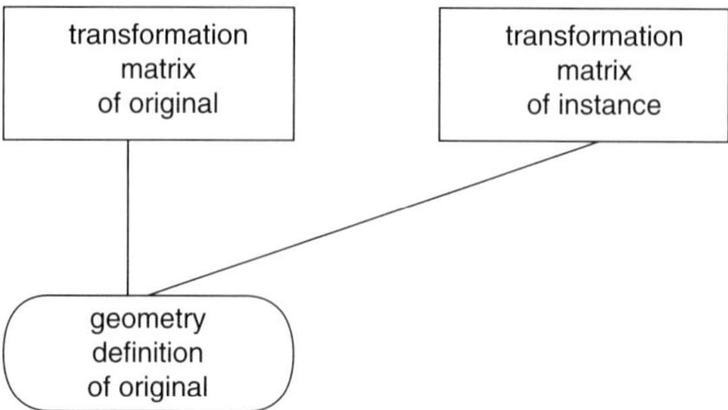

Figure 1-54. An instance has its own transformation matrix, which points to a shared geometry definition.

A major advantage of instantiation is that it affords tremendous economies of geometric data. In a situation where you have ten identical chairs in a room, you need to create and store the geometry for only one of them. All the other chairs share this same geometry. This means you deal with one-tenth the geometric data you would have dealt with had you duplicated the geometry for each chair.

Another, less obvious advantage of instantiation is that, since all the chairs share the same geometry, you very easily can make changes to the design of the entire collection of chairs. Any change you make to the original geometric definition immediately and automatically changes in each of the instanced chair models. This can be especially useful in large modeling projects such as architectural structures or outdoor scenes.

Common Modeling Techniques

A number of techniques for modeling surfaces are so simple and so powerful that you find them in almost all 3D modeling programs. These techniques are common to programs based on polygonal modeling and to programs based on patch modeling.

One such technique was inspired by a standard woodworking technique known as "turning," or "lathing." This woodworking technique involves a machine called a lathe, which clamps a piece of wood into place and then rotates it about the long axis of the piece of wood. As the wood rotates, the woodworker holds a chisel to the wood, cutting the wood symmetrically around the axis of rotation. This technique is used, for example, to form the rounded legs of chairs and tables.

Within computer graphics, you produce a **lathed surface** by drawing a curve in space and rotating it around some axis. The trace left by the curve as it rotates around the axis becomes the surface you are generating. Since rotating the curve around an axis is also referred to as "revolving" the curve around the axis, an object produced in this way is also called a **surface of revolution**, or sometimes simply a **revolve**.

In Figure 1-55a, the straight vertical line in space, represented as the darker line, is revolved around the Y axis a full 360 degrees. The surface that results from this revolution is a cylinder. In Figure 1-55b, a more irregular, S-shaped curve is revolved around the Y axis, producing a vaselike surface. Notice that if the original, or **generating**, curve touches the axis of revolution at some point, then the revolved surface will be closed at that point. This is what happens at the bottom of the vase shape in Figure 1-55b. If the original curve is some distance from the axis of revolution, as at the top of the vase, the surface will be open at that end. In Figure 1-55c, an even more irregular curve, which touches the axis at both ends, is drawn. This curve, when revolved around the Y axis, yields what might be a chair leg, as produced by a wood-turning lathe.

In principle, the generating curve can revolve around any axis. In practice, however, most systems limit the choice of axes. The most common restriction is that the axis of revolution must be one of the three perpendicular axes of the coordinate system—X, Y, or Z. In these systems, you produce a revolved surface along one of these axes, transforming that surface afterward to whatever position and orientation you need. A few more complex software systems allow you to specify any arbitrary axis by indicating the starting and ending points of a straight line. This line is then interpreted as the axis of revolution.

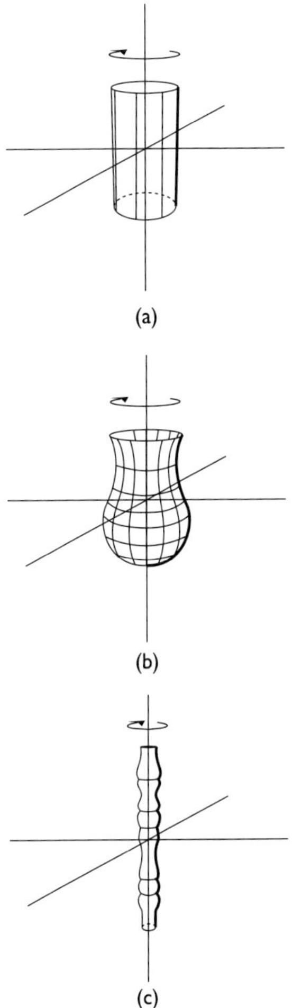

Figure 1-55. Surfaces of revolution generated by rotating a curve around an axis.

Another modeling technique found in almost all 3D packages is equally simple conceptually. In this technique, you draw a generating curve and push it straight back in space. The trace left by the curve as it moves through space becomes the surface. This technique is called **extrusion**. Objects modeled with this technique also are called extrusions or sometimes **extruded surfaces**.

A real-world example of an extrusion is a cookie cutter. The cutting edge of the cookie cutter corresponds to the generating curve, and the depth into the dough that you push the cookie cutter corresponds to the depth through space that you push the curve. For example, the Christmas-tree-shaped surface in Figure 1-56a was generated by a **closed curve**, which closes upon itself by ending exactly where it begins, like a circle. The surface in Figure 1-56b was generated by an **open**, or **unclosed, curve**.

Notice, however, the difference between a cookie cutter and a computer graphics extrusion. In a computer graphics extrusion, the trace left by the curve when it is extruded through space generates a surface that corresponds to only the *sides* of the cookie . There is no front or back to the extruded surface, whereas cookies, being made of solid material, have fronts and backs in addition to sides.

Most modeling systems allow you to address this problem in the following way. Instead of extruding just a curve, you extrude a flat surface in the shape of the generating curve. A flat surface is often called a **face**. When this is done, the generating face produces the front and back of the final extru-

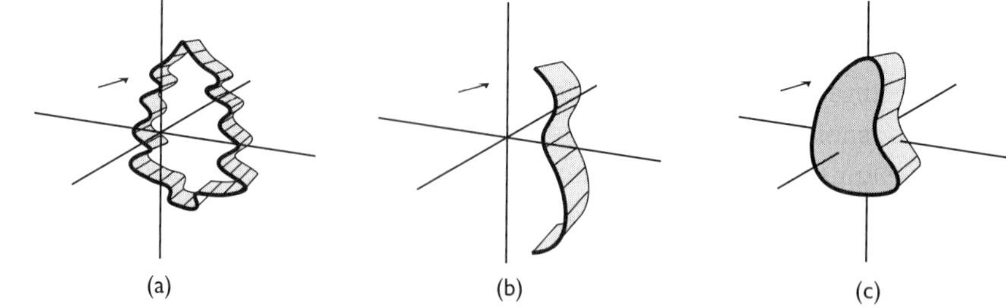

Figure 1-56. Extruded surfaces. If a face is used as the generator, the extruded result has a front and a back.

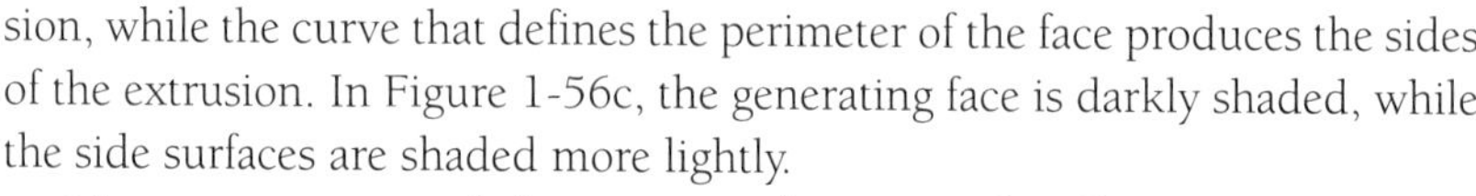

sion, while the curve that defines the perimeter of the face produces the sides of the extrusion. In Figure 1-56c, the generating face is darkly shaded, while the side surfaces are shaded more lightly.

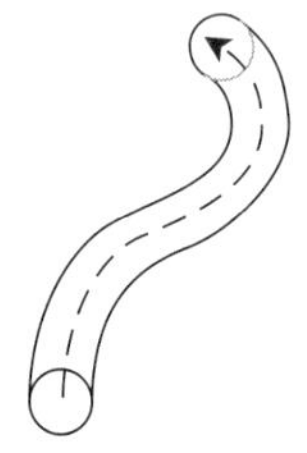

Figure 1-57. A circle extruded along a curved path to form a hoselike surface.

Many systems extend the concept of extrusion by allowing you to push the generating curve back into space in a direction other than a straight line. Instead of specifying the distance that you want to extrude your curve, you specify a path along which the curve will be extruded. This path is drawn as a second curve. In Figure 1-57 the circle is the first and generating curve. The long, snaking curve, rendered here as a dotted line, is the second curve and serves as the path of extrusion. The result is an extruded surface that resembles a snaking garden hose.

You can extend the extrusion technique further if you transform (see *Transformations*) the generating curve at the same time that it moves along the extrusion path. For example, you might scale or rotate the generating curve as it moves along the extrusion path. (Normally, you can't perform a translation transformation on a generating curve, because the movement of the curve along the path is already bringing about a translation.) When you sweep the curve along the path in this way, the surface is called a **swept surface**, or a **sweep**. For example, look back at the extrusion illustrated in Figure 1-56c. Suppose that, at the same time you push back the kidney-shaped generating curve of that figure into space, you also scale it up—say by a factor of two—to increase the size of the generating curve as it is swept. The result is that the final surface is wider at the back than in the front (Figure 1-58a).

Similarly, you could rotate the generating curve as it is swept along the extrusion path. Suppose the generating curve is a square. If you rotate this square at the same time that you move it along a straight path, you produce a twisted oblong surface (Figure 1-58b).

Combining scaling and rotation transformations with a subtly modeled generating curve and moving that curve along a complex three-dimensional path, you can quickly and easily generate some very complex and beautiful forms.

Another modeling technique found in virtually all 3D software packages was inspired by the contour maps geographers use (Figure 1-59). In these

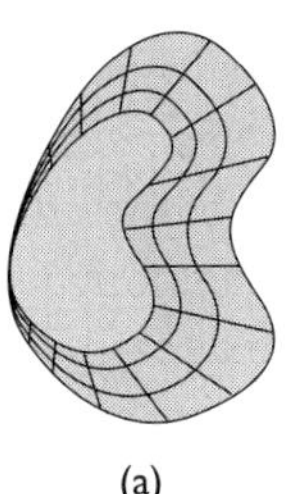
(a)

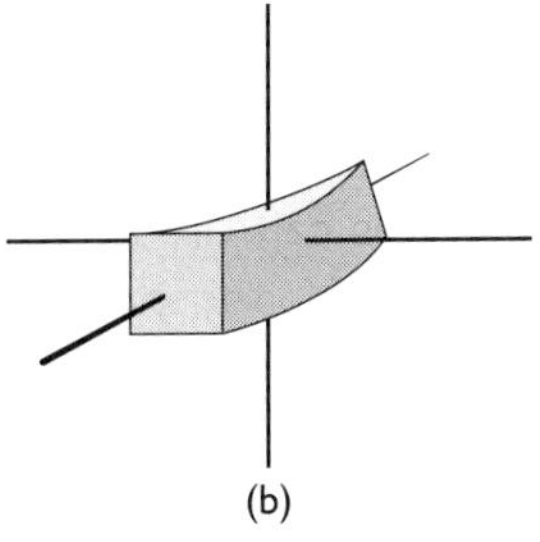
(b)

Figure 1-58. Swept surfaces generated by transforming curves as they are extruded through space.

maps, a series of concentric rings indicates the shape of a land mass, with each ring representing an increase in the height, or altitude, of the land.

In computer graphics, using an adaptation of this concept, you draw a series of curves, which may be either open or closed. You then position each curve, lofting it to some height above the previous curve. Finally, you specify the order in which these curves, or contours, are to be connected. The software system then produces a **lofted surface**, or **skin**, connecting the contours.

Figure 1-59. A contour map. Each concentric curve indicates the altitude of the surface of the land.

In Figure 1-60, both the boat hull (a) and the mountainous form (b) were generated as lofted surfaces. When creating a surface like this, the easiest way to fine-tune the model usually is to delete the model if it doesn't look right, adjust the contour curves—either by moving them up or down or by manipulating the control points—and then regenerate the form. You can repeat this process as often as necessary.

Lofting is an extremely powerful technique for generating surfaces that otherwise would be very difficult to model. The success of the technique, however, depends on how carefully you draw the contour curves and how precisely you position them in space. Notice also that the contour curves used to generate a lofted surface are effectively cross sections of the final surface. This fact makes the lofting technique very useful for digitizing physical objects (see *Digitizing Techniques*).

A final modeling technique commonly found in 3D modeling packages entails drawing curves to specify the edges, or boundaries, of a surface. With these edges defined, the software then forms a surface between the boundary curves. Since this technique works best for spline patches, surfaces generated with this technique usually are called **boundary patches**.

There are two standard approaches to the boundary-patch technique. The first is simply to draw two **boundary curves**, sometimes called **end curves**, each at an opposite end of the intended patch. You then instruct the system to calculate the surface patch that connects these two curves. Notice that the two end curves in Figure 1-61a are identical copies of each other, with the same curvature. This produces a patch that is symmetrical from one generating boundary curve to the other. In Figure 1-61b, however, the two end

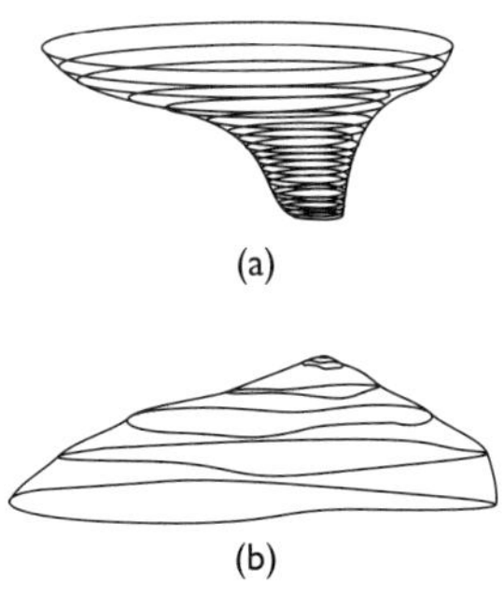

Figure 1-60. Lofted surfaces generated by connecting a series of contour curves.

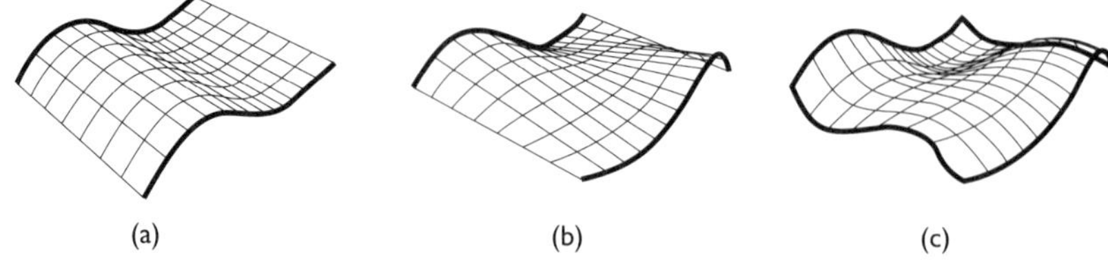

Figure 1-61. Boundary patches formed from either two or four boundary curves.

curves have radically different curvatures, and the resulting patch is much more irregularly curved. In both examples, the edges of the patch not defined by end curves are straight lines.

The second standard approach to making boundary patches is to specify four boundary curves, one for each edge of the patch. This approach can yield surfaces with much more complicated curvatures, since none of the edges of the patch need be a straight line (Figure 1-61c).

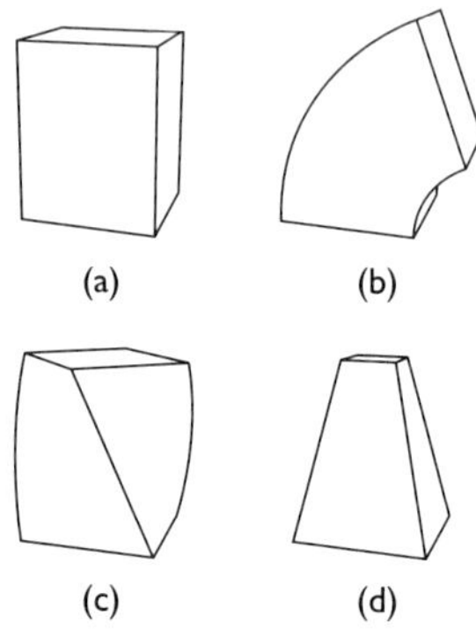

Figure 1-62. Common deformation techniques include bend, twist, and taper.

In addition to the techniques just described for generating models, there are also a number of techniques for modifying the shape of an existing object. Because they change the shape of an object, they are frequently referred to as **deformation techniques**. The most common of these are **bend**, **twist**, and **taper**. In Figure 1-62a you see the original, undeformed object, a rectangular box. Figure 1-62b, c, and d show the result, respectively, of bending, twisting, and tapering that box.

All these deformation techniques allow the animator to simply and usually with one mouse stroke relocate the points that define the surface of an object. (This approach is discussed in more detail in the *Shape Changes* section of chapter 3.) For a polygon model, these points are the polygon vertices of the surface. For a patch model, they are the control points of the surface. Since deformation techniques such as bending, twisting, and tapering operate on these points, any model that is going to be deformed in these ways must have enough points—either vertices or control points—to permit a smooth deformation. If there are too few points, the model will deform in undesirable ways (Figure 1-63). The cylinder in Figure 1-63a has only three horizontal rows of points. As a result, when it bends, it "creases," rather than bending smoothly. By contrast, the cylinder in Figure 1-63b has nine horizontal rows of points, which is enough to permit it to bend smoothly.

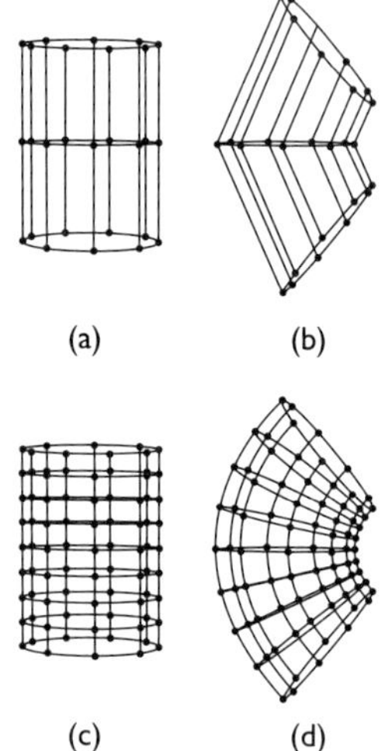

Figure 1-63. If a model has too few points defining its surface, it will not deform smoothly.

In using deformation techniques it is also important to carefully place the local origin, or pivot point, of the object. As you saw in the section on *Transformations,* the placement of the local origin affects the way an object transforms, since transformations are calculated with reference to that local origin. The same principle applies to the transformation of the points of an object; the placement of the local origin can radically affect the final result of a bend, twist, or taper operation. An undeformed object is shown in Figure 1-64a. In Figure 1-64b, c, and d the placement of the local origin is indicated by small crosshairs. Depending on the placement of the local origin, the cylinder bends in very different ways.

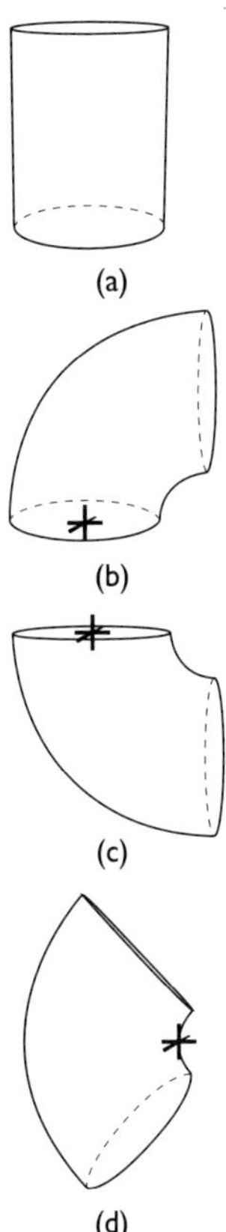

Figure 1-64. The placement of the object's local origin affects the way it will deform.

Hierarchies

Earlier in this chapter you learned how to move, rotate, and scale objects—that is, to "transform" them. All of the examples in that section dealt with individual objects in isolation from one another. You moved a sphere, you rotated a cube, and so on.

Most objects in the real world, however, and most models that you develop in a computer modeling system, are not that simple and cannot be thought of as single, undifferentiated objects. Many objects consist of several pieces, and models that consist of several parts can present problems when you try to transform them.

A table, for example, consists (at a minimum) of a top and four legs. Figure 1-65a shows a table in a side view, with only two of the legs visible. A cross marks the pivot point, or local origin, of each of the five elements—the top plus the four legs. Suppose you want to rotate the entire table around the Z axis. If you rotate the elements individually, each element rotates about its individual local origin, yielding the result on the right side of Figure 1-65a. Even though you rotate each of the elements the same number of degrees in the same direction, the placement of each element relative to the other elements changes because the local origins, or pivot points, are located at different points in space.

The same sort of thing happens if you try to scale all the elements of the table. Each element scales about its individual local origin, and as a result the legs and the top of the table are no longer positioned correctly relative to one another Figure 1-65b).

Clearly, in a situation like this you want to treat the entire table as a single, unified object. You want to rotate or scale the entire table and retain the original relationships of the parts to one another. In order for this to happen, the entire table and all of the parts must transform about a single local origin.

At the same time however, since you may need to increase the length of the legs or change the thickness of the top, you still want to be able to operate on each of the elements individually, relative to its individual pivot point.

A possible solution to this problem involves relocating the local origins of all of the elements to exactly the same point—say, to (0,0,0)—which allows you to rotate all the elements of the table uniformly and in the proper orientation. Taking this approach, however, creates other problems. If you later want to adjust the size or shape of one of the elements, you have to return the local origin of that element to the original location. If you still later want to

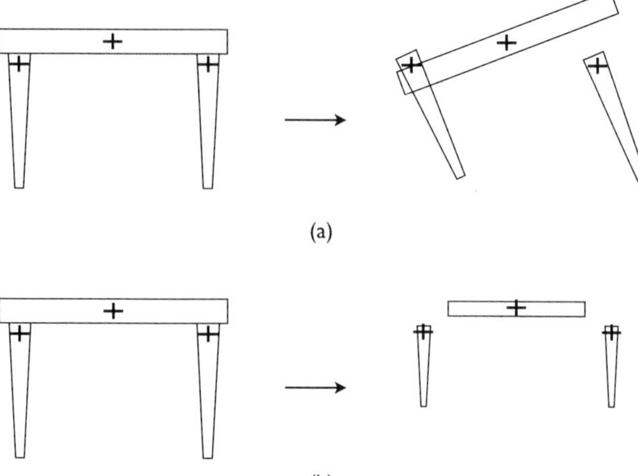

Figure 1-65. Transforming several objects around the individual pivot points of each object can cause problems.

rotate the whole table a second time (as you surely will), you have to make sure that all the pivot points are back at (0,0,0). And so on.

This process becomes very cumbersome very quickly, especially if there are a lot of elements to your model. Imagine, for example, trying to use this approach on a model of an ornate eighteenth-century table. You would have to move, and then move back, and then move back again the pivot point of every piece of molding and every piece of filigree.

The solution is to organize your model into a hierarchical structure. This is called **hierarchical modeling**. In the case of the table, you define the whole table to be the top, or "master" level of the structure. You define the separate elements of the table to be the lower levels of the structure. The mathematics of hierarchical modeling is such that now you can operate on the model as you wish to; that is, you can control the transformations either as a group or individually. If you operate on the top level, you affect the entire table as a unit. If you operate on the lower levels, you affect only the individual elements at those levels.

Remember that when you define an object, it automatically has its own local coordinate system. A similar thing happens with each level of a hierarchical model. When you define the hierarchy for a model, each level of the hierarchy automatically has its own separate local coordinate system and a separate local origin. Transformations applied to each level of the hierarchy thus take place around the local origin of that level. For example, say you define the local origin of the top level of your table hierarchy to be on the floor between the legs. Any transformation to the whole table happens with respect to this local origin. Since you defined the top level to consist of all the various pieces of the table, all of these pieces transform as a unit with respect to this one point in space. Likewise, if you locate the local origin of each leg

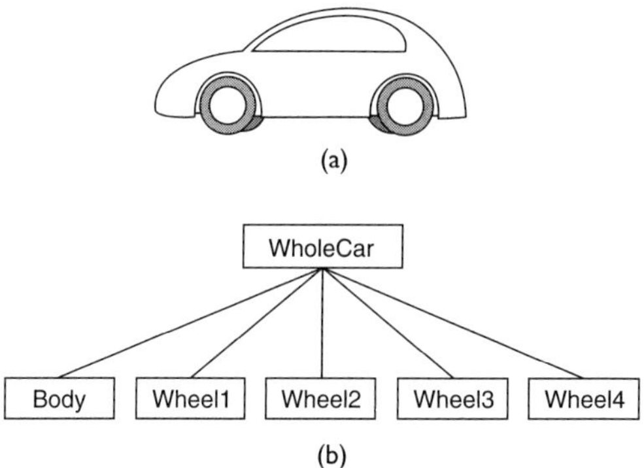

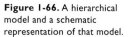

Figure 1-66. A hierarchical model and a schematic representation of that model.

at the top of the leg (see Figure 1-65), when you operate on one of these lower-level objects, it transforms individually around that one point.

To elaborate on this concept: suppose you model a car consisting of a body and four wheels (Figure 1-66a). Each of the four wheels and the body of the car has a local coordinate system and a local origin, as does any surface. Another way of saying this is that each element has a separate transformation matrix and can therefore be transformed individually as need be. Each of the five elements functions independently of the others. For example, the local origin of each of the wheels is located in the center of the wheel, allowing the wheel to be rotated around an imaginary axle. *Wheel1* rotates without causing any of the other wheels or the body to rotate, and so on.

All five of these elements, however, are grouped hierarchically into a higher-level element, in this case called *WholeCar*. This level has its own local coordinate system and local origin and is controlled by another, separate transformation matrix. Any transformation applied to the *WholeCar* level also affects the lower-level elements, since they are grouped logically within *WholeCar*. The transformations of *WholeCar* "propagate downward" to the lower-level objects. These transformations, however, are always relative to the local origin of *WholeCar*, so that if the entire car is picked up and translated, the wheels translate with it. A simple diagram, or **schematic representation**, makes clear this hierarchy of transformations (Figure 1-66b).

Within such a hierarchy, each element is often called a **node**, and in this instance there are six nodes: one node at the top level and five nodes at the next level down. A node hierarchically just below another node often is called a **child** of the higher node, just as the higher node often is called the **parent** of the lower, child node. *WholeCar*, therefore, is the parent node of the other five nodes. These nodes—*Body*, *Wheel1*, and so on—are children of *WholeCar*.

Suppose that the car is rolling down the road. You want the entire car to translate, and perhaps rotate a bit about Y, as it moves. At the same time, you want each of the four wheels to rotate about its own axis. The structure just diagrammed allows you to do this. To operate on a given wheel—say, *Wheel1*—you put a transformation into the transformation matrix of *Wheel1*

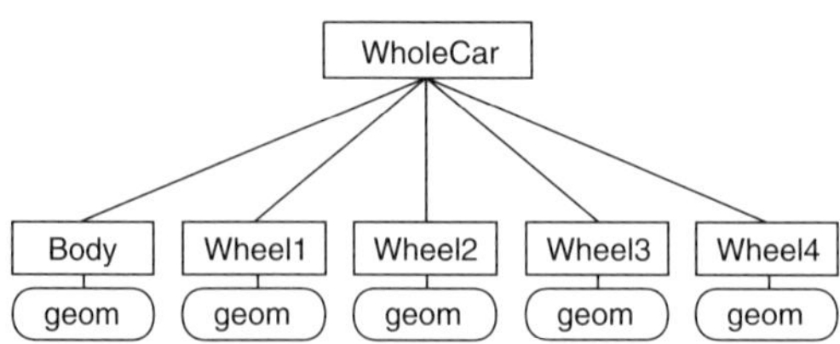

Figure 1-67. A schematic representation showing the presence or absence of geometry at each node of the hierarchy.

on the lower level. The rotation of *Wheel1* has no effect on any other node of the hierarchy, since *Wheel1* is not a parent of any other node. Next, to move the entire car, you transform the *WholeCar* level. Since this *WholeCar* level is a parent of the other nodes, any transformation you apply to it propagates downward and transforms the lower-level nodes as well. For example, if you translate *WholeCar* in X, the wheel and body nodes translate in X with it—that is, all the parts stick together, as they should.

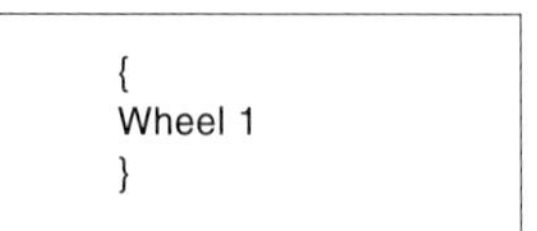

Figure 1-68. Each node of a hierarchy can be represented textually as enclosed within curly brackets.

Another possible representation of this same hierarchy of transformations includes some additional, potentially useful information (Figure 1-67). Not only does this diagram illustrate the fact that parent nodes encompass and affect lower-level child nodes; it also illustrates the fact that a given node may or may not include an actual surface. Surfaces are often referred to generically as "geometry," and in this representation an oval (and the abbreviation "geom") indicates the presence of geometry. A rectangle represents the presence of a transformation matrix.

Notice that the five lower-level nodes (*Body*, *Wheel1*, etc.) all consist of both a transformation matrix (a rectangle) and some geometry (an oval). The highest level, *WholeCar*, by contrast, consists of a transformation matrix but no geometry. *WholeCar* is a purely logical construct. There is no "shape" to *WholeCar*, no surface associated with *WholeCar*. *WholeCar* is a logical grouping of several subelements, the grouping accomplished by the definition of a transformation matrix that propagates effects downward to the lower levels of the hierarchy.

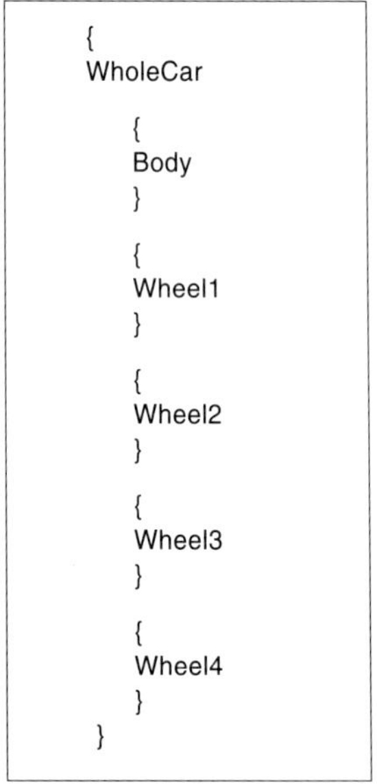

Figure 1-69. Placing a set of curly brackets inside another set indicates that the transformations of the outer set propagate downward to the inner node.

Another very common representation of transformation hierarchies is a textual representation, the syntax of which is derived from the *C* programming language, the language most commonly used for writing graphics programs. In this representation, the name of each node is enclosed within an opening and a closing **curly bracket** (Figure 1-68). The levels of a hierarchy are represented by the placement of a lower-level node within the brackets of a higher level node (Figure 1-69). (Indentation improves legibility, but is not necessary.)

Notice that the *WholeCar* node begins with an opening curly bracket, on the first line, and ends with a closing curly bracket, on the last line. Notice also that each of the *Wheel* and *Body* nodes consists of an opening curly bracket, a node name, and a closing curly bracket, and that each of the nodes appears inside the *WholeCar* node. The fact that they are inside the *WholeCar* node indicates that they are influenced by whatever transformations are applied to *WholeCar*.

Such a textual representation becomes particularly useful when you want to see the specific numerical values associated with each transformation, or node (Figure 1-70). (Wherever you see <*geometry of* . . . > would be the actual geometric information defining that particular surface.) From these specific transformation values you can tell that each of the wheels has been rotated some amount around its local Z axis. The *Body* of the car has been scaled, within its local coordinate system, to the desired size. And finally, the *WholeCar* (which, remember, itself has no geometry—only a transformation matrix) has a translation, a rotation, and a scale, all of which propagate downward through the hierarchy and affect all the lower levels, moving, rotating, and scaling them as a unit relative to the local coordinate system of *WholeCar*.

```
{
translate 22, 0, 0
rotate 0, 45, 0
scale 2,2,2
    {
    scale 0.7, 2.1, 1.8
    <geometry of Body>
    }

    {
    rotate 0, 0, 342
    <geometry of Wheel1>
    }

    {
    rotate 0, 0, 222
    <geometry of Wheel2>
    }

    {
    rotate 0, 0, 129
    <geometry of Wheel3>
    }

    {
    rotate 0, 0, -327
    <geometry of Wheel4>
    }
}
```

Figure 1-70. Specific transformations data can be included in the textual representation of the hierarchy.

Representing the hierarchy and the transformations of the model in this way helps make clearer the propagation of the transformations from one level to another. The idea is that any transformation is still in effect as long as it has not been "stopped" by the closing curly bracket that signals the conclusion of that node. Thus, in this example, the translation, rotation, and scale transformations of the upper-level node, *WholeCar*, continue to be in effect (that is, they are propagating downward) all the way to the last line of the text, where they are stopped by the curly bracket that closes the upper-level node. In other words, the transformations on *WholeCar* affect all the subelements (lower-level nodes) of *WholeCar*—which is exactly what you want to happen.

By contrast, the scale transformation applied to the *Body* node (line six of the text) is stopped immediately after the geometry of *Body* (line seven) by the closing curly bracket of the *Body* node (line eight). Again, you want this to happen, because you don't want the scale transformation of *Body* to have any effect on the subsequent wheel nodes.

This starting and stopping of a transformation are referred to in computer science as, respectively, a **push** and a **pop**. The opening curly bracket "pushes"—puts into effect, turns on—the transformation. The closing curly bracket "pops"—turns off—the transformation.

The "push" and "pop" terminology derives from the image of plates stacked on a spring device such as you might find in a cafeteria (Figure 1-71). As you place plates onto the stack, the stack becomes heavier and the plates sink down, so that the topmost plate always stays at the same level, ready for the customer. If you place a plate on such a stack, the stack is *pushed* down. If you take a plate off the stack, the stack *pops* back up a little.

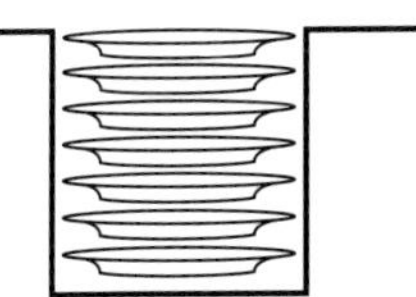

Figure 1-71. Adding a plate to the stack "pushes" the stack down. Taking one off the stack "pops" the stack up.

Pushing a plate onto the stack corresponds to turning on a transformation with an opening curly bracket. Popping a plate off the stack corresponds to

```
push
translate 22, 0, 0
rotate 0, 45, 0
scale 2, 2, 2

    push
    scale 0.7, 2.1, 1.8
    <geometry of Body>
    pop

    push
    rotate 0, 0, 342
    <geometry of Wheel1>
    pop

    .
    .
    .
pop
```

Figure 1-72. The "push"/"pop" terminology can replace the curly brackets to indicate the starting and ending of a transformation node.

turning off a transformation with a closing curly bracket. In fact, the term **transformation stack** often is used to indicate the collection of all the transformations currently in effect and how they propagate onto one another. Making even more explicit use of this stack imagery, systems sometimes substitute the words "push" and "pop" for "{" and "}" in the textual representation of a hierarchy of transformations (Figure 1-72).

Example: The Human Figure

The human figure is one example of a model that you need to organize hierarchically. It is a particularly good example because it is so familiar and so complicated (Figure 1-73).

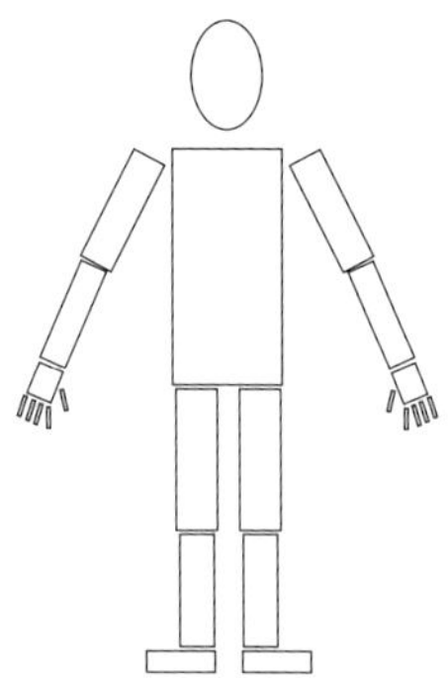

Figure 1-73. A human-figure model must be organized hierarchically in order to function properly.

Think about positioning just one arm of this figure (Figure 1-74). First you might rotate the whole arm around the pivot point located in the shoulder joint. All of the elements of the arm—upper arm, forearm, hand, and fingers—should rotate together. Having rotated the whole arm, you might bend the arm at the elbow. This rotation causes all the elements below the elbow joint (forearm, hand, and fingers) to rotate, but does not affect the upper arm. Next, you might rotate the hand and, along with it, of course, the fingers. And finally, you might slightly rotate each of the fingers. (If the model were more detailed, you could continue down a few more levels to the individual joints of the fingers!)

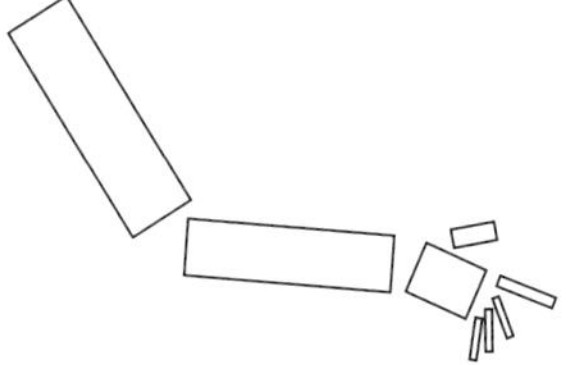

Figure 1-74. Transformations must be applied to each level of the "arm" hierarchy in order to position the arm.

To accomplish all of this, you need to structure the hierarchy of the model so that each node (finger, hand, forearm, etc.) affects or does not affect the other nodes in just the way you want them to. For example, you do not want a rotation of a finger to affect the whole arm, but you do want a transformation on the whole arm to affect, or propagate downward to, the fingers. Figure 1-75 is an appropriate hierarchical structure for this arm model, though for the sake of simplicity, the diagram contains only the rectangular transformation matrices, omitting the oval geometry icons.

Notice that you do not need to define a separate transformation matrix, or node, for the upper arm. This is because in human anatomy the upper arm cannot rotate, or translate, independently of the whole arm. The upper arm would be represented simply as some geometry included under the *WholeArm* transformation.

The hierarchical structure for each of the limbs of the model would be similar to that of the one arm.

In addition, you might want to develop a hierarchy that allows the figure to bend at the waist (Figure 1-76). This structure should reflect the fact that when a person bends at the waist, his or her arms and head move as well.

Notice again that you do not need to define a separate transformation for

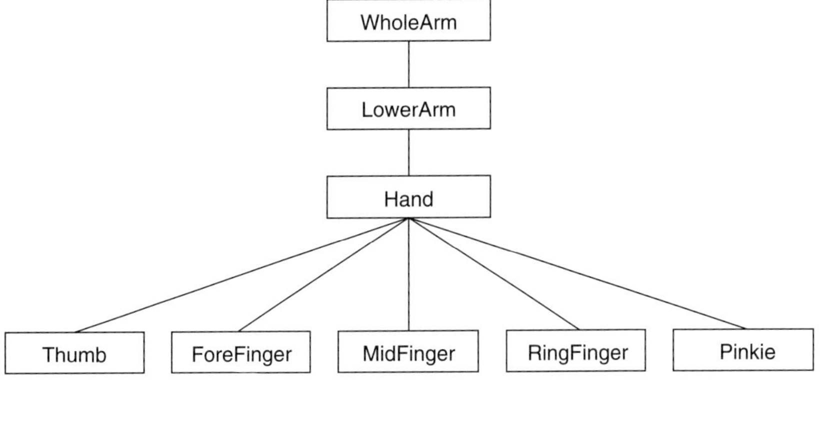

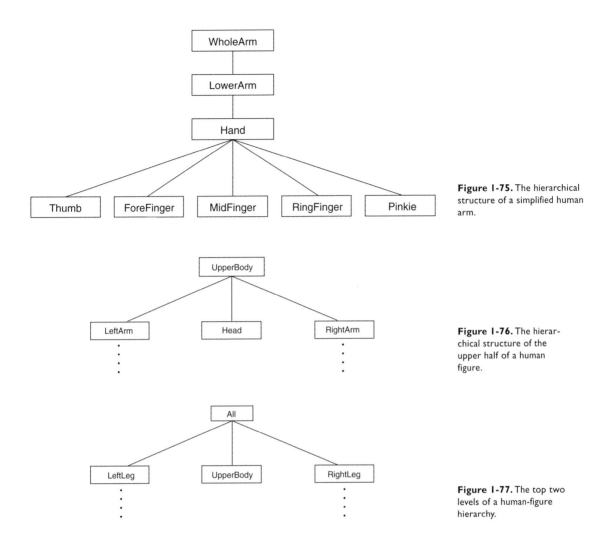

Figure 1-75. The hierarchical structure of a simplified human arm.

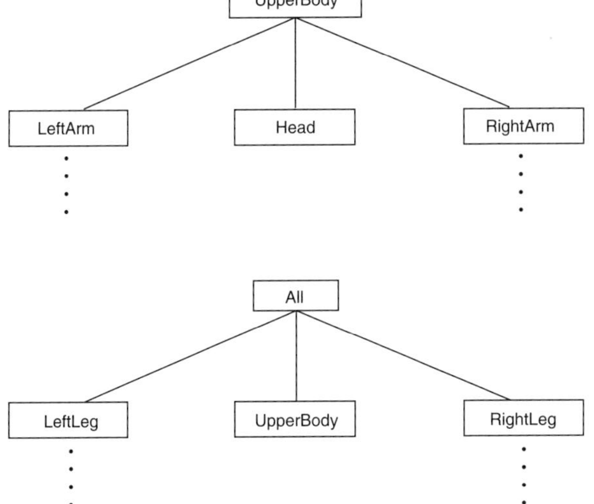

Figure 1-76. The hierarchical structure of the upper half of a human figure.

Figure 1-77. The top two levels of a human-figure hierarchy.

the torso, since that segment cannot move independently of the entire *UpperBody*. Also notice that *LeftArm*, *RightArm*, and *Head* are all on the same level, so that each can be transformed independently of the other. Since they are all children of *UpperBody*, however, they all will be affected by whatever happens to that higher-level node.

Adding a topmost level to the hierarchy allows you to transform everything in the figure: the *UpperBody* and everything in it, the *RightLeg* and everything in it, and the *LeftLeg* and everything in it (Figure 1-77).

Attaching all the levels of the structure produces a workable transformation hierarchy for the entire model (Figure 1-78).

It is very important to understand that in developing a computer model like this, there is no "correct" structure. In the case of the human figure, for

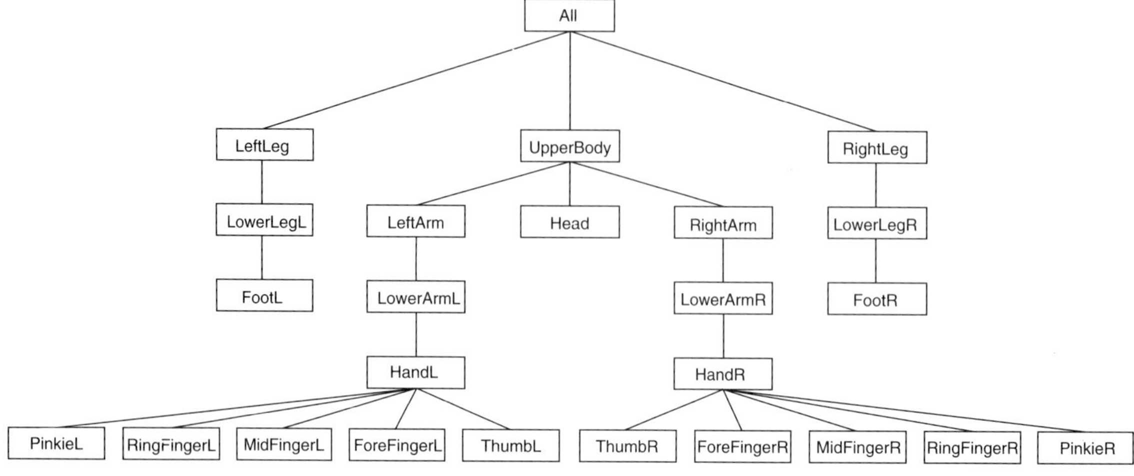

Figure 1-78. The entire hierarchy of the human model illustrated in Figure 1-73.

instance, you probably do not need to move both of the legs as a unit. In most situations humans don't do so. Consequently, the two leg nodes are not grouped together under a separate node. If, however, your model represented an acrobat, who might frequently move both legs as a unit, then you might insert an extra node, perhaps called *BothLegs*, which would have under it both of the leg nodes. In this way you could move the legs individually, by operating on the *LeftLeg* and *RightLeg* nodes, or you could move both legs as a unit, by operating on the *BothLegs* node. The hierarchical structure you choose depends on what you want to be able to do with your model; that is, on how you want your model to move.

Boolean Operations and Trims

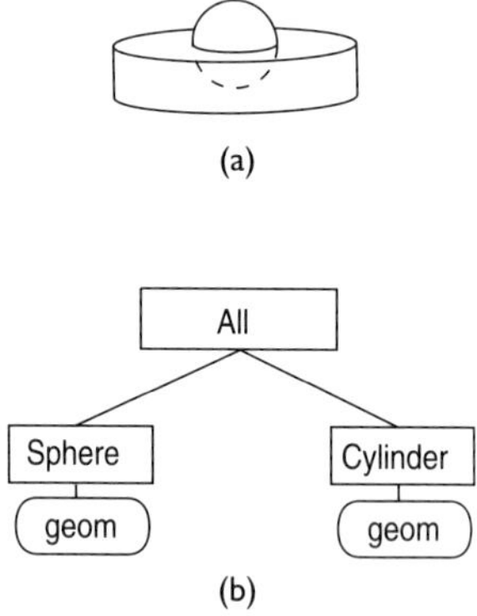

Figure 1-79. Combining two objects hierarchically means retaining the original two pieces of geometry.

In the previous section you saw that it is possible to combine several simple objects into a single, more complex object by structuring the objects into a hierarchy. There are some situations, however, where this technique turns out to be limiting. Suppose, for example, that you want to combine a cylinder and a sphere to form a larger object (Figure 1-79a). If you do this by grouping the two objects hierarchically, the result remains *two* objects. That is, your single object is composed of two distinct pieces. They can be moved about as a unit, since they exist in a hierarchy, but they remain distinct. In Figure 1-79b, "Cylinder" and "Sphere" are grouped under "All" but each retains its own geometry.

Suppose, further, that having joined the two objects, you want to modify in some fashion the surface area where they meet, perhaps producing a smooth, rounded transition between the surfaces. This proves very difficult to do with the two-piece model, since the area where the two objects meet is actually two surfaces, not one. (Another problem might arise if you want to apply a single pattern of color continuously across the whole object as described in *Surface Texture Mapping* in chapter 2.) Because you have two distinct objects this technique would not work.

For these and other reasons, sometimes you want to join several objects in various ways and produce a single piece of geometry—a single surface (Figure 1-80a). A **Boolean operation** allows you to do this. Notice that there is only one geometry element in the schematic diagram of this new configuration (Figure 1-80b). The shape of this geometry now includes, within the one geometric definition, both the hemispherical dome and the cylindrical base.

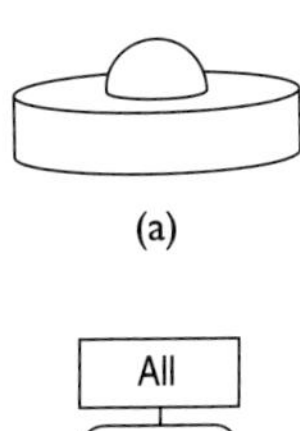

(a)

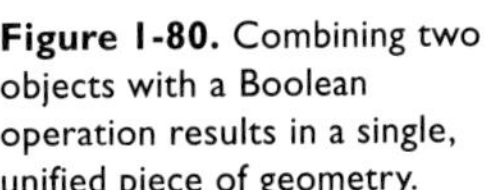

(b)

Figure 1-80. Combining two objects with a Boolean operation results in a single, unified piece of geometry.

The term "Boolean" honors the British mathematician and logician George Boole, who developed much of the logic on which these operations are based. This logic deals with combining in various ways the contents of different sets, or collections, of things. When Boolean operations deal with spatially defined sets, as in computer graphics, they are also known as **spatial set operators**. These operators, as they are applied to surface models, are actually derived from the Boolean operators used in solid-modeling systems, where they are often referred to collectively as **constructive solid geometry**, or CSG. When adapted for surface modelers, these operations lose some of the precision and exactness they have in the solid-modeling systems. Still, they remain very useful as surface-modeling tools and because of this are found in most high-level 3D animation systems.

There are three distinct Boolean operations. The first is the **addition**, or **union**, of two objects to form a third object. To the right of the two overlapping cubes in Figure 1-81a, for instance, is the result of a Boolean addition. Notice that the overlap—the volume that had been occupied by both of the cubes—has been modified so that only a single object occupies that space. This modified state, of course, corresponds to what happens in the real world, where two objects cannot occupy the same space. The fact that objects *can* do so in computer graphics is one of the great advantages of computer modeling. But if your modeling requires that you eliminate the unrealistic overlapping of two objects, a Boolean addition can do it for you.

The opposite of a Boolean addition is a Boolean **subtraction**, accomplished by the **difference operator**. As the name suggests, a Boolean subtraction takes away from an object the space occupied by another object. Notice, for example, that a piece of the lower cube in Figure 1-81b has been cut out where the upper cube had overlapped it. The upper cube acted, in effect, as a chisel to remove a portion of the lower cube.

There is a difference, however, between performing this Boolean subtraction and simply cutting a hole in the cube. Since the models here are defined by surfaces and are not solid models, cutting a hole in the cube results in an

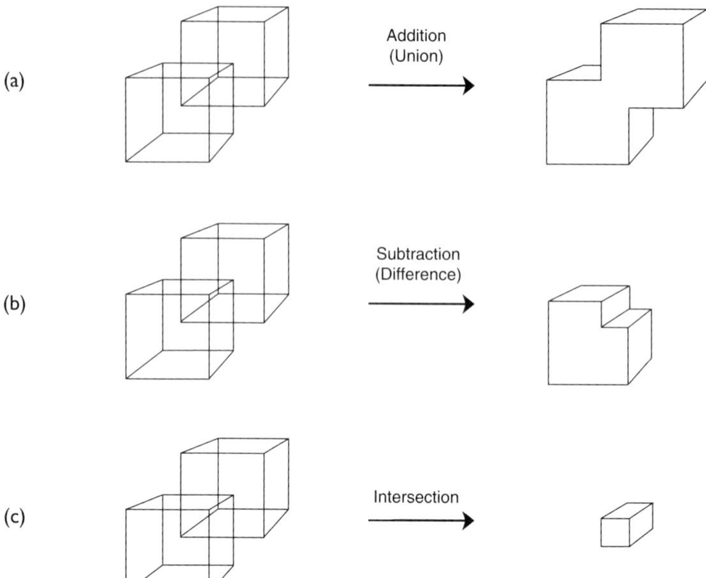

Figure 1-81. The three Boolean operations.

empty space through which something could pass into the lower cube. The Boolean subtraction, on the other hand, closes off this space with new surface area. This happens because the cutting cube, the upper cube, has surface area in that location.

The third Boolean operator is the **intersection operator**. Given two objects, such as the overlapping cubes in Figure 1-81c, the intersection operation finds those parts that are shared by both objects and produces a new object consisting of only those shared areas. In this case the intersection operation saves the space shared by the upper cube and the lower cube.

Among surface modelers, Boolean operators are found most commonly in polygon-based systems. This is because the surfaces that result from Boolean operations often are not readily parameterized into the UV space demanded by spline-based systems. Since polygons do not need to be organized into a UV directional system, an irregular shape such as the cylinder-sphere combination in Figure 1-80a presents no problem to a polygon-based modeler. The same combination does present a problem, however, to a UV-parameterized spline-based modeler.

One solution to this difficulty, presented by some software packages, is to convert all spline-based models to polygon-based models before performing any Boolean operation. This of course places a great burden on the software, because it requires that the software system support both spline-based and polygon-based modeling capabilities. Only a few systems do this.

For those systems based solely on splines and patches, there is another—although very limited—solution. Such systems often provide a function,

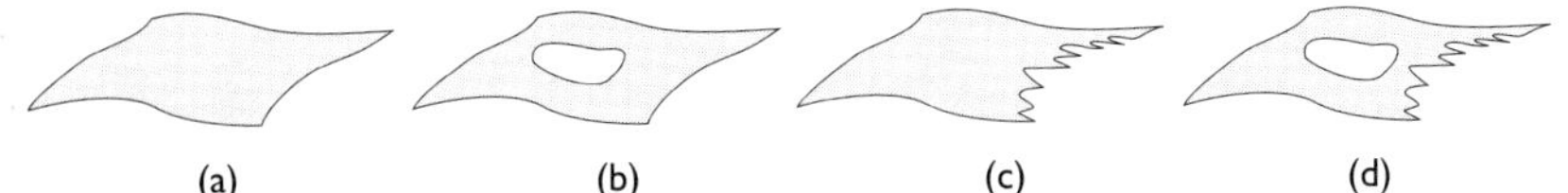

Figure 1-82. Three examples of trimming a surface.

somewhat similar to the Boolean difference operator, usually referred to as **trimming**. This function consists of cutting some pattern into a surface patch.

Figure 1-82a shows a parameterized surface patch. Figure 1-82b shows this patch with a circular hole cut in it by a trim operation, while Figure 1-82c shows the patch with a jagged edge left from trimming. And Figure 1-82d shows the patch with two trim operations—that of (*b*) and that of (*c*)—performed on the same surface.

The first of two techniques for creating a trim on a patch is to draw a curve in space and project it onto the surface you want to be trimmed. Say, for instance, that you want a normal cylinder to be trimmed (Figure 1-83a). First you draw a curve, here indicated as a heavy black line. The arrows indicate the direction in which this line projects back in space along the Z axis. Notice that as the curved line projects back along Z, it intersects the cylinder, producing a new curve around the perimeter of the cylinder. This curve is called the **curve of intersection**. Once the curve of intersection has been calculated, the trim operation itself can be performed. The trim operation cuts the original cylinder along the curve of intersection, leaving only a portion of the original surface (Figure 1-83b).

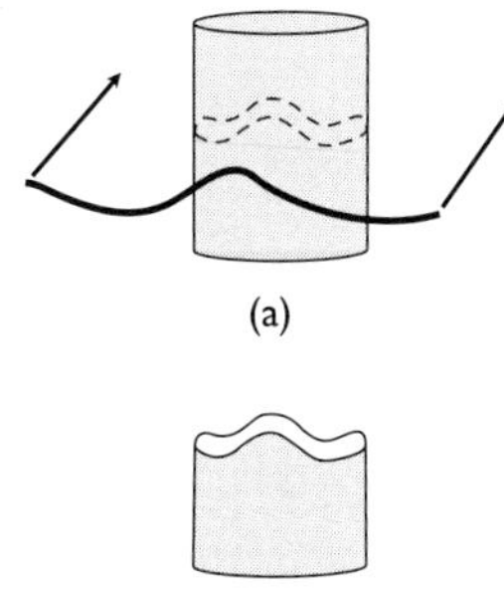

Figure 1-83. A trim can be produced by projecting a curve through space to calculate a curve of intersection on the original object. The object is then trimmed along this curve.

The second method of performing a trim operation is to use two objects, inserting one object into the other in order to calculate the curve of intersection. In Figure 1-84a the surface to be trimmed is the cone. The sphere, placed so that it overlaps the cone, determines the shape of the curve of intersection. That is, the border where the sphere touches the cone marks the curve of intersection. The trim operation cuts the original surface, the cone, along the curve of intersection to produce a new surface—a cone with a hole cut in it (Figure 1-84b).

Although you use some of the same words to describe a trim operation and a Boolean difference operation, and although the results of each look somewhat similar, a trim operation is *not* the same as a Boolean subtraction. A trim operation (see Figure 1-84b) simply cuts a surface. It does not add geometry to a surface, whereas a Boolean subtraction (see Figure 1-81b) does generate new surface area. In the case of the trimmed cone, the hole is just a hole. Because there is no surface in that area, you could stick your hand through the hole into the interior of the cone. If you had cut the cone with a Boolean difference operation instead of a trim operation, you would have produced a surface where the sphere gouged out a portion of the cone.

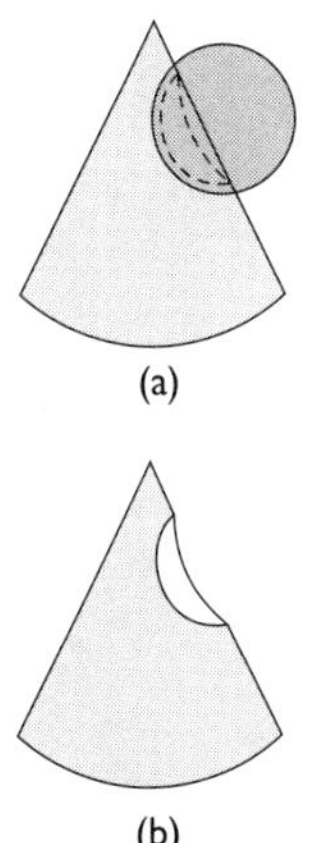

Figure 1-84. The curve of intersection can also be calculated from the intersection of two objects.

This limitation of trimming is not insurmountable, however. To address it, you do two trim operations, the first of which is a trim of the cone by the sphere. The second operation is a trim of the sphere by the cone, and this trim produces the orange-peel-shaped surface. If you then hierarchically group this new surface with the surface of the cut cone, you produce a cone with the desired scalloped surface. Notice, however, that you still have *two* surfaces, whereas a Boolean difference yields a single surface.

Fractals

In the 1970s, a French mathematician named Benoît Mandelbrot began refining an unusual new branch of mathematics, which has turned out to be extremely rich in possibilities for computer graphics. He termed this new mathematics **fractal** mathematics, because it involves the possibility of writing mathematical equations for geometries of fractional dimensionality. Normally, you think of dimensionality in terms of whole numbers: a point in space is 1-dimensional, a drawing on a piece of paper is 2-dimensional, a wooden box is 3-dimensional, and so on. In Mandelbrot's system, it is possible to think of something that is 1.76-dimensional, for instance, or 2.24-dimensional.

It is common for mathematicians to make visual representations, or graphs, of their mathematical formulas. To take a simple example, the visual representation of the equation $y = x^2$ is a parabola. This curve can be plotted by listing several *x* values, calculating the *y* value for each *x* value, and then drawing a mark at each (x,y) combination.

The images that result when fractal equations are plotted are much more complex than this simple example, and mathematicians working with fractal mathematics soon discovered that visual representations of their fractal equations produced some very intricate, unexpected, and beautiful results. Most interestingly, they found that graphs of fractal equations produce imagery that captures some of the characteristics of natural phenomena. That is, fractal imagery often has an irregularity and an unpredictability, an intricacy of detail, and a similarity of detail to overall form reminiscent of forms found in nature (Figure 1-85).

As fractal mathematics developed, computer graphics researchers began to develop techniques that took advantage of these characteristics by producing both two-dimensional pictures and three-dimensional models. Today, these fractal techniques have become useful enough and well enough understood that the software of many higher-end 3D modeling and animation systems includes significant fractal capabilities.

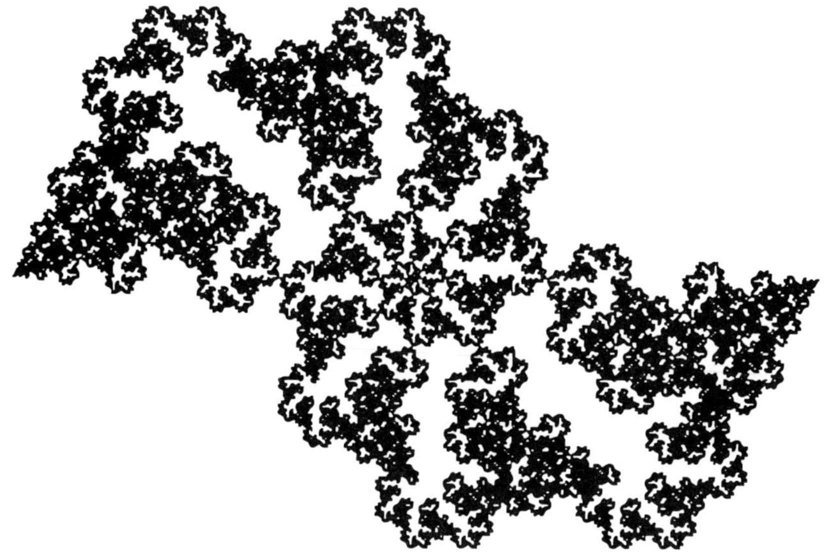

Figure 1-85. A pattern generated by plotting an equation of fractal mathematics. (Bathsheba L. Grossman, 1985)

One of the most important characteristics of fractals is that at any level of detail you can see similarities in the forms. The forms at the most minute level bear a resemblance to the forms at grosser levels, and these in turn look similar to forms at even higher levels. This characteristic, called **self-similarity**, belongs to many phenomena in nature as well. The large-scale crags and peaks of a mountain are similar in shape to the smaller abutments that make up those crags. Individual rocks on the mountainside have a similar "cragginess" to them, but on a much smaller scale. The pebbles that break off from such rocks have similar forms, and if you examine one of these pebbles with a magnifying glass, you would find miniature "crags" similar to the cragginess of the mountain itself.

To see how self-similarity works in a fractal image, take a simple and common example, called the **Koch curve**. You start generating this fractal curve with a simple straight line (Figure 1-86a). Next you break this straight line into a pattern, which is called the **generator** (Figure 1-86b). Breaking each of the four straight lines that make up the generator into yet smaller versions of the generator pattern yields a new pattern consisting of four occurrences of the generator (Figure 1-86c). Subdividing each straight line of that pattern into the generator pattern yields the next "generation" of the curve (Figure 1-86d). You can repeat this process of subdivision indefinitely, creating ever more detailed and refined repetitions of the generator pattern.

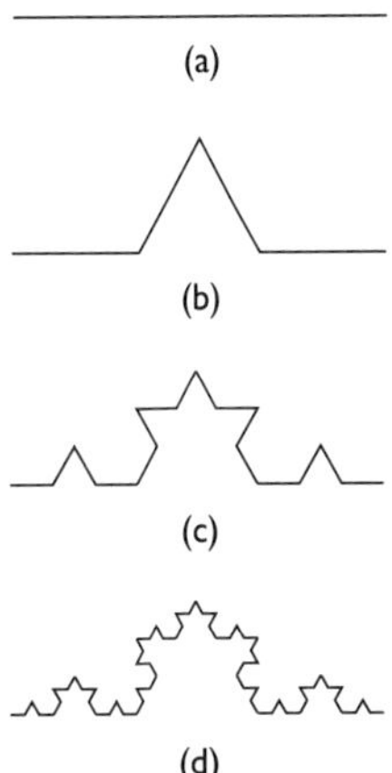

Figure 1-86. A Koch curve exemplifies the two fractal principles of self-similarity and recursion.

Notice that each new generation of the Koch curve is defined in terms of a previous Koch curve. For example, Koch-curve generation number 22 consists of Koch-curve generation number 21 with a generator pattern sub-

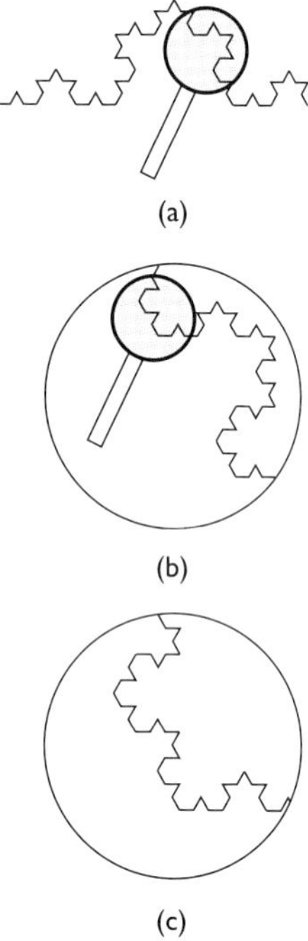

Figure 1-87. A fractal image has, as part of its definition, an infinite amount of detail. No matter how much you magnify an image, you will always see additional detail.

stituted for each straight line of number 21. In other words, in order to create a Koch curve, you first must create a Koch curve: the definition is self-referential.

This process of defining something in terms of itself is called **recursion** and the process is said to be **recursive**. Because it is self-referential, a recursive process in principle can go on forever. A common example of recursion in the physical world is what happens when two mirrors are placed face to face. If you look in the first mirror, you see yourself reflected in the second, which in turns reflects an image of yourself looking in the first mirror and being reflected in the second, which in turn reflects an image of yourself in the second mirror looking at yourself in the first mirror and being reflected in the second, which is being reflected in the first—and so on.

In a fractal curve there can be an unlimited number of generations—that is, it contains an unlimited amount of detail, even if you cannot see it. Beyond a few additional generations, for example, you could not see any more detail in Figure 1-86d. The image on the page is simply too small for your eye to pick up such tiny detail. For this practical reason, therefore, you probably would not attempt to draw too many additional generations. It is important to understand, however, that by definition these additional generations of the curve are there, even if you choose not to draw them.

If you imagine magnifying a section of the curve, you can understand more clearly that no matter how much you magnify a section of a fractal curve, there will always be, if you choose to draw it, more detail to see. Imagine that you place a magnifying-glass over a section of a Koch curve (Figure 1-87a). Notice that even at a magnified level the same amount of detail is available (Figure 1-87b). If you zoom in yet again, as indicated by the magnifying-glass icon, the resultant image again has a full level of detail (Figure 1-87c). The definition of the original curve includes all of these levels of detail—that is, all of these generations.

If you now imagine trying to model the mountain described at the beginning of this section by using the nonfractal modeling techniques discussed earlier in this chapter, you can see that none of those techniques allows you very successfully to simulate the infinitely craggy quality of the mountain. First, complexity and irregularity make the forms involved tremendously difficult to model by positioning polygon vertices or patch-control points. Second, trying to model these forms in enough detail to make them look convincing both from the altitude of an airplane and from the height of a person walking on the surface of the mountain is impractical.

Moreover, if, through some tremendous exercise of saintly patience, you manage to create such an exceedingly detailed model, you will produce a wasteful rendering situation. Since all of the details of this model have to be dealt with, the rendering process will spend a lot of time rendering detail that is not visible. From the height of the airplane, the renderer will render even the tiniest details, even those details too small to be seen in the final picture. Conversely, from the height of a person's eye, the renderer will process a vast quantity of model data, much of which is off screen.

Fractal models solve both the theoretical problem of whether it is possible to create such a complex model, and the practical problem of how to render it once you have created it. On the theoretical side, fractals are by definition very irregularly shaped and contain an unlimited amount of detail, so a fractal technique can, in fact, solve the problem of how to model a mountain. On the practical side, fractal techniques offer control over how many generations of a pattern are going to be created. Depending on the level of magnification needed, the software creates more or fewer generations, in the same way that you increase or decrease the number of generations—that is, the level of detail—in the Koch curve. The most common technique for applying fractal mathematics to three-dimensional modeling is very similar to the approach illustrated by the Koch curve. This process is called **recursive subdivision.**

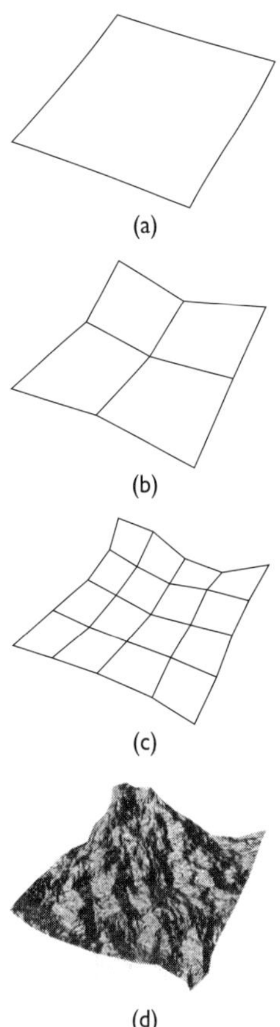

Figure 1-88. A fractal terrain model can be developed by recursively subdividing and displacing a patch.

Imagine that you have a simple rectangular patch (Figure 1-88a). If you subdivide this patch into four smaller subpatches, and then displace the corners of each patch some irregular amount, you produce the model in Figure 1-88b. If you then subdivide each of these subpatches into four smaller patches, with the corners irregularly displaced, you produce a model with more displacement (Figure 1-88c). By repeating this process many times, you can model a very irregular, terrainlike surface (Figure 1-88d). Further, depending on how much detail you need to see on the surface from a given point of view, using this modeling procedure the modeling software can produce a higher or a lower generation of the fractal geometry. A lower generation is suitable for viewing the terrain from a distance. A higher generation is suitable for a close-up view.

An interesting application of fractal modeling and rendering techniques appears in color plate 7. There, the fire around the rings was created through a fractally generated transparency map. The patterns inside the ring were also fractally generated.

Digitizing Techniques

All the modeling techniques described so far have pertained to models being designed and constructed entirely within the computer. In some situations, however, a physical model or some other real-world data already exist, and you want to develop a digital model from that given model or data. Say, for example, that you want to include a very realistically modeled human head, perhaps even a portrait of a specific person, in an animation. The best way to do this is to take measurements from the person and bring that information into the 3D modeling software package. Or if you are developing an architectural model or animation for which detailed data, perhaps in the form of architectural drawings, already exist, you undoubtedly want the digital model to accurately reflect these data.

Such applications require some method of getting information from the physical world into the computer modeling program. This process is known as **digitizing**, since it involves the conversion of real-world information into the digital form required by computer programs. A variety of digitizing techniques exists. Some of these techniques work from two-dimensional representations of three-dimensional data, and some of the techniques work directly from three-dimensional physical models.

One technique that works directly from physical models is a **3D digitizing pen**. Touching the tip of this pen to the surface of the object to be digitized produces a set of three-dimensional XYZ coordinate values, which the computer records. Each time the tip touches the surface, the location of another point is recorded. In this way, you compile a list of three-dimensional coordinates representing all the critical points on the surface of the object. The modeling software then uses these coordinates to build a surface, most commonly a polygonal model, that corresponds to the surface of the original object.

In order to produce data that have some regularity and are not randomly placed over the surface of the object, when using a 3D digitizing pen you should plan out exactly which points you want to record, and in what order. You can do this by either drawing or taping lines onto the surface of the object. Using this pattern, you then guide the pen to precise locations.Drawing the pattern of lines in a grid permits points to be recorded in an orderly fashion.

On the left in Figure 1-89 is a physical object to be digitized—in this case, a sculpted head. The head has been marked all over with a pattern of lines, and the pen is about to touch one of the intersections of this pattern. Notice that the pattern of points does not have the same spacing throughout. It is denser where the curvature of the object changes abruptly in significant ways. For example, the areas around the eyes, nose, and mouth have a relatively dense pattern of lines applied to them. This density allows the digitizing process to capture the detail of those areas. By contrast, the top of the head is marked with a less dense pattern. This area has fewer significant changes of surface curvature, and consequently fewer points are needed to replicate it satisfactorily.

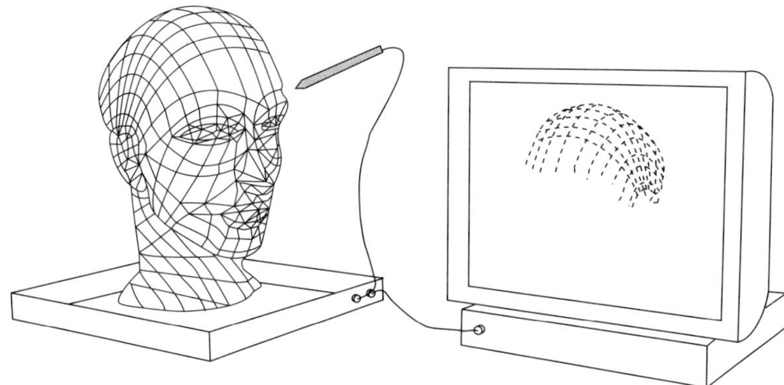

Figure 1-89. A 3D digitizing pen can be used to produce a list of polygon vertices.

Notice also that the head is sitting in a shallow box. Most 3D digitizing pens make use of inaudible sonic waves as a means of keeping track of the location of the pen. A boxlike device emits sonic waves simultaneously from different directions. The digitizing device, like a bat locating an insect by sonar, locates the pen within this sonic field by measuring the amount of time it takes each sonic wave to reach the tip of the pen.

Finally, on the right in this figure, some of the individual digitized points are displayed on the computer screen. After all the points have been digitized, the digitizing software generates a polygonal surface, converting each digitized point into a polygon vertex.

A very different type of three-dimensional digitizing technique works on the principle of building up a surface from contour curves. This makes use of the lofting process (see *Common Modeling Techniques*). First, a sequence of contour curves is developed, with each curve at a progressively higher Y location. Once these curves are in place, a lofted surface can be generated from them, either as a polygonal mesh or as a parametric surface.

The central issue of such a digitizing process, of course, is how to generate the contour curves. The most common approach, often referred to as **laser contour scanning**, is to use a laser beam to scan around the surface and generate a list of points as it goes (Figure 1-90). The object to be digitized is placed on a turntable that slowly rotates. A laser beam is projected onto the surface of the object, and the distance the beam travels to the object is recorded. This continues for one complete 360-degree rotation of the object, producing one contour curve, which is displayed on the computer screen. Then the beam is lowered a bit, the object completes another 360-degree rotation, and another contour curve is recorded. When all the curves have been completed, a lofted surface is built from them.

In order to make the illustration clearer, the distance between each contour curve in Figure 1-90 is greatly exaggerated. In actual practice, the laser beam is

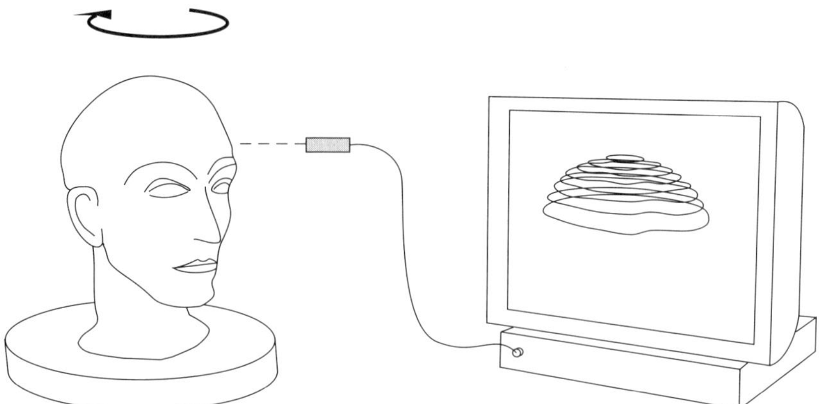

Figure 1-90. A succession of laser scans along the surface of an object produces a sequence of contours, which can be lofted to form a surface.

capable of producing extremely fine readings, with only a fraction of an inch between contour curves and with many, many points on each curve. For this reason, laser contour scanning can produce extremely accurate and detailed digitized models. A disadvantage of this refinement, however, is that the technique can also produce extremely large and unwieldy sets of data. The more refined the resolution of the laser scanning, the more data generated. Consequently you may use a process, called **thinning**, or **culling**, that selectively throws away some data in order to make the remaining data more manageable. This process requires that you specify a maximum number of points allowable on each curve. Some of the original digitized points are then discarded, and a new curve is recalculated. Of course, there is a trade-off between accuracy and quantity of data. The more points discarded, the more manageable the data, but also the less accurately the recalculated curve represents the original surface.

Notice also that the laser-scanning process is a relatively dumb, brute-force technique, in that it produces an admirable amount of detail but makes no attempt to decide where that detail is needed and where it is not. For example, the same density of points appears on the top of the skull, where you do not need it, as appears around the eyes.

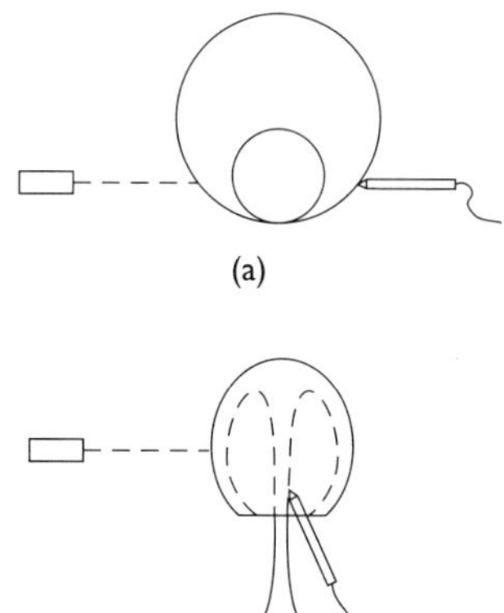

Figure 1-91. Both 3D digitizing pens and laser scanners have limitations. Certain surface configurations are inaccessible to both techniques.

Both the 3D digitizing pen and laser contour scanning can be extremely useful, depending on the nature of the original model and what you want to do with the digitized result. Both of them, however, suffer from one notable limitation: they digitize only the *exterior* surfaces of objects. If the object you want to digitize consists, for example, of a steel ball within a semitransparent plastic ball, with either a pen or a laser beam you can reach (and therefore digitize) only the exterior plastic ball (Figure 1-91a).

In some situations even exterior surfaces are inaccessible to either technique. A mushroom-shaped object, for example, presents difficulties, because neither a laser beam nor a digitizing pen is able to reach the top of the stem of the mushroom (Figure 1-91b).

This limitation can be significant for some applications. Many sculptural objects, for example, involve inward-curving forms similar in principle to the mushroom shape. And in many scientific applications it is crucial to be able to see and model surfaces within surfaces.

In fact, a number of digitizing techniques have been developed to handle such situations in science and, especially, medicine. These techniques are based on the idea of creating a series of **cross-sectional slices** and building a model by stacking the slices. The effect is the same as when you slice Swiss cheese. That is, viewing the cheese from the outside, neither you nor a 3D digitizing pen, nor a laser beam can see the holes inside the cheese. But when you cut the cheese into slices, these holes become apparent on each slice.

Several medical technologies implement this technique , including X rays, Magnetic Resonance Imaging (MRI), and Computerized Axial Tomography (CAT) scans. Each of these technologies involves the emission of a signal capable of passing through certain materials of our bodies. When the signal reaches an interior material of a different character, it sends back information to the computer about the location in depth of this material.

A variation on this digitizing technique is possible even for those computer modelers and animators who do not have such extremely elaborate and expensive medical equipment at their disposal. A sort of poor person's CAT scan, this technique works with very simple objects. If the object to be digitized is cut into slices, both the interior and exterior contours are revealed on each slice. Tracing around these contours with a digital pen device digitizes the shape of each contour. By stacking these digitized curves, offsetting them by the thickness of each slice, you can generate a three-dimensional lofted surface.

On the left in Figure 1-92 is the mushroom-shaped object from Figure 1-91b. Here the object has been sliced into several slabs. The first three of these have already been digitized, and the digitized shapes of these slabs appear on the computer screen. The fourth slab is lying on the 2D digitizing tablet, in the process of being traced. Notice that this cross-sectional technique captures the contours defining the space between the stem and the inner surface of the bell. A significant disadvantage to this technique, however, is that at several stages of the process it is subject to human error. If the slabs are not cut uniformly or if the tracing is not done with extreme care, accumulated error can distort the final digitized version of the model.

When you digitize cross-sectional contours by hand in this way, you also must properly align each slab with the slabs above and below it, and you do

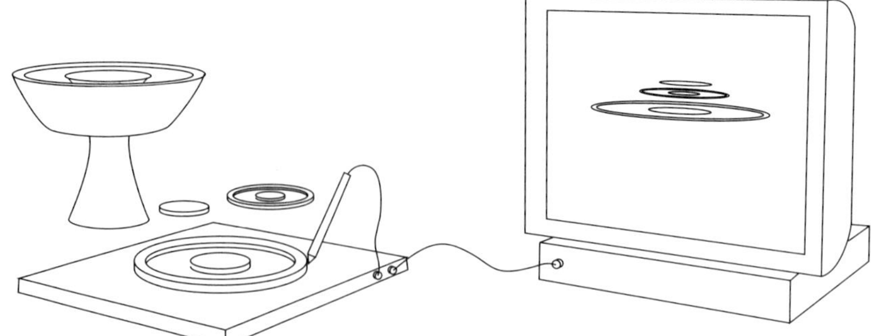

Figure 1-92. Cutting an object into slices produces contour data. Any surface of any complexity can be digitized with this approach if the slices are fine enough.

this by putting **registration marks** on all of the slabs. By aligning registration mark number 1 of slice A with registration mark number 1 of slice B, and so on, you can position all the digitized contours relative to one another.

Two-dimensional tracing plays a key part in another digitization process, provided by some 3D modeling systems, called **orthographic reconstruction**. This technique is related to the production, notably in architecture and industrial design, of scale drawings. These drawings are done orthographically—that is, without perspective foreshortening—and from three different right-angle views: front, side, and top.

The process begins with the digitization of each of the two-dimensional drawings. That is, you place each drawing on the 2D digitizing tablet and trace over the key elements with a digitizing pen. As with the hand-drawn cross-sectional contours, you must properly register the drawings to one another. In the case of three orthographic drawings (Figure 1-93a), this usually is done by defining **fiducial points**, which are located within the drawing space of the paper and which remain constant through each of the three drawings. (The word "fiducial" means "something you can trust.") Once the

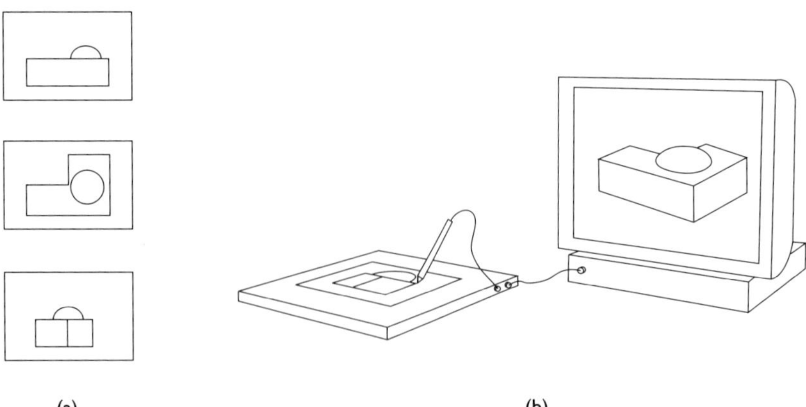

Figure 1-93. Three orthographic drawings can be used to reconstruct a three-dimensional object.

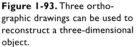

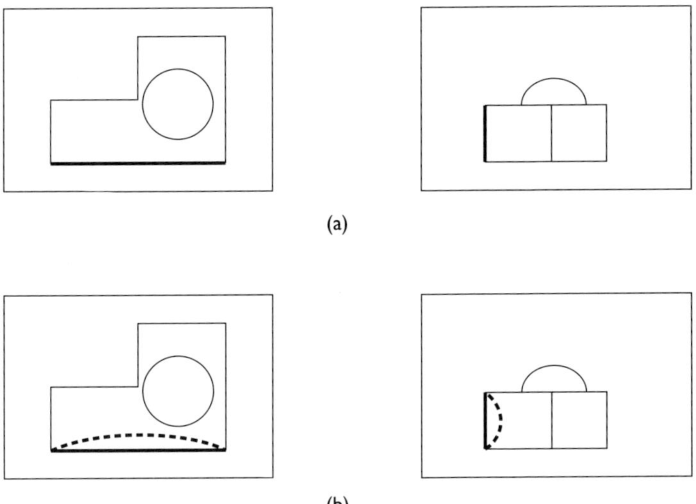

Figure 1-94. In order to deal with ambiguous forms, the orthographic reconstruction technique must make assumptions about the nature of the forms.

data from the three orthographic drawings have been entered into the computer, the software then reconstructs an object consistent with the three sets of data (Figure 1-93b).

It is important to understand that any orthographic reconstruction process makes significant assumptions about the nature of the shapes involved. The silhouette information in the orthographic drawings in and of itself does not indicate whether the front wall of the previous example is flat (Figure 1-94a) or whether it is has a slight bow in it (Figure 1-94b). The orthographic drawings cannot resolve this ambiguity because the critical information—the bowing of the concavity as it would be seen from the side and top—is hidden by the other walls of the structure.

The orthographic reconstruction on the screen in Figure 1-93b, in other words, is based on the assumption that all walls are flat unless a silhouette suggests otherwise. For the majority of designs in the architectural and industrial worlds, of course, this assumption is perfectly reasonable and the orthographic reconstruction technique works well. For some applications, however, the assumptions of the orthographic reconstruction process are too limiting and the process is ineffectual.

Plant Generators

As you saw earlier in this chapter, almost all 3D software packages provide functions that generate certain simple forms—such as the cube, the cylinder, and the cone—called "geometric primitives." To use these functions,

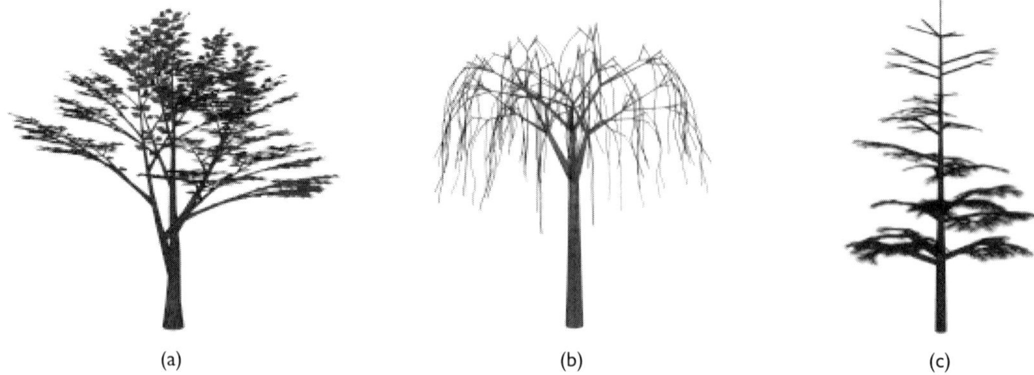

Figure 1-95. Trees modeled three-dimensionally by a plant-generator function. The artist specified the species of tree.

you do not explicitly define each surface of the form to be modeled. You do not, for example, draw a curve and revolve it to form the side of a cone. Rather, you simply indicate that you want a cone and specify certain parameters to control size and location. Employing an internal definition of what a cone is, the "cone" function then automatically generates the appropriate form.

In principle, a computer programmer could apply this approach to forms other than the geometric primitives. A function to generate hats, for example, would include an internal definition of what a hat is (a brim, a circular interior, a band around the rim, etc.). The function could be set up so that certain parameters would be specified by the user to control the style, size, and shape of the hat. A *style* parameter might contain such possibilities as: *Panama*, *Baseball Cap*, *Navy Watch Cap*, and so on, and these settings would be equivalent to the *Cube*, *Cone*, and *Cylinder* settings in a "geometric primitive" function. Unlike the geometric primitives, though, which are very useful to a great many people, hat forms are used only rarely, so there is very little demand for a "hat" generator function.

A few advanced 3D systems come equipped with functions that generate certain other forms, namely the forms of plants, which *are* in great demand. Not only are the forms of bushes, trees, and flowers very common, but these forms tend to be very difficult to model well. The shape of a maple tree, for example, is complex. To model, surface by surface, a convincing maple tree requires a lot of work.

To use **plant generator functions**, you first specify a **plant-type** parameter. Having narrowed the category to a specific plant type, say a tree, you then specify the **plant species**. From among the category of trees, for example, you might choose a maple, a willow, or a spruce (Figure 1-95a, b, c). Bear in

(a)

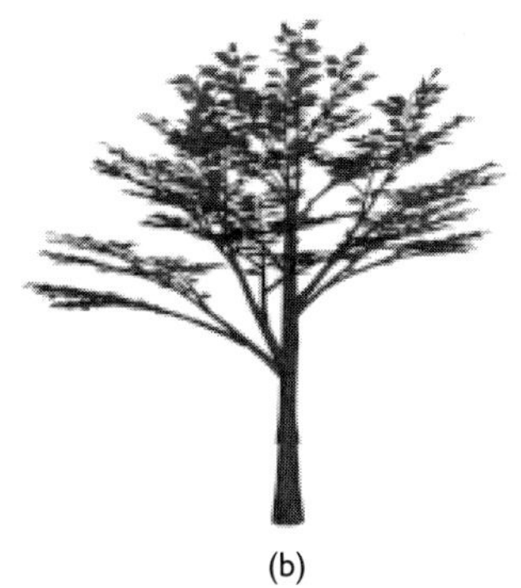
(b)

Figure 1-96. Often an age parameter can be applied to a plant model. Here are a young maple tree and an older maple tree.

mind that these illustrations look deceptively flat because the intended scale of the trees is so large. The trees modeled here are, indeed, *models*. That is, they are not merely pictures of trees, but have been defined as fully three-dimensional objects. When part of a 3D computer graphics scene, these models exist in all three dimensions, and you can move around them visually in the same way that you can move around a cube or a cone.

Having selected a species of plant, you next specify various parameters that control the size and shape of the plant. Usually, one of these parameters is **age**, and you normally specify this value in years. A relatively young maple tree (Figure 1-96a) looks substantially different from a maple tree that is many years older (Figure 1-96b), despite the fact that all the other parameters defining these trees are identical.

As you will see in chapters 3 and 4, good 3D animation systems handle any parameter as a variable whose value can be changed over time. Changing the value of a variable over time effectively animates the model. When the age parameter of a plant model is animated, the plant will appear to grow. Because of this, some sophisticated plant-generator functions are often referred to as **growth models**.

Randomness plays a role in all natural phenomena, and therefore is important in making plant models look convincing. Part of what makes the two maple tree models in Figure 1-96 look like real trees is the fact that their branches and leaves are not all of the same length or size and are not placed at regular intervals along the trunk. Because of the importance of this randomness factor, many plant-generator systems also offer a **randomness** or **noise** parameter to give you greater control over just how the final plant looks. When generating grass with a "grass" function, for instance, by employing a randomness factor you can control both the length of the blades of grass and how irregularly they splay out from the center (Figure 1-97).

Figure 1-97. This grass model was generated by a "grass" function. A degree of randomness is critical to producing convincing models of this sort.

Given the complexity of modeling individual blades of grass or individual leaves and branches, this type of form-generating function is terrifically useful. It is reasonable to expect, moreover, that other form generators will find their way into commercially available software packages. Someday, for example, you may find "house" generators and "automobile" generators available in 3D systems.

CHAPTER 2

Rendering

Introduction

So far you have been reading about techniques for defining "geometry," or the data that describe the three-dimensional shape of an object. This process constitutes the modeling of an object and involves thinking and working spatially, in the round, in all three dimensions.

It is an irony of three-dimensional computer graphics, however, that when you sit at a computer graphics workstation and work three-dimensionally, you see on the screen a two-dimensional picture of your model. That is, the computer processes the three-dimensional data that define your model to produce flat, two-dimensional representations of the model. As you work, you react to these two-dimensional pictures.

The process of producing a two-dimensional picture from three-dimensional data is called **rendering**. The word is used here in the same way that an architect speaks of producing two-dimensional "renderings," or drawings, of an architectural design.

The simplest computer graphics rendering approach represents an object as if the object had no surfaces at all, but instead were composed only of wire-like edges (Figure 2-1a). **See-through wireframe** rendering, or simply **wireframe rendering**, is very easy and fast for a computer to calculate and therefore is part of all 3D computer animation systems. Most systems can calculate wireframe rendering fast enough to allow **real-time interaction** with the model, which means that at the same time that you manipulate a device, such as a mouse, a pen, or a joystick, the image on the screen changes.

The disadvantage of see-through wireframes, however, is precisely that they are transparent. Almost all of the objects you might be interested in modeling do, in fact, have surfaces, and the see-through wireframe cannot represent these surfaces. Moreover, wireframes of this sort can be ambiguous, in that sometimes it is difficult to tell which of the "wires" of an object are to the front of the object and which are to the rear.

A second rendering approach overcomes these limitations by taking into account the fact that an object has surfaces and that these surfaces hide, or occlude, the surfaces behind them (Figure 2-1b). In **hidden-line rendering**, the edges of the object are still represented as lines, but now some of these lines are hidden by the surfaces in front of them.

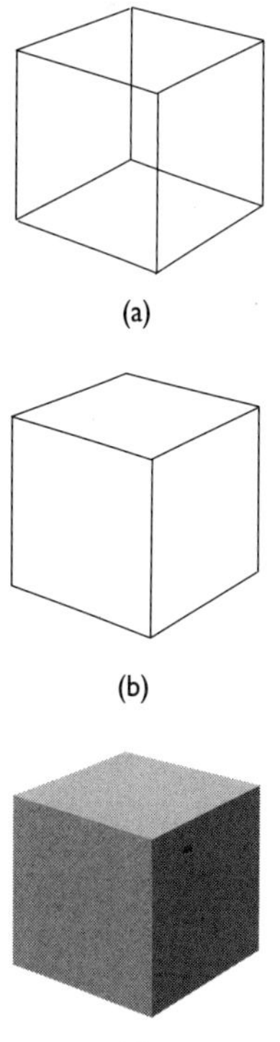

Figure 2-1. Three rendering approaches: see-through wireframe, hidden-line, and shaded rendering.

Hidden-line rendering is computationally more complicated than wireframe rendering. In order to know which lines should be hidden, the system performs certain calculations to determine which surfaces are in front of other surfaces. As a result, hidden-line renderings take longer than see-through wireframe renderings, and they are less often a part of systems that place a premium on real-time user interaction. Another disadvantage is that while hidden-line renderings recognize the existence of surfaces, they tell you nothing about the character of those surfaces: the color of the surface, the shininess of the surface, and so on.

A third rendering approach overcomes even these limitations and is, predictably, still more complicated to compute and therefore slower to render. This approach provides information about various surface characteristics and about lighting and shading, and therefore is called **shaded-surface rendering**, **shaded rendering**, or—since it corresponds to the use of the word "rendering" outside of computer graphics—simply **rendering** (Figure 2-1c). (All the color illustrations in this book are examples of shaded-surface rendering.)

A number of hardware manufacturers have developed special-purpose computer graphics machines capable of producing simplified shaded-surface renderings in real time. These machines allow you interactively to rotate and move your model at the same time that you view it as a shaded rendering. You normally use this kind of equipment with high-end three-dimensional modeling and animation packages.

More complex and higher-quality shaded renderings, however, take a long time to compute. An extremely high-quality, very sophisticated rendering of a complicated model might take anywhere from a few minutes to more than an hour to calculate, depending on the speed of the computer. The advantages of high-quality shaded rendering, however, clearly outweigh the disadvantages, and all 3D animation systems provide some means of producing such renderings.

In general terms, you can think of the process of producing a two-dimensional rendering of a three-dimensionally defined scene as involving five major components (Figure 2-2). The first of these, as you saw in chapter 1, is the geometry of the model, the three-dimensional shape of the model. The remaining components are the point of view from which you see the scene (also referred to as the "camera"); the lighting of the scene; the definition of the surface characteristics of the model; and, finally, the specific technique, or algorithm, the system uses to calculate the two-dimensional picture once the other information is complete.

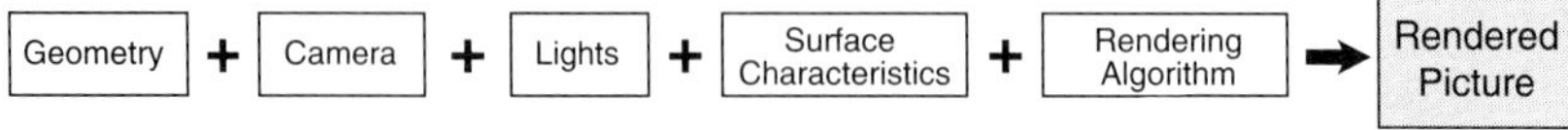

Figure 2-2. Rendering can be thought of as consisting of five basic components.

Remember that even though for the sake of conceptual convenience we are considering modeling and rendering separately, in practice it is impossible to segregate these two tasks. Normally you develop the geometry to a certain point, then develop some of the rendering characteristics, then return to the geometry, then return to the rendering, and so on. The modeling and the rendering *together* produce the final model.

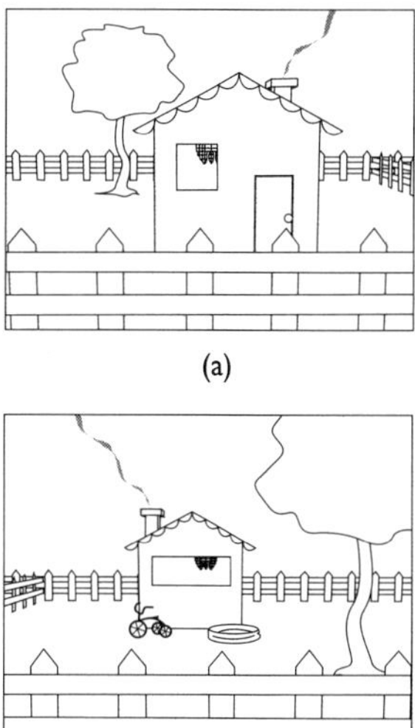

(a)

(b)

Figure 2-3. In these two views, the point at which you are looking remains the same, but the location of your eye changes.

The Camera

When you look at a scene in the real world, what you see—that is, which portion of the scene and how much of that portion—is determined by your point of view. When you create a computer rendering of a three-dimensional scene, you first define the point of view from which the scene is to be observed.

A point of view consists of two factors: where you are standing, and where you are looking. Suppose the scene you want to render is your friend's house and the grounds around it. If you stand in front of the house and look at the dining room chandelier, you see one image (Figure 2-3a). If you stand behind the house and look at the same chandelier, you see a very different image (Figure 2-3b). This example is an illustration of changing the "where you are standing" factor, while keeping the "what you are looking at" factor the same.

Now reverse the situation and keep the "where you are standing" factor constant, but change the "what you are looking at" factor. In the first instance, you stand in front of the house and look at the dining room chandelier (Figure 2-4a). In the second instance, you stand in the same spot but look at the chimney (Figure 2-4b).

In computer graphics, the point of view is part of what is called the **camera**, or, to emphasize that it is not physical, the **virtual camera**. The definition of the camera incorporates both of the components of a point of view.

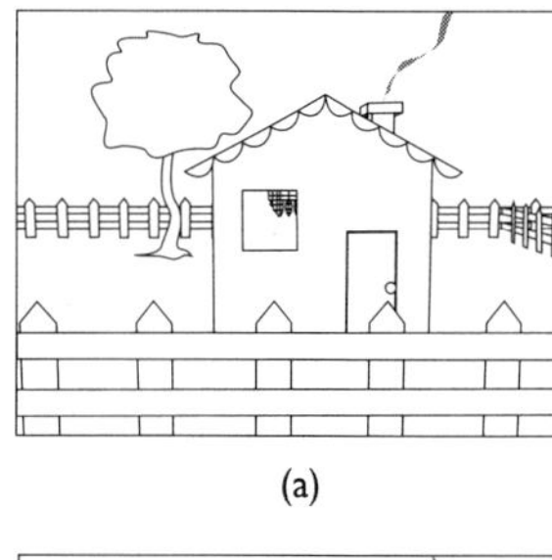

(a)

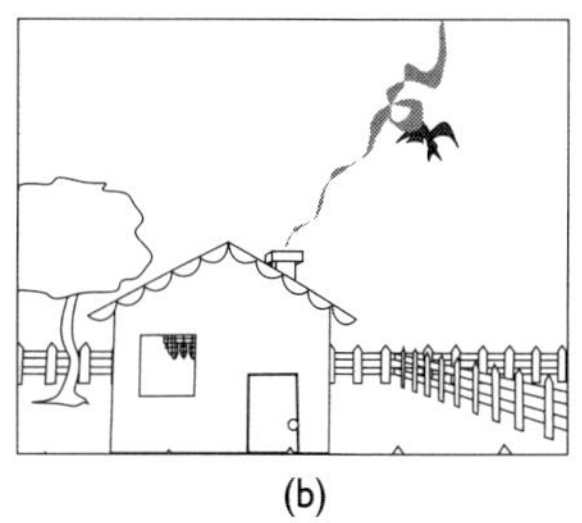

(b)

Figure 2-4. Here, the location of your eye remains constant, but the point at which you are looking changes.

The first factor—where you are standing—usually is called the **camera location** or **eye location**. The location of the camera is a point in space and as such is specified as a triplet of XYZ coordinate values. You might say, for example, that your camera is located at (–10, 2.5, 17.6). Most three-dimensional computer graphics systems allow you to specify this camera location either by typing in those number explicitly or, more commonly and more conveniently, by interactively positioning the eye/camera with some device, such as a mouse. Usually as you move the location of the camera you view the scene as it appears from that vantage point, changing in real-time.

You can deal with the second factor—where you are looking—in either of two ways. The first way, used throughout this book, is to think of "where you are looking" as an actual point in space, as in "looking at the chandelier." This point in space is called the **center of interest** or **camera interest** and,

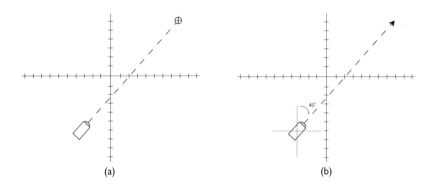

Figure 2-5. Two different methods of representing where the camera is looking: as a point in space, or as a rotation of the camera.

like the camera location, is specified as a triplet of XYZ coordinate values. You can change the center of interest in the same ways that you change the camera location: either by interactively repositioning the center, or by typing in numbers. (In Figure 2-5a, the rectangular icon represents the location of the camera—where you are standing. The circle with the cross hairs represents the camera's center of interest—where you are looking.)

A second, less common approach is to think of "where you are looking" in terms of rotation of the camera—in other words, pointing the camera in a certain direction. When you use this rotational approach, the system specifies the **camera direction** as a triplet of XYZ rotational values: *rotate (0,–40,0)*, for instance (Figure 2-5b).

If you stand in one spot and turn your head to the left or to the right or up or down, this is equivalent to keeping the camera location fixed and moving the center of interest. Such a **camera move** is called a **pan**, a term taken from the film industry. Figure 2-6a is a diagram of a camera pan as seen from above, while Figure 2-6b shows the two-dimensional renderings that might result from such a pan.

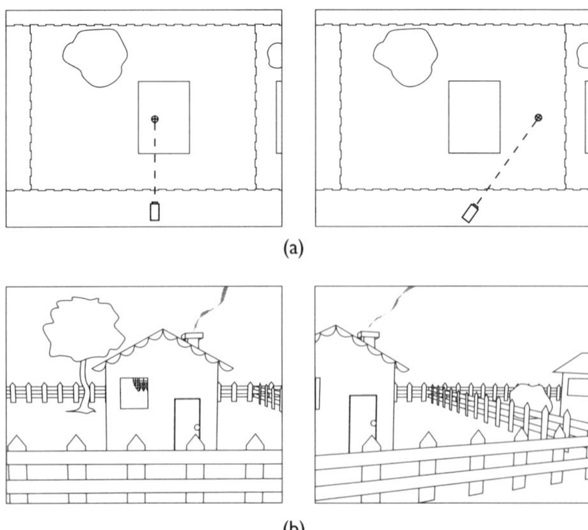

Figure 2-6. A camera pan.

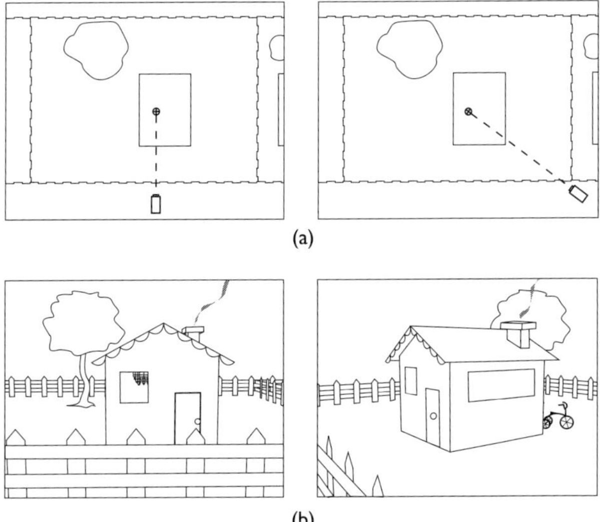

Figure 2-7. A camera tumble.

The opposite of a pan, called a **tumble** or **orbit**, keeps the center of interest stationary while moving the camera location. This corresponds to fixing your gaze on one point in space while walking around it. Figure 2-7a is a diagram of a tumble as seen from above, while Figure 2-7b shows the two-dimensional renderings that might result.

Another standard camera move, called a **track**, involves changing the camera location and the center of interest at the same time, as a unit (Figures 2-8a, 2-8b). Again the term comes from filmmaking, in which a "tracking shot" is often made by sliding a wheeled camera along a railroadlike track.

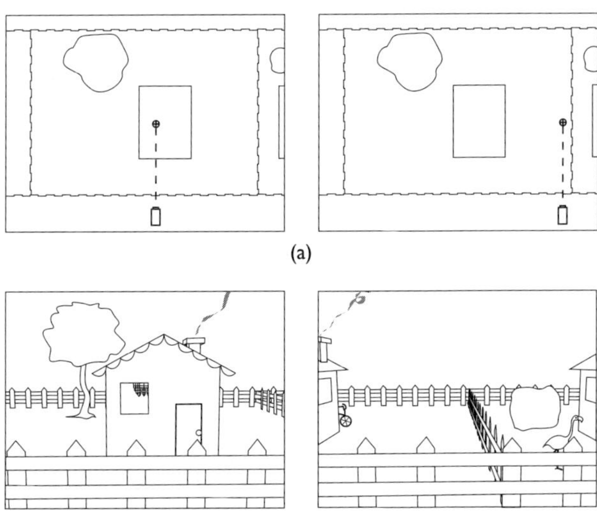

Figure 2-8. A camera track.

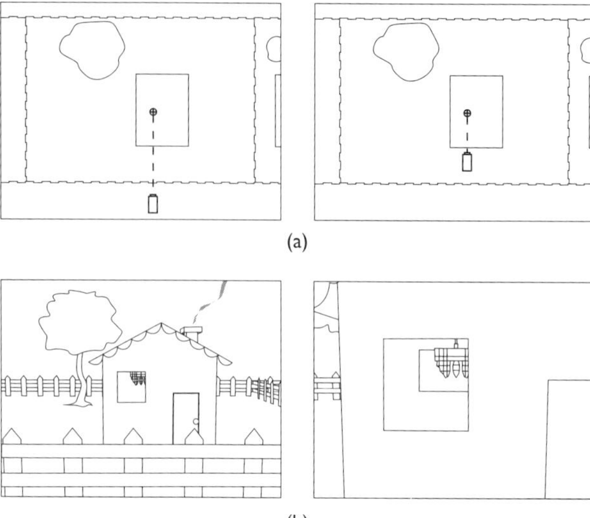

Figure 2-9. A camera dolly.

If both the camera location and the center of interest are moved in or out—that is, along the Z axis—the movement is called a **dolly** (Figures 2-9a, 2-9b).

If a system uses the rotational approach rather than the center-of-interest approach to specify where the camera is looking, these same moves apply, but the moves are specified in terms of rotations of the camera. A pan is a rotation of the camera about an origin located at the camera location (Figure 2-10a). A tumble is a rotation of the camera about an origin located at the center of interest (Figure 2-10b).

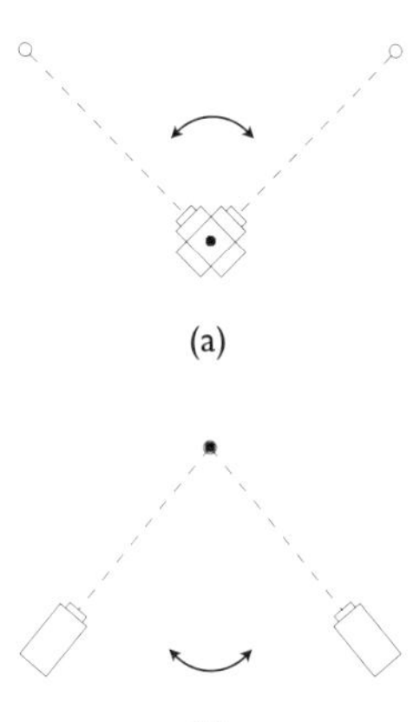

Figure 2-10. A pan and a tumble involve rotations of the camera around different pivot points.

Although the terminology used to describe these camera moves is largely taken from the film industry, occasionally a three-dimensional computer graphics system uses terminology taken from aviation. This is especially likely if the system was developed primarily for engineering applications. In such a system, **pitch** is a rotation of the camera around the X axis, **yaw** is a rotation of the camera around the Y axis, and **roll** is a rotation around the Z axis. The "rolling" of the camera around the Z axis is like what happens in aviation when a plane banks or, in extreme cases, turns upside down. In the more common center-of-interest approach, the same effect is called **tilt** and describes what happens when you tilt your head: the image you see changes. This is most noticeable when you tilt your head 180 degrees—that is, when you stand on your head. The image of the world you see is upside down. In Figure 2-11, all three renderings employ the same camera location and the same center of interest. Only the tilt of the camera varies.

If a system uses the rotational approach to defining the camera, tilt is specified automatically by the rotation around Z. If a system uses the center-of-interest approach, however, you need additional information to indicate how

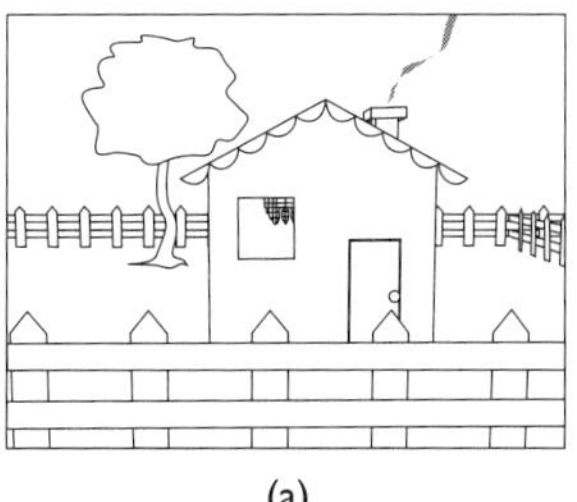
(a)

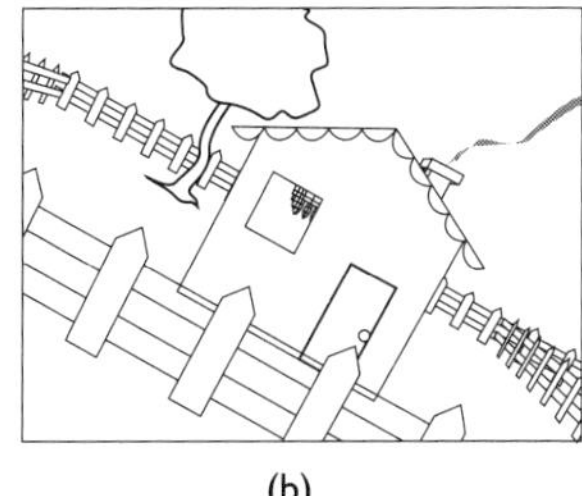
(b)

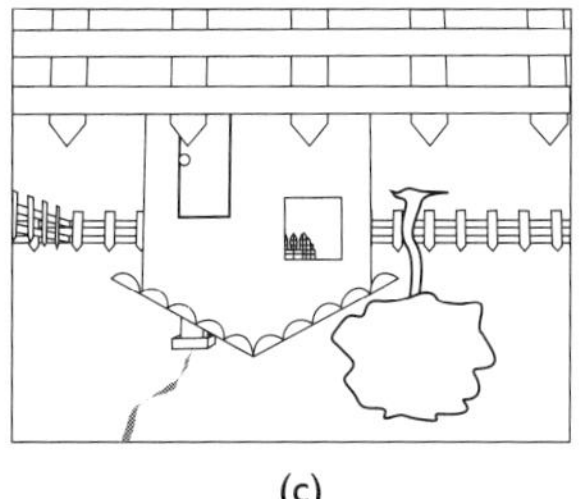
(c)

Figure 2-11. A camera tilt.

the camera is tilted. One technique is simply to borrow from the rotational approach and specify the tilt as a separate rotational value. A more common technique is to specify a point in space that indicates the **top** or **up direction** of the camera (corresponding to the top of your head). In Figure 2-12a the tip of the arrow icon, which is the "up" point for that camera, is directly above the camera and the camera is upright. In Figure 2-12b the up point has moved to the side, causing the camera to tilt correspondingly. Notice that the length of the arrow is not significant; the direction of the arrow controls the camera tilt. Placing the up point anywhere along the arrow has the same effect on the camera tilt.

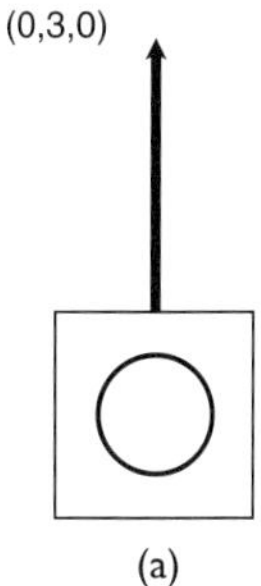

(a)

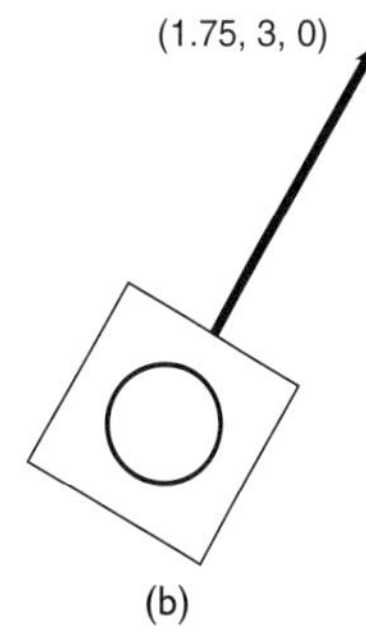

(b)

Figure 2-12. The tilt of a camera can be represented by an "up" point in space.

All of these factors—the location of the camera, the point at which the camera is looking, and the tilt of the camera—constitute point of view, and as such become part of the definition of the virtual camera. Several additional factors, however, can be part of that definition. Lower-end systems may not permit you to control all of these factors. Such systems may use fixed default values instead. Higher-end systems commonly allow you to change the values of these additional camera parameters as you wish.

One additional camera parameter, called simply **zoom**, simulates the effect of a zoom lens. In photography, changing the zoom on your camera has two effects. First, it makes objects appear closer or farther away. This effect is reflected in the terminology used, as in "zooming *in*" and "zooming *out*." It is important to understand, however, that a photographic zoom really does not involve any movement in or out of either the camera or the scene: zooming in only *magnifies* the image.

The second effect of a photographic zoom is to exaggerate the perspective with which you view a scene. Think of the classic example of converging railroad tracks as an example of perspective: you have "more perspective" where the convergence is greater and "less perspective" where the convergence is lesser. In this sense, a zoom-in creates more perspective and a zoom-out creates less perspective.

Both of these characteristics of the photographic zoom—the apparent increase in size of the objects, and the increase in perspective distortion—are replicated in computer graphics by the zoom parameter of the virtual camera. Figure 2-13a shows a scene as it would appear with a "normal" zoom, which

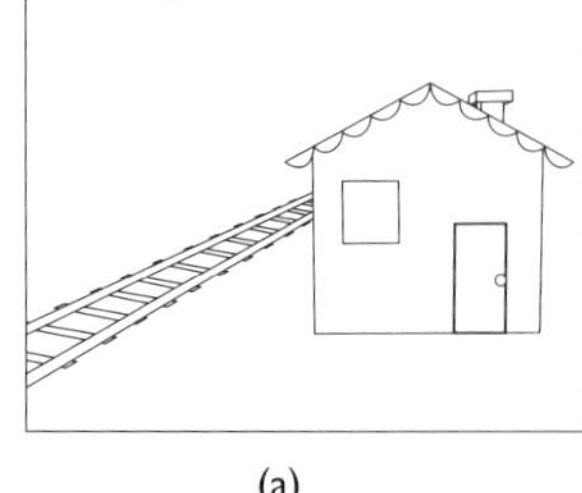
(a)

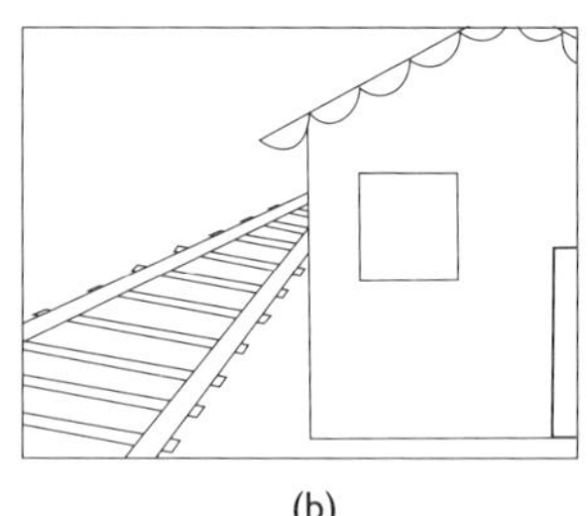
(b)

Figure 2-13. A camera zoom both magnifies and changes the perspective of an image.

approximates what your eyes see naturally. Figure 2-13b is the same scene zoomed in, as with a wide-angle photographic lens. Notice that the size and the perspective of the image have changed.

When working with the zoom parameter, however, you must remember what zoom really does and does not do. A zoom-in on a scene is not the same as a dolly into the scene. A dolly, as you saw above, involves translating the camera location into the scene along the Z direction. A zoom, on the other hand, involves no movement of the camera location. Because of this, the visual results of a zoom are quite different from the visual results of a dolly. These differences might be hard to detect when the changes in the zoom or dolly values are small. With larger changes, however, the differences become apparent. A zoom involves a change in perspective, while a dolly keeps the perspective the same at all times. A substantial zoom-in on a scene creates a noticeable distortion of perspective. Figure 2-14 shows a cube rendered three times, each time with a different zoom factor. (In order to isolate the effects on perspective, the magnification effect of the zoom has been counteracted with a simultaneous dolly-out.) In Figure 2-14a the camera has been zoomed out extremely far, producing a rendering with almost zero perspective—that is, an orthographic rendering. Figure 2-14b is a rendering with a normal zoom. Figure 2-14c is a rendering with an extreme zoom-in, which produces an extreme exaggeration of the perspective.

(a)

(b)

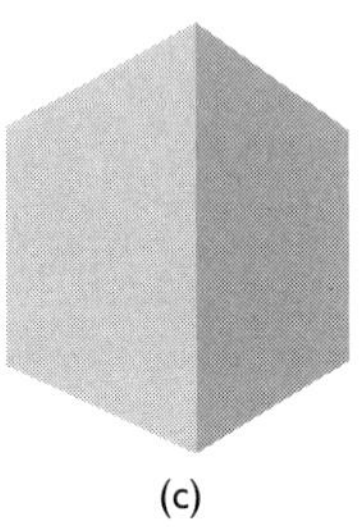
(c)

Figure 2-14. Three renderings that illustrate the perspective distortions of zooming.

Whether a zoom or a dolly is the more appropriate camera move depends on the effect you want to achieve. If you intend to simulate a person walking through a scene, a dolly is appropriate, being an actual translation of the camera through the scene. If you intend to create the effect of someone focusing his or her attention on a detail of a scene, a zoom may be more appropriate.

Systems generally allow you to change the zoom interactively with a mouse device. In addition, many systems provide the option of typing in numerical values to control zoom. In order to understand the significance of the values used to define zoom, you must understand a bit about how a zoom is calculated in computer graphics.

When you look at the world around you, objects too far to the left or right or too far above or below you are not visible. They are outside the range of your peripheral vision, or your **field of view**. The human field of view (for each eye) can be thought of as a cone-shaped area, often called a **cone of vision** (Figure 2-15). Objects that lie within your cone of vision (such as the cube in this figure), are visible to you. Objects that lie outside your cone of vision (such as the cylinder) are not visible.

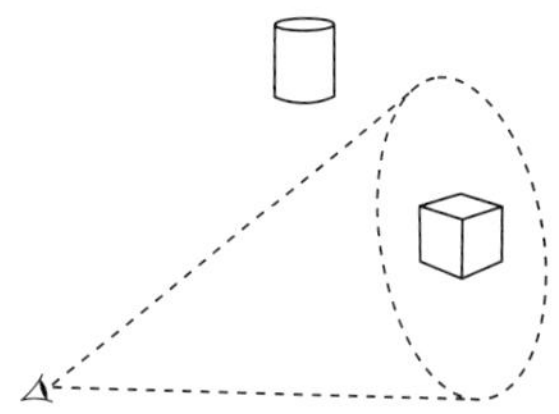

Figure 2-15. Objects that lie within the cone of vision are visible. Those that lie outside the cone of vision are not.

In computer graphics, the cone of vision becomes a **pyramid of vision**, in order to conform to the rectangular shape of computer monitor screens. One of the factors that determine the shape of this pyramid is the angle from top to bottom of the pyramid (Figure 2-16). Usually referred to in computer graphics as the **field-of-view angle** or simply the **field of view** or even more simply the **fov**, this angle is measured in degrees.

A change in the *fov* angle causes a change in zoom. A very large *fov* angle results in the same extreme perspective distortion as a wide-angle lens. A very narrow *fov* angle produces a "flattened" rendering with very little perspective distortion. The reasoning behind this relationship is that everything that the eye, or virtual camera, "sees" within the pyramid of vision must be distorted by perspective calculations so that it fits onto the rendered screen of the computer system. A large field of view produces a pyramid of vision that is very wide at the back. Since everything within the pyramid of vision, including those objects at the back of the pyramid, must fit onto the rendered screen, a more extreme perspective distortion is necessary for those pyramids that have wider backs.

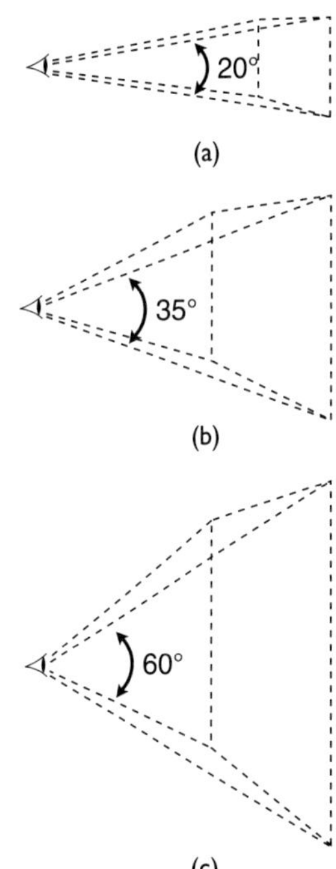

Figure 2-16. Increasing the field-of-view angle of the pyramid of vision produces a zoom-in.

When you view a scene, either through a photographic camera or with your eyes, some objects appear in focus and some appear out of focus. Some rendering programs reproduce this effect through a parameter called **depth of field** (a term borrowed from photography). The most common method for specifying depth of field is to give two numbers: the first represents the nearest distance at which objects will be in focus, and the second represents the farthest distance at which they will be in focus. Sometimes you specifiy a third parameter to indicate just how out of focus objects might become. Figure 2-17a is a schematic representation, as viewed from the top, of a camera and a scene. The dotted lines emanating from the camera icon represent the field of view of the camera. The parallel dotted lines within this field of view represent the near and far values of the depth of field. The shaded area between these two values is the area within which objects are in focus. In this example, the cylinder and cone are out of focus, since they lie outside of this area (Figure 2-17b). The cube, on the other hand, is in focus.

One last characteristic of the computer graphics camera has no direct parallel either in photography or human vision: when a program renders a scene, it must restrict that scene to a finite three-dimensional space. This is necessary because a program dealing with the infinite space of an endless Cartesian coordinate system would continue rendering forever. That is, the program always would be looking at some new area of space to see if any objects

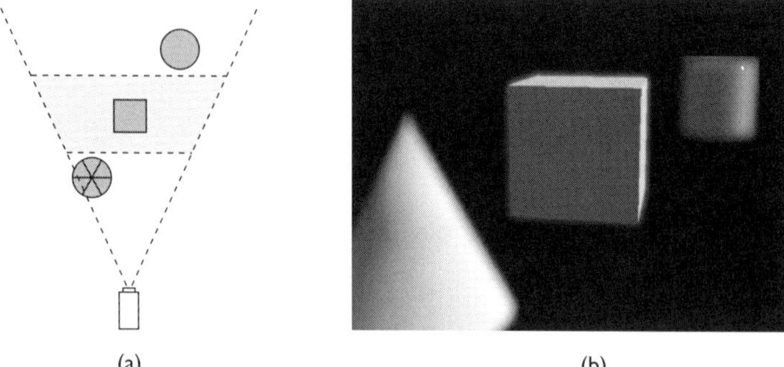

Figure 2-17. Depth of field can be specified, causing objects to be rendered in or out of focus.

within that space needed to be rendered. You can think of the limited world that a rendering program deals with as the "viewable" world.

The most basic restriction that a rendering program imposes in order to limit the viewable world is the restriction imposed by the four edges of the computer screen. The rendering program looks through this screen as if through a window, then deals with only that space viewable through the window.

Figure 2-18a is a diagram, as seen from above, of a modeled scene. The short dark line represents the screen on which this scene is rendered. Beyond the screen is the virtual camera. The dotted lines extending from the camera past the edges of the screen represent the field of view and demarcate the viewable world of the camera. Of the objects in the scene, only the cube lies within the viewable world of the camera, and so only the cube is rendered (Figure 2-18b). The sphere and the cone, which lie outside the viewable world, are not considered by the rendering program and are said to be **clipped**.

This example illustrates how the viewable world is clipped on the right, left, top, and bottom. But what about the space extending in the Z direction? If this space is not also limited in some way, the rendering program could, in theory, look forever through this space to see if there were any other objects—a million miles away and beyond—that should be rendered.

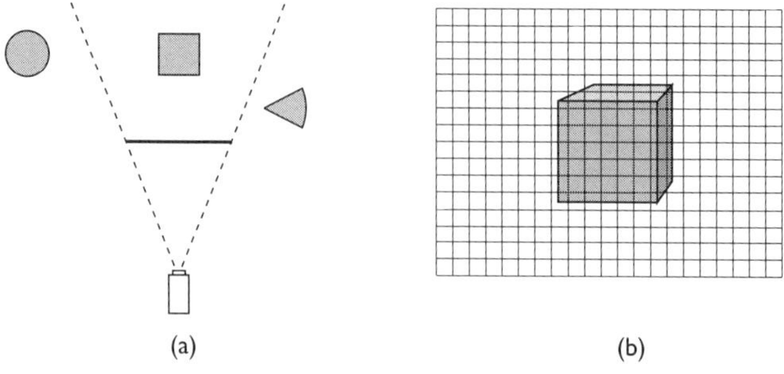

Figure 2-18. The viewable world of the virtual camera is clipped by the edges of the screen.

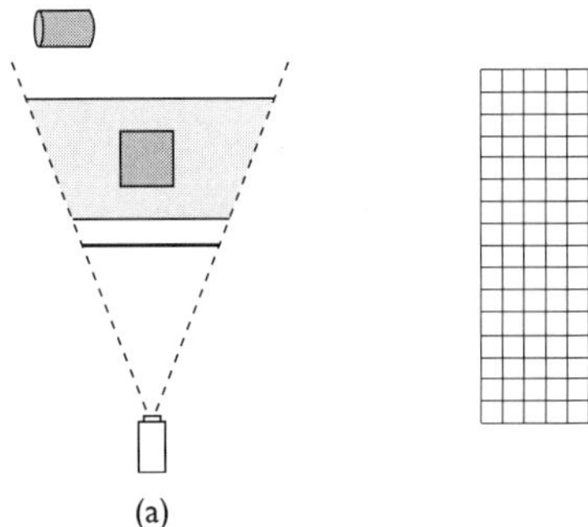

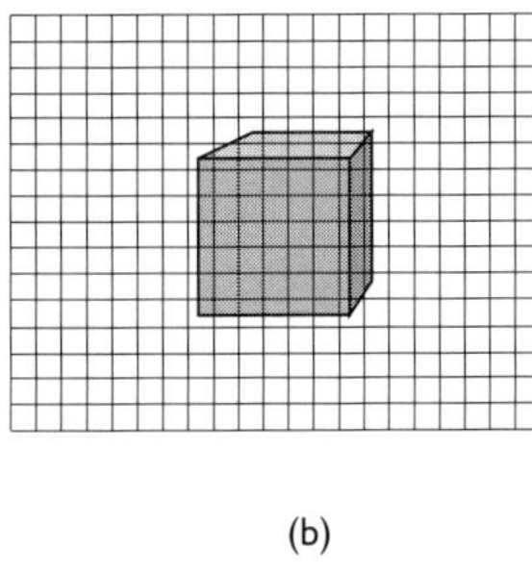

Figure 2-19. The viewable world is also clipped in the Z direction by the near and far clipping planes.

To handle this situation, computer graphics programs include an invisible vertical plane, called the **far clipping plane**, beyond which nothing is renderable. Objects farther away than the far clipping plane, like objects that lie beyond the edges of the screen, are clipped. In the same way, a **near clipping plane** prevents objects closer than the near clipping plane from being considered by the rendering program.

In Figure 2-19a the screen is represented as a heavy horizontal line. The two thinner horizontal lines represent the near and far Z clipping planes. The shaded area between these lines is the space viewable by the camera. The cube is "seen" by the camera and is rendered (Figure 2-19b). The cylinder, however, lies beyond the far Z clipping plane and therefore is not viewed by the camera, even though the cylinder lies within the viewable pyramid created by the edges of the screen. The pyramidal volume of space created by the clipping from the edges of the screen has been truncated at both front and back by the Z clipping planes. Any object that lies outside this truncated pyramid is clipped, not rendered, by the rendering program.

This concept of a truncated pyramid is important. If you combine the clipping of the viewable world by the edges of the screen and the clipping of the same world by the near and far clipping planes, you end up with a viewable world in the shape of a pyramid with its top and bottom cut off (Figure 1-20). This volume is called the **viewing frustum**, and in any given scene only those objects that lie within the viewing frustum are renderable.

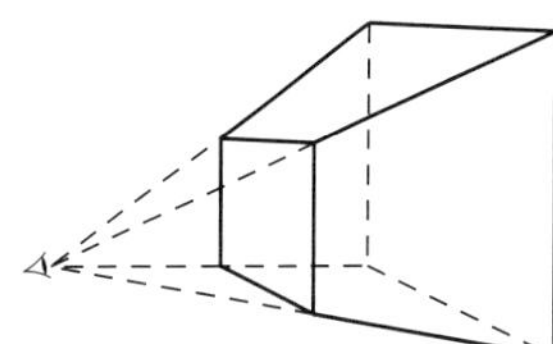

Figure 2-20. The combination of all the clipping planes produces a viewing frustum. Only objects lying within the viewing frustum are visible.

Notice also that the near clipping plane need not coincide with the placement of the screen. In Figure 2-19, for example, the near clipping plane is slightly farther away from the camera than is the screen itself. Most high-end software packages allow you to position the near and far clipping planes wherever you want, either interactively with a mouse device or by typing in numbers to indicate the depths of the planes.

A curious effect of Z clipping planes is that an object straddling one of the Z clipping planes appears to be sliced in half, because only the portion of the object inside the viewable space is visible. In Figure 2-21a the solid parallel lines represent the near and far clipping planes, and the shaded area is the

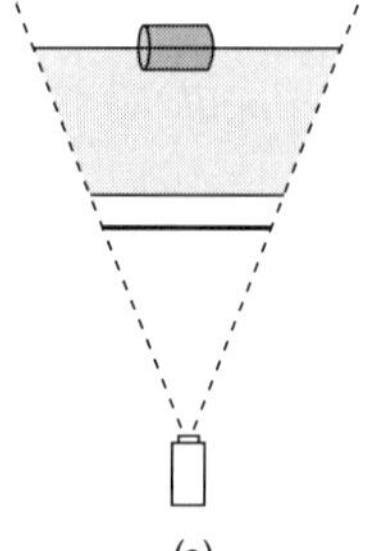
(a)

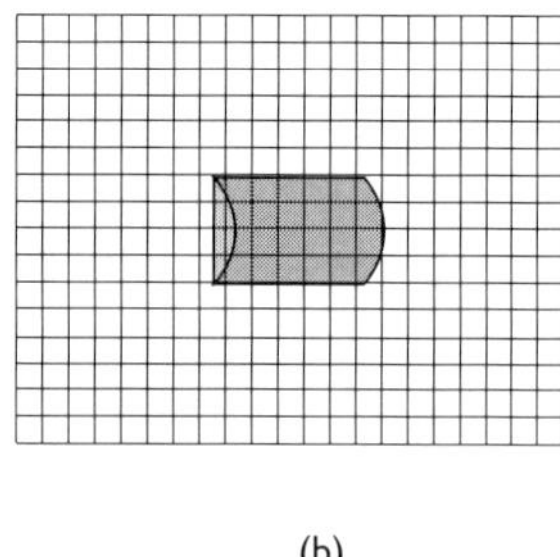
(b)

Figure 2-21. If an object straddles one of the clipping planes, part of it will be visible and part of it will be invisible.

viewable volume between them. Notice that the cylinder sitting atop the far clipping plane is partially rendered, the front half lying within the viewable area and therefore visible, the rear portion lying beyond the far clipping plane and therefore invisible (Figure 2-21b).

Lights

In an environment where there is no light at all—for example, a windowless room, with the lights turned off—you can see nothing. The rendering of a three-dimensional computer graphics scene is similar. In order to "see"—that is, to render—a scene or any objects within that scene, you must define lights.

When defining lights with a 3D software package, you define many of the characteristics that lights possess in the real world. The first of these is **location**, which you usually specify either by positioning the light interactively with a mouse device or by typing in values (that is, a triplet of XYZ coordinates) with the keyboard. Placing a light at *(0,0,0)*, for example, locates the light at the center of the world. Placing it at *(9,4,0)* locates it to the right and up a bit.

Another parameter to be defined for all lights is **intensity**, which you usually specify as a range of numbers. The higher the number, the brighter the light. For example, if the range is 0.0 to 1.0, then an intensity value of 1.0 produces an extremely bright light, a value of 0.5 produces a moderately bright light, and a value of 0.0 turns the light off.

You usually specify a third parameter, the **color** of the light, as three numbers, one for each of the three primary colors of the standard computer graphics color system: red, green, and blue. These are referred to as **RGB**, for short. The most common method of defining RGB values is to use numbers ranging from 0 to 255, with 0 being no color and 255 being full color. Intermediate numbers produce colors that lie between these two extremes. For example, RGB = (0,0,0) describes pure black—no red, no green, and no blue. RGB = (255,255,255) is pure white; RGB = (255,0,0) pure red; RGB =

(0,255,0) pure green; and so on. RGB = (150,23,192) produces a purplish color composed primarily of red and blue.

Sometimes a software system combines the specifications for color and intensity into one parameter, asking you to indicate both color and intensity in one RGB triplet. In this case, the magnitude of the numbers indicates the intensity, while the ratio of these numbers to one another indicates the color. Thus, Light = (255,0,0) is a very bright, pure red light, while Light = (128,0,0), the red component of which has been decreased by half, is a pure red light of only half the intensity. Similarly, Light = (255,255,255) is a very bright white light, while Light = (70,70,70), also a white light (because all the color components are equal), is rather dim.

In addition to determining the location, the intensity, and the color of a light, you also must think about the type of light. In the real world, there are many different types of light, such as fluorescent light, incandescent light (the glow of standard light bulbs), daylight, and candlelight. Most 3D computer systems offer a range of light types that attempt to simulate the different types of real light.

The most common type of light in computer graphics systems, a **point light**, simulates the effect of a bare light bulb hanging from a wire. Located at a specific point in space, it radiates light equally in all directions: up, down, and to the sides (Figure 2-22a).

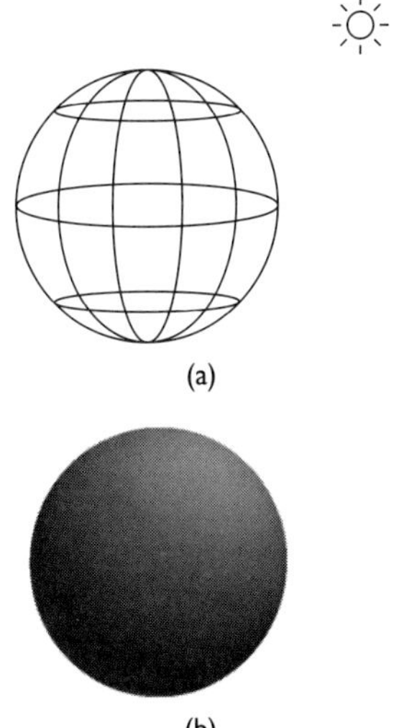

Figure 2-22. A point light emits light equally in all directions.

In addition to location, color, and intensity parameters, point lights often have another parameter associated with them. Intended to simulate the fact that the light from a light bulb does not travel forever, but fades with distance, this parameter often is called **decay** or **falloff**. A decay value of zero means that there is no decay—the light continues forever at the same intensity (a very unrealistic situation). The larger the decay value, the more quickly the light fades as it moves away from the point light.

Unlike a real light bulb, however, a point light does not have any size or any shape. In other words, it has no geometry. It is formless. In a computer graphics rendering you normally do not see a point light. You only see the effects the point light has on objects in the scene (Figure 2-22b).

Even though a point light has no geometry and does not render as an object, most 3D systems allow you to treat the point light as a *logical* object. This means that you can select it, delete it, move it, and even, if you choose, group it hierarchically with other objects. In order to allow you to do this, most systems provide some iconic representation of the light (see Figure 2-22a).

Hierarchically grouping a light becomes especially important if you want to have an actual light-bulb model in your scene. In order to do this, you first model the geometry of the bulb, perhaps using a surface of revolution. Next,

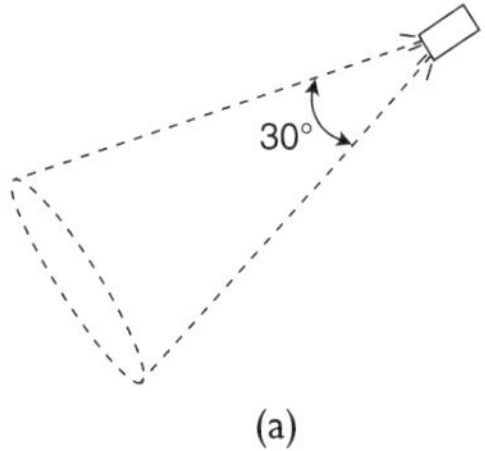

(a)

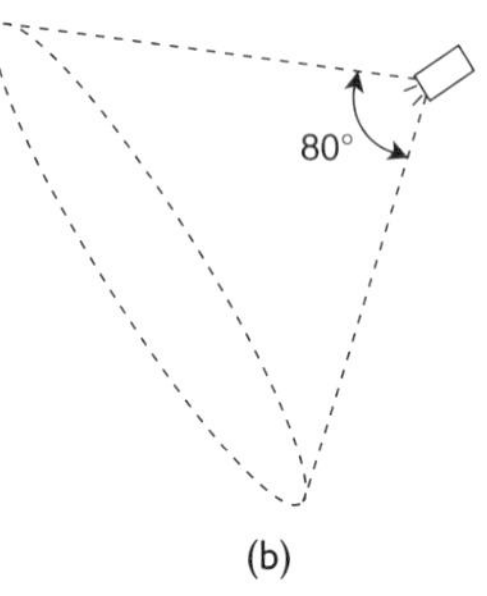

(b)

Figure 2-23. The spread of the cone of a spotlight can be adjusted.

you define a point light to be located at the center of this geometry—that is, inside the bulb. Finally, to make sure that the bulb geometry and the point light stay together, you hierarchically group them. In this way, if you move the bulb geometry, the light within the bulb moves with it.

Like the point light, a second common type of light is located at a specific point in space and has intensity, color, and decay parameters. You specify these parameters in the same ways that you specify them for a point light. In addition to these parameters, however, a **spotlight** has several additional parameters, which simulate the effect of a spotlight in the physical world. For instance, a spotlight throws light in a cone-shaped beam, and this cone of light can vary in width. In computer graphics a parameter, usually called **spread**, controls the width of the cone. The spread of a spotlight is the measure of the angle between the opposite sides of the cone. An angle of 30 degrees, for example, produces a rather narrow cone of light (Figure 2-23a). An angle of 80 degrees produces a much broader cone (Figure 2-23b). Objects that lie outside of the cone do not receive any of the light from the spotlight.

A spotlight also throws light in a certain **direction**, and in some systems a line or an arrow emanating from the spotlight icon indicates this direction. In most systems the same cone that indicates the spread indicates the direction. You change the direction by rotating the spotlight. As the spotlight rotates, the directional arrow or cone points this way or that way, clearly indicating which way the light will fall.

Just as you do not see an actual point light in a scene, however (see Figure 2-22b), you do not see a spotlight nor its cone of light (Figure 2-24a). You see only the *effect* of that light on objects (Figure 2-24b). This makes sense within the artificial world of 3D computer graphics, in which the only things that are rendered, and therefore the only things that are visible, are surfaces. In the real world, you see a cone of light in the air because the light from the spotlight hits the surfaces of thousands of tiny dust particles that float in the air. If you do not model any such surfaces in a computer scene, you typically cannot see the cone of light as it passes through the air. It is possible, however, to render this sort of effect by using special techniques that simulate the presence of the myriad tiny surfaces that constitute a real-world atmosphere. Several of these techniques are discussed in the section on *Atmospheric Effects* later in this chapter. Another approach to the same problem is discussed in the section on *Particle Systems* in chapter 4.

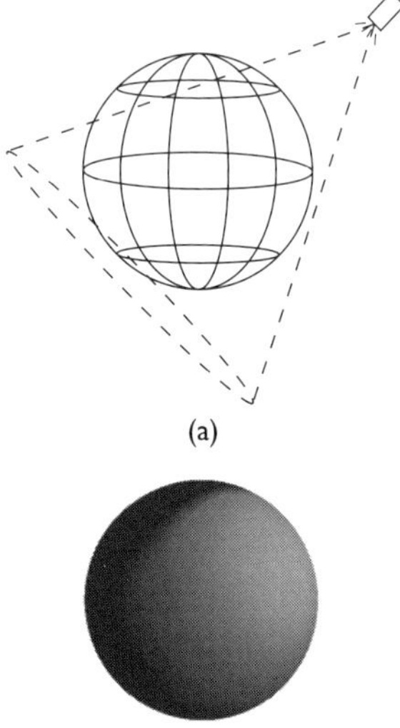

(a)

(b)

Figure 2-24. Anything outside the cone of the spot light is not illuminated.

You have seen that point lights fade with distance, and that decay parameters control this sort of fading. Spotlights also fade in this way and also normally have decay parameters. However, spotlights fade in another way as well. In the real world, the intensity of light fades not only with distance from the light source, but also with distance from the center of the light cone. That is, the intensity of the light decreases from the center of the light cone to the edges of the light cone. The parameter that controls this effect is often called **dropoff** (Figure 2-25). The larger the dropoff value, the more quickly the light fades toward the outer edges of the light cone. A dropoff value of zero produces no such fading. A dropoff value of zero would have produced a hard-edged demarcation between the dark and light portions of the sphere in Figure 2-24b, for instance. Instead, a dropoff value greater than zero produced a gradual change from dark to light and a certain fuzziness.

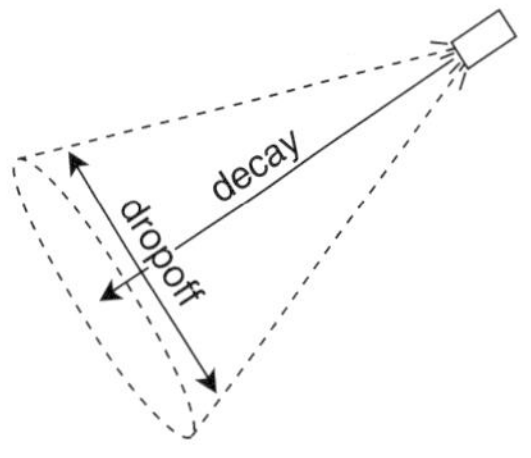

Figure 2-25. The light from a spotlight fades in two directions and is controlled by two parameters.

Yet another type of light provided by some of the more advanced 3D systems simulates the effect of an entire area, rather than a single point, emitting light. Two examples of this type of lighting are the banks of fluorescent lights in the ceilings of some offices, and the screens of television sets. Whereas the light from a spotlight begins at a point and emanates in a conical beam (Figure 2-26a), the light from an **area light** begins at a rectangular area and emanates in a rectangular beam (Figure 2-26b).

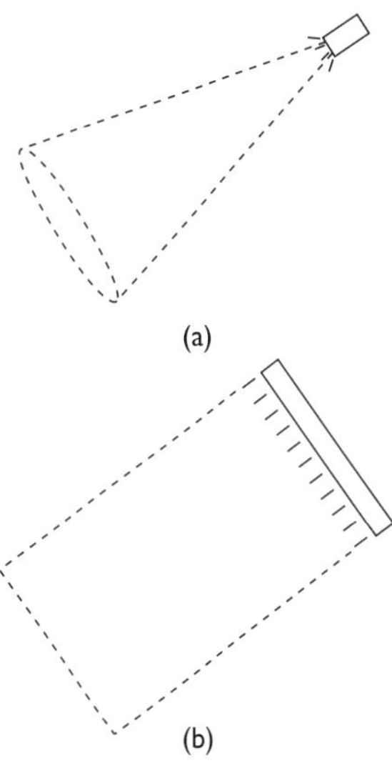

Figure 2-26. An area light emits a rectangular area of light.

The lights presented so far—point, spot, and area—are readily comprehensible to us, but calculating the effects of each light represents a different level of complexity for the computer. That is, it takes more time for a rendering program to calculate the effect of an area light than it takes to calculate the effect of a spotlight. And it takes more time to calculate the effect of a spotlight than to calculate the effect of a point light. Therefore, when you choose a light, consider the impact on rendering time of the different types of light. This becomes especially important when you render a large number of frames for animation, since any increase in rendering time is multiplied by the number of frames to be rendered. Often, a little experimentation with simpler light models can produce a result that looks as good as, but renders much faster than, a more computationally complex set of lights.

Another type of light, called **ambient light**, simulates the overall amount of daylight (or lack of daylight) in the world around you. An ambient light does not emanate from a specific location in space, nor does it flow in a specific direction. It is simply an overall level of light, present everywhere in the environment. Consequently, when defining an ambient light, you specify only the intensity parameter and the color parameter. You might use a low-intensity purplish light, for example, to simulate twilight, or a high-intensity white light to simulate full daylight.

In reality, of course, no light, including daylight, behaves like this. The sun has a location, and sunlight arrives on Earth from a specific direction. The ambient light of computer graphics is a convenient abstraction, an easy way to alter the overall level of lighting in a scene.

The artificial, directionless quality of ambient light has a curious result. If the only light in a virtual 3D computer graphics environment is ambient light, all sides of all objects are lit equally, since the ambient light is present equally

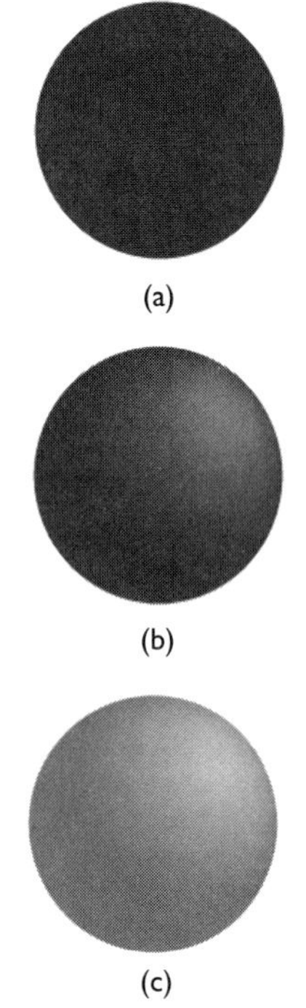
(a)
(b)
(c)

Figure 2-27. Ambient light is the overall level of lighting in a scene. It comes from no specific direction or location.

everywhere. A sphere, for example, rather than being darker on one side or the other, is lit equally on all sides and thus appears as a disk (Figure 2-27a). By itself, therefore, ambient light cannot provide a realistic rendering of a three-dimensional situation. Instead of using it in isolation, you must use ambient light in conjunction with other lights, of whatever different types you choose. Combining a point light and ambient light, for example, produces a very reasonable rendering (Figure 2-27b). Increasing the intensity of ambient light, while keeping a point light as is, increases the overall light and makes an object in the environment lighter (Figure 2-27c).

Infinite light, sometimes called **directional light**, is considered to be located infinitely far away (simulating, in effect, the great distance of the Sun). In this it resembles ambient light, which has no location. However, an infinite light, unlike an ambient light, has directionality, in that it moves from right to left, or from upper left to lower right, and so on. In this, it more accurately simulates sunlight, which comes from a certain direction. However, unlike other lights—such as spotlights and area lights—that also have directionality but that throw light within only circumscribed regions, an infinite light throws equal amounts of light everywhere. The light comes from a specific direction, but it comes from that direction equally throughout the scene.

On the computer screen an arrow icon often indicates an infinite light. The location of the arrow is insignificant. Only the direction of the arrow—that is, the angle of the arrow—matters. In Figure 2-28, the heavy arrow is the icon for the infinite light. In addition, a number of lighter arrows indicate that this infinite light projects down equally throughout the entire scene from the indicated direction. Thus, all objects within the scene—the sphere as well as the cylinder—receive equal amounts of light, and this light arrives at the same angle on all the objects.

One advantage of infinite lights is that it is very easy to get a reasonable (though not subtle) rendering with only a single infinite light. For this reason, many systems define an infinite light as the default lighting environment.

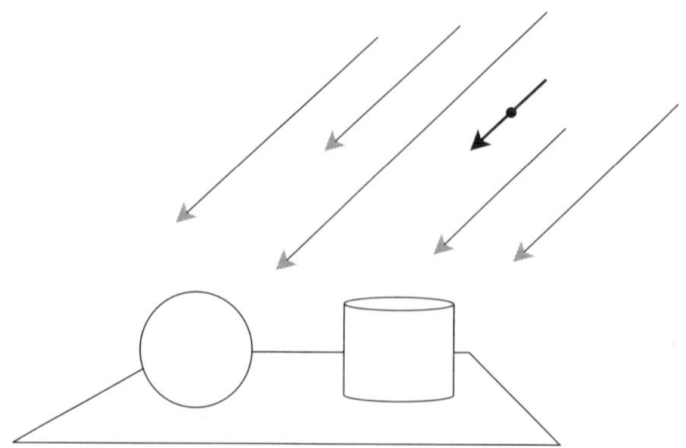

Figure 2-28. Directional light throws light equally throughout the scene from a given direction.

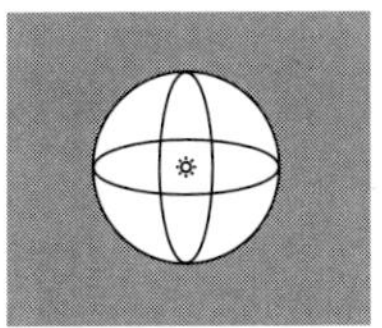
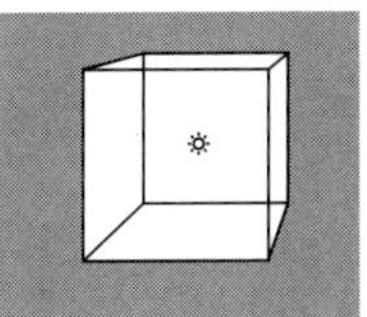
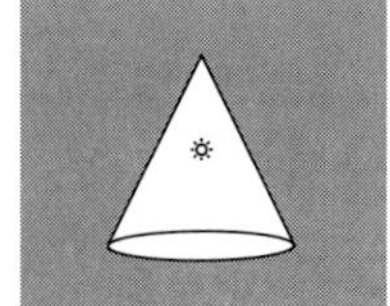
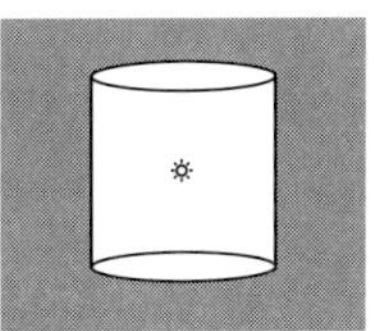

Figure 2-29. The light cast by a volume light is restricted to a clearly defined volume of space.

Another advantage is that it is very easy and not very time-consuming for the computer to calculate the effects of an infinite light.

Another type of light offered by some software packages is a **volume light**. The light cast by a volume light is restricted to a clearly defined volume of space, defined as one of several possible geometric forms. Figure 2-29 illustrates four of the most common volume shapes for volume lights. Illumination cast by the volume light illustrated in (a) is restricted to a spherical volume of space. The illumination of (b) is restricted to a cubic volume of space, that of (c) to a conical volume, and that of (d) to a cylindrical volume.

Volume lights are an extension of the basic concept of a three-dimensional light already discussed in this section. Since all lights in 3D computer graphics cast their light in a fully three-dimensional space, all lights effectively create volumes of lights. This is most obvious, perhaps, when we speak of the "cone of light" of a spotlight. What distinguishes volume lights, however, is that they make use of a very clearly and unequivocally delineated volume. A spotlight, for example, creates a cone of light, but its light might be cast infinitely far, creating an unending cone, if you will. Similarly, a point light emits its light equally in all directions and therefore can be thought of as emitting its light in a spherical pattern, but its light does not necessarily end abruptly at the edge of a specific sphere.

Figure 2-30. Only objects lying within the light's volume receive illumination from it.

The clear delineation of a volume light's volume is one reason for its usefulness. Any objects that lie outside the volume of the light's illumination will not receive any light at all from the volume light. This provides a convenient way to limit the effect of a light within a scene. In Figure 2-30, for example, the table and vase lie within the light's cubic volume and are therefore illuminated. The other objects in the scene, however, receive no light at all from the volume light. In the section on *Atmospheric Effects*, you will see how some volume lights can also be used to render fog.

In the earlier discussion of spotlights, you saw that the cone of a spotlight is not visible. A similar problem arises when a light glows. A candle flame, for example, has a distinct glow around it. In order to address this situation, some sophisticated software packages include a **glow** parameter, which can be adjusted for point lights. In Figure 2-31, for example, a point light has been placed at the tip of the wick. This light illuminates the models in the scene—that is, the candlestick and the wick. The glow parameter of this point light has been adjusted to create the luminous effect. How intense the glow

Figure 2-31. Some software systems permit a light to be rendered with a glow effect. (Courtesy, Dongho Kim.)

Figure 2-32. The light in this scene has been given a very intense glow factor. In addition, the angle of the camera and the location of the light produce a lens flare.

is, how far the glow spreads, and even what shape the glow is can be controlled. These controls are separate from the intensity or decay of the point light itself. The light proper may have an intensity of 3.0, while the glow has an intensity of 2.5. If the glow intensity is turned down to 0.0, no glow is visible, but the point light of intensity 3.0 still illuminates objects in the scene.

Another specialized lighting effect, available in advanced systems, enables you to simulate the **lens flare** that sometimes occurs on the lens of a camera facing directly into a light. If the camera points toward a light whose lens flare parameter has been turned on, a "hot spot" of light will be rendered (Figure 2-32).

So far, you have considered lighting objects that are rendered in isolation, a deliberate simplification. In most scenes, however, there are many objects to be rendered, and this raises the distinction between "shading" and "cast shadows."

Shading is the effect of light on the surface of an object as the surface goes from lighter to darker. When one portion of a sphere is darker because the portion faces away from the light, this portion is shaded. If there are several objects in a scene, however, the situation can become more complex, in that each object not only is shaded but might also create **cast shadows** on other objects. All objects in a scene have shading, but not all objects necessarily have cast shadows.

The calculation of shading is fairly straightforward and is provided automatically by all 3D computer graphics systems. Cast shadows, however, are much more difficult to calculate, and consequently most systems provide this capability as an option that you may turn on or off. The most common way to turn shadowcasting on or off is through a parameter associated with each light. When you define any type of light, you specify whether or not this particular light casts shadows. The reason you make this choice on a per-light basis, rather than globally for all lights, is that often the look you are after can be achieved by having only one or two lights casting shadows. This situation is much less complicated mathematically, and therefore faster for the rendering program to calculate, than if you were to turn on shadow casting for all the lights in the scene.

Most programs offer two methods of calculating cast shadows. One uses a **ray-tracing** algorithm (see the section on *Rendering Algorithms* later in this chapter for a more complete discussion of ray tracing). This method calculates the movement of light beams as they bounce from object to object in the scene, or even as they pass through transparent objects. The ray-tracing approach to casting shadows produces very accurate shadows, but can be quite time-consuming and may slow down your renderings considerably.

An alternative method for calculating cast shadows is to use a **shadow depth map**. Here the software begins by calculating what the world looks like from the point of view of the shadow-casting light. Information about which objects are in front of which other objects is stored, pixel by pixel, in an internal image called a **depth map** (for a more detailed explanation of this technique, see the description of Z-buffering in the section on *Rendering Algorithms*). Since most 3D software systems use the Z axis to represent the depth of a scene, this internal image is also called a Z **map**. Such an image is illustrated in Figure 2-33b. Figure 2-33a shows the scene as viewed normally from the camera. Notice the spotlight icon in the upper right. Figure 2-33b shows the depth information of the scene as it is viewed from the shadow-casting spotlight. In this depth-map image, objects that are farther away from the spotlight are represented as lighter, while objects which are closer to it are darker.

Once the Z depth information has been calculated, the software then uses it to calculate how objects that are closer to the light project backwards onto objects that are more distant. The projection of each object backward becomes the shadow it casts onto those objects behind it.

The shadow depth map approach to shadow casting can be much faster than ray tracing. However, it is also less accurate. In order to refine its accuracy, most software packages allow you to adjust the resolution of the preliminary Z map image that is produced. The higher the resolution, the more accurate the shadow calculations. Of course, the higher the resolution, the slower the rendering, as well.

Cast shadows add a substantial degree of realism to a scene. They also can be crucial in conveying information about the three-dimensional placement of objects. Notice, for example, that in Figure 2-34a, with shadow casting turned off, you cannot tell that the sphere is hovering just above the large, flat surface. In Figure 2-34b, with shadow casting turned on, you can tell that the sphere is hovering by the way its shadow is cast onto that surface.

In addition to adding realism to a scene, cast shadows can generate a powerful emotional effect when used carefully. In Figure 2-35 the exaggerated shadows cast on the floor and wall create an air of hyperreality that works to great effect with the dreamlike modeling of the scene.

An alternative technique that can nicely simulate cast shadows is **projector lights**. Projector lights function like a standard home slide projector—that is, they project light through an image. With a computer graphics projector light, however, the image is a picture file that you tell the software to use. The software then does its calculations as if that image were placed in front of the light, with the light shining through it. The result is that the image is cast, or projected, into the scene and onto any objects in its path (Figure 2-36).

The image that you project can be a full-color image, in which case the projection of that image onto the scene will also be full-color. However, one

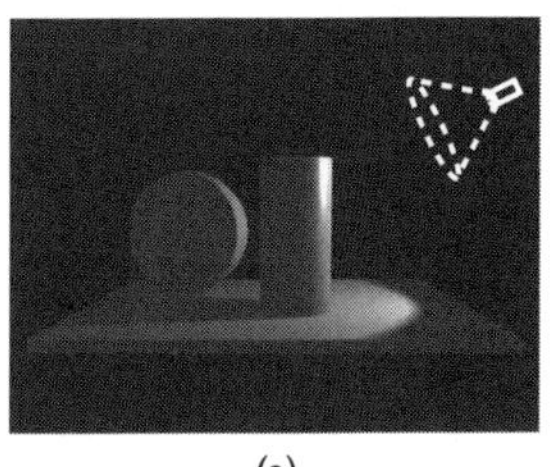

(a)

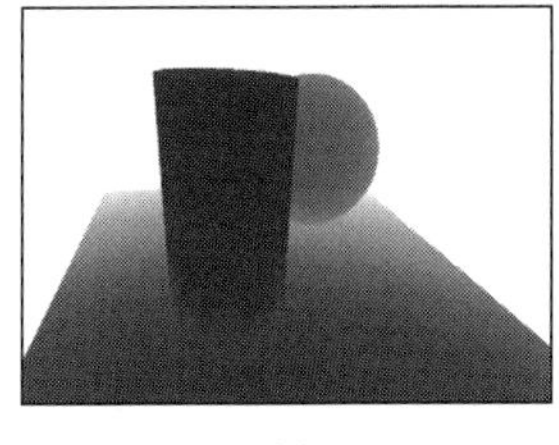

(b)

Figure 2-33. A shadow map uses a Z depth representation of the scene as viewed from the shadow-casting light.

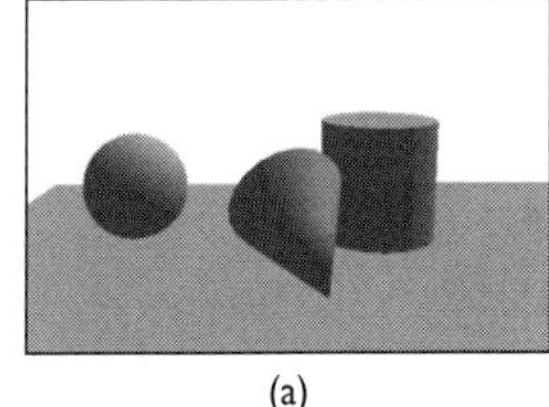

(a)

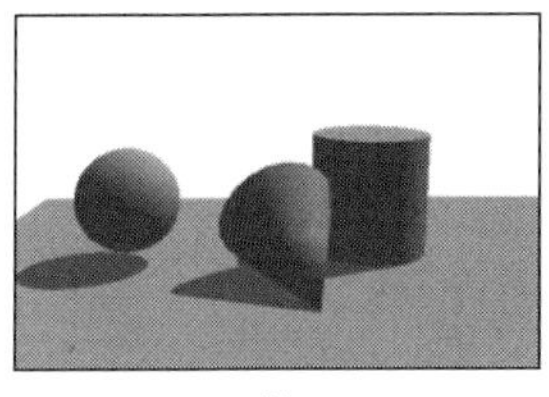

(b)

Figure 2-34. Cast shadows can lend an important degree of realism.

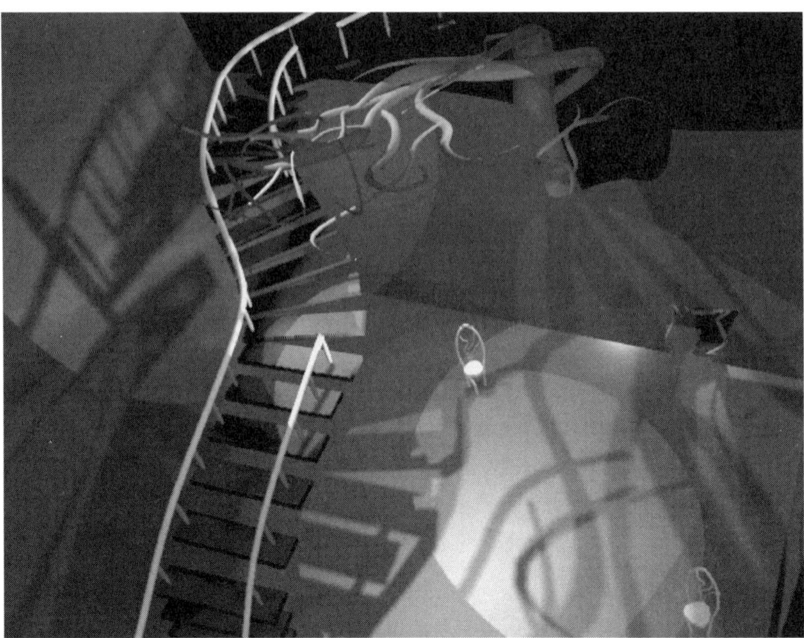

Figure 2-35. Lighting and shadows can be used to great emotional effect. (Courtesy, Seung Hye Choi)

of the most useful applications of projector lights is the creation of cast shadows through the use of a black and white grayscale image rather than a color image (Figure 2-37). Figure 2-37a shows a black and white image of tree branches, the image to be projected. In Figure 2-37b this image has been projected by a spotlight through a rectangular window into a room, creating the illusion of a tree's shadow on the objects in the room. This technique is a much more economical way to create a complex shadowing effect than modeling a tree and casting shadows from the tree model onto the floor. The projector-light technique not only allows you to avoid modeling the tree altogether; it also significantly reduces the rendering time for this scene, since projected images are much faster to calculate than true cast shadows. Notice, however, that it is only possible to employ the projector-light technique here because the tree itself is not visible in the scene. If the shadow casting objects are visible in the scene, as they were in the image in Figure 2-35, the use of a projector light would not be possible, or would be far less effective.

Color plate 8 shows another, very sophisticated example of a projector light. Here, rather than simulating cast shadows, the projector light projects an image proper—the film image shown playing on the movie screen. The image is, in fact, just one frame of a live-action film that was digitized and projected, frame by frame, through the projector light, giving the effect of a movie within the animation.

To give you additional control over the lighting of a scene, some 3D computer systems provide the option to have a given light either affect or not

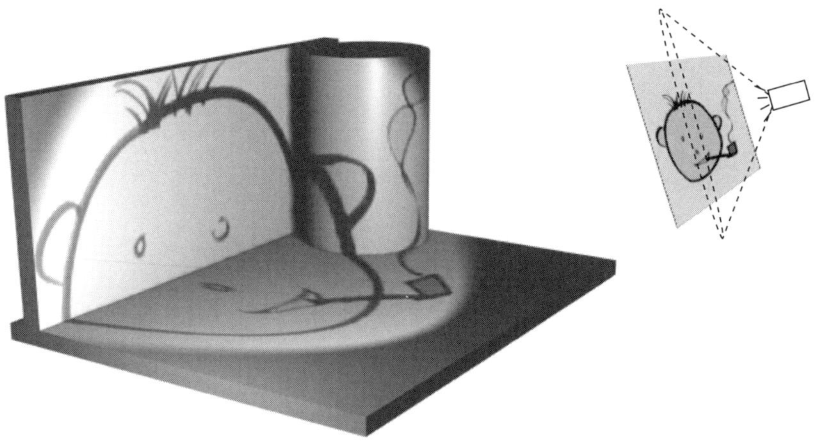

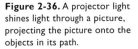

Figure 2-36. A projector light shines light through a picture, projecting the picture onto the objects in its path.

affect a given surface. This, of course, does not correspond to what happens in the real world, in which a light that is turned on affects all surfaces that are close enough to it. In computer graphics, however, it is possible to create an artificial situation in which, for example, a spotlight over a table affects the table and the book on the table, but not the pencil lying on the book. This technique often is called **light linking** or **light association**. In the example just given, the spotlight is linked to the table and the book, but not to the pencil. Lights linked to specific objects are sometimes said to be **exclusive** or **selective** lights. Lights not linked to any specific objects are assumed to affect all objects.

The technique of linking lights to specific objects becomes especially useful when you have your lighting worked out for an entire scene, but one object (for example, the pencil) doesn't look quite right. If you did not have light linking, the addition or subtraction of a light to improve the lighting on the pencil would disrupt the otherwise perfect lighting on the rest of the scene. By making use of light linking, restricting the effect of the light to the objects that need it, you avoid having the new light affect the rest of the scene.

Like so much of three-dimensional computer graphics, lighting is very simple in concept but extremely subtle in practice. Most scenes require the placement and careful definition of anywhere from a few lights of various types to up to ten or twelve lights. That this work calls for a great deal of skill and, sometimes, patience should not surprise you. Think about the art forms of still photography and cinematography, in which setting up the lights for a shot is crucial, time-consuming, and highly demanding. In film making, it is common to have a specialist devoted to lighting, and to spend an hour setting up and fine-tuning the lights for a shot, which then may take only a few minutes, or even seconds, to shoot.

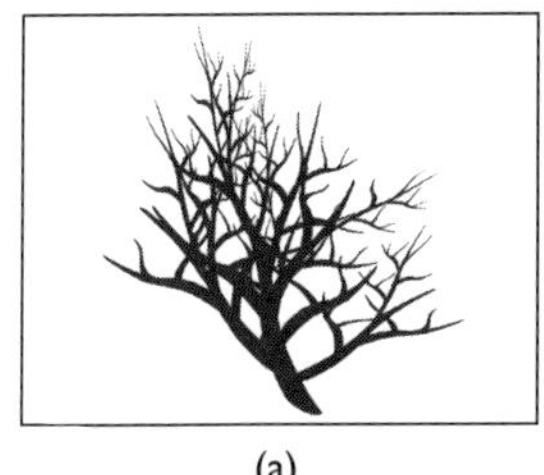

(a)

(b)

Figure 2-37. A projector light can be used to easily simulate complex cast shadows.

It is not difficult to explain to someone the basic techniques of applying paint to a canvas. It is another matter entirely for that person to paint a masterpiece. Lighting a virtual 3D computer scene can be similarly demanding. It can also be stunningly effective, and the time and patience you devote to it extremely rewarding.

Surface Characteristics

The next major element needed to produce a rendering of a scene is the definition of the surface characteristics, such as color and shininess, of the objects in the scene. Often the surface characteristics of a particular surface are treated as a conglomerate. When this grouping is done, the set of characteristics of a particular surface usually is called a **shader**. A shader for a given surface includes the definition of the color for that surface, the definition of the shininess of that surface, and so on.

One benefit of organizing a group of surface characteristics into a shader is that you then can save this shader independently of the surface for which you originally designed it. Later, when you work on another model, you can select the saved shader and assign it, with all of the defined characteristics, to a new surface. Both the original surface and the new surface will have exactly the same set of characteristics.

In fact, many 3D systems allow you to create an entire **shader library**. You can call up at any time any of the shaders saved into this library, and either assign that shader to a new model, or edit it to produce a variation on the original shader.

When you define the properties of a given surface, you normally think first of the **color** of that surface, and you normally do so in terms of the three primary colors of the RGB color system—that is, red, green, and blue, described earlier in *Lighting*. Most systems allow you to use the RGB system to define the color of your surface in some convenient, interactive way, such as by manipulating a **slider bar** for each of the color components (Figure 2-38). As you drag (usually with a mouse device) the "button" of the slider bar for a particular color, you increase or decrease the amount of that color component in the final color. The final color is updated and displayed at the same time, so you can see at each moment what the current color is. This technique allows you very precisely and easily to define a color without having to think in numerical terms.

Sometimes, of course, it is more convenient to think in terms of the actual numerical values that compose an RGB color. Consequently, almost all systems allow you to type in those numbers, usually using a range of 0 to 255 for each color component.

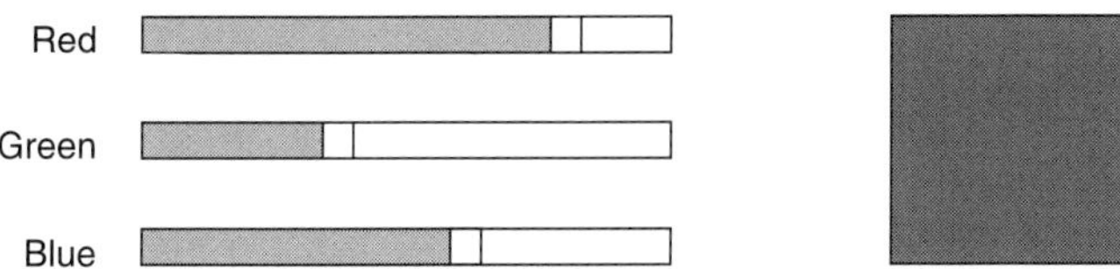

Figure 2-38. Slider bars can be used to define surface parameters.

Some programs also offer you the possibility of defining the color of a surface according to a different color system. This color system, known as **HSL**, uses three different variables—hue, saturation, and luminance—to define a color. You specify hue, saturation, and luminance values in the same ways that you specify the red, green, and blue values of the RGB system—either interactively (for example, with a slider) or by typing in numerical values.

Hue is the "color" of the color, in the sense that one red may be a purer red than another. A pure red contains only one hue, while an off-red contains several hues. Related colors—for example, crimson and vermilion—are related because they are close in hue.

Saturation is the amount of the hue in a color. A very saturated red will be brilliant. A "desaturated" red will be dull. As saturation increases, colors tend to take on a kind of neon look. As saturation decreases, colors tend to approach gray. A fully desaturated color, in fact, *is* a tone of gray.

Luminance is the brightness of a color. A color of a given hue and a given saturation can be made lighter or darker by changing the luminance.

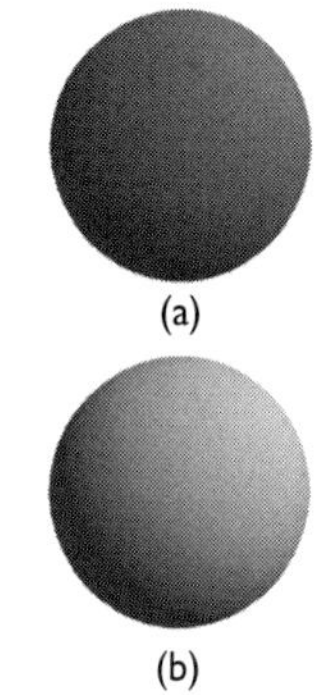

Figure 2-39. The diffuse component of a surface controls how much light bounces off a surface—that is, the overall tendency to brightness of that surface.

In addition to determining the color of a surface, you must define the way that light bounces, or reflects, off the surface. You usually define this phenomenon through a combination of several parameters, the first of which is **diffuseness**, the measure of how much light reflects, overall, from a surface. A surface with a small diffuse component will be darker (Figure 2-39a), because it reflects less light, than a surface with a large diffuse component (Figure 2-39b), even if both surfaces are defined to have exactly the same color and are lit by exactly the same lighting. You usually specify diffuseness, often with a slider bar, as a number between zero and one. A value of zero means that no light reflects off the surface, and the surface renders as black. A higher value means that more light reflects off the surface.

Diffuseness controls the overall brightness of the surface, but does not produce highlights on the surface. If you activate only the diffuseness parameter, the surfaces you generate will be perfectly matte—without any highlights—like a piece of cardboard.

To create highlights, you activate several other parameters. The first of these controls how shiny the surface is, and is called **specularity**. To say that a surface is very specular means that it has very bright highlights. For instance, metallic surfaces, shiny plastic surfaces, and soap bubbles have high specularity, while unfinished wood, paper, and cloth have low specularity.

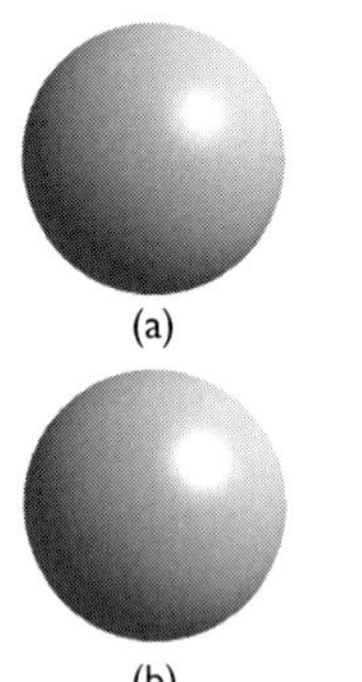

(a)

(b)

Figure 2-40. Specularity controls how shiny an object is.

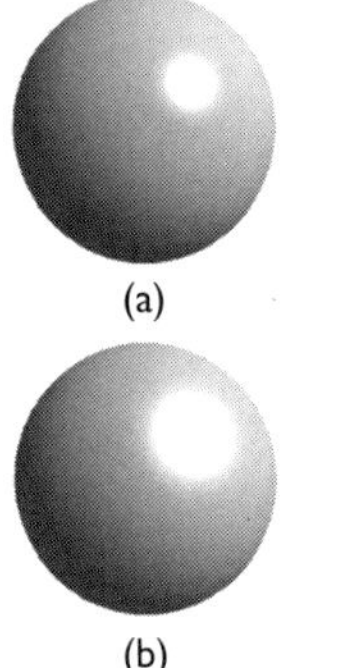

(a)

(b)

Figure 2-41. Highlight size can be used to fine-tune the surface definition of a shiny object.

You define specularity in conjunction with diffuseness, first supplying a diffuse value to control the overall brightness of the surface, then supplying a specular value to control the brightness of the highlights. You specify the value for specularity in the same way that you specify the value for diffuseness.

The sphere in Figure 2-40a has a specular component of 0.2, for example, while the sphere in Figure 2-40b has a specular component of 0.6. Both spheres have exactly the same diffuse component and are rendered with exactly the same lights, but the higher specular component of the sphere in Figure 2-40b produces the much brighter highlight on that sphere.

Many systems provide additional control over highlights with a second parameter, called **highlight size**. At first, it might not be obvious why you need this. It might seem that if you want to make a surface shiny, you just increase the brightness of the highlight with the specular component. However, different materials produce highlights of different sizes. A highlight on a very shiny chrome surface is not only very bright but also very condensed —that is, small and focused (Figure 2-41a). A highlight on extremely shiny plastic, on the other hand, while also very bright, is broader and less focused (Figure 2-41b). Using both the highlight size parameter and the specularity parameter, you can define surfaces that closely resemble specific materials.

Again, it might not be obvious why you need yet another parameter for defining highlights, but different materials actually have slightly different **highlight colors**. Plastic of any color, for example, tends to reflect a white highlight. Aluminum, on the other hand, tends to reflect a highlight of the same color as the color of the aluminum. To specify highlight color, you usually use the standard RGB slider.

These last three parameters—specularity, highlight size, and highlight color—all help define how shiny a surface is. Shiny surfaces, in addition to having highlights, however, also tend to be reflective, that is, the environment around them may be visible on them. An extreme example of this effect is a mirror.

Not all shiny surfaces are equally reflective. For instance, an extremely shiny plastic is less reflective than an equally shiny stainless steel, which is largely why you perceive stainless steel as stainless steel and not as silver-colored plastic. Some systems provide a parameter called, appropriately enough, **reflectivity**, to control this condition. As with the other surface parameters, you usually specify reflectivity as a value ranging from zero to one, with zero being a surface that does not reflect the environment at all and one being a perfectly reflective mirror. Thus, in Figure 2-42a the tabletop on which the bowl sits has no reflectivity. In Figure 2-42b the tabletop is slightly reflective. In Figure 2-42c the tabletop has a very high reflectivity value.

A surface also can be either opaque or transparent, and a **transparency** parameter allows you to control this characteristic. In most software systems, you again use numbers from zero to one, with zero creating no transparency at all—that is, complete opacity. A shower curtain might have a low transparency value, for example, making it slightly (and discreetly) transparent, while a wine glass would have a high transparency value. When using transparency, beware of making an object 100 percent transparent—it will be totally invisible!

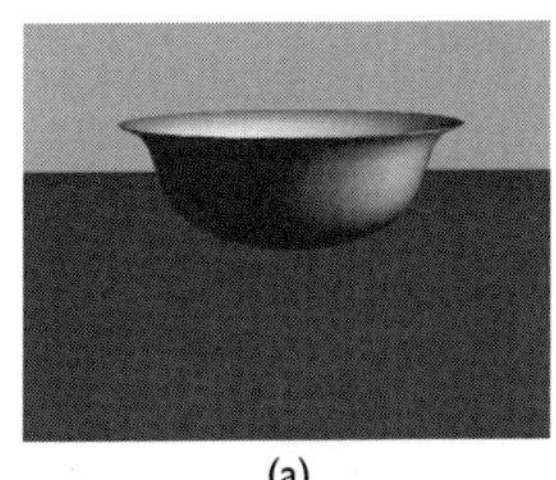
(a)

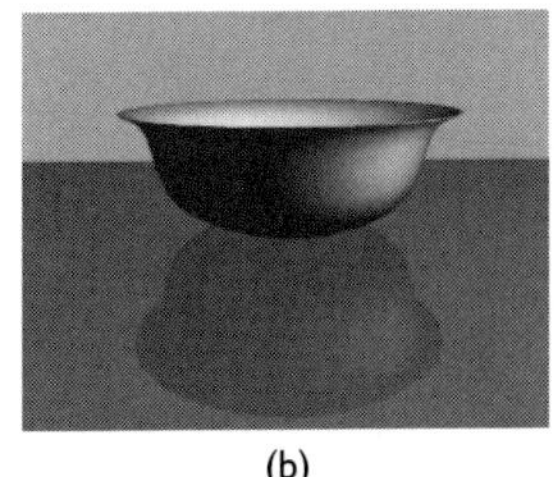
(b)

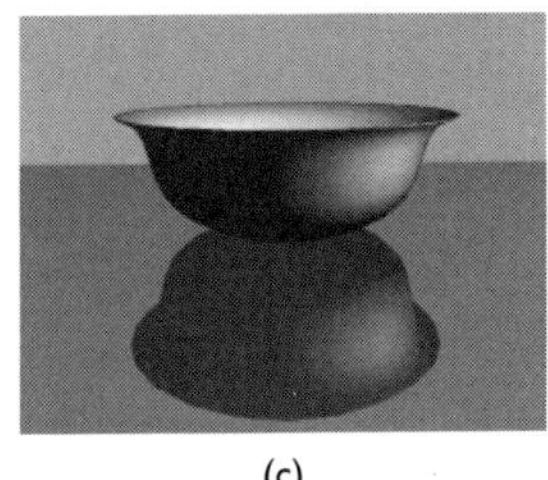
(c)

Figure 2-42. A surface can be defined as more or less reflective.

When you define a surface to be transparent, the color of that surface is rendered by combining the color of the transparent object with the color of whatever is behind the object. In some rendering situations, there is nothing behind the transparent object—only a black background. In this case, the effect of transparency is to combine the color of the transparent object with the black of the background, producing a rendering of the object that simply looks darker, not more transparent. Transparency is most effective, in other words, when there are other modeled objects or a background of various colors behind the transparent object. It is least effective when the background is of some uniform color.

Another unexpected result of transparency can be a decrease in the effect of any highlights you have defined. In fact, an object that displays a clearly visible highlight when opaque may have no highlight at all when rendered as transparent. This is because the highlight, as well as the normal surface color, blends with whatever color is behind the object. Often you can solve this problem by substantially increasing the specularity parameter for the transparent surfaces.

Another surface characteristic that some, though not all, systems allow you to specify has to do with how light bends as it passes from one material to another. A classic example of this phenomenon is the straw that appears to bend as it enters water in a glass. Many rendering programs are not capable of calculating this bending of light, which is known as **refractivity**, but ray-tracing programs (discussed further in the next section) provide a **refractive index** parameter.

Physicists have determined experimentally the refractive index values for materials in the real world, and rendering programs that make use of refractivity also use these values. Air, for example, has a refractive index of one. Refractive indices other than one cause light to bend and therefore create distortions as you look through the material in question. Indices larger than one bend the light one way, and indices less than one bend light the opposite way. If you model a transparent sphere and give it a refractive index of one, light will not bend as it enters that surface, because both the air and the sphere have the same refractive indices (Figure 2-43b). If the

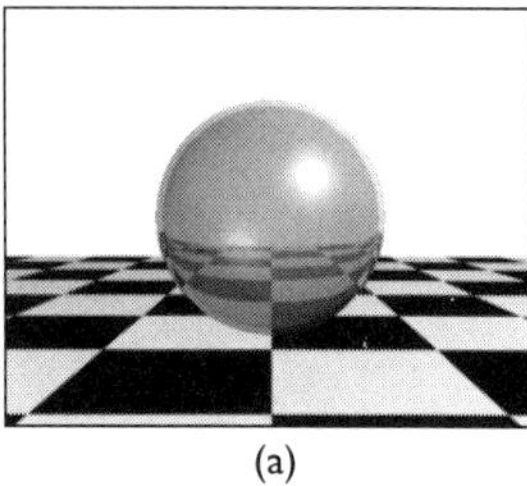

(a)

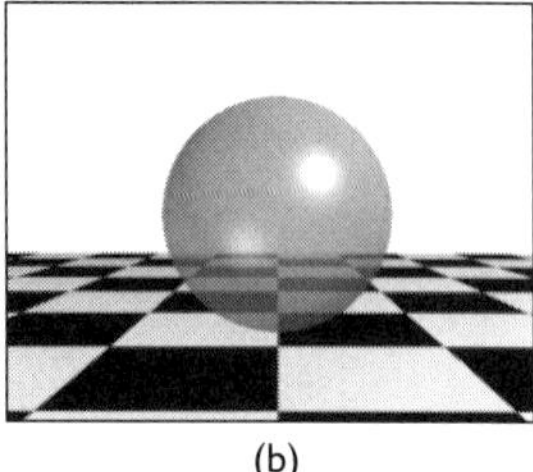

(b)

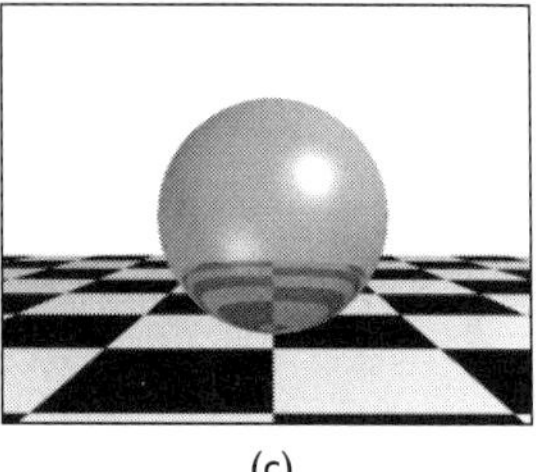

(c)

Figure 2-43. The refractive index controls how light bends as it passes through a transparent object.

sphere has a refractive index slightly less than one (Figure 2-43a), or slightly more than one (Figure 2-43c), the light will bend.

Most surfaces in the world absorb and reflect light, but only a few surfaces emit light. A light bulb is one example. To better render light-emitting surfaces, some systems provide a parameter called **incandescence**. This parameter, usually specified with a number from zero to one, adds a certain amount of brightness to the original color of the surface. The larger the incandescence value, the more brightness is added and the more the surface appears to glow. Note that incandescence is a different quality than the "glow" effect discussed in the previous section, however. Incandescence applies to surfaces, while glow effects apply to lights, which are not surfaces.

The upcoming sections on texture mapping present many more techniques for defining the characteristics of a surface, but in this section you have seen the most essential surface characteristics. Understand, however, that in defining a given shader you do not necessarily define all of the parameters discussed here. Many shaders can be defined very effectively with only a handful of parameters. It is, in fact, to your advantage to keep your shader definitions as simple as possible while still achieving the desired look, because each additional parameter increases the time required by the rendering program to calculate the final picture.

Another reason for being conservative in your use of shader parameters is that people tend, simply because it is so easy to do and creates such stunning effects, to use lots (or all) of the shader parameters much (or all) of the time. This results in trite computer graphics images. To paraphrase a remark Ernest Hemingway made about writing, "The difficult thing is not knowing what to render, but knowing what not to render."

Rendering Algorithms

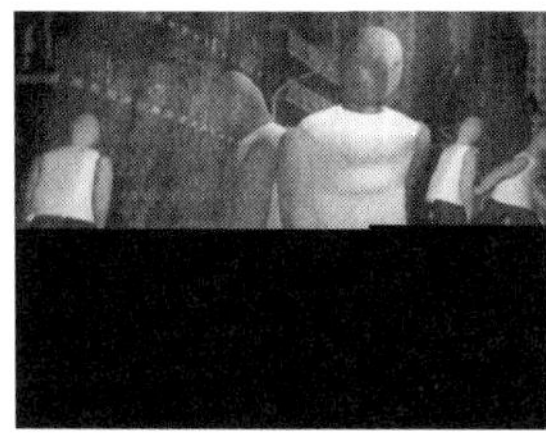

Figure 2-44. Scan line rendering steps through the pixels of an image pixel by pixel and scan line by scan line. (*Iggy's Dream #123*, © Michael O'Rourke.)

The word **algorithm** means a well-thought-out, logical procedure for doing something. A **rendering algorithm**, therefore, is the procedure that a particular program uses to calculate a picture. There are many algorithms for rendering a 3D scene, and none is "correct." Different rendering algorithms have different advantages, and each produces a different look.

Most rendering algorithms in commercially available software packages use a general approach known as **scan-line rendering**. Any digital image is composed of a fine grid of individual picture elements, or **pixels**. Each row of these pixels is a **scan line**. Scan-line rendering means that the program looks at each pixel, one after the other, scan line by scan line, and calculates the color that pixel should be rendered.

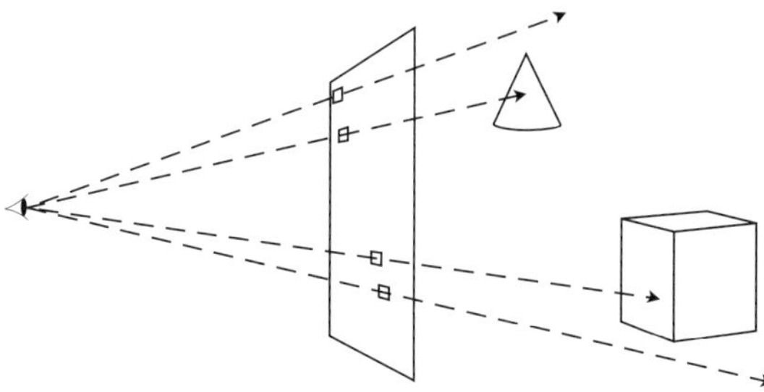

Figure 2-45. The ray casting algorithm casts a single ray through each pixel. If the ray strikes a surface, the color of the surface is calculated and assigned to the pixel.

One telltale sign of this methodical, scan-line-by-scan-line approach is that a partially completed picture consists of some lines that have been rendered (usually from the top down), and some that remain unrendered. This characteristic of the scan-line process can become useful: when you render an extremely time-consuming image, you can complete different "slices" of the image—that is, different sets of lines—individually on different machines and later assemble the pieces to form the whole picture.

Some 3D software systems that use scan-line rendering allow you to view a picture as it is being rendered (Figure 2-44). You can see the pixels filling in one by one and line by line. The as yet unrendered bottom portion of the image you see is pure black, black being the standard default color for unrendered pixels.

How does a rendering program determine what color a given pixel should be? One common approach to answering this question is a process called called **ray casting**. From the point of view of the camera, which is also referred to as the "eye," a ray is cast through the first pixel of the first scan line, as if the eye were looking through a tiny, pixel-sized window into the three-dimensional world on the other side of the screen. The eye then follows the ray until the ray either hits the surface of an object or exits from the viewable world. (Exactly what constitutes the viewable world was discussed in *The Camera)* If the ray hits an object, the program calculates the color of the object at the point where it has been hit. This color becomes the color of the pixel through which the ray had been cast. Having completed the calculation for the first pixel, the ray-casting algorithm then moves on to the second pixel and goes through the same steps. The algorithm steps through all of the pixels of the image in the same fashion, casting a ray through each one and calculating the color of the pixel.

In Figure 2-45 each pixel has one ray cast through it. (The illustration shows only four of those rays, for the sake of simplicity.) The topmost and bottom-most rays hit nothing when cast, so the pixels through which those rays were cast have no color. The two middle rays hit surfaces, so the pixels are colored, each with the color of the surface at the point hit by the ray.

This general description of the ray-casting algorithm still does not fully answer the question, "Once the program knows that a beam hits a surface,

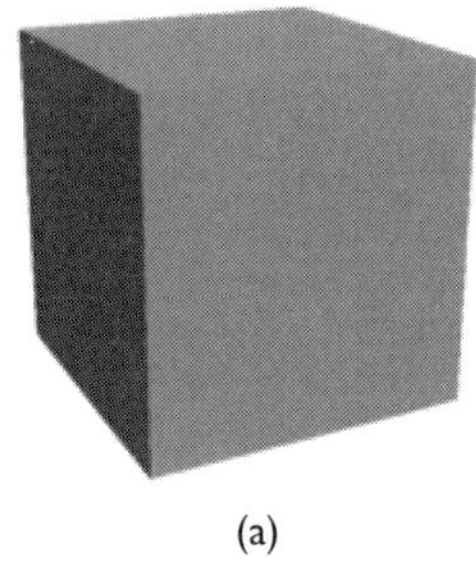

(a)

(b)

Figure 2-46. Examples of faceted shading. Each face of the cube (a) has been rendered with a single color. In the polygonal approximation of a sphere (b), each polygon has been rendered with a single color.

how does it calculate the color of the surface at that point?" There are many ways that it can do this, and each of them involves another algorithm. More specifically, these algorithms are called **shading algorithms** or **shading models**, since they are techniques for calculating the shading of a surface. Shading algorithms are implemented as subalgorithms within the broader ray-casting approach.

All shading algorithms represent simplifications of what happens in the real world, where the complexity of lighting and shading is enormous. Light passes through objects and around objects. Light bounces off objects. Objects are shaded by other objects, and so on. In order to render these effects, any algorithm must make assumptions that allow it to manage the otherwise overwhelming complexity of the process. The closer the assumptions are to the real-world situation, the more natural the renderings look. However, the closer the assumptions are to the real-world situation, the longer the rendering process takes.

One such simplifying assumption is that any flat surface is the same color at every point on the surface. This is not necessarily true in the physical world, where a flat surface might be darker at one end than at another. Rendering each flat surface with only one color gives objects a faceted look (Figure 2-46), and therefore the approach that makes this assumption is known as **faceted shading**. Faceted shading results in very fast renderings and consequently appears in many 3D packages.

The concept of faceted shading introduces another concept important to all shading algorithms. In order to calculate the color of a given surface, any shading algorithm must know whether the surface it is about to render faces or does not face the light, because the surface will be darker or lighter depending on its orientation. If, for example, a surface faces in exactly the opposite direction from the light, it receives no light and appears a very dark shade of whatever color it is. If the surface faces slightly toward the light, it receives some light and appears a lighter shade. If it faces the light directly, the surface receives a great deal of light and appears an extremely light shade.

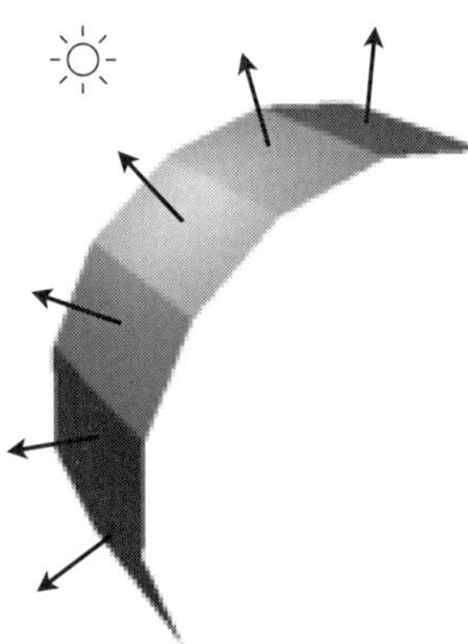

Figure 2-47. The surface normal indicates the orientation of each surface, which in turn affects the brightness of the surface.

In order to measure the direction a surface faces, computer graphics programs employ a concept called **surface normals**. A surface normal is a line (or, more specifically, a vector—a line with both length and direction) perpendicular to a surface at a given point on that surface. A surface normal is usually represented as an arrow coming off the surface. For a flat surface, a single surface normal suffices to indicate the orientation of the entire surface, since all points on a given flat surface face in the same direction.

With the information provided by surface normals, a rendering program can compute the exact angle at which a surface is oriented toward the light. In Figure 2-47, for example, several flat surfaces are connected, and a surface normal appears on each of them. Those surfaces that face most directly toward the light—that is, on which the normals point most toward the light—are brightest. Those surfaces that face farthest from the light, as indicated by the direction of the surface normals, are darkest.

Although all points on a flat surface face in the same direction (Figure 2-48a), a curved surface is more complicated (Figure 2-48b). Many normals are necessary in order to describe the orientation of a curved surface, because each point on the surface faces in a different direction. Because it is so much easier to determine a single normal for a flat surface than to determine a great many normals for a curved surface, many 3D software packages that use truly curved, spline-based patch geometry actually convert curved surfaces into polygonal approximations just before rendering. By converting a curved surface into a polygonal approximation of the curved surface, the rendering program can take advantage of the fact that each polygon requires only one surface normal.

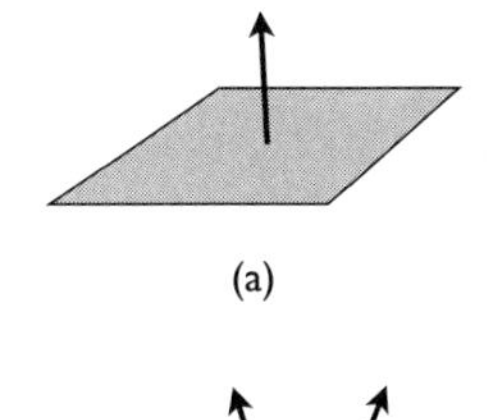

(a)

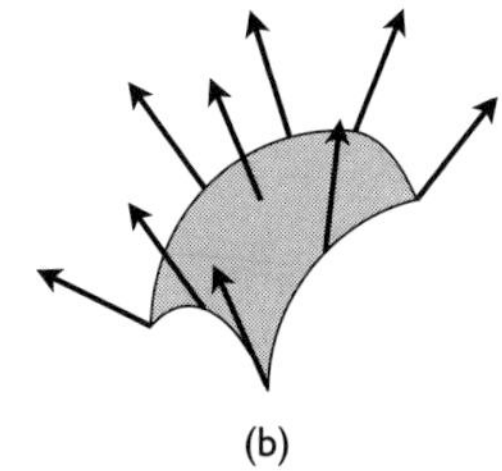

(b)

Figure 2-48. Representing the direction of a flat surface requires only one surface normal. Representing the directions of a curved surface requires many normals.

Part of this process, called **triangulation**, subdivides the curved surfaces into triangular polygons. Triangles are used because a triangular polygon is necessarily flat. Polygons of more than three vertices may or may not be flat.

Polygonal approximations, however, can present a problem. If the polygons are rendered with faceted shading, the actual shape of the polygons is apparent. This is not a problem if you want to see the shape of the polygons, as you do, for example, with a cube. But if the surface you are rendering is smoothly curved, you probably want it to *look* smoothly curved, not faceted.

Several shading algorithms have been developed for rendering polygonal surfaces so that they look smooth. As a group, these are referred to as **smooth-shading** algorithms. All of them make use of one critical observation, which is that the surface normals for a smoothly curved surface change gradually over the length of the surface (Figure 2-49a). By contrast, the normals of faceted surfaces change abruptly from one flat surface to the next (Figure 2-49b).

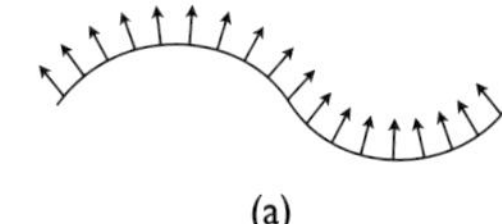

(a)

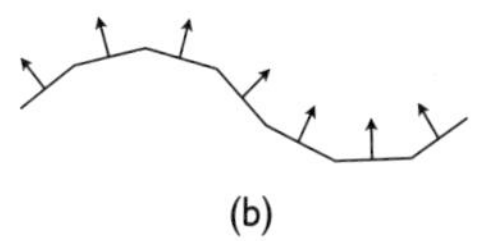

(b)

Figure 2-49. The normals of a truly curved surface change much more gradually than the normals of a polygonal approximation of that surface.

One of the most common smooth-shading algorithms is **Gouraud shading**, named after Henri Gouraud, who invented it. Gouraud shading creates a smooth look on a polygonally approximated surface by artificially adjusting the surface normals of the polygons. First, the algorithm positions a normal at each corner, or vertex, of each polygon. This normal is, as it should be, perpendicular to the surface of the polyon. Figure 2-50a, for example, shows a side view of the same polygonally approximated curved surface you saw in Figure 2-47. At each vertex where two polygons touch, two surface normals—one for each of the two polygons involved—are drawn as gray arrows. Each of these is perpendicular to the corresponding surface.

The Gouraud algorithm then calculates an average of the normals at a given vertex. This new, averaged normal is drawn as a black arrow in Figure 2-50a. Notice that the averaged normals look more like the gradually

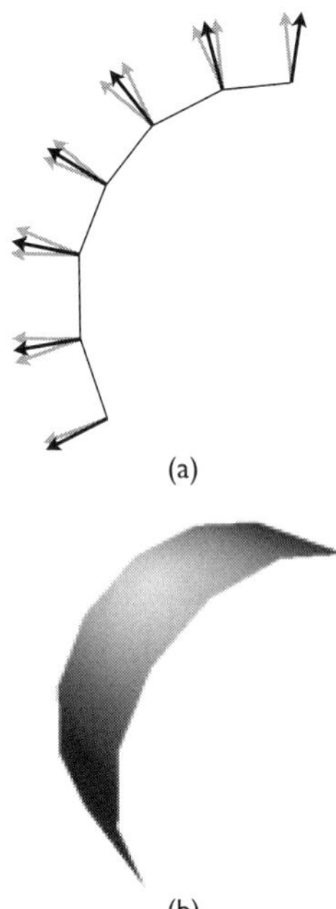

(a)

(b)

Figure 2-50. The Gouraud-shading technique artificially adjusts the normals of polygons to create the appearance of a curved surface.

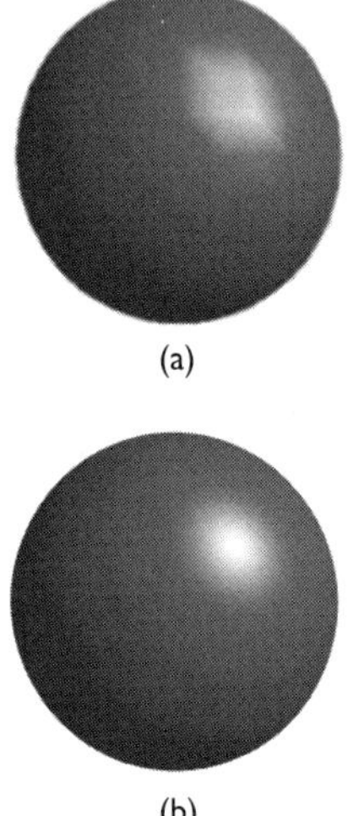

(a)

(b)

Figure 2-51. Gouraud and Phong shading compared.

changing normals of a curved surface than like the abruptly changing normals of a faceted surface.

Finally, the Gouraud algorithm calculates the color at each vertex, based on the averaged surface normal at that vertex. Once all of these corner colors have been calculated, the colors between vertices are calculated by interpolating from one corner color to another.

Notice, in the rendered version of the polygonally approximated surface (Figure 2-50b), that the Gouraud technique produces a smooth progression of the color along the surface. Even though the surface is made up of flat polygons, you see it as being smoothly curved. Notice also, however, that the underlying polygonal structure of the surface is still apparent at the edges of the surface. If the polygons are large enough, you see flat edges from certain angles, even though the interior of the model looks smooth.

While not as simple as faceted shading, Gouraud shading is very simple, and programs that use the Gouraud-shading algorithm are often very fast. Some high-end workstations, in fact, incorporate Gouraud shading into their hardware so that you can perform real-time updating of smooth surfaces. In other words, with a joystick or mouse device you can turn the smoothly Gouraud-shaded objects around on the screen in real time.

But Gouraud shading has its limitations. Most serious, the technique of interpolating one vertex color to another sometimes makes the seams between polygons visible (Figure 2-51a). A seam is most apparent when it is near a bright highlight.

In order to overcome this limitation, a technique called **Phong shading** was developed. Named after Bui Tuong Phong, who invented it, Phong shading averages surface normals at each polygon vertex, just as Gouraud shading does. However, instead of interpolating the colors between these vertices, Phong shading adds another step, calculating interpolated surface normals between vertices. From those interpolated surface normals it then calculates the colors of the surface. This approach yields a more accurate calculation of the colors, a more accurate rendering of the highlight, and invisible seams along the edges of the polygons (Figure 2-51b).

As always, however, an improvement in quality is matched by an increase in rendering time. The same scene rendered with Phong shading, which is very commonly used in 3D rendering programs, can take substantially longer than if it were rendered with the simpler Gouraud-shading algorithm.

So far you have seen only the rendering of single objects—a deliberate simplification for the sake of clarity. Most scenes, however, contain several, sometimes many objects. Remember, too, that in the ray-casting algorithm used by many programs, a ray is cast from the eye through the three-dimensional space of the environment. What happens if several objects, one behind the other, are in the path of the ray? How does the rendering program know which of these objects is the one to be rendered? How does it know which objects are in front of, which are obscured by, other objects?

One approach to this problem is to sort all the objects by depth before rendering begins, so that the rendering program then can start rendering those objects that are farthest away. Once rendered, each new object covers up distant objects that already have been rendered. This procedure resembles the way a painter might complete the background of a scene before painting the apple in front of it. In fact, the technique of presorting objects by depth so that the objects rendered last are the objects closest to the eye is often called the **painter's algorithm**.

To presort by depth can be very time-consuming, though, particularly when a scene involves a large number of objects. Not only does each of these objects have to be sorted by depth, but each polygon of each object has to be sorted by depth! An alternative, and very common, solution to this problem is known as the **Z-buffer algorithm**.

When a computer graphics picture is rendered, the digital information for the picture is stored in a large block of memory called a **frame buffer**, which organizes the color information for the picture on a pixel-by-pixel basis. The Z-buffer algorithm makes use of a similar block of memory, called a **Z-buffer**. Like the frame buffer, this area organizes information on a pixel-by-pixel basis. Here, however, the information being stored is not the color of a surface but rather the distance of the surface from the eye. If a point on the surface is far away, the Z-buffer stores a large number. If a point on the surface is close, the Z-buffer stores a small number.

The Z-buffer algorithm renders objects in any order, without presorting them according to depth. When a ray is cast through a pixel, that ray might hit any one of several objects that lie in its path. Since the objects are not presorted by depth, the ray could hit an object in the back of the scene before hitting an object in the front of the scene. No matter the order of the encounters, as the ray hits each object, the depth in Z of that object is calculated and stored in the Z-buffer, at the Z-buffer pixel corresponding to the pixel through which the ray was cast. For example, if a ray cast through pixel one of scan line one hits some object, the depth value of that object is stored in pixel one, scan line one of the Z-buffer.

When the same ray encounters a second object, the depth in Z of that object is calculated and compared to what is already in the Z-buffer. If the new value is less than (that is, closer than) the old value, it overwrites the older, more distant value in that pixel. By comparing the Z values of the different objects at each Z-buffer pixel in this way, the rendering program can determine at every pixel which objects are in front of which other objects.

The depth information written into a Z-buffer normally is not viewed as a picture, but it can, in fact, be displayed as such. Figure 2-52a shows the

(a)

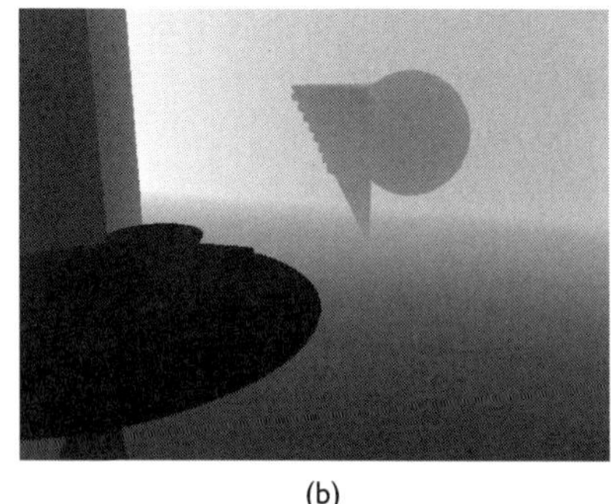

(b)

Figure 2-52. A Z-buffer stores depth information for a scene by storing a number at each pixel—larger numbers (brighter pixels) for more distant objects, and smaller numbers (darker pixels) for closer objects. (Courtesy, Punyapol Kittayarak.)

normal rendering of a scene. Figure 2-52b shows the Z-buffer image of that same scene. Notice that the large numbers assigned to distant objects become bright pixels in the Z-buffer image, and the small numbers assigned to closer objects become dark pixels. The result of displaying such a Z-buffer image is a gray-scale image in which near objects appear darker and distant objects appear lighter.

The Z-buffer algorithm is very powerful and very commonly used in 3D rendering programs. Higher-end workstations and graphic accelerator cards often incorporate Z-buffering into their hardware so that depth sorting can be done in real time. But the approach is also very flexible, in that Z-buffer information can be used in a number of ways besides depth sorting for standard rendering. It can also be used to calculate cast shadows, as discussed in the section on *Lighting*, to produce mattes for compositing (see *Digital Techniques* in chapter 5), and to produce maps for such techniques as bump mapping (see the next section, *Surface Texture Mapping*).

All the algorithms you have seen so far, even though they address different aspects of the rendering process (depth sorting, shading, etc.), fall within the general category of ray-casting algorithms. Ray casting can produce very sophisticated renderings, as you can see, for example, in color plate 9. In this image the furniture in the foreground was rendered with great subtlety. The colors, shading, and highlights were all rendered using ray-casting algorithms.

All ray-casting algorithms, however, have one fundamental limitation: they deal with the shading of each object in the scene as if it existed in isolation, as if there were no other objects in the scene. Even in the case of depth sorting, once it has been determined which object is closest to the eye, the more distant objects do not have an effect on the object being rendered.

As a result, creating reflections becomes a problem, since reflections involve the reflection of *other* objects onto one object. Another problem is cast shadows. In order to take into account a shadow being cast on an object, you must know of the existence of another object in a position to cast a

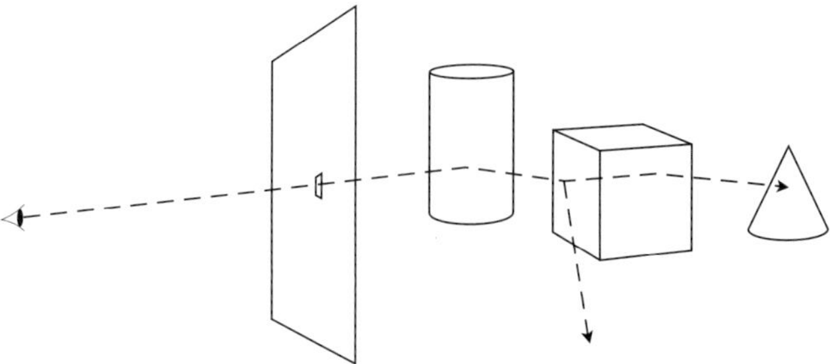

Figure 2-53. The ray-tracing algorithm traces a light ray back as it bounces off objects in the scene.

shadow. And a third problematic issue is transparency, which involves looking through one object and seeing some other object or objects behind it.

You can address these problems through various ray-casting "tricks": simulating reflections through environmental reflection mapping (see *Solid Texture Mapping* later in this chapter), generating shadows through a clever use of the information stored in Z-buffers, simulating transparency by rendering several objects into one pixel and combining the colors of the different objects. Researchers have developed all of these techniques to the point that they are quite effective and usually very easy to use. But the fundamental problem remains that the ray-casting technique does not in and of itself produce these visual effects in a physically accurate way, because it concerns itself with only one object at a time.

A different category of rendering algorithm, called **ray tracing**, addresses this fundamental weakness by dealing with all of the objects in a scene simultaneously. When you look at a specific point on a surface, the color at that point is being affected not only by the light falling from the light source onto that particular surface, but also by the light bouncing onto it from nearby surfaces—or perhaps even, if the object is transparent, by the light traveling through other objects in the scene. In other words, every point on a surface is affected not merely by one light ray, but by many light rays hitting it from many different parts of the scene. If you are to get an accurate rendering of that surface point, you need to trace these different rays back to their sources to see what contributions they are making to the final color of the surface.

Figure 2-53 shows the tracing of a ray that might be needed to render a single pixel. As with the ray-casting technique, a ray is projected from the eye through the pixel and into the scene. The ray hits a first surface, the cylinder. Because the cylinder has been defined as somewhat reflective, the ray bounces off the cylinder and hits the cube, which has been defined as partially reflective and partially transparent. This contact generates two ray paths. Because the cube is partially reflective, one ray bounces off the cube and travels toward the bottom of the picture. In this simple example, the ray travels without hitting anything until it disappears off the edge of the world. Meanwhile, because the cube is partially transparent, a portion of the light coming from the cylinder passes through the cube and changes direction slightly, as light does when it passes through objects. When this ray emerges from the cube, it changes direction again and continues until it hits the cone. Since the cone has been defined as 100 percent matte, with no reflection, the ray stops traveling when it hits the cone.

In order to calculate the color of the cylinder at the point where the ray first hit it, you begin by calculating the color of the cube at the point indicated, since light bounces from the cube to the cylinder. But in order to calculate the color of the cube at the point indicated, you need to know the color of the cone, since light from the cone passes through the transparent cube and contributes to the color of the cube. You also need to know the color of the space around the cube, since one of the rays hitting the cube has come from the empty space around the scene. In short, in order to calculate the one point on the surface of the cylinder that you are interested in, you first must calculate the color of the cone, then the color of the background space, then the color of the cube.

The examples given here, though very simplified, illustrate both the complexity and the power of ray tracing. A much more complex rendering technique than ray casting, ray tracing requires the calculation of many surfaces in order to arrive at the final calculation for a single surface point. For each pixel, you have to trace many rays, and consider many contributing surfaces. As you might expect, all these extra calculations take time, and ray tracing can be much slower than ray casting.

Consider the result, however. Because the calculation of each surface point takes into consideration all the different surfaces in the scene, the effects of all those surfaces show up in the final rendering. Cast shadows, reflections, and transparency are all automatically calculated by the ray-tracing technique. Notice the reflections throughout the scene in color plate 10, for example, especially on the salt- and pepper shaker. Notice also the shadows cast by the different objects onto the table. Finally, notice the bending, or refraction, of light as it passes through the transparent water in the glass, causing the flower stems to distort.

In a complex scene with a great many objects, ray tracing can become immensely complex. If you continue tracing the path of a ray in such a scene, the ray can go on bouncing off and through hundreds of objects, creating a tree of ray paths so complex as to be impractical to render. In fact, a ray in this situation could, in principle, continue bouncing forever, in which case your rendering would never finish! Consequently, most ray-tracing programs ask you to define the maximum number of bounces that each ray should be followed. This is called the **depth** of the ray tracing. The larger the depth number, the more accurate, but also the more time-consuming the rendering. If the depth is zero—that is, if no bounces are followed—the ray tracer becomes effectively the same as a ray caster.

Some software systems expand on this concept of tracing depth by providing several depth parameters to control different aspects of the rendering. For example, there might be a parameter to control how many rays should be followed when calculating shadows. Another parameter might be provided to control the number of rays followed when calculating reflections.

In ray-tracing, the shading algorithms discussed earlier still apply. That is, within a ray-traced environment, some surfaces may be rendered using the Phong algorithm while others are rendered using a Gouraud algorithm.

Although the ray-tracing algorithm handles many optical effects very well, it does not handle well the diffuse reflection of light from one surface to another. This effect happens, for instance, when you hold a piece of red cardboard next to a white wall. Even though the wall is not specular (you see no highlights in it) and not reflective (you see no reflections in it), it nonetheless is affected by the color of the cardboard. The white of the wall takes on a pink hue because light bounces not in a concentrated way but in a very scattered way from the surface of the cardboard to the surface of the wall. The cardboard in turn picks up some of the color of the wall.

A **radiosity** algorithm handles this situation by breaking down every surface into a number of smaller surfaces. In Figure 2-54, where the large shape represents the wall and the small shape represents the piece of cardboard, each of these rectangular shapes has been subdivided into a number of smaller rectangles in such a way that, after all the radiosity calculations are done, the pieces fit together seamlessly.

The subdivision of each surface into smaller subsurfaces is necessary because the variations in color that result from diffuse reflection do not occur equally over the entire surface. Only a small portion of the white wall is visibly affected by the red cardboard. Subdividing the surface enables the radiosity algorithm to deal with this uneven distribution of light. Once the surfaces have been broken down into sufficiently small subsurfaces, the algorithm determines how much any one subsurface affects any other subsurface; that is, how much of each subsurface is "visible" from the point of view of each of the other subsurfaces. The result of this calculation is called the **form-factor**. If two subsurfaces are close to each other and facing each other, approximately 100 percent of each surface is visible to the other: the number of the form-factor is approximately one. In Figure 2-54 the two subsurfaces highlighted with heavy lines have a very high form-factor. If two surfaces are at an extreme angle to each other or are far away from each other, a much lower percentage of surface area will be visible from one surface to the other, and the form-factor is a number closer to zero.

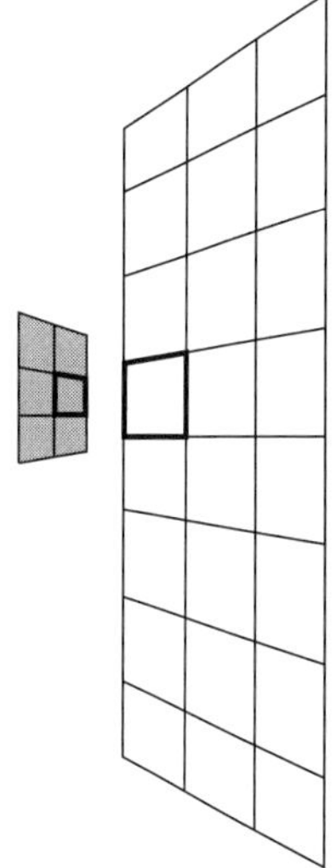

Figure 2-54. The radiosity technique subdivides each surface in order to calculate the diffuse reflections between these surfaces.

With this information, the radiosity algorithm calculates the color of each subsurface, taking into account the effect each of the other subsurfaces has on it; that is, taking into account the diffuse reflections between these subsurfaces. This calculation can be very time-consuming. However, unlike the calculation of specular highlights and reflections, which move about as you move your point of view, the calculation of diffuse reflections is unaffected by the position of your eye. Because form-factors are derived purely from the geometrical relationship of the surfaces to one another, the only time form-factors (and consequently diffuse reflections) change is when the surfaces themselves actually move. Because the calculation of diffuse reflections is independent of the camera, then, the radiosity algorithm can calculate the diffuse reflections for an entire scene just once, no matter how many frames of the scene are going to be rendered (again, assuming the surfaces themselves do not move). The rendering program can then store this information in memory. As it renders each new frame, the program retrieves the radiosity information and then performs the rest of the shading calculations (hidden surface removal, specularity, and so on).

Surface Texture Mapping

A set of techniques, known collectively as **texture mapping**, permits you to enhance the definition of the surface characteristics of a model with great subtlety. Earlier, in the discussion of surface characteristics, each surface was defined as having only one color; it might be blue or red or green, but not different colors simultaneously. In real life, of course, many surfaces are multicolored. Part of what makes wood look wooden is color variations caused by the grain. Clothing, to take another example, is as often multicolored as not, frequently with patterns and images printed on it. Perhaps a bit more subtly, a plain gray concrete wall is almost certainly not the same shade of gray at every point on the surface, but is more likely to range from a very light gray to a very dark gray, depending on the wear and tear of the wall.

The most basic kind of texture mapping is **surface texture mapping** in which a two-dimensional picture is applied to the surface of a three-dimensional model. The two-dimensional picture is the "texture." Texture in this context means something like "pattern," rather than the minuscule bumps you might associate with the term.

A texture image can be generated in any number of ways. It can be scanned into the computer from a photograph or other hardcopy image. It can be painted directly within the computer using a digital paint program. Or it can be generated procedurally (that is, generated by a small subprogram) within the 3D software package by choosing a menu selection—a selection to create a grid pattern, for example.

The process of applying a texture to a surface is known as "mapping." Mapping may be implemented in two ways: by projecting the texture image or by stretching it onto the surface. In **projection mapping** the texture image is projected through space. Wherever the texture image "hits" the surface of the model, the surface takes on the colors of that section of the texture image. Think of an image projected by a slide projector: if you place an object in the path of the projected image, the object takes on the colors of the slide image wherever those colors hit the object.

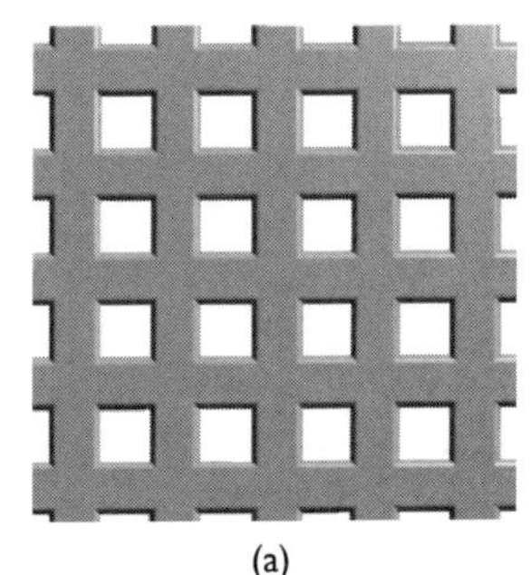

(a)

(b)

(c)

(d)

Figure 2-55. Planar projection mapping.

In Figure 2-55a the grid pattern image is the texture image to be projected. In Figure 2-55b the projection has come from the left; in Figure 2-55c the projection has come from above, and in Figure 2-55d the projection has come from the right. In these examples of **planar projection mapping**, the texture image, in this case the grid pattern, has been projected along each of the three axes—X,Y, and Z.

This sort of projection mapping is very simple conceptually, and so it is a very commonly found mapping technique. Notice, however, a severe limitation of the projection-mapping technique just described. Since the texture image is projected in only one direction, it streaks along the sides of the mapped object. In each case in Figure 2-55, only one side of the cube receives a reasonable mapping. All of the other sides are streaked. The streaking on these sides is so extreme, in fact, that it results simply in straight lines, and a complete loss of the grid pattern, because each of these other sides is parallel to the direction of the projection. Only if the surface of a model is perpendicular to the direction of projection does that surface receive a completely accurate mapping of the texture image.

You can alleviate the streaking problem somewhat by rotating the model relative to the direction of projection. However, the price of doing this is that now *no* side receives a completely accurate mapping, since no side is exactly perpendicular to the projection.

In an effort to solve this problem, most systems offer two ways of projecting a texture image simultaneously in several directions. The first of these multidirectional projection techniques is **cylindrical projection mapping**. Here, the two-dimensional texture image is bent into an imaginary cylinder before any projection takes place. The object to be mapped resides within this imaginary cylinder, and the image is projected inward from the surface of the cylinder to the axis of the cylinder.

In Figure 2-56a the model being mapped is a cylinder, the cylinder has been mapped using planar projection, and the grid pattern has been projected from the left. This process produces a reasonable mapping on the left

(a)

(b)

(c)

Figure 2-56. Cylindrical projection mapping is more effective for approximately cylindrical objects.

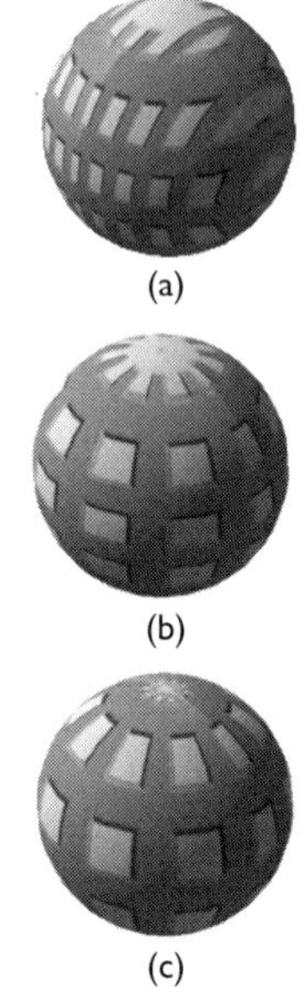

(a)

(b)

(c)

Figure 2-57. Spherical projection mapping is more effective for approximately spherical objects.

side of the cylinder. (The far right side, if you could see it, also would look reasonable.) However, the grid pattern on the side of the cylinder closest to you is quite noticeably stretched. On the top of the cylinder the stretching is even worse.

In figure 2-56b the grid pattern has been mapped onto the cylinder using cylindrical projection. Notice that the grid pattern looks correct all the way around the cylinder, but on the top of the cylinder the pattern is still badly deformed, although in a different way. This streaking happens on the top and bottom of any model because the cylindrical technique projects the texture image in from the sides of the imaginary cylinder. If the model has no top, as in Figure 2-56c, the cylindrical technique can work very successfully.

Another technique offered by most systems, **spherical projection mapping**, sometimes can eliminate difficult streaking problems. Here, the two-dimensional texture image is bent into an imaginary sphere before being projected, and the image is projected inward from the sides of the imaginary sphere to the center. The projected pattern is mapped onto the surface of an object placed within this imaginary sphere

In Figure 2-57a, a sphere has been mapped using planar projection. Projected from the left, the grid pattern appears streaked on the side and the top of the sphere. Figure 2-57b, in which the grid pattern has been mapped onto the sphere using the cylindrical technique, shows a marked improvement, as you might expect, since a sphere is symmetrical along the Y axis just as a cylinder is. However, cylindrical mapping fails to do an adequate job at the top of the sphere. Mapping the sphere with spherical projection, as in Figure 2-57c, improves on this considerably. Now both the sides and the top of the sphere receive a reasonable mapping of the grid pattern.

Each of these projection techniques—planar, cylindrical, and spherical—has particular uses. Planar projection is most effective when the object to be mapped is relatively flat, such as a rug. Cylindrical projection works best when the object to be mapped is itself roughly cylindrical in shape, such as a vase. And spherical projection is most effective for an object that requires mapping from all directions, such as a cube or a ball.

All projection-mapping techniques are limited by the tendency to streak, but in spite of that fact they appear in many systems, because they are relatively easy for the computer to calculate. This is especially true of planar projection. Because of the limitations of projection-mapping techniques, the second technique of mapping, called **parameterized texture mapping**, also commonly appears in 3D software packages.

Parameterized texture mapping is most readily understood through an analogy. Imagine that you wish some three-dimensional surface to be multicolored. Imagine also that you have a flat sheet of flexible latex onto which you print a multicolored image—that is, a texture. If you stretch this flat sheet of latex tautly over the three-dimensional surface, covering it entirely, the three-dimensional surface will look as if it were colored with the two-dimensional image. This stretching of the texture image onto a three-dimensional surface is the basic concept of parameterized texture mapping.

The picture of a face in Figure 2-58a is a two-dimensional pattern, or texture. In terms of the analogy, this image would be on the flat sheet of latex. Figure 2-58b shows a three-dimensional surface, a curved patch, onto which the two-dimensional texture has been "stretched." The process of stretching the two-dimensional texture onto the three-dimensional surface corresponds to the mapping of the texture onto the surface.

Figures 2-58c and 2-58d show two other three-dimensional surfaces—a sphere and a revolved surface—with the same two-dimensional texture image mapped onto them using the same parameterized-mapping technique. Notice first that there is no streaking of the sort you saw with projection mapping, since the image is stretched rather than projected onto the surface. Notice too, however, that the more the shape of the three-dimensional surface differs from the shape of the original two-dimensional texture image, the more the image may be distorted as it is stretched to cover the three-dimensional surface. The two-dimensional texture image is normally rectangular, so any three-dimensional, nonrectangular surface causes some distortion in the mapping process. (Later in this section you will learn about ways to avoid this distortion.)

You have just seen the simplest case of 2D parameterized texture mapping. In practice, many subtleties are possible with this sort of mapping. In order to understand how these variations work, you need to understand in more detail what happens during the mapping process.

A two-dimensional computer graphics image is, by its nature, divided up into a discrete number of tiny rectangular areas, called **pixels**. These pixels exist in a two-dimensional Cartesian coordinate system, with the pixel in the lower left of the image normally said to be located at XY = (0,0). If the image is 512 pixels wide by 512 pixels high (a standard image size for texture maps), then the pixel in the upper right corner of the image is located at XY = (511,511) (Figure 2-59).

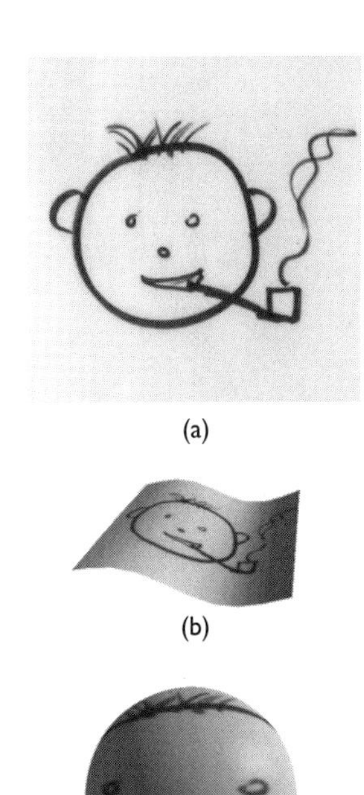

(a)

(b)

(c)

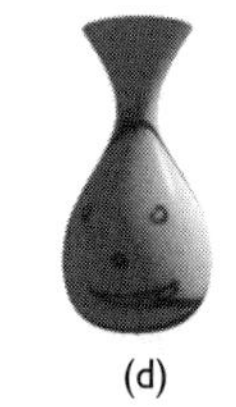

(d)

Figure 2-58. Parameterized texture mapping.

Figure 2-59. The texture image is organized into an XY grid of pixels.

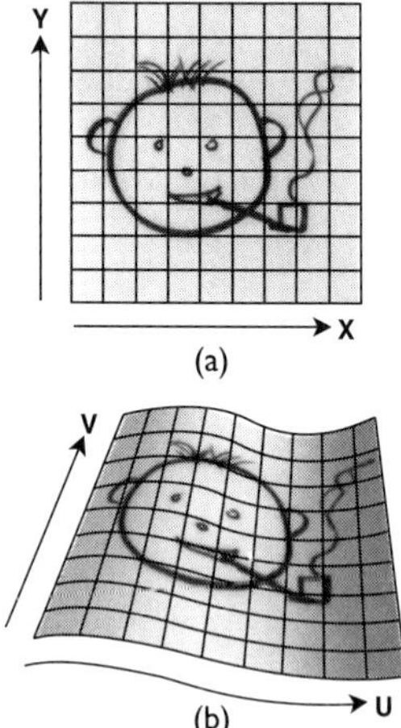

Figure 2-60. Each pixel in the XY space of the texture image maps to a rectangular area in the UV space of the surface.

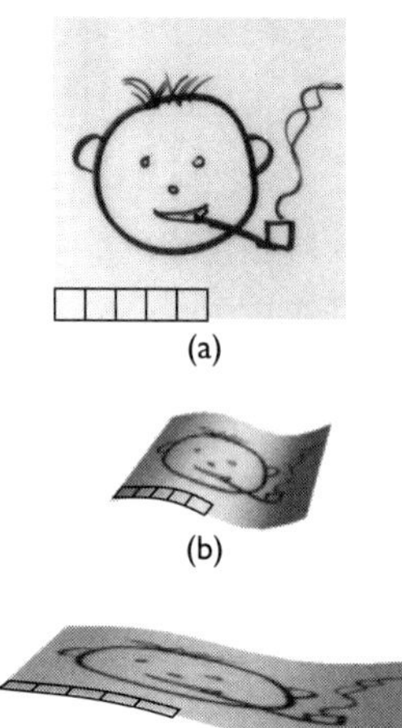

Figure 2-61. A texture image may stretch as it maps to a surface.

The basic idea of parameterized texture mapping is that each area, or pixel, of the two-dimensional image is applied to (mapped to) a corresponding area of the three-dimensional surface. This requires that the three-dimensional surface be divided into the same number of rectangular areas as there are pixels in the texture image. In order to divide the three-dimensional surface into the correct number of discrete rectangular areas, you step along the surface in two different directions in the same way that you step along the two-dimensional picture in the X and Y directions (Figure 2-60a). Since a surface patch is defined in terms of two directions, or parameters, called U and V, you step along the surface of a patch in the U direction and in the V direction (Figure 2-60b).

The color in the rectangular area located at XY = (0,0) on the two-dimensional texture image maps to, or is applied to, the rectangular area located at UV = (0,0) on the three-dimensional surface. The color of the texture area located immediately to the right of XY = (0,0) maps to the area on the three-dimensional surface immediately to the right of UV = (0,0), and so on. This mapping continues area by area, stepping simultaneously across both the two-dimensional texture image (Figure 2-61a) and the three-dimensional surface (Figure 2-61b).

Thinking of the mapping process in this way explains image distortion on many three-dimensional surfaces. When a surface is very differently shaped (say, longer and narrower) than the original rectangular configuration of the two-dimensional texture image, the subdivision of the three-dimensional surface into rectangular areas can result in each of those areas being stretched, since there must be the same number of areas on the surface as there are on the texture image (Figure 2-61c). (For the sake of clarity, both the texture image and three-dimensional surface in the figure are subdivided into only a handful of rectangles.)

In all the mapping examples so far, both parameterized and projected, the texture image was mapped exactly once to the three-dimensional surface. In practice, however, you have considerable control, both with parameterized mapping and with projection mapping, over where and how large the two-dimensional image maps onto the three-dimensional surface.

The first form of control that most computer graphics systems permits is the ability to specify the **scale**, or size, of the final mapped image. The default (seen in the examples so far) is a scale of 1.0—that is, the two-dimensional texture image covers 100 percent of the three-dimensional surface (Figure 2-62a). If the scale were 0.5, the image would cover only 50 percent of the surface, in both the U and V directions (Figure 2-62b). A scale factor of 0.25 would cause the image to cover only 25 percent of the surface in each of the directions (Figure 2-62c).

When the mapped image covers less than 100 percent of the three-dimensional surface, the area of the surface not covered by the texture image retains whatever color was originally assigned to the surface before any mapping took place. For example, if the original color of the three-dimensional surface in Figure 2-62 was orange, then all but the lower left quadrant of the surface would be orange in Figure 2-62b.

In addition to controlling the scale of the final mapping, most systems allow you to control the **placement** of the mapped image. For UV-mapped images, placement controls make use of the U and V coordinates of the parameterized mapping. For projection-mapped images, most programs provide slider bars that simulate the UV space of true parameterized mapping. In either case, you usually begin by specifying where on the surface the mapping process should begin. By default, the process begins at UV = (0,0). By choosing some other point in the UV space of the surface, however, you offset the mapping. Most systems consider the UV space of a surface to range from 0.0 to 1.0. Using this system, if you keep the scaling of your map at 0.25 (Figure 2-63a), you can change the starting, or offset, point of your mapping from the default UV = (0,0) to UV = (0.5,0) (Figure 2-63b). If you change the offset to UV = (0.75,0.75), you place the image toward the upper right corner of the surface (Figure 2-63c).

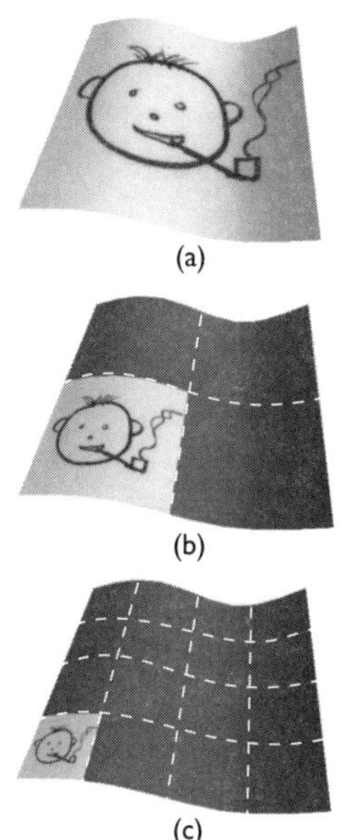

Figure 2-62. The texture image can be scaled as it maps onto a surface.

In the previous examples, the scale was very small, so the image never went over the edge of the surface. Imagine, however, changing the scale back to 1.0 and using a nondefault offset. When UV offset = (0.0,0.0), the image covers the surface exactly once, starting in the lower left corner (Figure 2-64a). When UV offset = (0.5,0.0), the image starts halfway across the surface in the U direction, but then, because it is so large, wraps around, so that the right half of the texture image appears on the left half of the surface (Figure 2-64b). Further, when UV offset = (0.5,0.5), the image wraps around in both the U and V directions (Figure 2-64c)

Many systems provide a variable, often called either "wrap" or "repeat," that allows you to turn on or off this **wrapping** effect. If wrap is turned off, depending on the offset values you get one of the results in Figure 2-65.

If the two-dimensional texture image is a representational image, like the face in these examples, you probably do not want the image to wrap around to the other end of the surface. On the other hand, if the texture image is some repeating pattern, such as the design on a rug or some wallpaper or a piece of cloth, the wrapping of the pattern may be precisely what you want.

In addition to controlling the scaling, placement, and wrapping of a texture image onto a three-dimensional surface, you can control the **effect** of the mapping. In the case of color texture mapping, the effect of the color mapping is the saturation of the colors. Many systems allow you to scale this

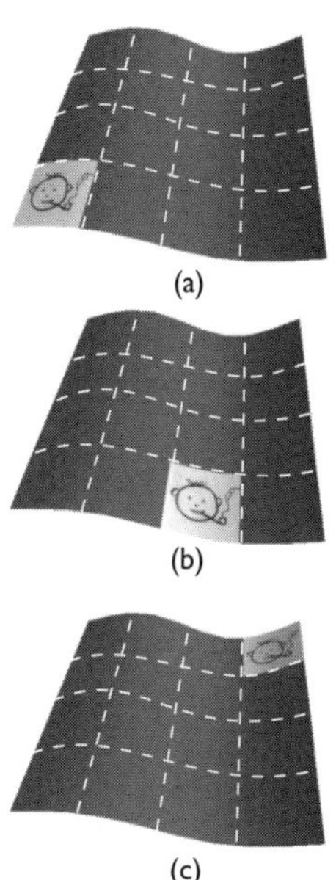

Figure 2-63. A texture image may also be positioned on a surface.

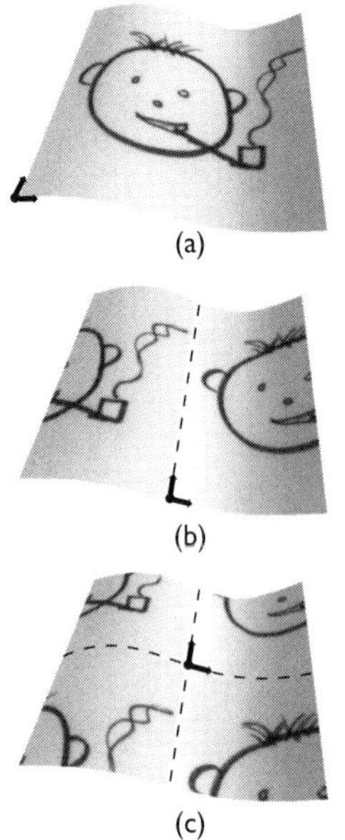

Figure 2-64. A texture image may wrap around a surface.

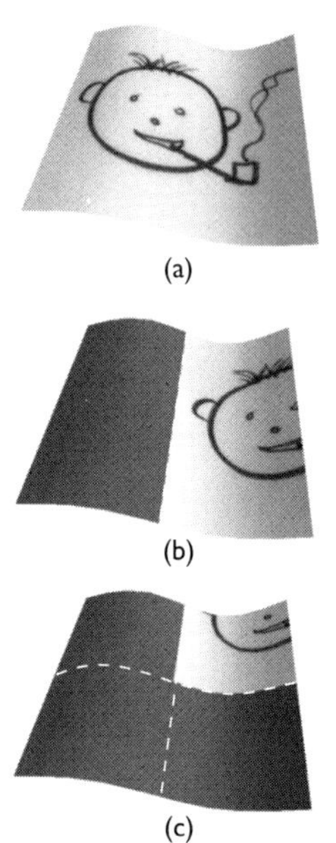

Figure 2-65. The wrapping of the texture image can be turned off.

effect—that is, to increase it or decrease it—by multiplying it by some factor, usually in the range 0.0 to 1.0. When you scale up the effect of color texture mapping, you increase the saturation of the colors. If, for example, the color of a particular pixel in the two-dimensional texture image is RGB = (100,0,40), scaling the effect of the color mapping by a factor of 2.0 produces color values of RGB = (200,0,80). Scaling the color by a factor of 0.5 desaturates the color of the pixel by half, producing a color of RGB = (50,0,20) on the surface. Many systems allow you to scale each of the three components of an RGB color individually, in order to make the mapped color "redder," or "greener," for example.

Since a scaling operation is a multiplicative one, a curious thing happens when you scale the color effect by 0.0. No matter what the RGB values of the original colors on the texture image, all of the pixels—and all the area on the three-dimensional surface—become a pure black, RGB = (0,0,0).

All of these controls—scaling, placement, wrapping, and effect—can usually be specified either by typing in numbers directly or by adjusting slider bars. In addition, higher-end programs allow you to make adjustments visually and in real time by using the mouse. As you drag the mouse, you see the texture slide across the surface of the model, change size, and so on.

However you create your map and whatever process you use to manipulate it, the pixel values in the two-dimensional texture image can be interpreted in any number of ways, to produce any number of effects. In **color texture mapping** the pixel values are interpreted as color and consequently change the color of the three-dimensional surface onto which they are mapped. In the other applications of texture mapping, the pixel values are interpreted as, and therefore change, some other characteristic of the three-dimensional surface.

In **transparency texture mapping**, or simply **transparency mapping**, the brightness of each pixel in the two-dimensional texture image is interpreted as the amount of transparency of the three-dimensional surface. The brighter the pixel, the more transparent the corresponding area of the three-dimensional surface; the darker the pixel, the more opaque the area of the surface. When the circular pattern in Figure 2-66a is mapped onto a three-dimensional patch, for instance, with the pixel values of the texture image interpreted as degrees of transparency, the result is the surface you see in Figure 2-66b. The "hole" in this surface is not an actual geometric hole, but the result of the white circular area from the texture image, interpreted as transparency, creating a corresponding circular area of transparency on the patch.

When a pixel of the texture image is neither completely black nor completely white, but has a brightness of some intermediate value, the transparency of the corresponding area on the three-dimensional surface, such as around the rim of the circular hole in the patch, is of an equally intermediate level.

Another interesting example of this effect is shown in Figure 2-67, in which the flame of the candle was rendered using transparency mapping. The original surface of the flame is an approximately ellipsoidal shape. The texture pattern was a fractally generated pattern of irregular blacks and whites (see chapter 1 for a discussion of fractals). Because of the irregularity of the texture pattern and because of the subtlety of the tonal gradations in the texture image, a flamelike pattern of transparency is produced.

(a)

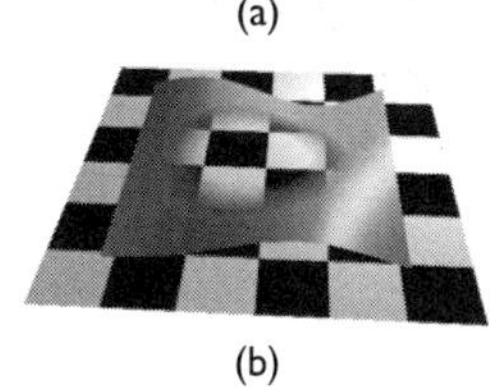

(b)

Figure 2-66. Transparency mapping.

Notice that for the purposes of transparency mapping, you do not need to have a full-color, twenty-four-bit RGB image as your texture image. A simple, eight-bit black-and-white image serves just as well, since the information the mapping procedure needs is simply brightness, which can as easily—in fact, more easily—be represented through a gray-scale as through a full-color image.

Bump texture mapping, or simply **bump mapping**, simulates the small bumps and irregularities of some surfaces. Examples of such surfaces—the individual bumps of which may be so small that you cannot perceive each one of them separately—include fabrics with a noticeable weave, dirt, coarse sand, the surface of a concrete wall. To try to model the myriad tiny bumps of these surfaces geometrically, by pulling control points or polygon vertices, would be both extremely tedious and wasteful.

Figure 2-67. The flame of the candle was modeled using transparency mapping. (Courtesy, Jia-Ming Day.)

To understand bump mapping, recall that how dark or how light a color is at a certain point on a surface depends largely on the orientation of the surface relative to the light sources. If it faces a light source, the surface is brighter. If it faces away from a light source, the surface is darker. The orientation of a given point on the surface is determined by the surface normal at that point. A perfectly flat surface has surface normals that point straight up, all across the surface (Figure 2-68a). A bumpy surface, however, has surface normals that point in all different directions (Figure 2-68b). Bump mapping works by "fooling" the rendering program. That is, it artificially tilts the surface normals (Figure 2-68c), so that the rendering program "thinks" the surface is bumpy when really it is not. This artificial tilting of the surface normals is called, amusingly, **perturbing** the normals. The bump-mapping technique interprets the brightness of each pixel of the texture image as more or less perturbation of the surface normal at the corresponding area of the three dimensional surface. If a texture pixel is very bright, the surface normal is perturbed a lot in one direction. If the texture pixel is very dark, the normal is perturbed a lot in the other direction. And if the texture pixel is some intermediate value of brightness, the normal is perturbed some intermediate amount.

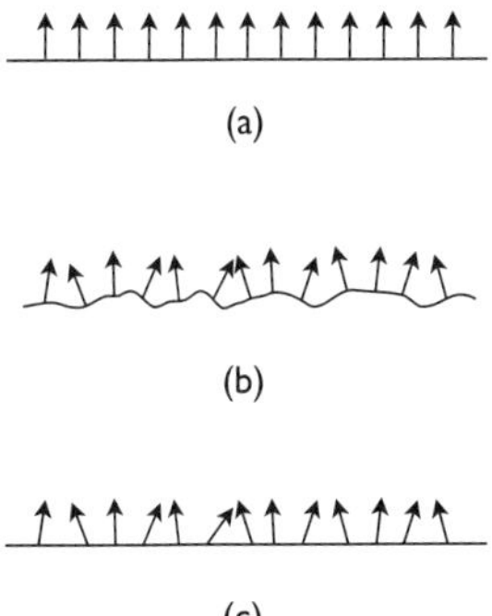

Figure 2-68. Bump mapping simulates the irregularity of surface normals by perturbing the normals.

When a rendering program encounters perturbed normals, it renders the surface exactly as it would if that surface were bumpy and had those same normals. The bumpiness you see on the surface in Figure 2-69a, for example, is entirely a result of bump mapping. The geometry of the surface is totally flat. A fractally generated texture pattern was used to create a black-and-white

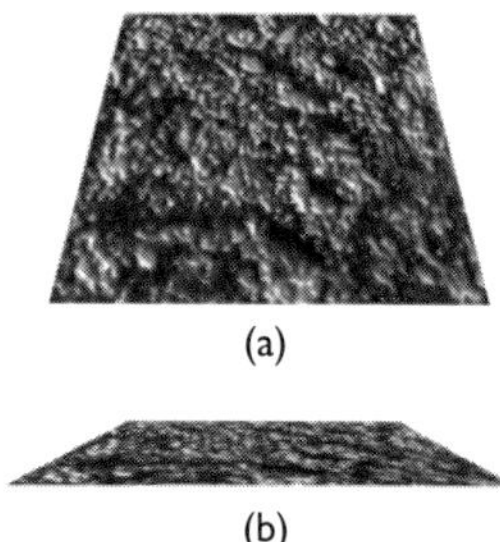

(a)

(b)

Figure 2-69. Bump mapping does not change the underlying geometry, as the straight edges of the surface show.

texture image, which was then interpreted as a bump map for this surface. One odd but important fact about this bump-mapping process is that if you tilt the surface a bit (Figure 2-69b), you see that the edges of the rendered surface are straight: the bumpy rendering of the surface has no effect on the underlying geometry.

Figure 2-70 illustrates the effectiveness of bump-mapping. The bumpy textures on both the chameleon and the branch were created by scanning in photographs and using them as bump maps.

Yet another application of texture mapping, called **displacement mapping**, deals with situations in which you want to model a lot of irregularities into a surface and you want the irregularities large enough to be individually noticeable. Examples of this type of model are a hilly terrain and the surface of an ocean.

Like transparency and bump mapping, displacement mapping uses the brightness of the pixels of a two-dimensional texture image as a source of information. In the case of displacement mapping, however, the brightness is interpreted as an actual geometric displacement of the height of the surface at that particular location. The brighter the texture pixel, the more the three-dimensional surface is displaced upward. A black texture pixel means no displacement of the surface at all. A white texture pixel means very great displacement.

In Figure 2-71a, the texture image is an irregular pattern created by a fractal procedure. The original, unmodified three-dimensional surface is the patch in Figure 2-71b. After the displacement mapping, the geometry of the three-dimensional surface is modified, producing the craggy, terrainlike structure in Figure 2-71c. Notice that, unlike bump mapping, displacement mapping does

Figure 2-70. Photographs of chameleon skin and tree bark were scanned in as maps in this sophisticated example of bump mapping. (Courtesy, Tim Cheung.)

change the geometry of the surface, as is apparent if you look at the edges of the displaced patch. In fact, of all the mapping techniques discussed, displacement mapping is the only one that actually modifies the geometry of the surface. All of the others are only rendering enhancements. In this sense, displacement mapping might be more properly considered a modeling technique than a rendering technique, though it fits here because the implementation of this technique derives from the other mapping techniques.

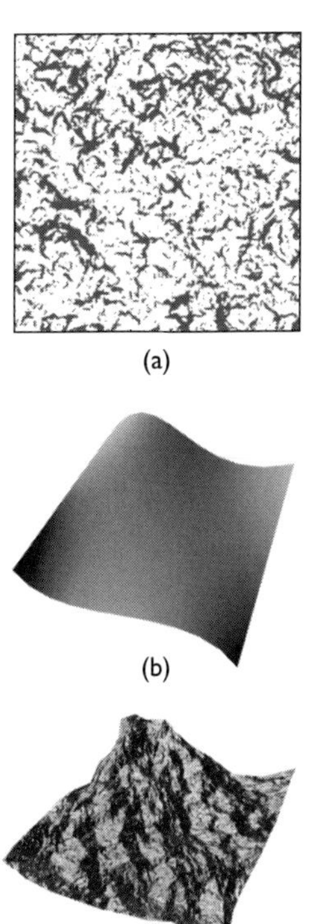

Figure 2-71. Displacement mapping alters the geometry of the mapped surface.

All of these mapping techniques—color, transparency, bump, and displacement—are implemented in such a way that you can manipulate all of the same control parameters discussed earlier in this section. That is, you can adjust the scaling, or size, of the mapping. You can control the offset placement of the mapping. You can make any of these maps wrap or not wrap. And you can alter the effect factor of any of them. Changing the scale, placement, or wrap for any of these varieties of texture mapping is easy to understand, but a few words are in order about changing the effect factor of a mapping.

In a transparency map, scaling the effect increases or decreases the overall range of transparency values for the surface. If the effect factor is set to two, then the transparency values at the various locations of the surface are twice as transparent as normal. If the effect factor is set to zero, the transparency mapping is effectively turned off, since transparency will be zero, or opaque, at every location of the surface. If the effect factor is made negative, all transparency values are reversed. That which was transparent becomes opaque, and that which was opaque becomes transparent.

Similar things happen with bump mapping. If the effect factor is zero, the bump mapping is effectively turned off and the surface appears without bump mapping. If the effect is scaled negatively, bumps that went up now go down (becoming hollows), and vice versa. Analogous sorts of things happen to a displacement map when the effect factor is changed.

There are a number of other, less common types of surface texture mapping in addition to those discussed in this section. Basically, any useful way of interpreting the pixel values of a texture image can be developed into a mapping procedure. For example, some systems provide **incandescence mapping**, in which the pixel values are interpreted as more or less incandescence—that is, a glowing brightness added to the color of the pixel. Sometimes you find **specularity mapping** and **reflectivity mapping**, in which the amount of specularity or the amount of reflectivity are made to vary across the three-dimensional surface. In effect, the numbers and types of surface texture mapping are theoretically unlimited.

Regardless of whether the mapping is done through the projection technique or through the parameterized technique, and whether the map is interpreted as color information, transparency information, bump information, or any other variety of texturing, in all cases the mapping begins with a two-dimensional image. How that two-dimensional image is generated, however, can vary. Very commonly it is scanned from a photograph or an actual object. It also can be painted in a two-dimensional digital paint program. Another extremely powerful approach to creating two-dimensional texture images is **3D paint programs**. These programs allow you to paint directly onto the surface of your three-dimensional model. As you do so, the 3D paint program automatically creates for you the predistorted two-dimensional texture image that would produce your three-dimensionally painted results (Figure 2-72).

A 3D paint program is sometimes incorporated as a subprogram directly into the main 3D animation software package. Alternatively, it may be a **plug-in**, a subprogram that is purchased from another vendor and that can be linked to the main program and run from within it. Finally, the 3D paint program may be a separate, or **stand-alone**, program that runs completely outside the main 3D software package. In this case, both programs use file formats that allow them to share data.

However they may be implemented, 3D paint programs function similarly. You begin by creating your model and defining its mapping (UV, spherical projection, planar projection, or cylindrical projection) in your 3D modeling program. Next, you read this model into your 3D paint program. Inside the 3D paint program, you can turn your model around interactively, usually with the mouse, just as you can inside a normal 3D program. At this point, the 3D paint program resembles a two-dimensional painting: it offers a selection of brushes, colors, and application techniques. Selecting these, you paint directly onto the surface of your three-dimensional model. In Figure 2-72a, for example, the model is a simple sphere. The animator has turned the model around and painted a human head on it. Notice that the painting has taken place all around the surface of the sphere. In this example, you might begin by painting the facial features on the front of the sphere. As you work on the beard, you would tilt the sphere up so that its underside is visible. To work on the hair, you would rotate the sphere to reveal the sides, back, and top as necessary.

At the same time that you are painting three-dimensionally in this way, the program is automatically and simultaneously producing a flattened, stretched two-dimensional texture image (Figure 2-72b). Recall that all surface texture mapping techniques, whether parameterized or projected, involve some amount of stretching, streaking, or distortion. In this example, which employs spherical projection, the distortion would be most noticeable at the top and bottom of the sphere, where the texture image will tend to pinch together. The advantage of a 3D paint program is that it predistorts the texture image automatically, allowing you to think only in terms of your final visual result.

You can see this effect most clearly in the beard and forehead hair. Notice how much these need to flare outwards in the 2D texture image of Figure 2-72b in order to produce the desired result in Figure 2-72a.

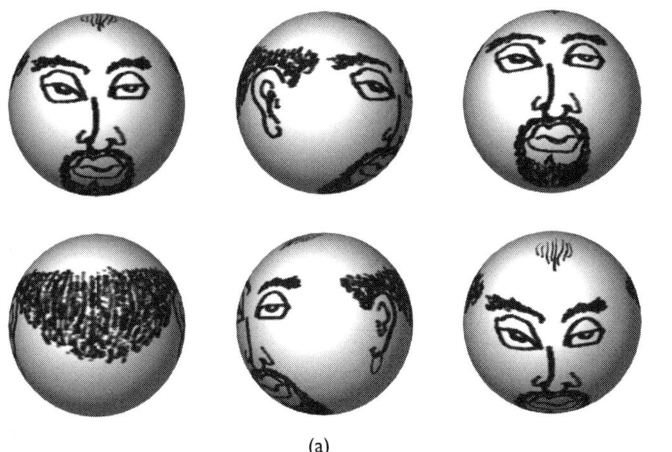

(a)

(b)

Figure 2-72. A 3D paint program allows you to paint directly onto the surface of a three-dimensional model, automatically creating the necessary distortion in the two-dimensional texture image.

Lacking a 3D paint program, if you want to create this texture on a sphere-man, you would have to paint the 2D texture directly in a 2D paint program, render it onto the sphere to see how it looks, then repaint the texture and rerender it, repeating this process many times until you finally achieved the desired mapping. With a 3D paint program, you paint the end result, and the program calculates the distorted 2D image necessary to give you that result.

The example used here is a simple color texture mapping: the colors of the texture become the colors of the model. But 3D paint programs allow you also to create any of the different varieties of texture maps—color, bump, transparency, displacement, and so on. Each different map is usually painted on a separate **layer**, in the same way that you compile your image layer by layer in two-dimensional drawing and painting programs. If you wanted your sphere-man to have a mole on his cheek, you might go into bump-texture mode and create a separate bump painting on a separate layer. Just as a predistorted 2D texture image was generated for your color mapping, the program would generate another predistorted texture image for your bump mapping.

A completely different approach to the problem of creating two-dimensional texture images is **procedural mapping**, in which the software system itself creates the image by means of a collection of procedures, or subprograms. When generating a map procedurally, you normally begin by specifying which procedure you wish to use. Your choices may range from a relatively simple procedure that calculates a grid pattern to a very sophisticated procedure that calculates a fractally based pattern of cloudlike elements. Some procedures are quite specific. A procedure might be designed, for example, to create an image that then creates the effect of water ripples when used as a bump map.

In selecting a procedure, you normally indicate values for a number of different variables, or parameters, that control the look of the procedurally generated two-dimensional image. For a grid-generating procedure, for example, you might be asked to indicate the number of horizontal bars, the number of vertical bars, the color of the bars, and the color of the background. For more complicated procedures, the number of parameters can increase dramatically. The aforementioned water-ripple procedure might have twenty or more variables that allow you to control various characteristics of the water image.

A good example of the power of texture mapping is color plate 4. In this image, the geometry of the scene consists simply of two flat surfaces. All of the effects in the image were created through various mapping techniques. The face image was achieved through a color texture map of a scanned photograph of a woman's face. On the same surface that received this color texture map, a displacement map was applied. The source image of this displacement map was a black-and-white painting of the same face, but with those portions of the head that are most distant painted darkest and those closest to the viewer (for example, the tip of the nose) painted lightest. The bubbly texture that surrounds the face was achieved by applying two maps to the second surface. This surface first received a bump map to create the bumpy, roiling surface. It then received a transparency map to make portions of it invisible, thereby allowing the surface of the face underneath it to be seen.

Solid Texture Mapping

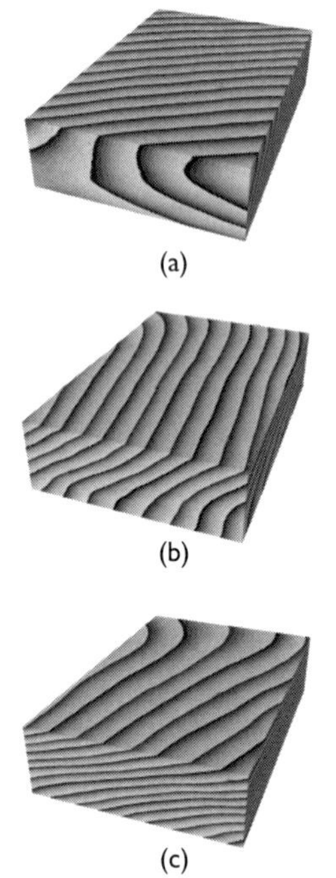

Figure 2-73. Wood-grain patterns are difficult to render effectively with two-dimensional mapping techniques.

All of the mapping techniques discussed in the previous section involve the mapping of a flat two-dimensional pattern onto a surface. A great many interesting effects can be created with the different varieties of this kind of texture mapping. Some rendering effects, however, do not lend themselves to this two-dimensionally oriented mapping approach, but require instead a more fully three-dimensional method. A good example of this is wood, which has a grain. When you cut or carve something out of wood, the grain of the wood is visible on all the exterior surfaces of the object. The wood-grain patterns vary, however, depending on the angle of each surface relative to the direction of the grain (Figure 2-73).

Surface mapping techniques (see the previous section), which either project a pattern onto a surface or wrap a pattern across the surface of an object, do not handle this kind of effect very successfully. To continue with the example of wood, the result of parameterized mapping would look more like a block wrapped in wood-grain-patterned paper than like a block made of wood. Nor would projection mapping work any better, since it would produce a streaking effect along some of the surfaces. Neither of these approaches produces the effect of an object made *of* the material. Surface mapping techniques, whether projected or parameterized, tend to produce the effect of a pattern placed *on* the object.

The technique developed to solve this problem is known as **solid texture mapping**. The idea behind this technique is that you create a virtual *volume*

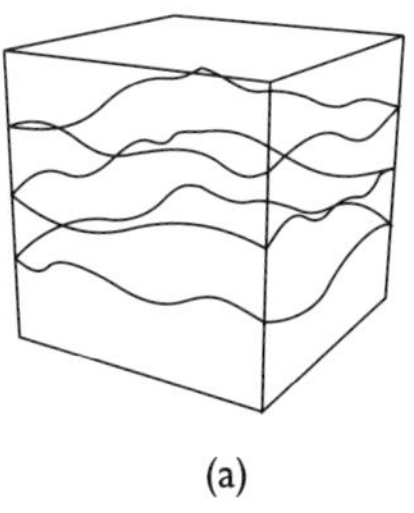

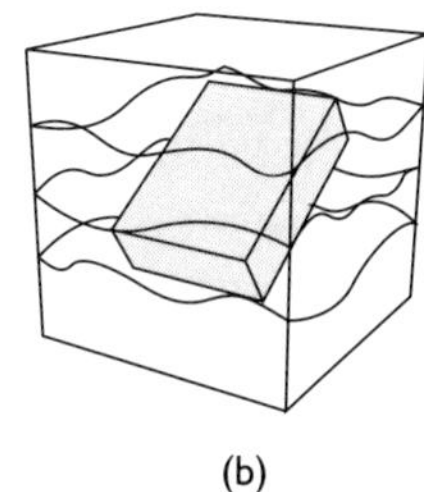

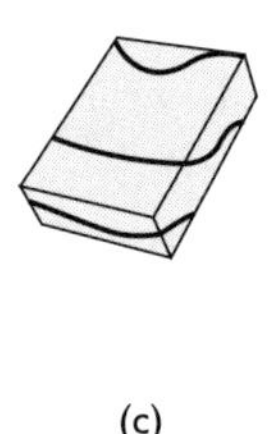

Figure 2-74. In solid texture mapping, the model is immersed in a volume of texture.

of texture and then immerse your object in that volume. Depending on how the object "floats" in the volume, it picks up different colors of the volumetric texture.

The simplified volumetric texture in Figure 2-74a consists of a few wavy lines projected back (with some irregularity) through space. In Figure 2-74b a block-shaped object has been dropped into this texture volume. Figure 2-74c shows the patterns on the surface of the object that result from this "immersion." Wherever one of the wavy lines went through the block, a pattern is left on the block.

Since the pattern of texture is a three-dimensional volume, the color patterns that end up on the surface of the mapped object can be altered simply by transforming the object within this volume in some way. In Figure 2-75a the block of the previous illustration has been given a rotation, which causes it to pick up a different pattern of lines. In Figure 2-75b, the block has been translated downward slightly, which produces yet another pattern of lines.

Just as the object can be transformed within the texture volume to produce a different pattern of marks, the texture volume itself can be trans-

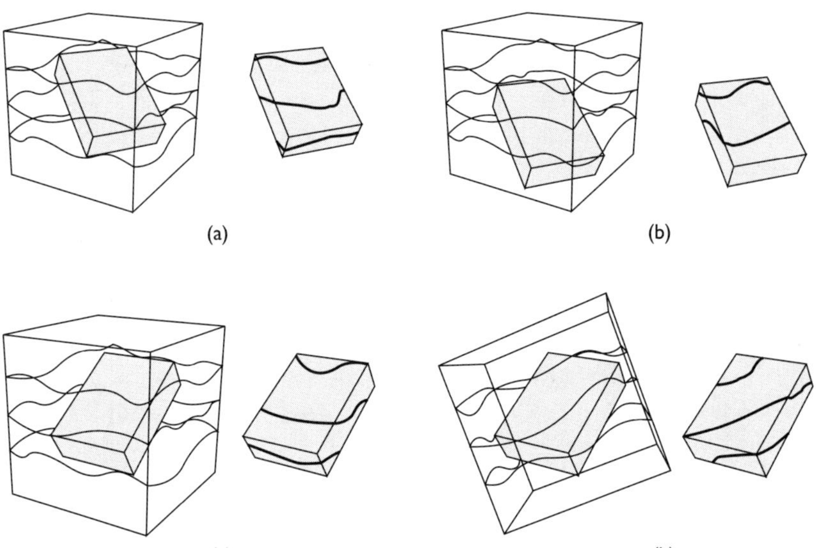

Figure 2-75. Transforming the model within the texture volume changes the patterns which appear on the surface of the model.

Figure 2-76. The texture volume itself can be transformed to produce a different pattern on the model.

formed to produce different marks on the object. Thus, in Figure 2-76b the block has not moved from the position it occupies in Figure 2-76a, but the entire texture volume has been rotated. This rotation causes a different pattern of lines to cross the block immersed in that volume. The different patterns on the rendered blocks are the result solely of this rotation of the texture volume.

Software packages that permit this kind of transformation of the texture volume also make it possible (usually through a menu selection) to link the transformations of the texture volume to the transformations of the object being textured. This is done by making the texture volume a hierarchical child of the object being textured (see *Hierarchies* in chapter 1). Thus, if the object moves to the right, the texture volume moves exactly the same amount to the right. If the object rotates, the texture volume rotates exactly the same amount and in the same direction. This linking of transformations is done to prevent the texture pattern from moving about on the surface of the mapped object whenever the mapped object moves. If the two sets of transformations are not linked, the pattern on the object shifts, as you saw in Figures 2-75 and 2-76. In an animation, this kind of shifting causes the patterns on the surface of an object to swirl and slide across the object as it moves about in space.

Figure 2-77. A procedurally generated solid texture that simulates marble.

With solid texturing as with surface texturing, you can adjust parameters to control the result of the procedure. A "wood" procedure, for example, includes a number of parameters for controlling the density of the wood grain, the color of the grain, the color of the wood pulp, and so on. A procedure that simulates the effect of marble includes various parameters for controlling the veining of the marble, the colors of the marble patterns, and so on. Notice how the vein patterns seem to run "through" the vase in Figure 2-77. This effect is especially apparent around the rim of the vase.

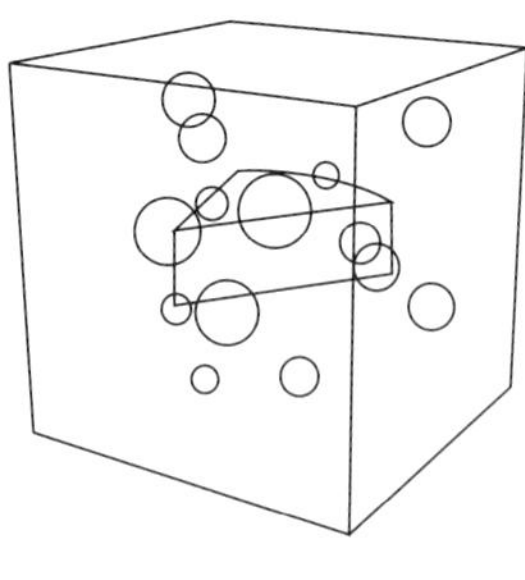

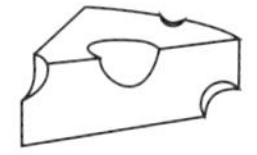

Figure 2-78. Solid texturing can also be used for transparency mapping.

Along with using solid texturing to generate patterns of color on the surfaces of objects, you can use solid texturing in numerous ways similar to the different interpretations of surface texture mapping. For example, the volume of texture might be interpreted as a pattern of transparency rather than of color. The result of this interpretation would be to make transparent holes in the surface of the rendered object (Figure 2-78). Bump mapping is another common application of solid texturing.

So far you have looked at the general principle of the solid-texturing process and the general effects of the process on an object, but you have not seen how you actually go about generating the volume of texture at the heart of the whole process. There are several ways that you normally can do this.

The first and simplest way to create a volume of texture is to create a flat two-dimensional image and to extrude that image straight back through space along the Z axis. In actual practice, this image usually is either digitally painted or scanned. In Figure 2-79a the original image is a pattern of three wavy lines. In Figure 2-79b you see this two-dimensional image pushed straight back through space to produce a cubic volume of three-dimensional pattern.

Notice that this is the same process used by the planar-projection-mapping technique discussed in the previous section. In fact, planar projection mapping, as well as all the other projection mapping techniques, create simplified volumes of texture, and are therefore in a certain sense "solid." The simplified volumes created by projection mapping, however, are so regular that there is no sense of solidity or true volume when they map to objects. What you see with these techniques has very much the feel of an *image* on a *surface*.

Remark, for example, the limitations of the simple extrusion in Figure 2-79b. Though the extrusion process produces a three-dimensional volume of texture, this texture has a regularity to it that is probably not desirable: the lines along the side walls of the volume are perfectly straight, for example. A simple extrusion of a two-dimensional image produces exactly the same pattern at every level of depth in the Z direction.

To make the patterns of texture volume more interesting and more useful, a **noise** parameter is added to the process in order to generate randomness as the image extrudes back through space. This parameter permits you to control how regularly or irregularly the extrusion takes place. As the noise is increased, the extruding pattern fluctuates more and more as it moves back through space. In Figure 2-79c the noise parameter has been given a low value, resulting in a slight wobbling of the image as it extrudes back along Z. In Figure 2-79d the noise parameter has been increased to produce a more pronounced wobbling and a much more irregular volume of texture.

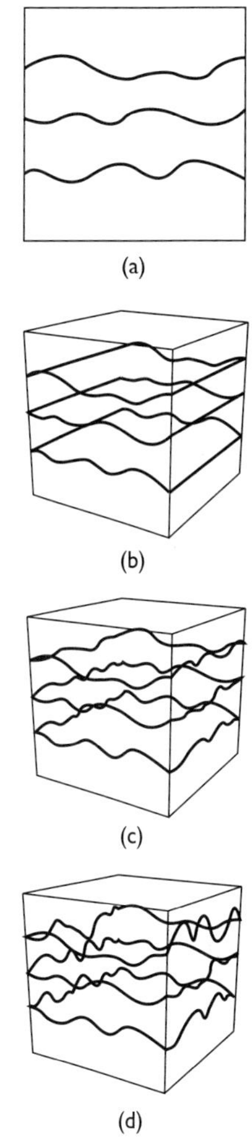

Figure 2-79. The volume of texture is generated by pushing a two-dimensional pattern through space. Randomness is added to create irregularity in the texture volume.

It is this irregularity of the volume texture that gives it the appearance of solidity. Because the texture is everywhere different within the volume, no part of a textured object receives the same texture. This avoids the streaking problem of projection mapping. At the same time, because the texture maps to the object according to the object's immersion in the volume, the stretching problems of parameterized mapping are also avoided.

The immersion approach of solid texture mapping also solves another problem encountered with surface mapping techniques, both parameterized and projected. With surface mapping, it can be extremely difficult to get a single texture pattern to map smoothly across the adjacent surfaces of two objects without a visible seam between the surfaces. In Figure 2-80a there is a noticeable discontinuity in the texture pattern where the top cylinder touches the bottom cylinder.

Some software packages, however, allow you to apply a single solid texture to an entire hierarchy of objects. Since the entire hierarchical object is immersed within one texture volume, the solid-texture-mapping technique

(a)

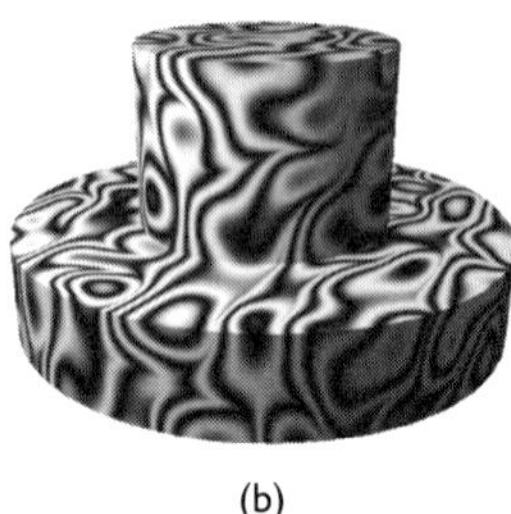

(b)

Figure 2-80. Solid texture mapping can produce continuous texture patterns across the seam between two objects.

now creates a smooth, continuous texture pattern across the seam between the two cylinders (Figure 2-80b).

Most high-end systems also allow you to produce texture volumes without explicitly providing a two-dimensional image. They accomplish this by generating the texture volume procedurally, in much the same way that two-dimensional textures are generated procedurally. Systems that offer this kind of solid texturing usually offer within menus several specific procedures to achieve specific effects. For example, a "marble" procedure might procedurally generate a volume of marblelike texture; a "cloud" procedure might procedurally generate a volume of wispy cloudlike texture. Many of these three-dimensional solid-texturing procedures make use of noise and randomness to achieve the desired irregularity in the texture. Many of them also make use of fractal mathematics (see *Fractals* in chapter 1) so that the irregularity and randomness of the solid texture is maintained no matter how much detail is seen in the final rendering. Figures 2-73 and 2-77 are examples of procedurally generated solid textures.

Environment Procedures and Reflection Mapping

Another situation that requires three-dimensional information for proper rendering is reflections. A highly polished piece of steel, for example, looks like steel not only because it is shiny (that is, has very pronounced highlights), but also because you can see other objects reflected in the surface of the steel. If the shiny surface of a car does not reflect the environment as it drives by, you feel that "something is wrong with this picture"—that perhaps the car is made of plastic, rather than steel. Generating this kind of reflection requires a three-dimensional approach when rendering the car. Since the reflections on the surface of the car come from the three-dimensional environment around the car, you somehow must bring that three-dimensional environment into the rendering process.

One way of doing this, as you saw in the section on rendering algorithms, is to use a ray-tracing program. Because ray tracers, by definition, trace each beam of light through the three-dimensional environment of the scene, accurate reflections are generated automatically, as part of the ray-tracing process.

But ray-tracing programs are computationally expensive and can be slow. As a consequence, many software packages use (either exclusively or in conjunction with a ray tracer) the simpler and faster ray-casting approach. The ray-casting approach does not automatically produce reflections, so you must use an additional technique to render them.

Plate 1. A whimsical example of 3D character animation. (Image created by David M. Kershner.)

Plate 2. Keyframed animation and motion dynamics were combined in this animation sequence. The character is animated with keyframing, the bowling balls with a motion-dynamics simulation. (*Iggy's Dream #819*, © Michael O'Rourke.)

Plate 3. In this stunning model, several particle systems were used to create the hairs of the tarantula. The parameters of the particles were carefully adjusted to control the length, thickness, density, and color of the hairs. (Courtesy, Gevel Marrero.)

Plate 4. An example of the power of texture mapping, this image was generated using only two flat patches of geometry. Bump, displacement, and transparency mapping, in conjunction with several fractal procedures, produced all the effects. (*Off the Map*, © 1991 Sylvain Moreau.)

Plate 5. This frame shows the effects of an extremely sophisticated command of technique as well as a wonderfully observant eye. The portions of the vines that are not animated were created through texture mapping. The portions that were animated were modeled three-dimensionally. (©1993 Nancie L. Atanasoff.)

Plate 6. The cars and gasoline pumps in this ad were animated by capturing the motion of professional dancers through a channeling system. (Courtesy, R/Greenberg Associates, Inc. Commercial for Shell Oil, created by Ogilvy & Mather, Houston, Texas, directed by David Lane of Savoy Commercials, New York.)

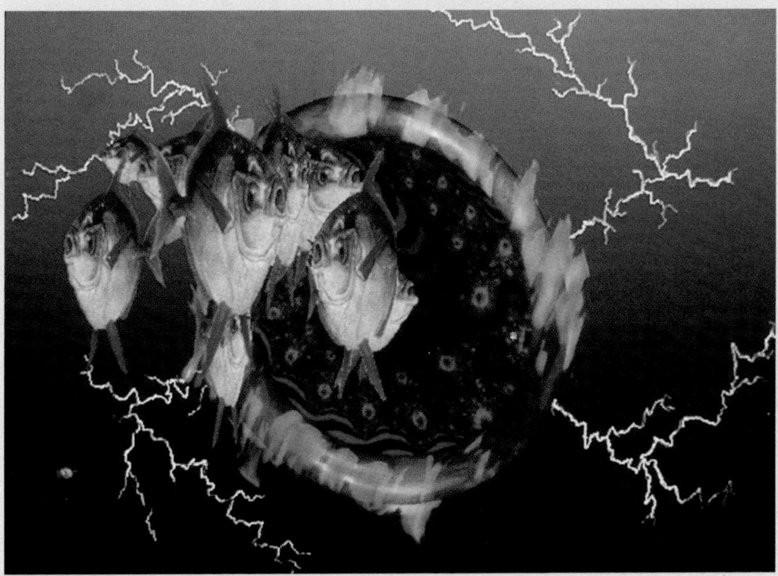

Plate 7. This image combines a number of techniques. The ring and fire were modeled and rendered three-dimensionally. The fish are a single two-dimensional image that was manipulated and matted after the rendering. The lightning was painted digitally, frame by frame. (*The Absolute Contingency*, © 1993 Brett D. Gardy.)

Plate 8. Several sophisticated lighting techniques create a densely composed frame in this powerful animation. A projector light with volumetric fog projects an animated sequence of digitized video frames onto the movie screen. The streaks of rain and the mist in the background are also created through volumetric fog lights. (*The Seventh Day,* Courtesy, Hamid Rahmanian.)

Plate 9. In this image, the lighting on the three-dimensional models in the foreground was adjusted to be consistent with the lighting in the background image. (Courtesy, Toolaya Silthumpithuk.)

Plate 10. The animator used ray tracing to create the stunning reflections and refraction of light as it passes through the glass that holds the flower. (© Kyeng-Im Chung.)

Plate 11. Lighting a scene in computer graphics demands all the subtlety and talent traditionally associated with photography. (Courtesy, Alan Chiou.)

Plate 12. This sophisticated polygonal model began as a simple sphere to which individual polygons were added and subtracted. The facial animation was created by repositioning polygon vertices and saving keyshapes. (Courtesy, Yukito Kurita.)

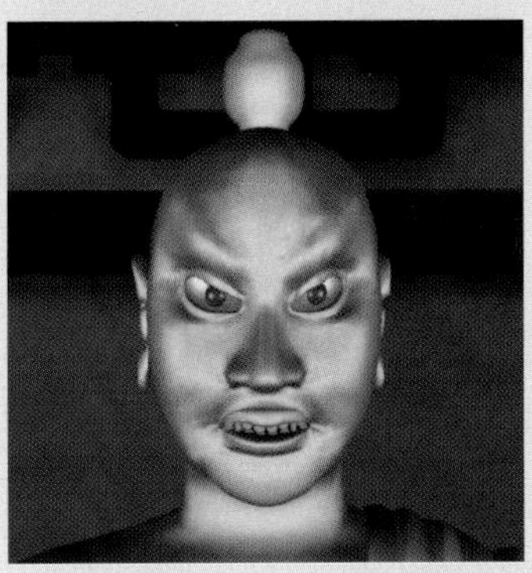

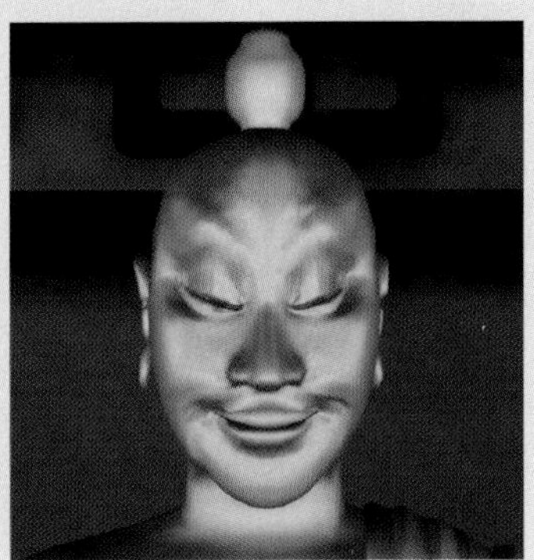

Plate 13. Motion-path animation allows the camera to follow the lines of this abstract form as it swirls and twists through space. This same form also was built as a physical piece of sculpture. (© Frank Stella.)

Plate 14. Shape deformation techniques accomplished the naturalistic modeling and animation of the body of the dolphin. The rendering used a blue "atmosphere" to simulate the effect of water on the color of the dolphin. (Courtesy, RGA/LA. Joseph Francis, creative director.)

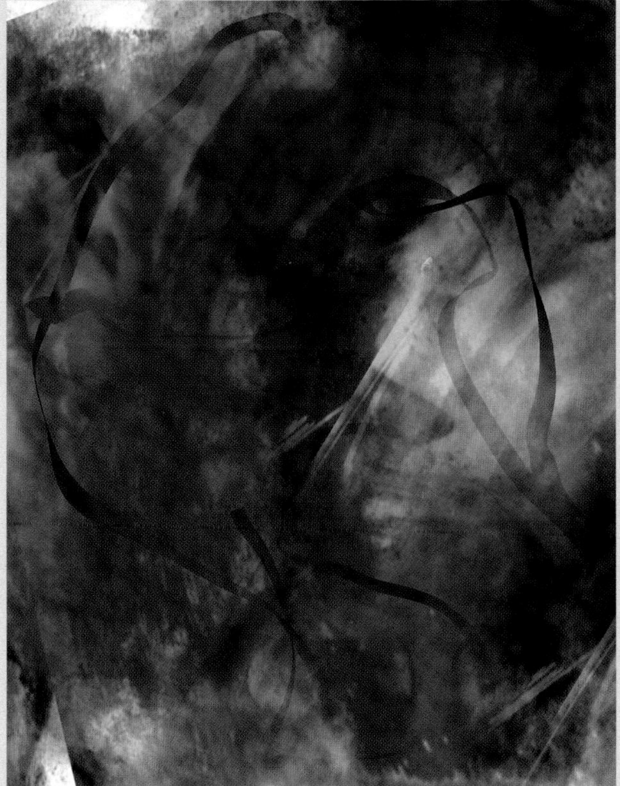

Plate 15. Initially developed in a 3D modeling and rendering program, this composition uses volumetric fog lights and transparency mapping to create a dense space. Once rendered, the image was color-adjusted in a 2D paint program and digitally printed as a large-scale, archival print. (© 1997 Michael O'Rourke.)

Plate 16. Radiosity is most useful for rendering indoor scenes, in which many matte surfaces (walls, ceilings, floors, etc.) reflect upon each other. (Copyright © 1992 Harold Zatz, Cornell Program of Computer Graphics.)

:03 Total:03

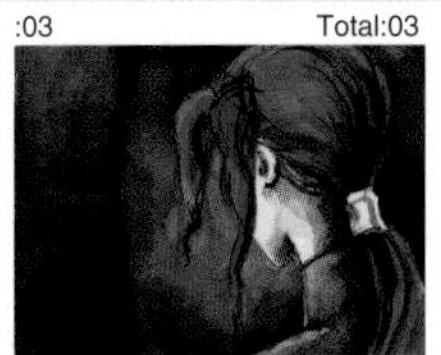

Fade up from black to close shot of figure in dark, cave-like room. Silence

:04 Total:07

Fade up of distant sound of people marching. Figure turns his head at sound.

:07 Total:14

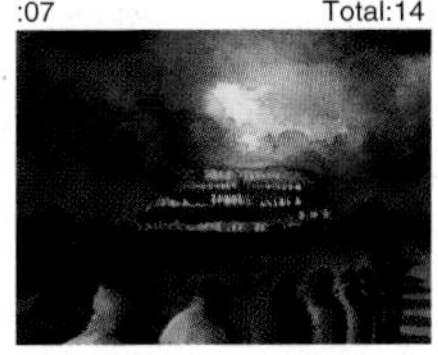

Cut to exterior long shot of building. Louder sound of same footsteps. Overcast skies, sound of blowing wind. A column of dark figures is marching toward building.

:04 Total:18

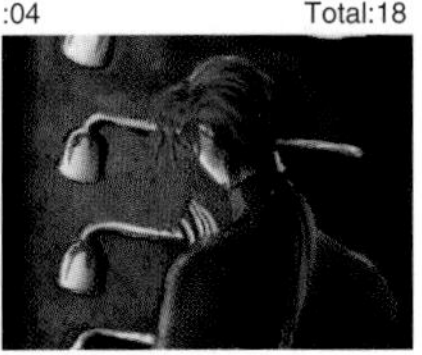

Cut back to interior shot. Figure reaches for candle extinguisher. Distant, faint sounds of marching footsteps.

:06 Total:23

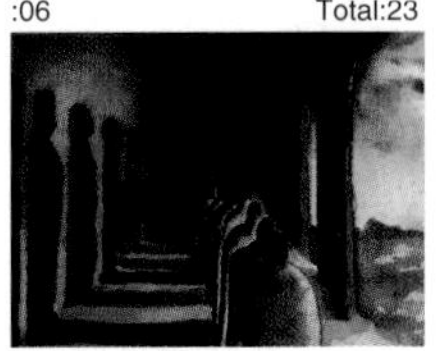

Cross-dissolve to column of marching souls, now entering building. Sound of footsteps and low moaning.

:07 Total:30

Cut back to figure. Shadows of marching souls pass by on wall. "Death" figure extinguishes candles one by one. As each candle goes out, one shadow disappears.

Plate 17. This storyboard segment illustrates the clear visuals, verbal descriptions, and timing and soundtrack notations that are key to good storyboarding. The 3D animation that resulted from this storyboard was very close in visual style to these watercolor panels. © Ayako Hayashi.)

Plate 18. An architectural application of 3D computer animation. The dome structure opens and closes to form a roof. The design for this structure was created as a three-dimensional computer model to demonstrate how the final structure would look and behave. (*Iris Dome*. Invention and design by Chuck Hoberman. Rendering by Andrew Holdun. © 1994 Chuck Hoberman and Andrew Holdun.)

Plate 19. The transformation of the dinosaur skeleton in this animation was accomplished through a digital wipe between a skeleton model and a chrome model of the dinosaur. (Courtesy, R/Greenberg Associates, Inc. Commercial for Philips, created by Backer, Spielvogel and Bates, New York. Directed by David Ashwell of BGCS, with visual effects by R/Greenberg Associates. Computer animation directed by Joe Francis.)

The technique you use for this purpose is called **environmental reflection mapping**, or sometimes just **reflection mapping**. The basic idea behind reflection mapping is that you create one or several two-dimensional pictures to provide a simplified representation of the three-dimensional environment. You then map these two-dimensional pictures onto the surface to be rendered.

The most common way of implementing environmental reflection mapping is through **cubic reflection mapping**. With this technique, six pictures, each on the interior face of an imaginary cube, represent the three-dimensional environment. This configuration simulates the effect you would see if you were standing inside a large cube and saw in each direction a picture of the environment as it looked in that direction (in Figure 2-81a the front face of the cube has been left off so you can see into the cube). Notice how this technique simplifies the true three-dimensional environment, yet retains some of its three-dimensional character. It is not truly three-dimensional, because each wall of the imaginary cube is a flat picture, like a theatrical backdrop. Yet when you look in different direction, it feels somewhat three-dimensional because you see a different "scene."

Cubic reflection mapping uses this approach in the following way. The object to be rendered—and to receive the reflections—is positioned inside and at the center of the cube (Figure 2-81b). For each point on the surface of the object, an imaginary line, or vector, is drawn perpendicular to the surface at that point. (This vector, as you saw in the section on rendering algorithms, is called the "surface normal" at that point.) Each of these vectors is then traced away from the surface until it bumps into some point on one of the six cubic pictures. The color of the picture at that point is the color that needs to be reflected onto the surface at the base point of the vector.

(a)

(b)

Figure 2-81. Cubic reflection mapping maps six pictures of the environment onto the surface of a model.

Note that the imaginary cube of reflection pictures must be positioned in such a way that the object to be rendered resides at the center of the cube. Because of this requirement, each of the scene's reflective objects must have its own cube of reflection pictures. Imagine, for example, that a second object, say a cone, were to be positioned in Figure 2-81 to the left of the house. This cone would require a very different set of cubic reflection pictures than does the sphere. While the sphere would reflect the front of the house, the cone would need to reflect the back of the house. In short, each object to receive reflections through the cubic reflection technique requires that a unique set of six cubic reflection pictures be calculated for it.

This leaves you with the question of how to generate the six cubic pictures. One possibility, of course, is to draw them by hand, perhaps with a digital paint program. When doing so, you must be aware of how seamlessly each image fits against the neighboring images on all four sides. Any discontinuity between the images—for example, if the mountains in the background of Figure 2-81 don't connect seamlessly with the mountains of the right panel—

shows up on the rendered surface of the object. The reflections will appear to have a line, or seam, running through them, destroying the sense of realism they were intended to convey.

A more useful technique for creating the six images needed for cubic reflection mapping is to render them from the three-dimensional data of your scene. The situation in Figure 2-81b—a sphere existing in isolation, onto which you map an imaginary environment—is rare. More often, such a sphere exists within a three-dimensionally modeled scene. For example, the tree in the right panel might be a three-dimensionally modeled tree positioned to the right of the sphere. In order to produce convincing reflections, you must render the reflected tree in exactly the same style and with exactly the same colors and lighting as the original tree is rendered. The best way to ensure such fidelity is to create six renderings of the three-dimensional scene, then use these six renderings as the six panels of your reflection cube.

In Figure 2-82a the entire environment—that is, the entire modeled scene—is represented as a panoramic line drawing. Hovering in the center of this environment is the virtual camera. The dotted lines emanating from the camera indicate the field of view of the camera and delineate the area of the environment that the camera sees as it faces to the right. Using this camera to render a picture produces the image on the right panel of the cube in Figure 2-81. Using the camera facing to the left produces the image on the left panel of the cube (Figure 2-82b).

Rotating the camera 90 degrees in each of the six directions produces the six cubic pictures you need for cubic reflection mapping. It is important to note that the field of view of the camera is a full 90 degrees (a very wide-angle lens). The field of view must be this full 90 degrees in order to ensure that the edge of each rendered panel matches up exactly with the corresponding edge of the adjacent panel.

Conveniently for the user, the process just described for creating the six cubic renderings necessary for cubic reflection mapping can be handled automatically by most software packages. Rather than positioning the camera and rendering each of the six views needed, you simply activate cubic reflection mapping through a menu selection, and the software does the rest, rendering the six cubic pictures for you automatically. There are some occasions, however, where you might want to exercise more control over this process, creating your own six cubic renderings by hand—either by rendering the three-dimensional scene as described above, or by drawing, painting, or photographing your own six pictures to generate a specific sort of reflection. For this reason, most 3D packages give you the option of either allowing the software to calculate the six pictures automatically for you, or having you specify them manually by typing in the names of the six picture files you wish to use.

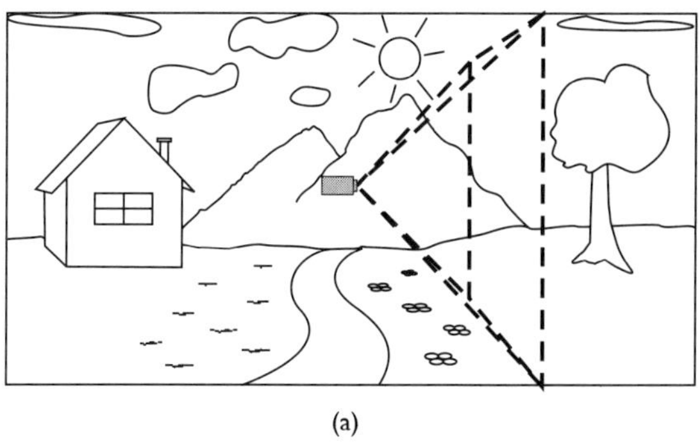

(a)

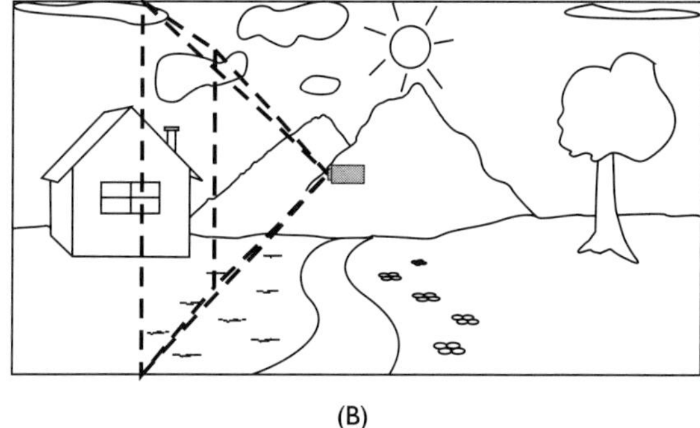

(B)

Figure 2-82. The six texture images of cubic reflection mapping can be generated by rendering the virtual three-dimensional environment from six points of view.

Even automatic generation of the six cubic pictures can be cumbersome, however. A simpler variation of environmental reflection mapping, **spherical reflection mapping**, attempts to address this problem. This technique replaces the six pictures of cubic reflection mapping with a single picture. This one picture represents the whole world as if the world were on the inside surface of a sphere. Thus, the top of the picture matches up with the bottom of the picture, and the right side of the picture matches up with the left. The result is an image of the whole world seen in all directions, compressed into one rectangular picture (Figure 2-83). Notice that the edges of this hand-drawn picture have been left bare of imagery, so that each side matches up cleanly with the edge on the opposite side.

A disadvantage of spherical reflection mapping is that it is extremely difficult to generate a single picture that corresponds accurately to the three-dimensional environment of a particular animation. In many situations, however, reflections on a surface do not need to be precise in order to be convincing. Sometimes the reflection of general color patterns is convincing enough. The blade of a kitchen knife will reflect something when you pick it up. You almost certainly cannot tell *what* is being reflected. If it is sufficient to show that *something* is being reflected on a surface in your animation, without being too precise about exactly what is being reflected, spherical mapping can work very satisfactorily. If so, the advantage of producing only a single map picture, instead of the six pictures required for cubic mapping, can be significant.

All environmental reflection mapping, whether cubic or spherical, is based on the assumption that the objects in the surrounding three-dimensional environment—that is, the objects creating the reflections—are stationary. If the objects are moving, you have a problem, because as the environment changes the reflections should change. If, for example, a tree sways in the wind, you cannot use the same set of six static pictures for the whole animation.

Figure 2-83. Spherical reflection mapping uses a single picture to represent the entire environment.

In short, if any object in the three-dimensional environment moves, you must render new reflection-map pictures for each frame of the animation. In the case of cubic reflection mapping, this means that all six cubic-reflection pictures must be rerendered for each frame of the animation. These, plus the

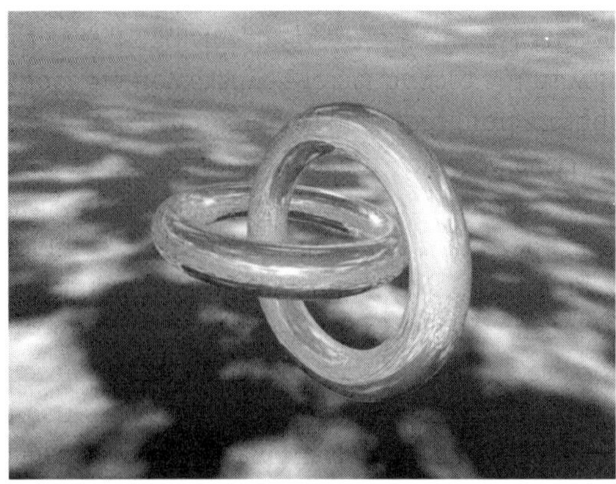

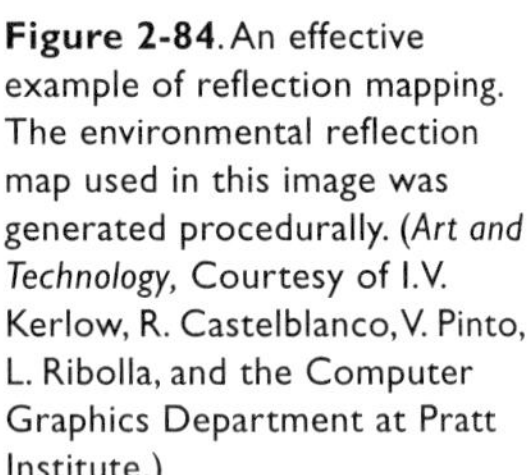

Figure 2-84. An effective example of reflection mapping. The environmental reflection map used in this image was generated procedurally. (*Art and Technology,* Courtesy of I.V. Kerlow, R. Castelblanco, V. Pinto, L. Ribolla, and the Computer Graphics Department at Pratt Institute.)

final animation frame itself, make a total of seven rendered pictures for each frame of animation. In such a situation, accurate reflection mapping becomes extremely time-consuming. Here ray tracing may be the more appropriate approach.

In the sections on *Surface Texture Mapping* and *Solid Texture Mapping* you saw that it is possible to generate a two-dimensional texture image procedurally. This is true of environmental reflection mapping as well. Many high-end software systems allow you procedurally to generate a three-dimensional environmental reflection map, which you then can apply to various models to produce convincing reflections.

Some procedures, however, do much more than merely create environmental reflections. Called **environment procedures**, they actually create an entire three-dimensional environment. This means that when you render a scene, you can see, in addition to the refections generated by the procedure, the actual environment that created those reflections.

Figure 2-84 shows a simple example of this: a sky environment procedure has been used to create a three-dimensional environment of clouds. In the rendered image you see both the clouds themselves, behind the rings, and the reflections of the clouds on the rings. The clouds in the background are not merely a two-dimensional backdrop picture pasted in behind the rings. Rather, they are one rendering of a fully three-dimensional world of clouds. If you were to look (that is, point your virtual camera) in a different direction, you would see a different configuration of clouds. Even though you cannot see the clouds that are, for example, behind you or far above the rings, they are there, created by the environment procedure and therefore reflected on the rings' surfaces.

Notice also in Figure 2-84 that the details of the reflection are vague because of the curvature of the rings. You can see that the surfaces of the rings are reflecting something, and if you look closely you can make out cloudlike images on parts of the rings. But you do not need to be able to see specifically what is being reflected for the image to be effective. That the surfaces are reflecting something cloudlike tells you what you need to know about the nature of the surfaces.

Some environment procedures have more capabilities than merely making clouds. Advanced environment procedures can also generate other elements of an environment, such as a sun, atmospheric color, haze, terrain, and so on. Each of these elements is controlled by a number of parameters, to permit you to define exactly what the environment will look like. The color of the sky, for example, could be defined by its Red, Green, and Blue component values, or by applying a two-dimensional texture pattern. The sun could be defined by specifying its size, color, and position in the sky. The amount and density of haze might be defined with slider bars.

The jacket of this book shows a sophisticated example of such an environment procedure; Figure 2-85 is a black and white version of that image. The sky and clouds were generated entirely procedurally, just as described above. You can tell that they are truly three-dimensional because the overhead clouds, which are invisible from our point of view, are nonetheless reflected on the screen of the monitor. Notice also the rising sun and the effect its light has on the clouds and the atmosphere.

Figure 2-85. Environment procedures create a fully three-dimensional environment that can include sky, clouds, sun, haze, and terrain. (Image by Marcus Meyer and Michael O'Rourke.)

Some environment procedures also allow a geographically accurate definition of an environment by permitting you to specify the latitude and longitude of the location, as well as the month, date, and time of day. The procedure then simulates the position, color, and brightness of the sun accordingly—for example, a 5:20 A.M. sky on the 14th of January, 1999, in New Delhi, India. This can be especially useful for architectural or scientific visualization applications.

With advanced environment procedures, all the myriad parameters that you set to define your environment are also animatable, usually as a simple keyframing operation (see chapter 3 for a discussion of keyframing). With this technique, you set the values for your parameters and make a menu selection to save those values at a particular moment in time. You then advance to another moment in time, set new values for the sky environment parameters, and save the new values. Using this approach, you might, for example, animate a sunrise, with the sun moving higher in the sky and changing color from a rosy-fingered pink dawn to a mustard-yellow early morning to a bright white midday sky. At the same time, you might animate a decrease in the amount and density of the early morning haze. If the software is sophisticated enough, it will also automatically change the apparent size of the sun as it rises, to simulate the magnification effect we experience when the sun is close to the horizon and seen through a great deal of atmospheric haze. The software may also diffuse the light of the sun according to how much and what sort of haze is present.

Recall, moreover, that all of this imagery that you render is being generated as a fully three-dimensional environment. You could, if you chose, move your camera through space as the sun rises, panning across the scene or looking around behind you to see the effect of the rising sun on the building you have just left.

Atmospheric Effects

Many 3D computer graphics images have a distinctive crystal-clear quality. Sometimes this clarity is intended by the artist and proves a very useful effect. But sometimes the hyperclarity of 3D computer imagery is not desirable and creates instead an appearance of unreality and falseness.

The reason so many 3D computer images have this crystal clarity is that they often fail to take into account an important optical effect. In the real world, the perceived colors of objects change depending on the distance of the objects from the viewer. The colors of a distant mountain range are muted by the atmosphere. This effect is sometimes known as **chiaroscuro**, which the painters of the Renaissance developed so effectively in their landscapes. In Leonardo da Vinci's famous painting known as the *Mona Lisa*, you can see the effect of the atmosphere on the colors of the countryside in the distance. The colors of distant rocks are much less vibrant than those of near-by rocks.

When light travels through the air, it loses some color as it travels. The farther the light travels, the more color it loses. This phenomenon causes the chiaroscuro effect. The light rays coming to your eye from the mountains in the distance are scattered along the way by the tiny molecules that make up the atmosphere. By the time the light rays reach your eye, some of the original green has been lost, and the remaining color has been modified, picking up some of the blue of the sky. This effect is even more pronounced if fog or haze (or smog, unfortunately) is in the atmosphere. The greater the density of molecules to deflect the light rays, the more severely affected the colors of objects. In a dust storm or underwater, the atmospheric effect on the color of the objects can be even more extreme.

Most 3D computer rendering programs do not render this sort of atmospheric effect automatically. When you model a scene—for example, a cube in the foreground and a cone in the far distance—the computer considers only the surfaces explicitly modeled to exist. There are no tiny molecule-sized surfaces in between the cube and the cone to deflect the light, so the cone in the far distance is rendered with the same clarity as the cube in the foreground.

To address this, many software packages offer techniques for generating atmospheric effects such as fog and haze and chiaroscuro. The best of these packages permit you to define various atmospheric parameters interactively from a menu window. The program includes these parameters in the color calculations when it renders the final frame, and the resulting frame displays the correct atmospheric adjustments.

The simplest and most common kind of atmospheric effect that you can define in these packages varies according to depth along the Z axis. With this sort of **Z-depth fog**, or **horizontal fog**, an object located at a Z depth of 100 meters is more obscured by the atmosphere than an object located at 50 meters. In most systems, the calculations done to determine how obscured an object is at a given distance are linear interpolations, which means that an object at 50 meters will be half as obscured as one at 100 meters and one-quarter as obscured as one at 200 meters.

In using an atmospheric rendering system, you normally specify the color of the atmosphere and the distance at which that color completely overrides the colors of objects. For example, to render a scene with a reddish haze, you might specify that the RGB components of the color are (200,100,100) and that objects at a distance of 1,000 meters are completely obscured by this reddish haze. These specifications mean that an object at a distance from the eye of 100 meters, for example, is one-tenth obscured—that is, one-tenth of the final color comes from the red of the haze and nine-tenths of the color comes from the original color of the object itself.

It is also possible to define an atmospheric fog that obscures objects along the vertical, or Y, axis. This sort of **vertical fog**, or **layered fog**, can be useful, for example, in rendering mountains, the feet of which may lie in fog while the peaks rise above the fog. The procedure here is usually similar to the procedure for defining fog along the Z axis. First you specify the color of the fog/atmosphere. Next you specify the range along the Y axis where this vertical atmosphere will be in effect. This latter specification usually involves a maximum and a minimum Y value: the fog is densest at one end of this range and dissipated completely at the other end.

The discussion so far has involved atmospheres of constant density, whether along the Z axis or along the Y axis. In reality, however, atmospheric density is rarely perfectly constant. The fog enveloping a mountain, rather than dissipating in a linear fashion as it moves up the mountain, instead may not dissipate at all up to a certain height, then dissipate very quickly for a while, then more slowly, and so on. On a smaller scale, the fog that hovers above the surface of a lake on a damp morning will vary in density, floating and drifting in the morning breezes. Most programs allow you to achieve such variable fog density through a **noise** parameter in the fog procedure's menu. By adjusting this parameter, often with a slider bar, you can cause irregularities in the fog's density, creating patches of more or less dense fog, making the patches larger or smaller, and making the patches nearer or

Figure 2-86. Introducing noise to fog creates variations in the density of the fog.

farther from each other (Figure 2-86). In most programs, noise can be added to both vertical fog, as in Figure 2-86, and to horizontal fog.

Another technique offered by some programs for creating irregularities in fog is controlling the density of the fog through a two-dimensional **density map** picture. This picture may be created procedurally—for example, with a fractal procedure or a ramp procedure (one that creates a smooth gradation from color to color, as described in the section *Final-frame Considerations*)—or by painting or photographing an image and scanning it. However it is created, variation in pixel brightness in the density map controls the variation in atmospheric density in the final rendering. For example, dark pixels at the bottom of the map imply a dense fog at the lowest Y values of a vertical fog. Lighter pixels higher on the map imply a less dense fog at higher Y values.

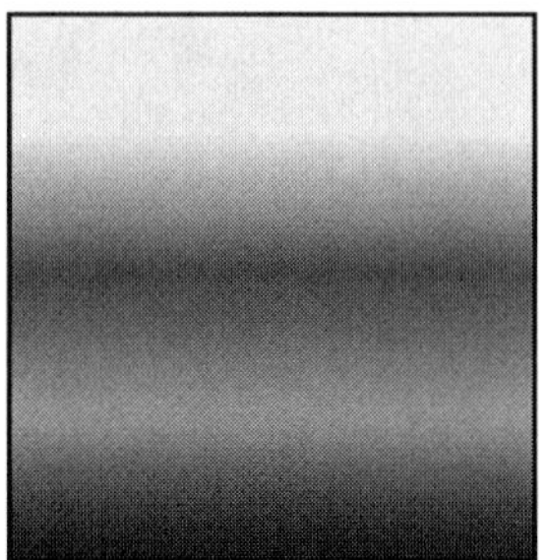

Figure 2-87. A map for controlling the density of a vertical fog.

Figure 2-87 shows a typical vertical density map. Notice that this map is darkest at the bottom, becomes lighter further up, then darker again, and finally lighter and lighter until it is almost white at the top. Using this variation in pixel values to control the density of fog in the type of mountain scene just described makes the fog very dense at the lowest altitudes (that is, at the base of the mountains). Slightly higher up, the fog dissipates a bit. Higher yet, corresponding to what is happening in the map, the fog becomes denser again, then dissipates almost entirely as it moves up to the mountain peaks.

Not only does this technique allow you to draw density variations, it also allows you very easily to cause global changes to the fog density. Making the entire density map somewhat brighter causes the fog to become less dense overall. Changing the contrast of the entire density map changes the rates at which the fog density changes. Increasing the contrast of the density map, for example, causes the density changes in the final rendering to be much more abrupt. Decreasing the contrast of the map creates much more gradual changes in the final rendering.

For example, the fog in Figure 2-88 at the feet of the walking figure dissipates as it rises. The density of this fog was controlled through a vertical

Figure 2-88. An example of vertical fog density in a rendering. (*Iggy's Dream #56*, © Michael O'Rourke.)

density map. A simple black-and-white ramp was created, ranging from black at the bottom to white at the top, and the contrast of this image was then adjusted until the fog fell off at the correct height around the figure. This image also illustrates the emotional effect that atmospheric rendering can have. If this figure had been rendered without any fog effect, but with the crystal clarity of many computer renderings, it would not have the same emotional impact.

All the parameters that determine the appearance of your fog—whether the color of the fog, its density, or the amount of noise in the fog—can be animated, creating a moving, shifting, or even swirling fog. This is usually done through simple keyframing (see chapter 3 for a discussion of keyframing).

Some software packages also let you take advantage of a density map picture to create special animated effects in fog. You do this by interpreting each column of pixels as the density map for a specific moment in time. Column 1 is the first moment, column 2 the next, and so on. If the brightness of a density map changes horizontally, these changes cause the density of fog to change over time (Figure 2-89). If the density map is 512 × 512, and the length of the fog animation is 300 frames, then column 1 of the map controls the fog density at frame 1, while the last column, column 512, controls the fog density at the last frame, frame 300. Frame 150 would be controlled by column 256, and so on. The result of this correspondence is that the several layers of densest fog rise and fall, shifting their thickness over the course of the 300 frames of the animation.

Figure 2-89. A vertical density map that varies in the horizontal direction can be used to animate vertical fog over time. Each column of pixels corresponds to a moment in time.

All of the techniques discussed so far for rendering atmospheric effects work very well for scenes that involve large distances, and this is, in fact, when you normally see atmospheric effects. If the distance between your eye and some set of objects is very short, the light rays coming from those objects do not have a chance to become scattered and there is no visible chiaroscuro effect. In a few situations, however, the effect of the atmosphere on light is important even at close distances—for example, when a spotlight is shined through the darkness. When this happens, the air in the path of the spotlight is illuminated, which is a critical visual cue for interpreting the scene. If you remove the illuminated air from the scene, leaving only the illumination of the spotlight on the objects it hits, the scene looks wrong, because your eyes expect to see that distinctive cone of spotlit air.

What makes this scene difficult to render is, once again, the lack of surfaces in the air. The reason the real-life spotlight creates a cone of light is that it is lighting thousands of tiny dust particles in the air. In the pristine world of computer graphics, there are (normally) no dust particles.

One solution to this rendering problem is to use a "particle system" procedure (as described in *Particle and Particle-like Systems*, in chapter 4). A much less effective, though sometimes serviceable technique is to model a cone, then

Figure 2-90. Shafts of light can be simulated by modeling a transparent cone for each spotlight. (Courtesy, Chiussu Chung.)

replace the tip at the location of the light source and angle it to simulate the angle of the light coming from the spotlight. If the cone is rendered as a semi-transparent object with no surface highlights at all, it fairly reasonably takes on the appearance of an illuminated cone of air (Figure 2-90).

The most effective technique for rendering this sort of localized atmospheric effect, however, is to use **volumetric fog lights**. In the section on *Lights* you saw that many software packages provide volume lights, in which the area lighted is restricted to a specific, geometrically shaped volume. Some packages offer volume lights that also produce fog, or atmosphere, within their volume. Figure 2-91 shows a spotlight whose conically shaped volume

Figure 2-91. Volumetric lights can be rendered with a three-dimensional fog within their volume.

(a)

(b)

Figure 2-92. Different sorts of noise can be applied to volumetric fog lights to create irregular patterns of density in the fog.

Figure 2-93. A volumetric point light with a spherical volume of fog, properly adjusted with noise, can simulate clouds.

has been rendered with fog in it. Notice that the fog is fully three-dimensional and volumetric. It not only fills the conical volume of the light, but also has shadows cast on it by the cylinder and the platform.

As with the horizontal and vertical fog discussed at the beginning of this section, you can apply noise to the fog of volumetric lights to create irregularities in the density of the fog. Figure 2-92a shows random noise applied to the fog to give it a less uniform, more smoky look. In Figure 2-92b, noise applied in a radial pattern creates the streaked effect of light streaming through a window.

Volumetric fog lights are not limited to the conical volumes of spotlights. Any volume light could have fog in it. Figure 2-92 shows a volumetric point light placed behind the objects. The spherical volume of the point light has been filled with fog. Adjusting various noise parameters made the fog look cloudlike. Notice also that the pronounced noise, by making the fog patchy, has also made the spherical shape of the volume light less obvious.

Color plate 15 uses several volumetric fog lights to create a sense of dense space, most noticeable in the upper left corner. Properly used, volumetric fog lights can be an important rendering tool for the artist.

Final-frame Considerations

When it comes time to render the final frames of an animation, you must think about several factors that affect the look and quality of the final images. One of the most basic of these factors is **resolution**. As you have seen, any digital picture is composed of a grid of tiny rectangular picture elements, or pixels. The density of this grid is called the "resolution" and is measured as the number of pixels in the horizontal, or X, direction by the number of pixels in the vertical, or Y, direction. Thus, an image with a resolution of 300 × 200 has 300 pixels in the X direction and 200 pixels in the Y direction. In terms of columns and rows, this image has 300 columns in the X direction and 200 rows in the Y direction.

Generally, higher resolutions result in better-quality renderings. An image rendered at 300 × 200 (Figure 2-94a) looks considerably cruder than the same image rendered at 600 × 400 (Figure 2-94b), and that image looks smoother yet if rendered at 1,200 × 800. The cruder, more "pixelized" look of the lower-resolution image is especially apparent around the edges of the objects.

In some cases, however, you accomplish nothing by increasing the resolution of a rendering. If the final image is displayed very small, a low-resolution rendering may do perfectly well. An animation produced for a four-inch screen at a bank automated teller machine, for example, gains nothing by being rendered at a very high resolution. The additional detail gained by a

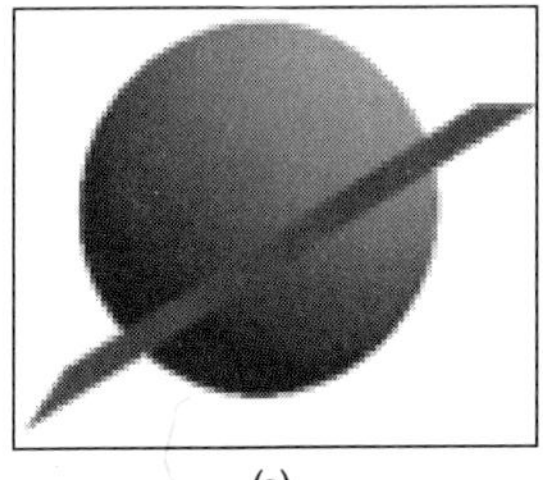

(a)

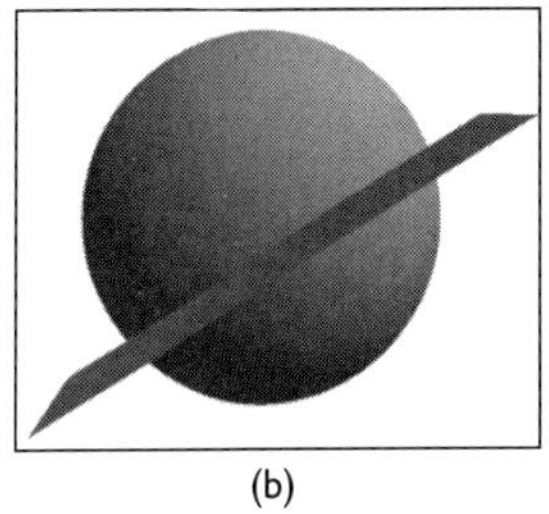

(b)

Figure 2-94. The resolution at which an image is rendered affects the final image quality. (For the sake of comparison, the lower-resolution image has been enlarged so that it is the same size as the higher-resolution image.)

higher resolution rendering would be imperceptible to the human eye. The same is frequently true in the game industry, where because of both screen size and the need to play the animations in real-time, rendering resolution is often deliberately kept low. On the other hand, if the image is displayed very large—for example, as a large-screen projection in a movie theater—then a very high-resolution rendering is critical. In this case, if the resolution is too low, the individual pixels become visible when the image is blown up to full size. A typical resolution for this sort of application might be a few thousand pixels in each direction.

Unfortunately, as in life, nothing in computer graphics comes free. The higher the resolution of an image, the longer the rendering takes. Remember that when a picture is rendered, a beam is projected from the eye through each pixel, and the system calculates what color that pixel should be. If twice as many pixels must be colored, twice as many calculations must be done, requiring twice as much time. In fact, increasing resolution increases rendering time even faster than you might think. If you double the resolution of a picture, you do not merely double the rendering time—you quadruple it!—because when you double resolution, you double it in both directions. For example, an image with a resolution of 300 × 200 has a total of 60,000 pixels to be colored (300 × 200 = 60,000). If you double this resolution to 600 × 400, you have a total of 240,000 pixels to be colored (600 × 400 = 240,000). The rendering for this second image thus takes four times as long as the rendering for the first image.

For this reason, it is important to be careful when you select a resolution. If a higher resolution gains you nothing, you save a lot of time and aggravation by working at a lower resolution. In fact, it is common practice to work at low resolution while performing rendering tests. Only when you know that everything is working to your satisfaction do you increase the resolution to produce the final frames.

The actual final resolution you use, however, is not arbitrary. Certain standard resolutions are used for specific purposes. Most 3D packages provide you with a menu that allows you to select any one of these standard resolutions.

When recording to video, for example, you must use one of several standard resolutions. Images with a resolution larger than the standard video resolution contain more information than can be recorded onto a frame of video and so are cropped when recorded to video. Images with a resolution that is too small, by contrast, do not fill the entire video screen. More detailed information about video recording appears in chapter 6, but for now you need to know that the standard resolution for the NTSC (National Television Systems Committee) video format, which is used in the United States, is usually 645 × 485, while the standard resolution for the PAL (Phase Alternation Line) video format, which is used throughout most of Europe, is usually 720 × 576.

The ratio between resolution in X and resolution in Y is called the **aspect ratio** of a picture. The aspect ratio of NTSC video, for example, is 1.33:1—that is, one and one-third times as long as it is high. The standard NTSC resolution of 645 × 485 yields this aspect ratio, or more exactly, a ratio of 1.3298:1. This slight variation from the true 1.33 ratio sometimes causes confusion. Because the aspect ratio produced by dividing the number of horizontal pixels by the number of vertical pixels does not always produce exactly the 1.33 ratio, some systems use a slightly different number of pixels: 645 × 484 yields a ratio of 1.3326:1, for example. The question of the exact number of pixels required for a given standard ratio is further complicated by the fact that the hardware of some computer systems does not use perfectly square pixels. If the pixels of an image are not square, the number of pixels required to achieve the correct aspect ratio changes. To address this situation, many systems permit you to specify the **pixel aspect ratio** at the same time that you specify rendering resolution. In this case, the pixel aspect ratio is usually specified as a single number between 0 and 1, with this number representing the width of the pixel. The height of the pixel is assumed to be 1. Thus, typing 0.8 would imply a 0.8:1 ratio—that is, a pixel that is 80 percent as wide as it is tall. Typing 1 would imply a 1:1 ratio—that is, a square pixel.

The concept of screen aspect ratio has an additional implication. When changing the resolution of an image for testing purposes, be sure to retain the same aspect ratio in the smaller, test resolution that you plan to use in the final renderings. If you fail to do this, the smaller test rendering will not frame the scene in the same way that it will be framed within the final, full resolution. For example, if the final frame is to be at an NTSC resolution of 645 × 485, make sure that your test renderings retain the same 1.33 aspect ratio as the original—for example, by halving both the X and the Y resolutions to 323 × 243 (and rounding off to whole numbers).

If you are recording to film, a different aspect ratio is involved. The aspect ratio of 35mm film is 1.5:1—that is, one and a half times as wide as it is high. When rendering a frame to be shot to 35mm slide film, therefore, choose a resolution that maintains this ratio. A typical resolution used for 35mm color slide film might be 2,048 × 1,365, which is high enough to produce a good-quality still-frame rendering and retain the correct 1.5:1 aspect ratio.

In the rendering of frames for 35mm motion-picture film, the issue is a bit more complicated, because there are two different standards in the film industry. One standard, called the **Academy aspect ratio**, leaves room in each frame for soundtrack information. The other standard, called the **Full Cine aspect ratio**, does not. Consequently the aspect ratios of the two different film standards are slightly different. A typical resolution for Academy frames might be 1,254 × 911, while a typical resolution for Full Cine frames might be 1,416 × 1,062.

When rendering your final frames it is also important to consider which **file format** to use for your picture files. A digital picture's information may be stored in a variety of ways. Each 3D animation software package usually has its own method, which produces its own **native** picture-file format. Most frequently, this format is the one you use while developing your animation within the 3D package.

Sometimes, however, you know in advance that you will need to export your animation frames to another set of software—perhaps in order to composite the frames with other images, or to edit them with other animation sequences, or to record them. (See chapters 5 and 6 for a discussion of all these techniques.) In these cases, you may need to store your picture files in a more standard file format, one that can be read by programs other than the one that created them.

Each of the formats has strengths and weaknesses. Some are more accurate in their preservation of color information. Others may produce smaller picture files. Some have sophisticated techniques for variably adjusting the compression of picture data, allowing you to choose how much compression you are willing to trade for how much loss of image quality. The formats that have become standard, however, all work very well. Your choice of file format is usually determined by the use you intend to make of your frames.

One of the standard formats, **PICT** (for "picture"), is very common and readable by most graphics programs. **TIFF** (Tagged Image File Format) is another common format. **EPS** (Encapsulated PostScript) format was specially developed to be device-independent—that is, to be readable no matter what hardware you are using. These three formats are especially common in printing applications. **TARGA**, an older format, was originally developed for a video hardware device of the same name.

JPEG (Joint Photographic Experts Group) format is one of the most commonly used formats with adjustable compression: you select the amount of compression of the picture data you want. The more compression, the smaller your picture files, but the greater the risk of losing color information. Another adjustable-compression format is **GIF** (Graphics Interchange Format),which is commonly used for the World Wide Web because of its compression capabilities.

Each of these formats is associated with a standard **file-name extension,** a sequence of letters appended, along with a period, to the end of a file name. You might call a file *test.pict, test.tiff, test.eps, test.tga, test.jpeg,* or *test.gif* depending on which of the above formats you use. Some operating systems prefer three-letter extensions, in which case you would substitute the names *test.pct, test.tif,* and *test.jpg* appropriately for the names above.

Many more picture-file formats than these are in use today, but these are the most common. To accommodate the number and variety of file formats, many 3D animation packages provide translation functions within their menu structures, to allow you to convert from one picture format to another. There are also separate file-conversion programs you can buy for the same purpose.

Another issue that comes up when rendering final frames is the **background** to be used in the rendering. By default, most three-dimensional computer systems render objects against a black background, because RGB values of (0,0,0) yield black. This standard black background gives the familiar floating-in-space look that so many computer images have. Most systems, however, allow you to control the background color, sometimes in very powerful ways.

The simplest way to change the background color from black to something else is through a menu selection that allows you to specify the red, green, and blue components of the color. This RGB combination then becomes the color that shows up on the screen anywhere there is not a rendered object.

Many systems also permit you to define the background as a **ramp** between two colors. A "ramp" in this context means a smooth interpolation from one color to another. Say, for example, you define the color at the bottom of the picture to be black and the color at the top of the picture to be a soft pale blue. The background of this picture will be a smooth transition, from black at the bottom through progressively lighter and bluer tints, finally reaching the soft pale blue at the top.

Most systems also allow you to use a previously existing image as a background. For example, you might take a photograph, scan it into the computer, and specify that this scanned picture is to be used as the background for your rendering. Objects then will be rendered on top of this background picture.

In color plate 9, for instance, only a few objects in the foreground—the couch, the coffee table, the two end tables, and the bottle and glasses on the coffee table—have been modeled in a three-dimensional modeling system. Everything else in the frame is part of the background picture, on top of which the modeled objects were rendered. What makes this image so effective is the precise match between the perspective, colors, and lighting of the modeled objects and those of the background picture. In fact, it is difficult to tell where the background ends and the modeling begins. This kind of matching is very difficult to do, but, as you see, can be very effective when it succeeds.

It is important to understand that a background picture, no matter how three-dimensional it may look, has no three-dimensional information attached to it. The process of rendering against a background picture is, therefore, really quite simple: for each pixel to be rendered, the color of the background picture at the appropriate place is first copied into the pixel. If the rendering program then needs to render some surface at that pixel, the background color is overwritten. If no surface is to be rendered at that pixel, the background color remains untouched. In other words, the background image is an unchanging backdrop on top of which things are rendered.

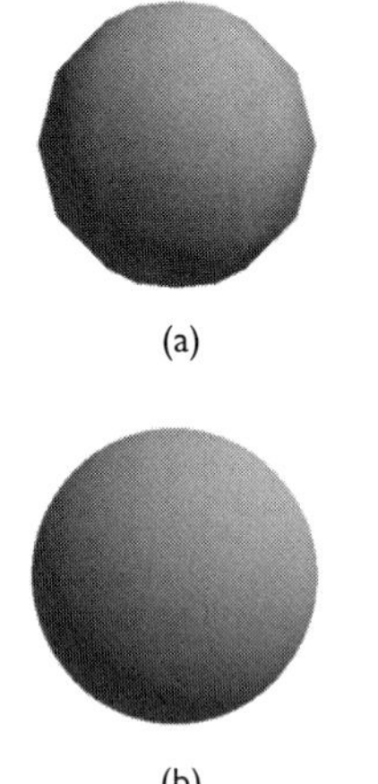

Figure 2-95. When patches are subdivided into polygons before rendering, the number of subdivisions affects the accuracy of the rendering.

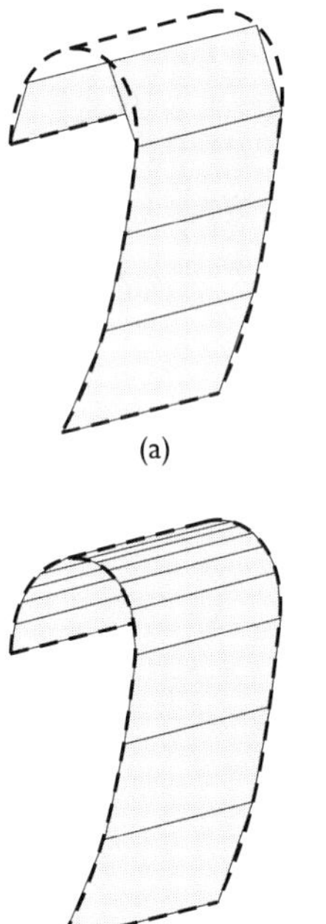

Figure 2-96. Rendering subdivision can be either fixed or adaptive.

You may recall (see *Rendering Algorithms*) that many 3D software packages convert spline-based curved surfaces into polygonal approximations before rendering, and that polygonal approximation grows more accurate as more polygons are used. A cylinder approximated by forty polygons around the sides, for instance, looks much more truly cylindrical than one approximated by eight polygons.

The process of converting curved surfaces to polygonal approximations prior to rendering is known as **polygon subdivision** or sometimes **rendering subdivision**. Most systems allow you to control the number of polygons used to approximate the patches. For testing, you might keep the subdivision level low in order to speed up the rendering. If each surface is approximated by fewer polygons, fewer polygons have to be rendered and the rendering takes less time. Later, when the final frames are about to be rendered, you can increase the subdivision level to improve the accuracy of the polygonal approximation.

Figure 2-95a shows a sphere rendered with a very crude level of polygon subdivision. The flat sides of the polygons are clearly visible at the edges of the sphere. In Figure 2-95b the same sphere is rendered with a much higher level of polygon subdivision. The polygon edges are no longer visible and the sphere looks truly curved. Note that the original patch geometry of both spheres is the same; only the level of rendering subdivision has changed.

The issue of polygon subdivision, however, is not so simple as "more is better." "More," as always, costs more, and the more polygons you use to subdivide a surface, the longer your rendering takes. Consequently, you should increase the level of polygon subdivision only where such an increase is necessary. If your sphere is being viewed from a great distance, you can get away with a very low level of polygon subdivision, since the sphere will be very small and the polygons will be too small to see. If, on the other hand, you move your camera very close to the sphere, even the number of polygons used in Figure 2-95b might no longer be sufficient, and you might have to increase the level of subdivision.

The first and conceptually simplest method of determining the level of polygon subdivision is to specify the total number of polygons along each direction of the patch. For example, you might specify that along the U direction of a given patch the number of polygons is twenty, while along the V direction of the patch the number of polygons is thirty-five. Sometimes you specify these numbers more indirectly, in terms of the number of polygons inserted between each pair of control points on the patch. In either case, you specify the number of polygons as a fixed number in the U direction and a fixed number in the V direction.

Some systems also offer another, more sophisticated way of determining the number of polygons. This approach takes advantage of the fact that some sections of a patch need far fewer polygons than do other sections. In relatively flat areas of a patch, only a few polygons are necessary to produce a good approximation. However, where the curvature of a patch changes abruptly, a lot of polygons are required to make the rendering look smoothly curved. Specifying the minimum and maximum number of polygons to be used in any given region addresses this problem. If the region is relatively flat, the minimum will be used; if the region is relatively curved, the maximum will be used. Because the number of polygons adapts to the curvature of the surface, this technique is called **adaptive subdivision**.

Figure 2-96a shows a patch subdivided into polygons with the nonadaptive method. Notice that the lower portion of the patch, where the curvature is relatively small, is very nicely approximated by only a few large polygons. In the area of greatest curvature, however, at the "crook" of the patch, polygons of the same size—that is, the same level of subdivision—prove insufficient. Because the approximation of the curvature is crude, you can clearly see the flat edges of the polygons in the area of the crook. When the same patch is subdivided with the adaptive method, the flatter areas again are represented by a just a few polygons (Figure 2-96b). At the crook of the patch, however, the number of polygons greatly increases, making the curve look smooth.

When rendering final frames, you also must consider the staircasing effect inherent to computer images. Because any digital image is composed of a grid of tiny rectangular pixels, a curved or slanted edge of an object tends to appear as a stepped pattern (Figure 2-97a). Often called the "jaggies," this effect technically is called **aliasing**, meaning that something appears to be other than it really is. For example, a truly curved line may appear to be a jagged line. Aliasing occurs when the system has too little information available for the phenomenon you want to represent. In this case, the phenomenon is a curved line and the information available is the rectangular grid of the pixels. Because the grid is too coarse, aliasing results.

The technique developed to handle this problem, **anti-aliasing**, consists of selectively blurring certain pixels along the aliased edge of a rendered surface. This blurring technique succeeds, even though the image is still composed of discrete pixels, because the color patterns of the pixels change very gradually, rather than abruptly, and the eye perceives the edges as smooth (Figure 2-97b).

Calculating the blurred pixels of an anti-aliased image requires additional time on the part of a rendering program. Because of this, you usually can turn anti-aliasing on or off. It is common practice, for example, when doing test renderings, to turn anti-aliasing off until you are ready to do the final renderings. In addition, many higher-end systems provide you with parameters for controlling the quality of the anti-aliasing. Some systems also permit you to select from among a variety of different anti-aliasing algorithms of differing qualities. As expected, the higher the quality, the more time required for the rendering.

Temporal aliasing is a problem related to the spatial aliasing just de-

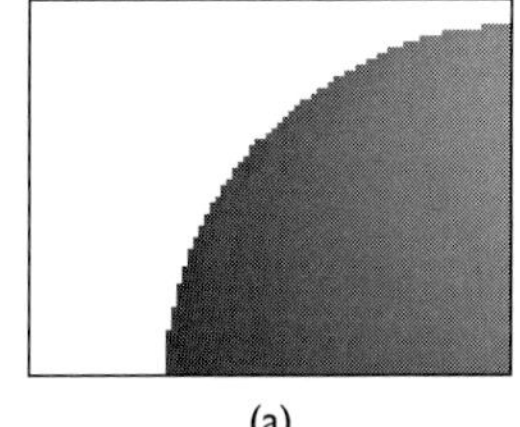

(a)

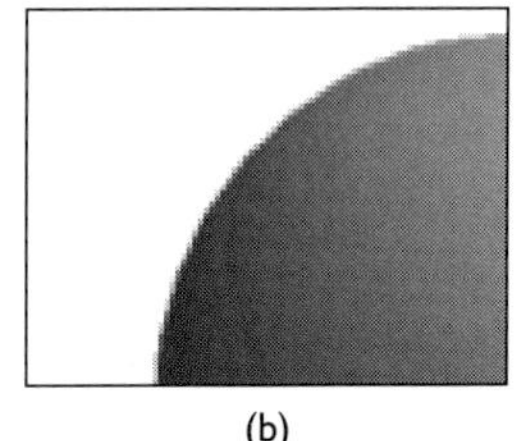

(b)

Figure 2-97. Aliasing, or the "jaggies," can be overcome by activating anti-aliasing calculations in the final rendering.

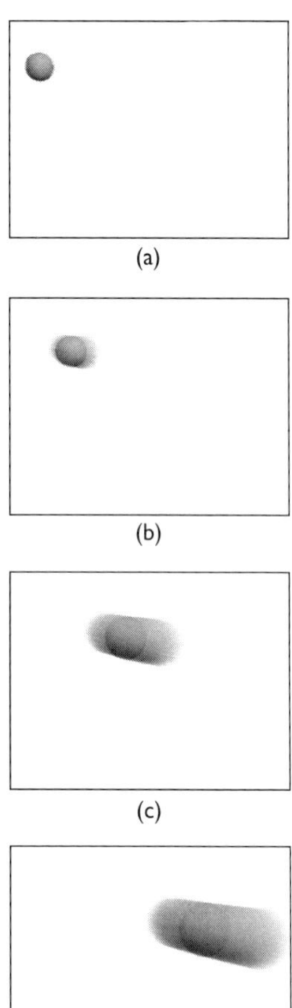

Figure 2-98. Very quickly moving objects may need to be rendered with motion blur to avoid jerkiness. Here the ball begins, in (a), at a standstill. Motion blur increases, from (b) to (c), as the ball begins to move more quickly, then increases further, in (d), when the ball is moving very fast.

scribed. It occurs when objects are moving very quickly. Sometimes the placement of an object within the frame changes drastically from frame to frame, and this produces a jerky effect when you play the animation back. In extreme cases, you see a strobelike effect. This variety of aliasing results from trying to represent the fast movement of an object with frames that are too coarse—that is, with frames rendered at intervals of one-thirtieth of a second.

One of the two ways of handling temporal aliasing takes place at the recording stage and involves a technique for creating and recording frames at smaller time intervals. (This technique and frame rates in general are discussed in *Video*, chapter 6.) The other approach, **motion blur**, is similar to the spatial anti-aliasing of a picture and involves rendering fast-moving objects with a slight blurring or repetition at each frame (Figure 2-98). Like the blurring of spatial anti-aliasing, this causes the eye to fuse the frames so that they appear smooth.

It is interesting to note that motion blur occurs automatically, as a by-product of the process, when shooting live-action film. Since each frame of film is exposed for a specific amount of time, an object moving very quickly during that time appears blurred in the developed frame. In computer graphics, by contrast, objects are frozen in time, producing images without any blur. Because of this, you must take specific steps to turn on motion blur. Usually you can do this through a simple menu selection.

Another factor you need to consider when setting up the rendering process is related specifically to the ray-tracing algorithm. Recall (from *Rendering Algorithms*) that the process of ray tracing involves following a light ray as it bounces from one object to another. The more the light ray bounces, the more physically accurate the shading calculations are. However, as usual, more calculations require more time, so you are in a position of having to balance precision against time. Most systems provide a parameter, often called **ray depth**, that controls how many bounces the rendering program will trace before performing the final color calculations for a given point on the surface. Setting the ray-depth parameter to zero causes the ray tracer to behave like a ray caster, tracing no reflective rays at all. In the interest of time, try to keep the ray-depth number as low as possible while still achieving acceptable visual results.

Some ray-tracing programs break down the ray-depth parameter into several component parameters, to give you more control. For example, one number may be used to limit the number of bounces a reflective ray may take, another number to limit the number of bounces a refractive ray may take, and a third number to limit the number of bounces a shadow-generating ray may take. As in all of these final-frame issues, you must make decisions which balance considerations of quality with considerations of rendering time.

CHAPTER 3

Animation

Introduction

Animation involves the production of a series of still images that, when played back in quick succession (usually on film or video), appear as continuously moving. This illusion is produced by a physiological characteristic of our eyes known as **persistence of vision**. That is, when human eyes are stimulated—for example, by a still image—a slight afterimage is left on the retina of each eye after the stimulus is taken away. As a sequence of still images, or frames, plays back, each eye retains an afterimage of each frame for a brief moment, and this afterimage fills in the minuscule gap between the frame just past and the frame yet to come. As a result, adjacent frames seem to flow together smoothly.

If the time between frames is too long, the afterimage does not persist long enough to fill in the gap between frames, and you see a staccato playback of individual images instead. In film, a playback rate of twenty-four frames per second works well. In video, the standard rate of playback is thirty frames per second. In either case, you must produce a lot of frames. A one-minute animation requires $24 \times 60 = 1{,}440$ frames on film and $30 \times 60 = 1{,}800$ frames on video. A one-hour animation requires 86,400 frames of film or 108,000 frames of video! This quantity is not difficult to produce using a live-action video or film camera: the actors walk around for one minute while the camera rolls, and frames are recorded in real time. If, on the other hand, an animator or team of animators must produce these frames one by one, an enormous amount of work and time can be involved.

In the early days of animation, and in particular at the pioneering Walt Disney Studios, a technique was developed to produce animation frames more efficiently. First a master animator would draw the most important, or "key," frames (called **keyframes**) of an animation sequence (Figure 3-1a and 3-1d). Then a number of less experienced animators would draw the **in-betweens**, or frames that fell between the master animator's keyframes (Figure 3-1b and 3-1c).

Almost all 3D computer graphics animation systems are based on this **keyframing** approach. In a computer keyframe animation system, the animator is the equivalent of the master animator. The animator sets up the keyframes, then instructs the computer to calculate the in-between frames. The computer, in other words, serves as an assistant to the human (master) animator.

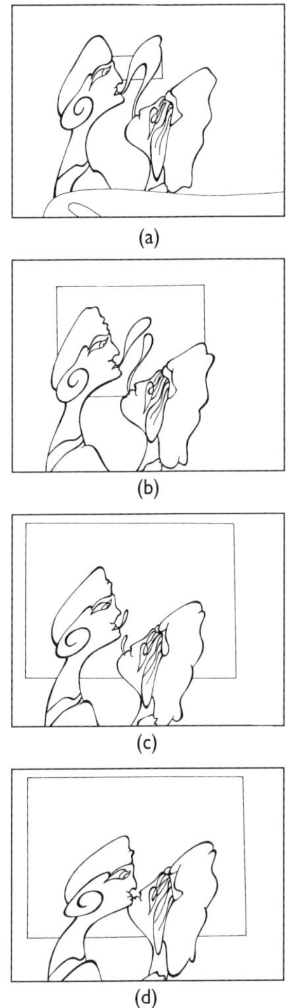

Figure 3-1. Some keyframes and in-between frames from a hand-drawn animation. Notice how the action changes gradually from one frame to the next. (*Dissipative Dialogues*, © 1982 David Ehrlich.)

Keyframing Simple Transformations

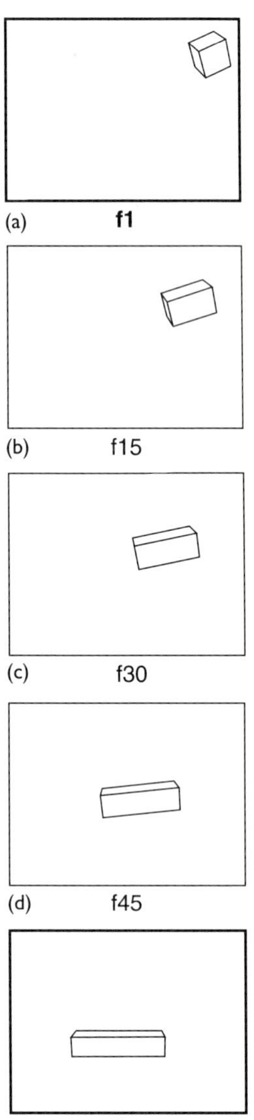

Figure 3-2. A sequence of computer-generated frames. Frames 1 and 60, outlined in bold, are keyframes explicitly defined by the animator. The other, in-between frames were automatically calculated by the computer.

You have already seen (in chapter 1, *Transformations*) that when a three-dimensional object is modeled digitally, a set of transformations, called a transformation matrix, is associated with it. Each transformation matrix consists of values for the nine basic transformations—*translation (x,y,z)*, *rotation (x,y,z)*, and *scale (x,y,z)*. The nine values of the transformation matrix control the overall placement, rotation, and size of the object. The simplest kind of keyframed animation involves changing the values of this transformation matrix over a period of time.

Imagine that you have modeled a cube, then positioned this cube by translating, rotating, and scaling it in some fashion (Figure 3-2a). With the cube transformed in some way that you like, you save this information as your first keyframe, keyframe 1. Saving the keyframe means that you save the values of the nine transformation parameters that define the configuration of the cube.

Having defined keyframe 1, you then reposition the cube—that is, translate, rotate, and scale it—as you want it to be for your next keyframe. Assume that you are making a two-second animation in video and that you want your next keyframe to be the final frame of the animation, frame 60. With the cube in that final position you save the transformations, and this becomes keyframe 60 (Figure 3-2e).

Once you have defined the keyframes for the sequence, you instruct the computer to calculate the in-between frames that should come between keyframe 1 and keyframe 60. The computer then calculates, for frames 2 through 59, the intermediate values for each of the nine transformation parameters. Calculating intermediate values is also called **interpolating** the values. These interpolated transformation values determine the intermediate placement, rotation, and size of the object at each in-between frame. For example, if the *translation x* of the cube is 6.0 at keyframe 1 and 0.0 at keyframe 60, then the interpolated value for the *translation x* of the cube at frame 30 (that is, halfway between frame 1 and frame 60) is 3.0.

In short, to say that the computer calculates an in-between frame means that it calculates the in-between, or interpolated, values of the nine transformation parameters for the object at that frame. When it does this for all of the in-between frames, you end up with a new set of nine transformation values in the transformation matrix of the object at each frame. With these transformation values the computer displays what the object looks like in each frame (Figures 3-2b, c, and d, for example).

Once keyframes have been defined and in-betweens calculated, you normally want to view the animation to evaluate it. In order to do this, you need to see more than just isolated still frames. That is, you need to play back the frames as continuous motion. All computer animation systems provide this capability, called a **motion preview**, in one way or another. More sophisticated systems display higher-quality images as the motion plays back and offer more controls over the playback than do less sophisticated systems.

Upon seeing the motion preview, you may decide to change the animation. For example, you might decide that at frame 60 the cube should be flatter. You then retransform the cube, scaling it flatter, and save this as a new keyframe 60, overwriting the old keyframe 60. Having redefined keyframe 60, you instruct the computer to calculate new in-betweens and to play back the newly calculated animation. By setting and resetting keyframes, recalculating the in-betweens, and looking at motion previews, you can refine an animation until you are satisfied with the movement.

In actual practice, of course, most animations are much more complex than the simple example used here. It is very common for an animation sequence to be several hundred frames long and to involve dozens of keyframes for each of many objects. The basic principles remain the same, however, regardless of complexity.

Interpolations

A keyframe-based software system creates the in-between frames of an animation by interpolating the transformation values from one keyframe to the next. The simplest kind of interpolation, **linear interpolation**, gets its name from the fact that if you draw a graph of the relationship between the two parameters (in this case, between frame numbers and transformation values), you get a straight line (Figure 3-3). In interpolating, say, from frame 1 to frame 60, frame 30, which is halfway between frames 1 and 60, receives transformation values that are half of the difference between the values at frame 1 and the values at frame 60. At frame 15, which is one-fourth of the way between frame 1 and frame 60, the transformation values are one-fourth of the difference between the values at frame 1 and the values at frame 60. The rate at which the value is changing stays the same over the length of the entire interpolation. Thus, if the *translation x*, or *TX*, value changes by –1.0—from 6.0 to 5.0—in the first ten frames of an animation, then *TX* also changes by –1.0 between frames 10 and 20, as it does between every set of ten frames.

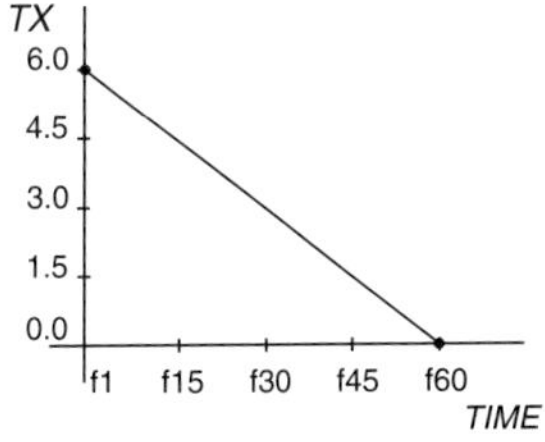

Figure 3-3. A linear interpolation of values between two keyframes.

If you imagine, however, having more than two keyframes in an animation, you can see the need for other kinds of interpolation. Suppose you want to extend your animation. The cube translates in X from 6.0 to 0.0 over the

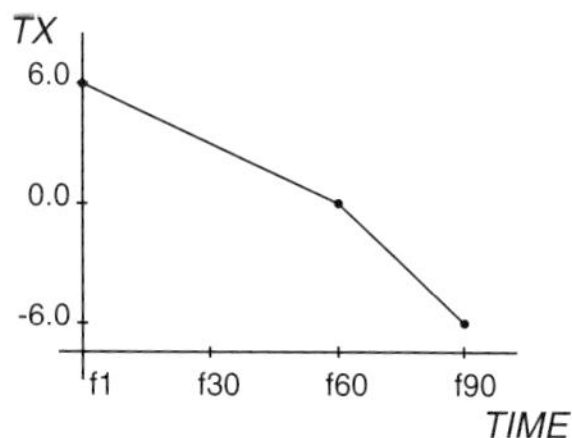

Figure 3-4. If there are more than two keyframes, a linear interpolation can result in an abrupt rate of change between keyframes.

first sixty frames, but you need to create a third keyframe at frame 90, where the *translation x* value will be –6.0.

A linear interpolation on the *translate x* parameter for this new animation shows that a potential problem lies in what happens at frame 60 (Figure 3-4). The graph shows that at frame 60, the rate at which the cube is translating abruptly changes. The rate of change is represented by the slope of the line, so that the steeper the line, the faster the change; the flatter the line, the slower the change. In this animation the cube moves smoothly and rather slowly from frame 0 to frame 60, but then at frame 60 it suddenly begins to move much faster. This may, in fact, be the movement you want to depict, but more likely, given the way things move in the real world, you want the cube to move smoothly through various positions, without any abrupt change in speed.

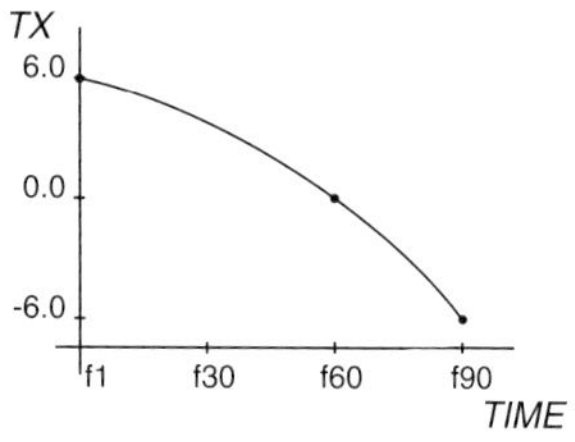

Figure 3-5. A spline interpolation through the keyframe values results in a smooth, continuous curve.

If you remember the discussions on curves and splines (see chapter 1, *Splines and Patches*), you can imagine the answer to this problem. The points on these interpolation graphs are effectively control points that determine the shape of a curve: in this example the "curve" consists of two straight lines connecting three control points. If you ask the computer to calculate a curve through these control points as a spline interpolation (in this case, an interpolating spline) rather than as a linear interpolation, you get the smooth curvature—the smooth change in *TX*—that you are looking for (Figure 3-5). Notice that there is no longer a sharp angle, or discontinuity, in the curve at frame 60. This means that there is no abrupt, or discontinuous, change in the rate at which *TX* is changing, so the cube translates smoothly from one point to another over the entire length of the ninety-frame animation.

The interpolating spline is not the only way to get a smooth interpolation through a series of values. Figure 3-6 shows another set of keyframe control points—here, for the translation in Y of some object—and the different interpolations that result when four different types of spline—linear, Cardinal, B-spline, and Bézier—are applied to those control points. Each of these interpolations produces a slightly different animation, even though all four have as initial data the same three keyframe values. Most 3D computer-animation systems provide at least several of these types of interpolation.

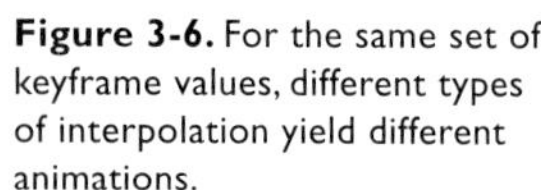

Figure 3-6. For the same set of keyframe values, different types of interpolation yield different animations.

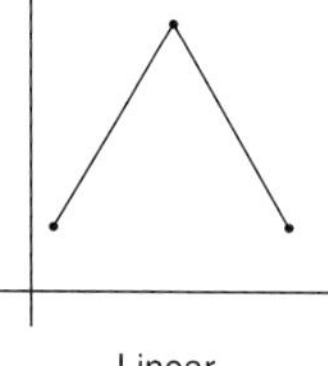

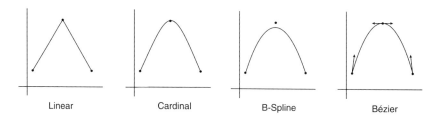

Linear

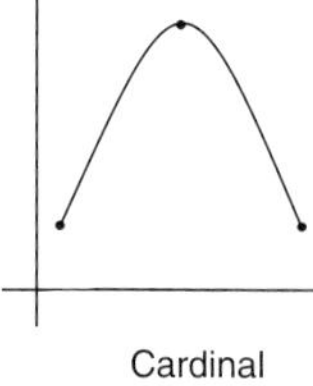

Cardinal

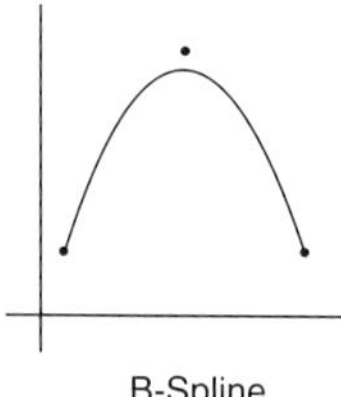

B-Spline

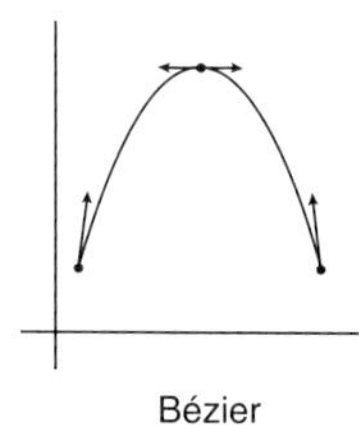

Bézier

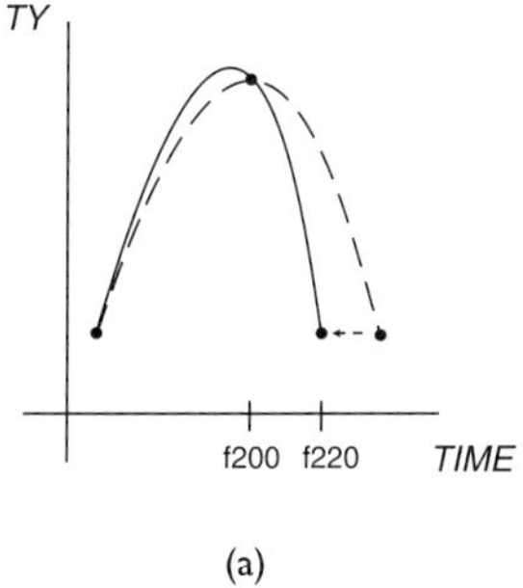

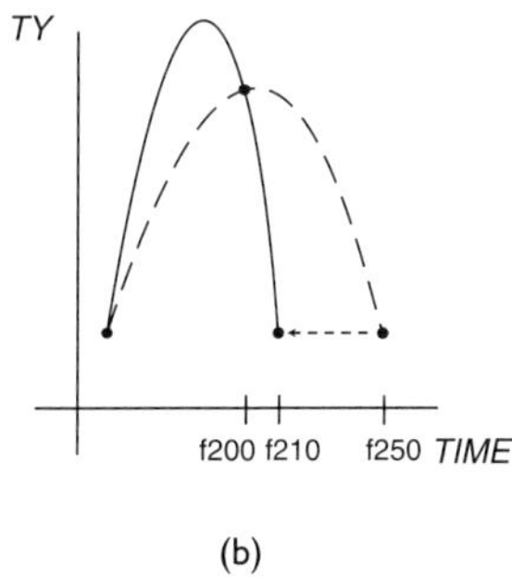

Figure 3-7. Spline interpolations can result in overshooting the intended values of a keyframe.

Now suppose that you modify the interpolation curve by moving the third keyframe closer in time to the second (Figure 3-7a). A problem occurs in the frames just before frame 200, the second keyframe. The spline interpolation must bend the curve upward above the value of the second keyframe so that when the curve comes down through the second control point (frame 200), the slope allows the curve to pass smoothly through the third control point (frame 220).

In a situation like this, you normally want the value at frame 200 to be the largest *TY* value that the object attains. The spline interpolation, however, forces the *TY* value to go higher, in the frames just before frame 200, than you probably intend. Suppose, for example, that the *TY* value represents the height of the ceiling in a room and your intention is to make the object rise until it touches the ceiling. The spline interpolation here unfortunately would cause the object to go through the ceiling in the frames preceding frame 200.

Notice also that this unexpected result is made even more extreme the closer the third keyframe is moved in time toward the second. If the last keyframe is advanced to frame 210 (Figure 3-7b), the curve has to bend up even more in order to come down smoothly through both frame 200 and frame 210.

This **overshooting** of keyframe values is a result of the requirement, built into the definition of a spline curve, that the curve always remain smooth, or **continuous**. Although the requirement of continuity is one of the great strengths of splines, in this instance it creates an unwanted side-effect, which you can adjust for by using a number of techniques discussed in the next section.

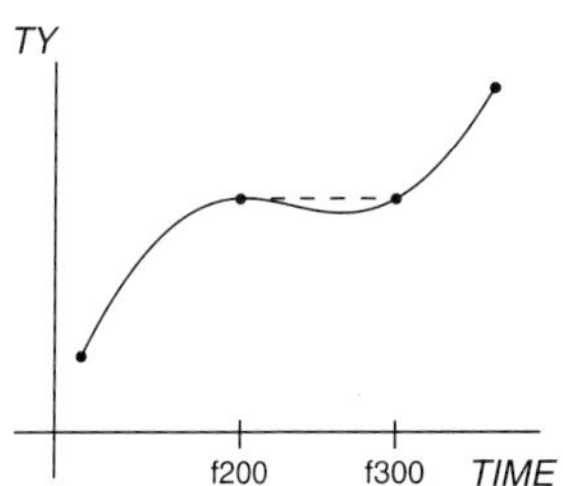

Figure 3-8. Spline interpolations by default produce a smooth curve, even if you intend a flat line.

Now suppose that you want an object to remain motionless across a certain range of frames. The normal way to do this is to give the object the same transformation value at the beginning of the range and at the end of the range. In Figure 3-8, for example, four keyframes have been defined. Two of these keyframes, frame 200 and frame 300, have the same *TY* value. If this *TY* value remains unchanged between these keyframes, the curve should be flat in that section, as indicated by the dotted line. Notice, however, that instead of the

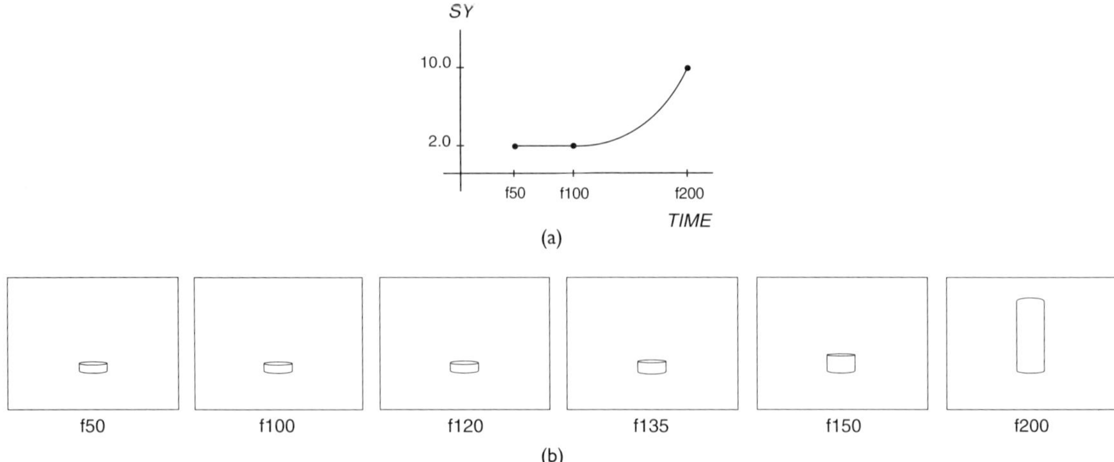

Figure 3-9. In some animations, you want an interpolation to yield a very gradual change in the interpolated value.

curve remaining flat, it bends. This, again, is because the obligatory continuity of the spline causes the curve to bend up above the *TY* value at frame 200, then come down below it and curve gently upwards toward frame 300 again. Techniques for handling this situation appear in the next section.

In addition to linear and spline interpolations, other interpolations—along with the distinct terminology attached to them—are commonly used. These interpolations are called **eases**.

In animation you often want some change to begin slowly and then increase in speed. Suppose, for example, that you want a cylinder, at first not changing at all, to increase in height (scale in Y). Usually you want the transition from no movement to some movement—that is, the curve—to be gradual and smooth, rather than abrupt (Figure 3-9).

Between frame 50 and frame 100, the flat line indicates no change in the *SY* value. That is, the height of the cylinder remains the same. At frame 100, the curve very, very gradually begins to slope upward, and in the animation you see an almost imperceptible change in the height of the cylinder in the first few frames after frame 100 (Figure 3-9b). Farther from frame 100 the curve begins to rise more sharply, meaning that the height of the cylinder is increasing more rapidly. By frame 200, the *SY* value of the cylinder is increasing, and the cylinder growing taller, quite rapidly.

The interpolation between frames 100 and 200 is called an **ease-out**, or a **slow-out**, because the value changes slowly as it comes out of frame 100 and then more and more quickly as it approaches frame 200 (Figure 3-10). The opposite of an ease-out is an **ease-in**, or a **slow-in**, in which the value changes more and more slowly as it comes into the second keyframe.

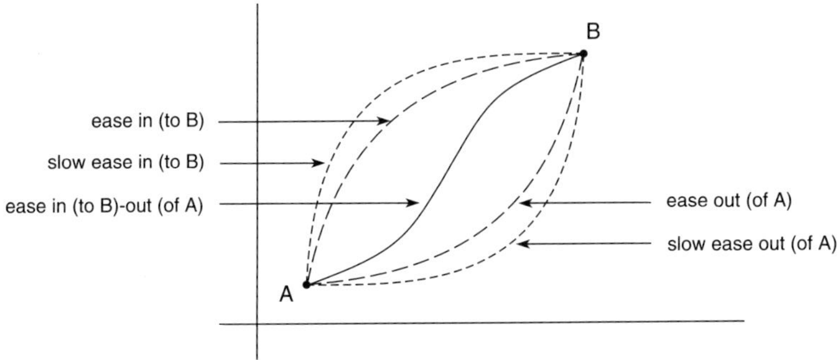

Figure 3-10. Different types of "ease" interpolations.

Combining an ease-in and an ease-out produces an interpolation called an **ease-in-out**, in which the value changes slowly at first, then more quickly, and then slowly again.

Some systems, in addition to these three basic eases, also provide what might be called a **very slow-in**, sometimes called a **slow ease-in.** The opposite is a **very slow-out**, or a **slow ease-out.** These interpolations are just exaggerated versions of the normal ease-in and ease-out.

A simple animation can illustrate all of the different types of interpolations discussed in this section (Figure 3-11). As you see in the storyboard, the animation begins with a cube sliding in from screen left to screen right. The cube is rotating all the while. This action continues for sixty frames, until the cube reaches the right side of the screen. The cube then slides back, over the course of thirty more frames, to the center of the screen, where it stops but continues to rotate. After it stops at center screen, the cube increases in size, slowly at first, then a little faster, and then slowly again, until it reaches full size at frame 150. All this while, it is still rotating around a vertical axis. At frame 150, when it reaches full height, however, all movement, including the rotation, stops and the cube just sits there for a few seconds until frame 200.

In a graphical illustration of the way each of the nine transformation values for the cube animates over time, each transformation parameter is illustrated as a separate graph (Figure 3-12). Notice first that curves representing the translation in Y, *TY*, the translation in Z, *TZ*, the rotation in X, *RX*, and the rotation in Z, *RZ*, are simply flat lines. This means that the transformation values of those parameters do not change at all throughout the entire animation.

The *TX* curve, on the other hand, has a Cardinal-spline interpolation going through keyframes 1, 60, and 90, causing the cube to start at a low *TX* value (that is, at screen left), increase the *TX* value (move to the right) up to frame 60, and then come back again until *TX* = 0.0, placing the cube at the center of the screen. After frame 90, the cube doesn't translate in X at all, so the curve is flat.

Now notice that the *RY*, rotation in Y, value has a linear interpolation from frame 1 through frame 150, meaning that the cube is rotating at a constant

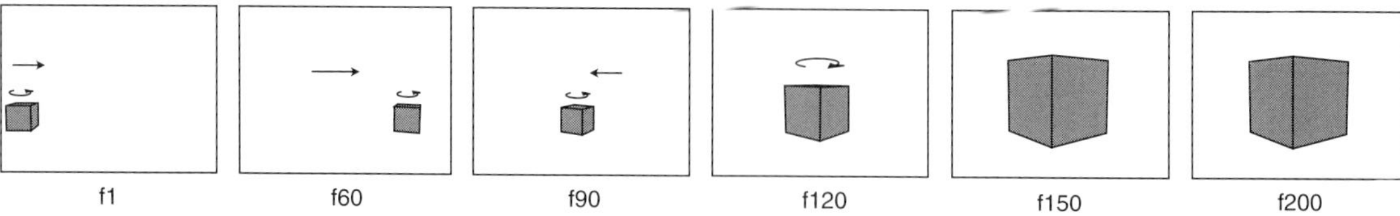

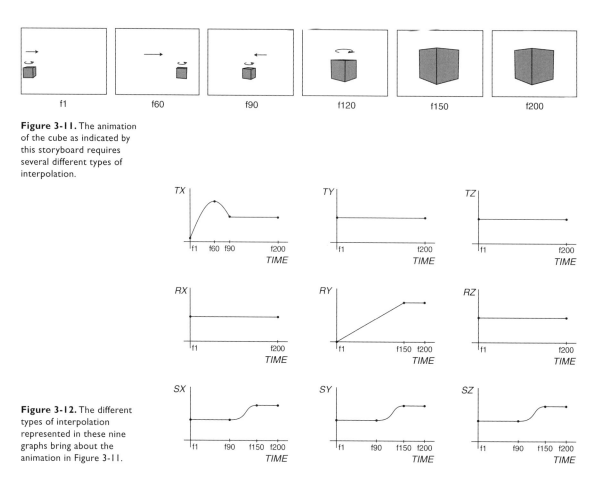

Figure 3-11. The animation of the cube as indicated by this storyboard requires several different types of interpolation.

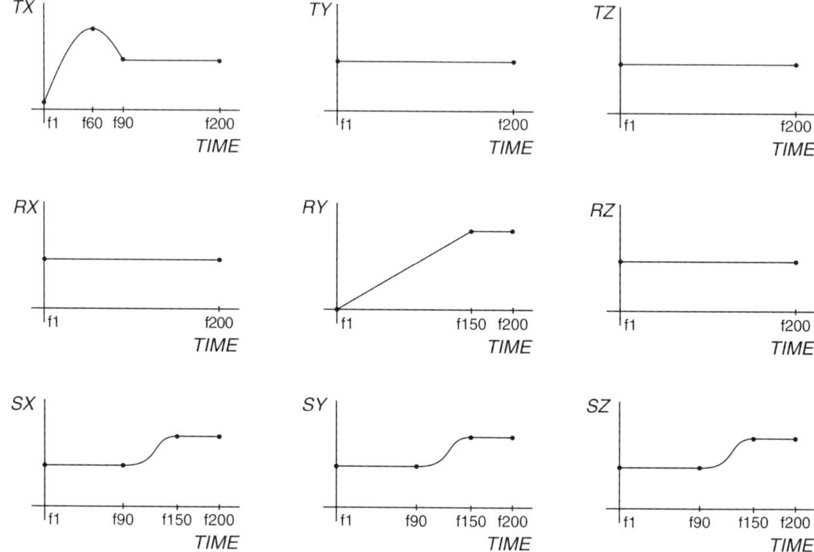

Figure 3-12. The different types of interpolation represented in these nine graphs bring about the animation in Figure 3-11.

speed all that time. At frame 150, which is where the cube reaches full size, the rotation stops, so the *RY* curve becomes a flat line.

The scale curves for this animation are all identical, since the cube increases in size equally in all three axes. From frame 1 to frame 90, the cube doesn't change size at all, so all three curves are flat. From frame 90 to frame 150, all three scale parameters have an ease-in-out interpolation, which is what causes the cube to grow in size—first slowly, then more rapidly, and then slowly again. From frame 150 to frame 200, the size of the cube does not change, so all three scale curves become flat lines again.

Parameter-curve Editing

Remember that in a keyframe-based animation system the most common way to define the movement and timing of an object is to transform the object until it looks right visually, and then to save each set of transformations as a keyframe. There is, however, another very common and very powerful

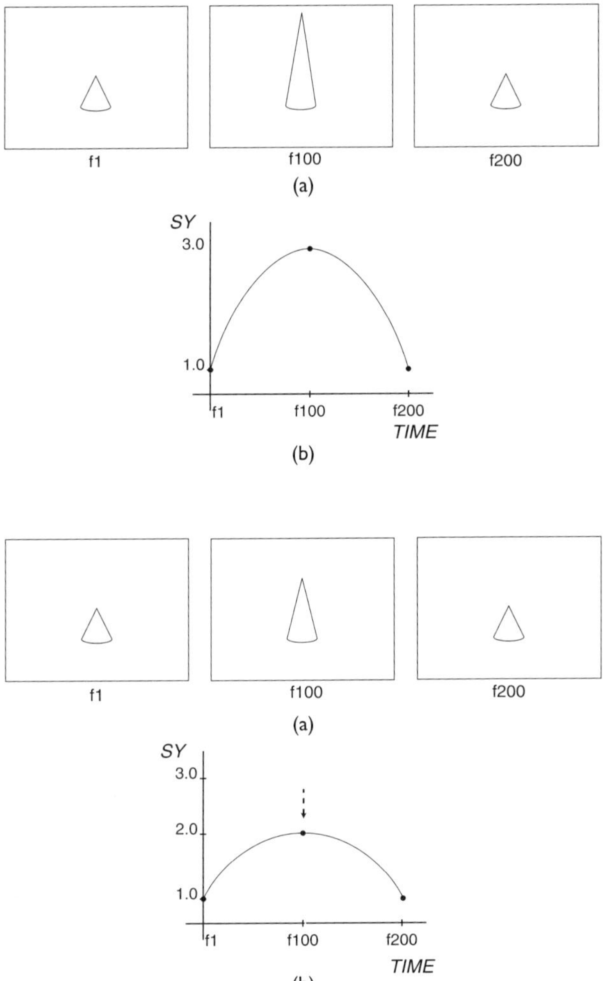

Figure 3-13. The graph of the animation of an object directly corresponds to the actual animation of the object.

Figure 3-14. By pulling a keyframe control point down along the vertical axis, you change the value of the parameter—in this case, the height of the cone.

approach to defining the movement and timing of an animation. You saw in the previous section that it is possible to represent the changes in a given transformation parameter as a graph, with the changes in the value of a parameter plotted against time. The alternate approach to defining animation takes advantage of this sort of graphical representation.

The underlying concept of this graphical approach is that any change made to the graph of some parameter causes a corresponding change in the animation. The graph, in other words, is a direct and immediate representation of the animation. If you change the graph, then you change the animation. Many 3D software packages allow you to modify, or edit, these parameter graphs and thereby to directly redefine, or edit, the animation itself.

Imagine that the height (that is, the scale in Y) of a cone increases and then decreases (Figure 3-13a; Figure 3-13b is the corresponding graph of the *SY* parameter). Using a system that allows parameter-graph editing, you can

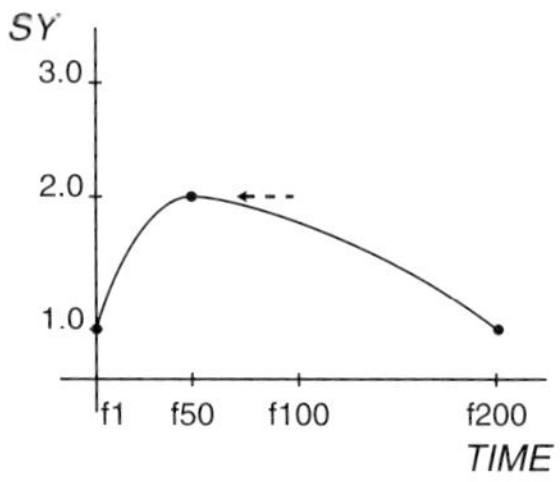

Figure 3-15. Moving a keyframe control point horizontally alters the timing of an action.

select the control point that represents keyframe 100 and pull it up or down to change the value of the *SY* parameter. Doing so immediately changes the height of the cone at frame 100. Pulling the control point at frame 100 down (Figure 3-14b), for example, lowers the height of the cone (Figure 3-14a).

It is also possible to push or pull a control point horizontally in the direction of time. For example, if you select and drag the control point at frame 100 to the left, leaving the point at frame 50, the height that the cone attains does not change (Figure 3-15). However, the timing of the animation changes, so that the cone achieves maximum height in only 50 frames, instead of the 100 frames it originally took—in other words, twice as fast as in the original animation. Moreover, the cone reverts to the lower height more slowly, in 150 frames instead of 100 frames.

In parameter-curve editing systems of this sort, it normally is possible to edit a curve in all the same ways that you might edit a curve for modeling purposes. For example, you might insert new control points into the curve, thereby changing the shape of the curve—as well as the animation controlled by the graph. To continue with the example of the cone, adding a new control point at frame 170 radically changes the animation, causing the cone to collapse almost to a flat circle at frame 170, where its *SY* value has been set to 0.1, before it returns to the original size at frame 200 (Figure 3-16).

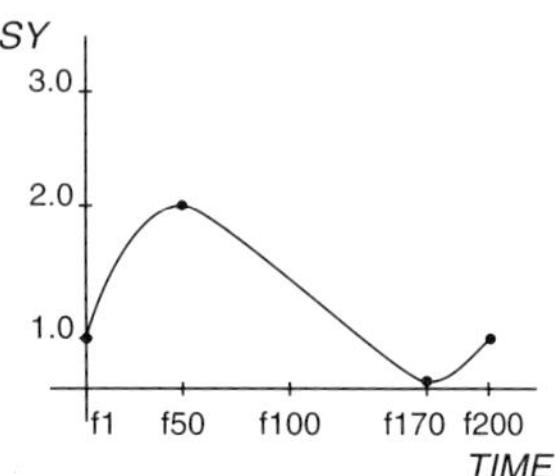

Figure 3-16. Additional control points can be inserted into a parameter curve to alter the shape of that curve and the animation it represents.

In chapter 1, *Splines and Patches*, you saw that some curve representations allow you to manipulate the tangent vectors of each control point in order to edit the shape of the curve. This technique usually is possible in parameter-curve editing systems as well. Editing the tangent vectors in this way changes the curvature, or slope, of the curve in the area of each control point.

For example, editing the tangent vectors of the control point at frame 50 of the previous example yields a new curve (Figure 3-17). The tangent vector of the control point at frame 50 has been adjusted so that the curve is flat in the frames immediately following frame 50. This change causes the cone to linger near the maximum height for a longer time after frame 50 before beginning to shrink.

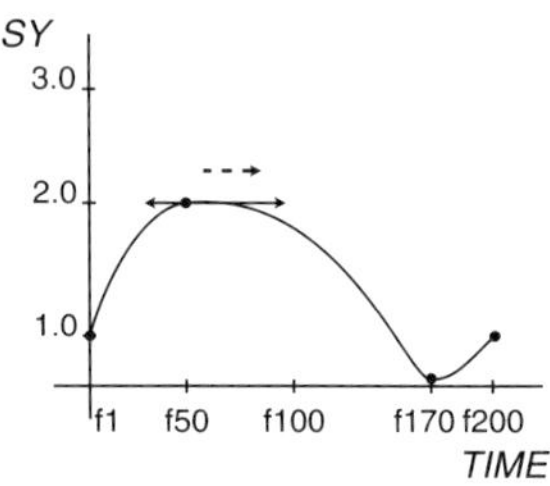

Figure 3-17. Adjusting the tangent vector of a control point changes the slope of the curve near that point. A change in the slope of the curve causes the changes in the action of the animation to happen more or less quickly.

Most systems also allow you to select the type of interpolation used between any two control points. Any combination of interpolation types may be used between frames. For example, between one pair of control points the interpolation might be a B-spline. Between another pair of control points the interpolation might be linear. This technique is particularly useful when you want an element of your animation to change for a certain amount of time, but then to remain unchanging for another period of time.

For example, suppose you want to modify the previous animation so that the cone returns to its lower height (with an *SY* value of 1.0) at frame 170, then remains unchanging until frame 200. First, you move the control point at frame 170 up to give it a value of 1.0 (Figure 3-18a). Notice, however, that the *SY* value does not remain absolutely constant between frames 170 and 200. As you saw in the previous section, the mathematics of spline interpolation (in this case, an interpolating Cardinal spline) always produces a smooth curvature from control point to control point. As a consequence, the curve is forced to dip below the value of 1.0 between frames 170 and 200 before returning smoothly to exactly 1.0 again at frame 200. In the animation corresponding to this curve, the cone returns to the lower height at frame 170, but then continues to decrease in height for a few frames, before finally growing to the original size at frame 200.

In order to correct this dip, you can change the interpolation between frames 170 and 200 to a linear interpolation (Figure 3-18b). This change produces the flat line—and constant *SY* value—that you need in order to keep the size of the cone constant during these frames.

It is very common to discover, during playback, that an animation or section of animation is too fast or too slow. Most systems provide you with some ready way to lengthen or shorten a sequence of animation, effectively changing the timing to make an action slower or faster. This editing capability usually is called **scaling the animation**.

One way to scale the animation is through a menu window, into which you type information such as the starting frame number of the sequence you want to scale, the ending frame number, and a scale factor. If the scale factor is two, for example, the sequence becomes twice as long—that is, twice as slow. This method allows you easily to scale an entire animation sequence, no matter how complex the sequence is or how many objects are in it.

A second approach entails using the parameter-curve editor to select a range of control points and stretch them out relative to some fixed control point. The fixed control point in this case effectively serves as the local origin about which the scaling operation is performed. In Figure 3-19a, for example, you see the original parameter curve. In Figure 3-19b the section of the curve defined by the last three control points has been scaled by 50 percent along the *TIME* axis. The fixed control point is the first of these—that is, the third from the right end.

This method of scaling an animation allows you more control over the scaling operation. Rather than performing a global scale on all the parameters of an object, you can scale specific parameters. If, for example, the whole animation sequence is fine, but the rotation of the cone around Y is too slow, you can scale just the *RY* parameter curve, without affecting the timing of any of the other parameters or any of the other objects. You also can control the scaling over a specific range of keyframes.

In addition to the operations described here, many systems allow you to cut and paste sections of parameter curves, to copy the curves of one object

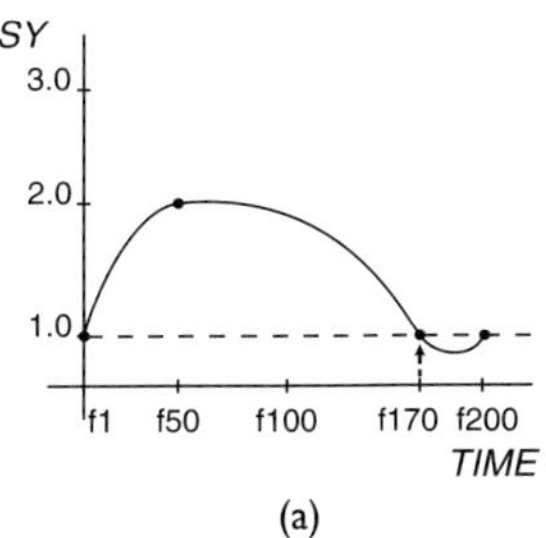

(a)

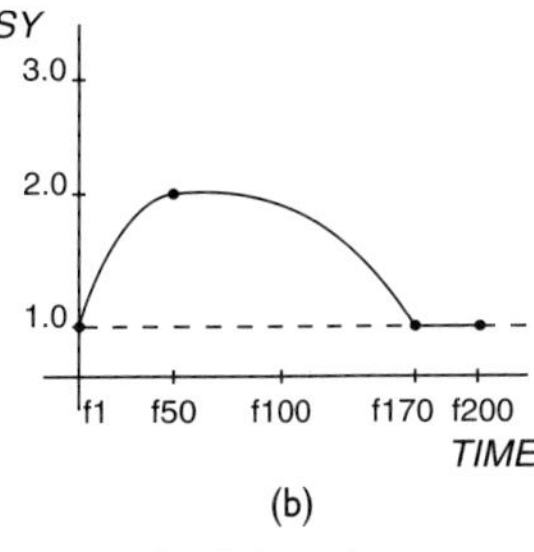

(b)

Figure 3-18. In order to cause an object to remain stationary between two control points, you can apply a linear interpolation to that portion of the curve.

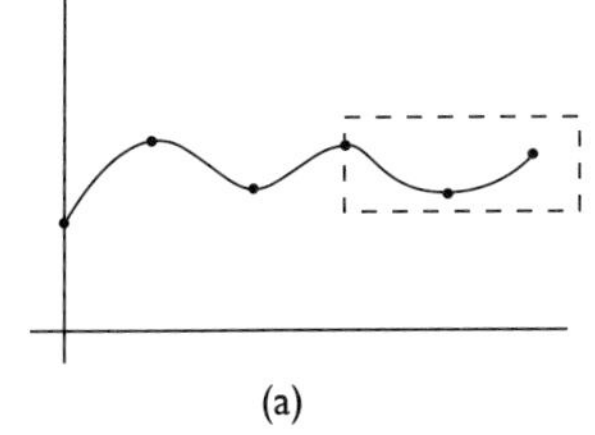

(a)

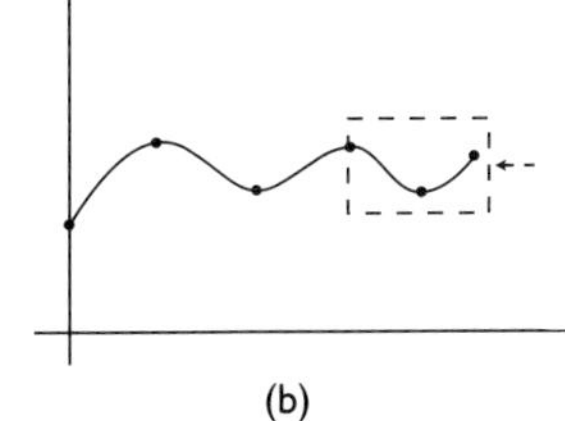

(b)

Figure 3-19. Curves, or sections of curves, can be scaled in time to slow down or speed up an action.

to another, to shift an entire curve up or down or left or right, and so on. Although the correspondence between the action of an animation and the graphic representation of that animation as a parameter curve may not be apparent to you in the beginning, with practice the correspondence becomes intuitive, and you will be able to use the power of parameter-curve editing to great advantage.

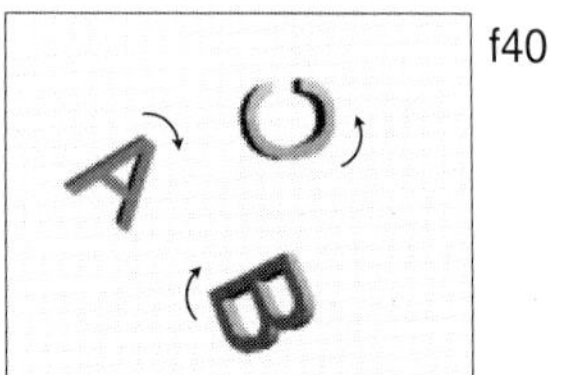

Figure 3-20. A storyboard of a simple animation that requires the use of hierarchical animation.

Hierarchical Animation

So far, you have seen examples of the animation of simple objects, such as a cube, a cone, or a cylinder. You have seen how each of the nine parameters in the transformation matrix of an object can be set and interpolated, and how the interpolation of the transformation values over time produces the animation of the object.

As you saw in *Hierarchies*, in chapter 1, however, many models are more complex than a simple one-piece object. Many models consist of several parts, which you need to organize into a hierarchical structure in order to gain more control over the transformations you apply to different elements of the model.

Animating a hierarchically organized model is conceptually just an extension of the technique of animating a simple one-piece model. What you do for the simple model in order to set keyframes and interpolate transformations you now do for *each node* of the hierarchical model. That is, for each node you position the model and set a keyframe, then reposition the model and set a new keyframe. You then tell the system to create interpolated in-between frames for that node.

For example, imagine an animation of a simple logo (illustrated in storyboard form in Figure 3-20). The animation begins with the letters coming from behind the viewer and tumbling forward, as you see in panels 1 through 3. When the letters reach center frame, they stop (panel 4, frame 90) and then, as a unit, spin quickly around the horizontal X axis (panel 5), coming to a stop again in panel 6, frame 210.

In order to create this animation, you must structure the elements of the model (Figure 3-21a) in an effective hierarchy (Figure 3-21b). Notice that the hierarchy is structured in such a way that you can either transform the entire logo by selecting the *Logo* node or individually transform any of the letters by selecting one of the lower-level nodes.

For the purposes of this animation you also must think carefully about the placement of the local origin of each node in the hierarchy. In order to get the tumbling effect of the individual letters, the local origin of each letter (one of the small crosses in Figure 3-21a) should be placed in the center of that letter. You also must place the local origin (the large cross) of the upper-level node, *Logo*. The local origin of this node controls the spinning rotation of the entire logo at the end of the animation. The most effective placement of this local origin is at the center-bottom of the whole structure.

Once you have structured your model properly, you define the animation. You probably begin by translating the entire logo—that is, the *Logo* node—to the initial position behind the viewer. You then save a keyframe for this node at frame 1. After that you translate the entire *Logo* node forward to the final position, panel 4, and save that transformation as frame 90. This series of steps defines the initial translation of the whole logo.

So far, however, the letters have not tumbled. You can go back to frame 1, rotate each of the three individual letters to the appropriate starting rotation value, and save this transformation as keyframe 1 for that individual node. You then view frame 90, which is where the tumbling of the letters ceases, and define—again, individually for each of the letter nodes—the appropriate final rotation value.

At this point, you have defined animation both for the *Logo* node and, separately, for each of the letter nodes, from frame 1 through frame 90. If you play back the animation now, you see the logo come forward, the letters tumbling as it does. This action continues for 90 frames, at which point both the forward movement of the logo and the tumbling of the individual letters stop.

Remember that *each* of the nodes must be positioned individually and that the position of each node must be saved as a keyframe. Some software systems provide a function that allows you with a single menu selection to save a given keyframe for all the nodes of a hierarchy. Many systems, however, require a separate "save keyframe" operation for each of the nodes. In either case, you must position the nodes individually.

The remainder of the animation entails a spinning movement of the entire logo so no additional keyframes need be set for the individual letters. You can create the spinning of the logo—the quick rotation about X called for by the storyboard—by selecting the *Logo* node and saving keyframes at the appropriate frame numbers. This is easy to accomplish, since you defined the pivot point of *Logo* at the bottom-center of the logo structure. Notice also that, because any transformation on a parent node propagates downward to the children nodes, the rotation you apply to *Logo* causes all of the individual letters to rotate with it as a unit.

In order to understand clearly what is happening when a hierarchical model is animated as described above, remember the concept of a local coordinate system (see the sections *Transformations* and *Hierarchies* in chapter 1). Remember that each node in a hierarchy represents a distinct transformation matrix, which functions relative to an individual local coordinate system. In

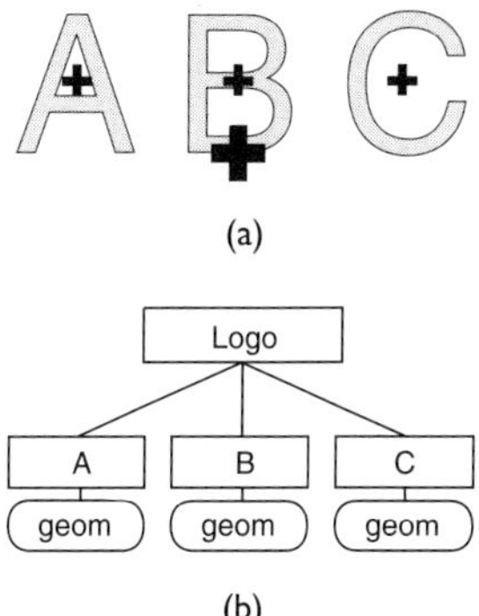

Figure 3-21. The hierarchy of the model is structured to allow the movements called for by the storyboard.

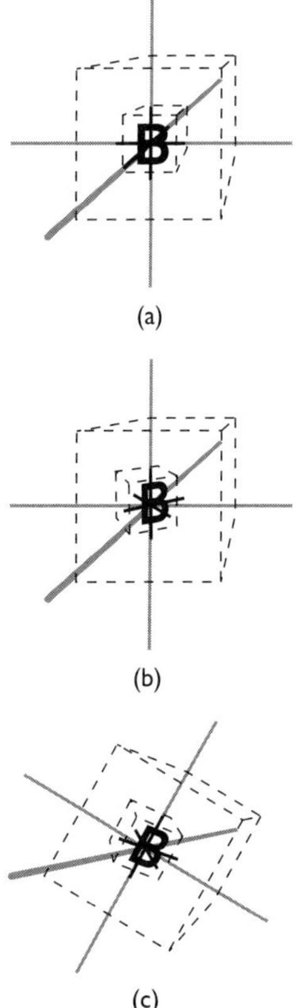

Figure 3-22. Each node of a hierarchy functions within an individual local coordinate system.

other words, each node of a hierarchy has a local coordinate system, and the transformations applied to that node are calculated relative to the local coordinate system.

Think of the local coordinate system of a child node as being contained within the local coordinate system of the parent node, like a box within a box. Figure 3-22 shows how, in the logo model discussed above, the local coordinate system of the *B* model fits within the local coordinate system of the *Logo* model. Each local coordinate system here is represented as a cube drawn with dotted lines. The larger dotted-line cube represents the local coordinate system of the whole *Logo* node.

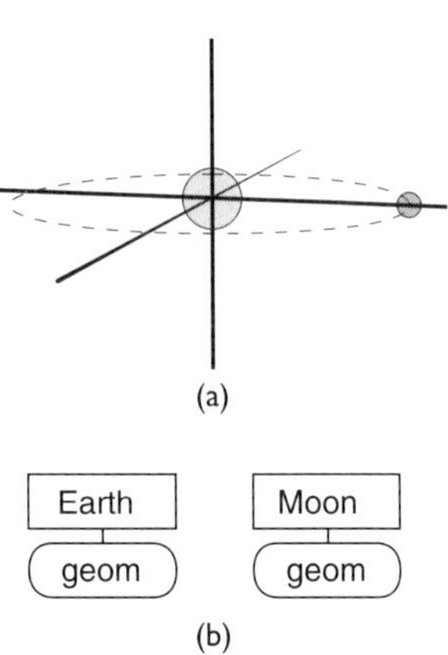

Figure 3-23. Animating the moon in a path that lies in the XZ plane does not require any hierarchical structure.

In Figure 3-22a the *B* and *Logo* models are untransformed. In Figure 3-22b the *B* has been rotated within its own local coordinate system. This rotation has no effect on the *Logo* coordinate system, since *B* is a child of *Logo*, not a parent, and transformations are transmitted only from parent to child. For a real-world analogy to this situation, think of rotating a shoebox within the larger box of your house. The rotation of the shoebox does not cause any other objects in the room to rotate, nor does it cause the house to rotate.

In Figure 3-22c the *Logo* node of the hierarchy has rotated, as represented by the rotation of the large dotted-line cube. Since this node is a parent of the *B* node, the *Logo* rotation causes the *B* to rotate along with it. To resume the shoebox analogy: rotating the house (the house movers have arrived?) causes all of the objects within the house, including the shoebox, to rotate. This concept of the transformations of local coordinate systems and the embedding of local coordinate systems within one another allows us to deal very easily with an animation problem that otherwise would be very difficult to resolve.

Suppose you want to animate a moon rotating in a circular path around the Earth (Figure 3-23a). Notice that the path of the moon lies conveniently in the XZ plane. This allows you to place the local origin of *Moon* at the center of the earth model and then rotate *Moon* around Y. A rotation around Y of 360 degrees causes *Moon* to rotate one complete orbit around the Earth. Notice, in the diagram of the structure of this scene, that you do not have to build a hierarchy in order to create this animation (Figure 3-23b).You can operate directly on the sphere object that is the moon.

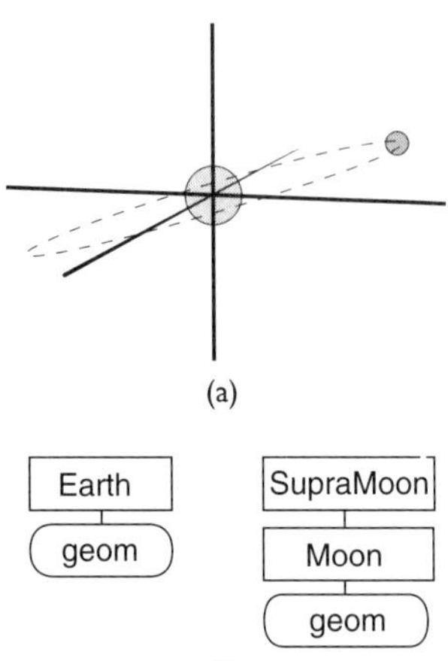

Figure 3-24. To achieve a rotation around an arbitrary axis, a dummy node can be created above the original node.

Imagine now, however, that you want the moon to rotate around the Earth at an angle (Figure 3-24a). This presents a problem. Since the orbiting path of the moon no longer lies flat in the XZ plane, you cannot do a simple rotation around Y, or any of the three axes, to produce the desired animation.

By making use of hierarchical animation, however, creating an additional hierarchical node directly above the *Moon* node, you can solve this problem (Figure 3-24b). A node such as this, which has no geometry connected directly to it, is sometimes called a **dummy node** or a **null node**, and in this example the dummy node is called *SupraMoon*.

Even though the *SupraMoon* dummy node has no geometry, it does have a local coordinate system. Initially, the local coordinate system of *SupraMoon* and the local coordinate system of *Moon* are in perfect alignment (Figure 3-25a). The local coordinate system of *Moon* is represented by the smaller of the two dotted-line cubes. The local coordinate system of *SupraMoon* is the larger cube, which encompasses the smaller.

Rotating *Moon* around Y still creates a simple rotation of the moon in the XZ plane. However, if you also rotate the local coordinate system of *SupraMoon* around Z (Figure 3-25b), you produce the tilted rotation of the moon that you want. In short, you produce a rotation around no particular global axis by creating a hierarchy of several embedded local coordinate systems.

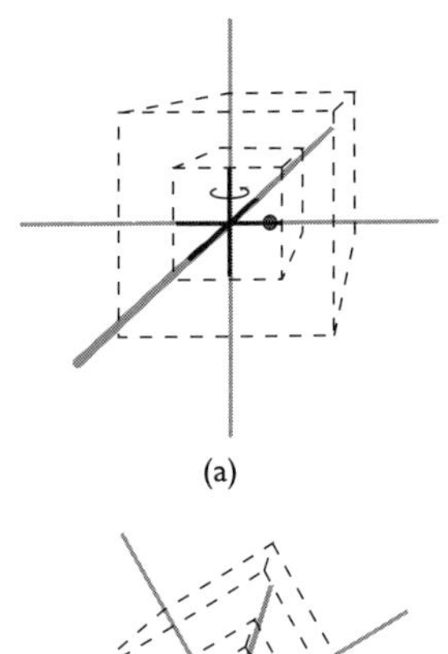
(a)

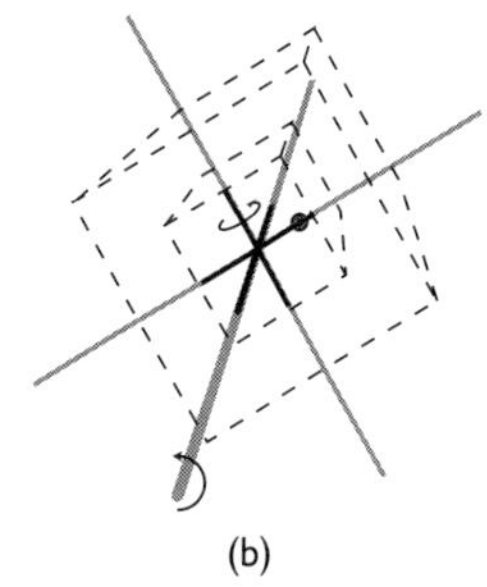
(b)

Figure 3-25. In hierarchical animation, a transformation in one local coordinate system is embedded within the transformation of another local coordinate system.

From a conceptual point of view, hierarchical animation is not complicated. That is, you animate each node of the hierarchy, positioning and saving keyframes. By carefully placing the pivot point of each node before you begin, you control the way the transformations affect that node. Also, by creating dummy nodes in the hierarchy, you divide one seemingly impossible transformation into several very simple transformations.

Hierarchical animation, however, can become very complicated when you have an elaborate hierarchical model. Suppose, for example, you want to animate a complex human-figure model with hierarchical animation. You would have to transform a great many nodes and then save those transformations in order to create each complete keyframe for the figure. If the figure is walking, for example, you have to position and save *LeftFoot*, *LowerLeftLeg*, *WholeLeftLeg*, *RightFoot*, *LowerRightLeg*, *WholeRightLeg*, *LeftHand*, and so on.

Fortunately, there is a technique, discussed in the next section, that tremendously simplifies the process of animating this sort of complex hierarchical model. Nonetheless, many animations require you to organize an elaborate model into a complex hierarchy. Each node of such a hierarchy must be transformed and saved individually. Time-consuming as this may become, the visual sophistication of the results can be stunning and well worth the effort.

Inverse Kinematics

In animating some hierarchical models, the procedure described in the previous section—that is, selecting each node of the hierarchy, transforming that node, and saving the transformation—makes perfect sense. In other situations, however, the structure and intent of your model make the process of selecting and transforming each node cumbersome. If you look at a simple arm model in one position (Figure 3-26a) and think about moving that

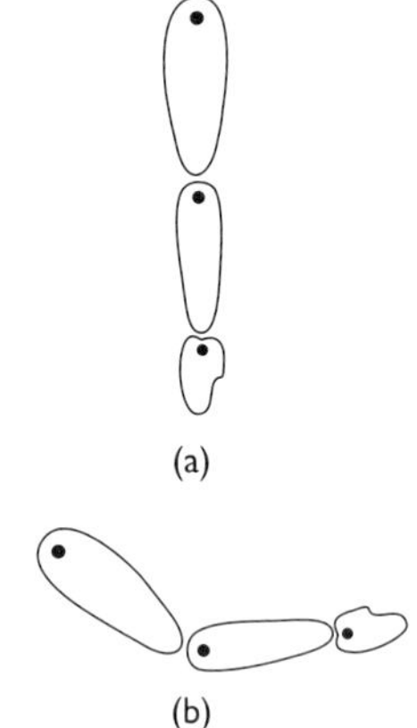

Figure 3-26. An arm model lends itself to the inverse kinematic technique.

model to another position (Figure 3-26b), for example, you probably want to do what you do in real life. That is, you probably want to move the "hand" end of the arm and have the rest of the arm follow. This is the way you intuitively think of this kind of movement: "I moved my hand from here to there," you think, not "I rotated my upper arm, then I rotated my lower arm, then I rotated my hand—with the result that my hand ended up there."

The standard approach to hierarchical animation, however, does force you to think this way. You can think in terms of transformations on specific joints, and you can animate this way, but it is not well suited to the sort of limbed model you usually find in figure animation.

In the real world, the position of the hand determines the position of the arm joints, because all the parts of the arm are connected and remain so as the arm moves. If the hand moves, the lower arm must follow. If the lower arm moves, the upper arm must follow. You know this intuitively, and that is why intuitively you want to place the hand and let the joints follow, rather than individually rotating each joint in order to get the hand to a specific location.

The technique that implements this approach is called **inverse kinematics**: "kinematics" refers to the mechanical study of motion, while "inverse" refers to the fact that the flow of transformations within the hierarchical model is calculated in the opposite direction to the normal calculation. Normally (as you saw in chapter 1, *Hierarchies*), you think of the transformations of a hierarchy as propagating *downward* through the hierarchy (Figure 3-27a). The transformations of *LowerArm* affect *Hand*, but those of *Hand* have no affect on *LowerArm*. The transformations of *WholeArm* effect both *LowerArm* and *Hand*, because the transformations for *WholeArm* travel downward through the hierarchy.

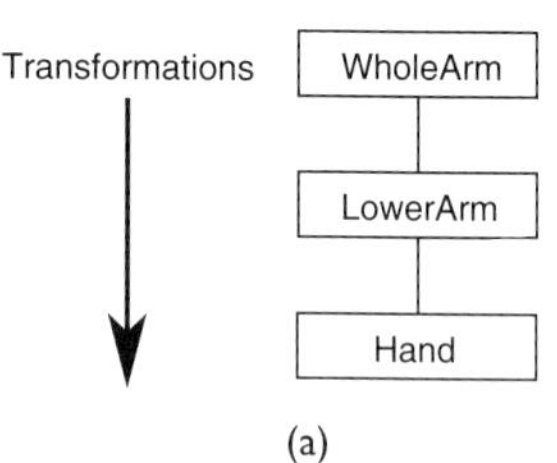

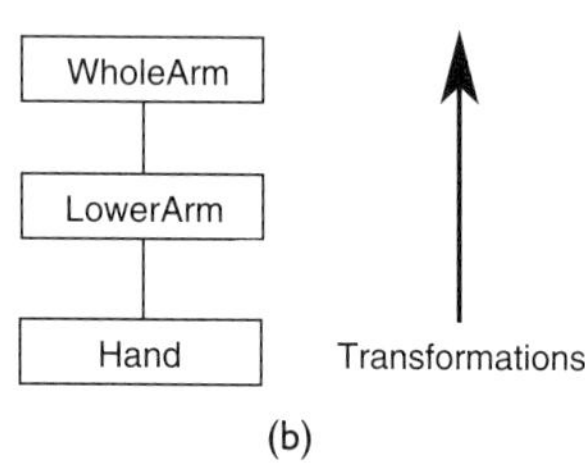

Figure 3-27. In standard hierarchical animation, transformations are calculated down the hierarchical tree. In inverse kinematics, the transformations are calculated upward from the bottom-most joint.

In an inverse kinematic model, however, the transformations applied to the lowest level, *Hand*, determine the transformations of *LowerArm*. The calculation of the transformations travels *upward* through the hierarchy, rather than down through it (Figure 3-27b). The standard downward propagation of transformations is sometimes referred to as **forward kinematics** to emphasize this difference.

Fortunately, 3D computer animation systems that provide inverse kinematic capabilities make all this mathematical calculation of transformations transparent to the animator. The animator can think simply in terms of "placing the hand at X" and let the system calculate as it will.

Because the animator does think in a different way when working with an inverse kinematic model than when working with a standard hierarchical model, a number of specialized terms are commonly used.

Since the hierarchy of an inverse kinematic model behaves in a chainlike fashion, with each joint necessarily following the movement of its neighboring joint, the hierarchy of an inverse kinematic model is often called a **chain**. Each joint, or node, of the hierarchy is then referred to as a **link** in the chain.

Using a different analogy, the hierarchical structure of an inverse kinematic model is sometimes called a **skeleton**, with each joint of the skeleton called a **bone**, since such a model is used very often for human and animal figures. It is not uncommon to find all of these terms—chain, skeleton, hierarchy, link, bone, joint, node—used within one system.

The end point of the final link in an inverse kinematic chain—the point that you move—is called the **effector**, because this point "effects" the transformations of the various joints. The starting point of the first link in the chain—the one point of the whole chain that is fixed—is called the **root** of the chain.

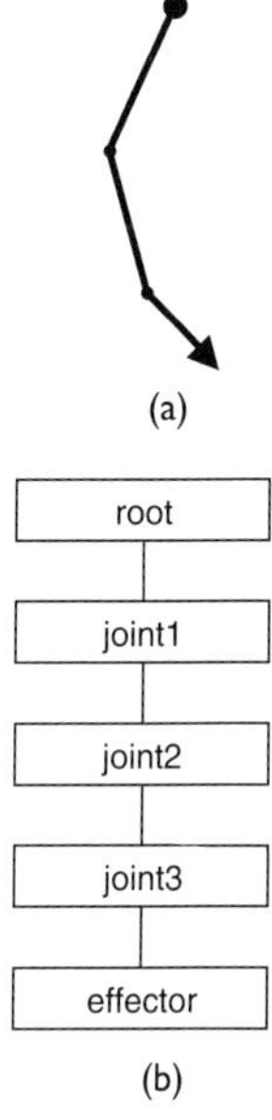

Figure 3-28. Two ways of diagraming the structure of an inverse kinematic chain.

Figure 3-28a shows these elements and their relationships to one another. Each of the links of the inverse kinematic chain is drawn as a straight line, and the starting point of each link is marked with a dot. This dot also represents the pivot point of that link. Remember that an inverse kinematic chain is actually a hierarchical model, and that each link of the chain is a node in that hierarchy. Each node of a hierarchy has an individual pivot point, or local origin, about which all the transformations on that node take place, and here the starting point, or dot, of each joint is also the local origin of that joint.

The local origin of the first link, the root of the entire chain, is represented here as a slightly larger dot, which means that it is also the pivot point of the entire chain. The end point of the final link in the chain is the effector, and is marked by an arrowhead. It is this effector point that you select and move in order to reconfigure the chain.

Figure 3-28b shows the normal diagram of a hierarchical model for this same structure. Both diagrams are accurate. They simply illustrate different aspects of the same model.

In principle, you can rotate the joints of a chain in any direction, and at a variety of very irregular angles (Figure 3-29a). Unrestricted rotations of this sort are appropriate if, for example, you model a rope (Figure 3-29b).

Inverse kinematics, however, is very frequently applied to human and other animal models. In the real world of animal flesh and bone, joints are not, in fact, capable of moving in unrestricted directions, as are the "joints" of a rope. Human and animal joints have constraints—points beyond which they cannot bend. The human elbow, for example, does not bend beyond approximately 180 degrees—that is, into a position where the upper and lower arms form a straight line. The same is true of the knee joint and most of the finger joints, and you find similar constraints in the joints of other animals.

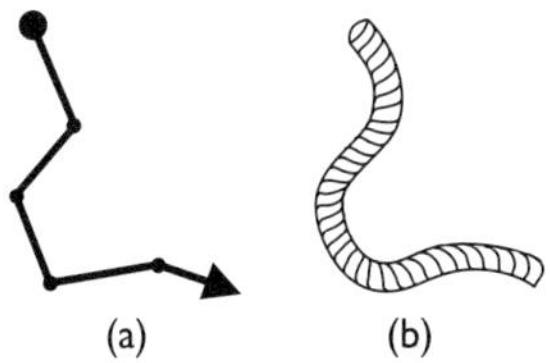

Figure 3-29. Unrestricted rotations of the joints of an inverse kinematic chain can be useful for certain types of models.

Because of this, it is common for a 3D animation system either to impose a 180-degree-rotation constraint on the joints of all inverse kinematic models, or, in more complex systems, to allow you to define the number of

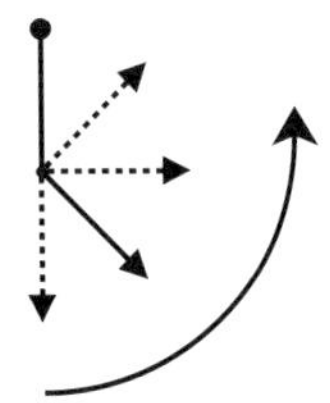

Figure 3-30. Some systems constrain the rotation of a joint in order to simulate the movements of the joints of our own bodies.

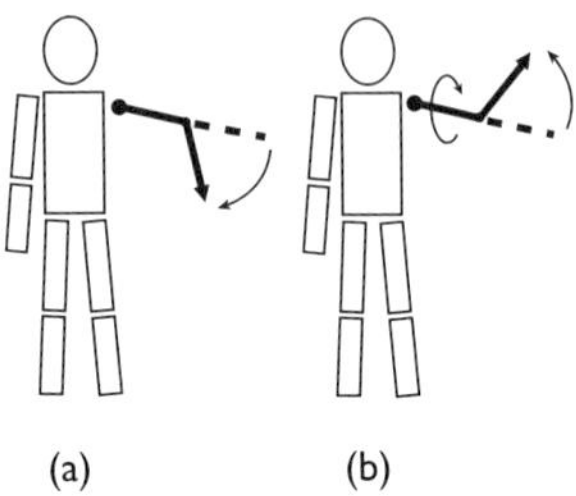

Figure 3-31. In order to overcome a 180-degree-rotation constraint, the entire chain can be rotated at the root.

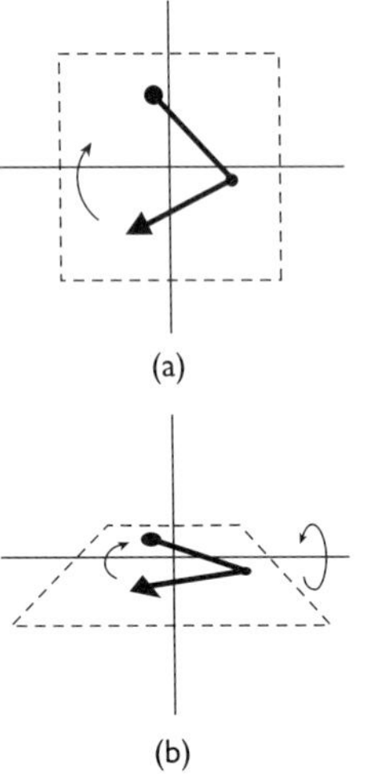

Figure 3-32. Some systems limit the rotations of a joint to rotations in a plane. In this case, the entire plane can be rotated to achieve a fully three-dimensional rotation.

degrees at which to constrain the rotation of a given joint. In practice, this means that most joints of a skeleton are able to bend in only one direction, like an elbow or a knee. In the simple two-joint model in Figure 3-30, the lower joint can bend only to the right. It is constrained from bending at all to the left, beyond an imaginary center line.

This 180-degree restriction might pose a problem when you want the bend of a limb model to change direction. In Figure 3-31a, for instance, the figure bends its lower arm joint up and down on the left side of the 180-degree dividing line, while in Figure 3-31b it bends the same joint on the right side of this dividing line. Both bends are reasonable human movements.

The solution to this seeming difficulty is the same solution you use in real life. In order to accomplish these movements, since your elbow joint really is constrained to approximately 180 degrees of rotation, you rotate your whole arm about the shoulder joint, in addition to rotating your elbow joint. In inverse kinematics, if you rotate the entire limb about the root pivot point, you produce the "reversed" rotation you want. In some systems you must keyframe the rotation of the entire limb. In more sophisticated systems, the rotation may be calculated automatically.

Another constraint that some systems impose on the movements of inverse kinematic chains has nothing to do with physical bodies. It happens to be much more complicated mathematically to calculate rotations about all three axes than it is to calculate rotations restricted to two axes. In other words, the rotations of a ball-and-socket joint that can move freely in all three axes are much more time-consuming to calculate than are the rotations of a hinge joint that moves in only the two axes of a plane. Since complex calculations translate into slower graphic displays, some systems restrict the movements of inverse kinematic chains to two-dimensional movements in a plane.

You can overcome this restriction, however, by rotating the entire chain, as you saw above. If, for example, you want to bend an arm in the XY plane and then later bend it in the XZ plane (Figure 3-32a), you can rotate the entire inverse kinematic skeleton 90 degrees about X (Figure 3-32b).

The discussion so far has centered on isolated inverse kinematic chains—one arm, one leg, and so on. In practice, of course, you need to combine these isolated chains if you want to model complete figures and other more complicated models. You do this with the normal hierarchical grouping techniques that all 3D computer animation systems provide. For example, a simple inverse kinematic human model might consist of one chain for each of the legs, one chain for each of the arms, a separate chain for a flexible backbone, and a final chain for the head/neck combination. Each of these chains is itself a hierarchy, and each chain can be grouped within the larger hierarchy that defines the entire figure. The result can be illustrated both as an inverse kinematic diagram (Figure 3-33a) and as a standard hierarchical diagram (Figure 3-33b).

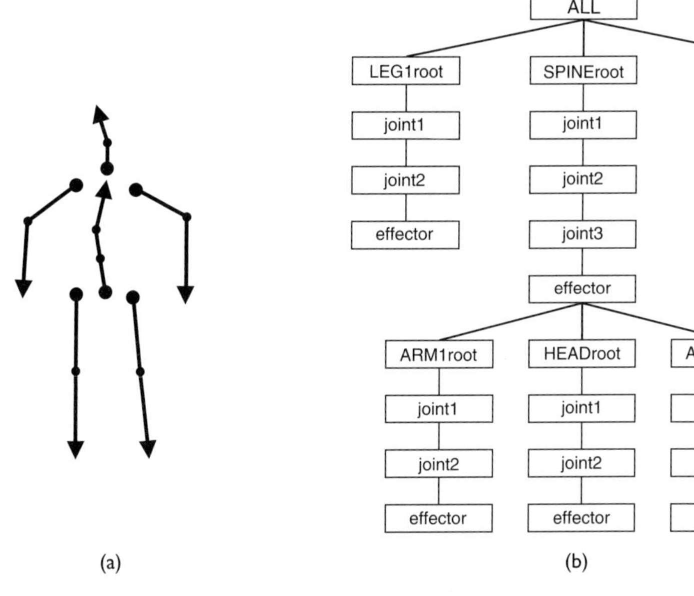

Figure 3-33. Individual inverse kinematic chains can be hierarchically grouped to form more complex structures, such as a human figure.

Whatever constraints a system imposes and whatever the complexity of the model, it is important that you define the structure/skeleton of your model in a way that allows you to make the kind of movements you want to make with your model. In order to do this, of course, you must first know what those movements are. How, for example, does a horse's foreleg move? And how is that different from the way a horse's hind leg moves? You also must be aware of the technical constraints of the system you are using. Are angles constrained to 180 degrees? Are rotations in three axes possible? With a combination of technical and visual acuity, you then can build a suitable inverse kinematic structure (Figure 3-34), one that reflects the thought you have given to the number of joints, the length of each joint, the relative angles of each joint, and the direction in which the joints bend.

The discussion so far has dealt with the structure of an inverse kinematic model, but what about the shape—that is, the geometry? In working with inverse kinematics, the development of the internal structure, or skeleton, of a model can proceed independently of any consideration of the geometry of the model. This is quite different from what happens with a standard hierarchical model, where you must define the geometry before structuring it into a hierarchy.

Once you have defined an inverse kinematic skeleton, you can associate some geometry with it in either of two ways. The first method is to model a separate piece of geometry (that is, some surface) for each link in the inverse kinematic chain. Suppose, for example, that you want a human-arm structure to become a cartoonlike arm made of sausage-shaped pieces. To do this, you first build the inverse kinematic skeleton (Figure 3-35a). Second, you build

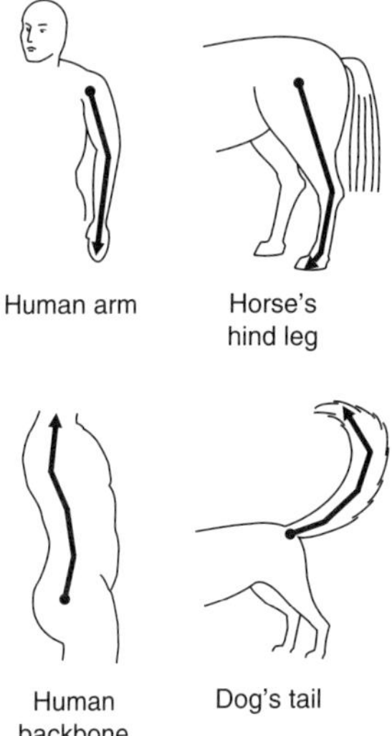

Figure 3-34. The structure of an inverse kinematic chain must take into consideration the form and the functionality of the model it will be animating.

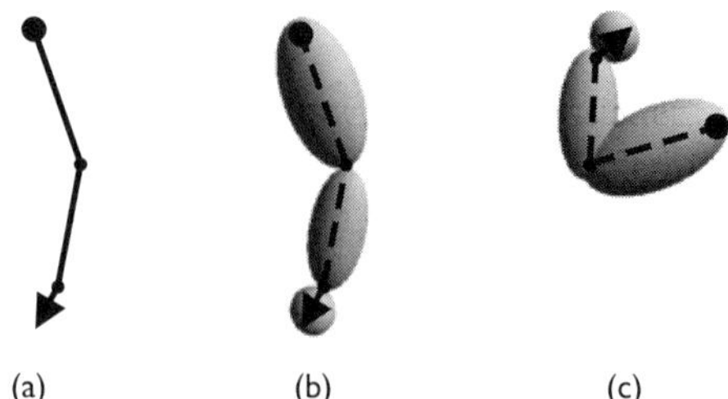

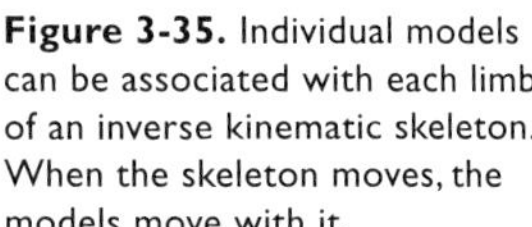
Figure 3-35. Individual models can be associated with each limb of an inverse kinematic skeleton. When the skeleton moves, the models move with it.

the three sausage-shaped surfaces, positioning them over the skeleton (Figure 3-35b). Third, you attach each surface to each joint. The act of "attaching" each object to a joint is actually a matter of hierarchically grouping the surface under the transformation matrix of that joint. You usually do this through a simple menu selection. Attached to the proper joints, the sausage-shaped objects follow the movements of the associated inverse kinematic joints. If you then select and move the effector, which is now at the tip of the "hand" sausage, you can reposition the skeleton as well as all the surfaces attached to it (Figure 3-35c).

When modeling the geometry to be attached, you must define it *in place*—that is, lying exactly on top of the skeleton—because the transformations of each link of the chain are propagated down onto the existing transformations of the associated surface. In this situation, the existing transformations of the surface and the new transformations of the joint are **concatenated**—that is, combined. Thus, if you initially define the surfaces off to the side somewhere (Figure 3-36a), they indeed will follow the movements of the skeleton, but all of these movements will be offset by the initial transformations (Figure 3-36b).

A second common way of associating geometry with an inverse kinematic chain is to put one smooth continuous surface, called an **envelope** or sometimes a **skeleton deformation**, around the entire chain. The simplest kind of envelope is made by creating a circular cross-section curve and effectively

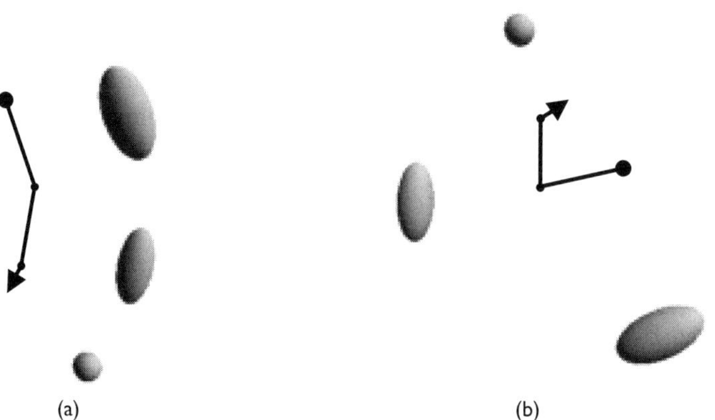

Figure 3-36. The initial placement of the models associated with each joint is critical.

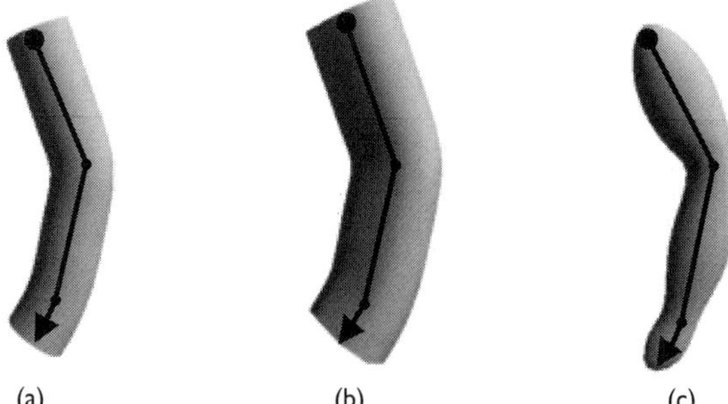

Figure 3-37. Several styles of deformable envelope can be built around a skeleton.

extruding it along the path of the skeleton (Figure 3-37a). Many systems also allow you to create envelopes from noncircular cross sections (Figure 3-37b). It is also possible in some systems to edit the shape of the surface of the envelope once it has been generated; for example, changing the shape of a simple circular envelope into that of a more naturalistically modeled human arm by pushing and pulling the control points or vertices (Figure 3-37c).

The crucial difference between the envelope technique and a standard extruded or lofted surface is that the surface of an envelope automatically deforms as the skeleton deforms. For instance, as the internal inverse kinematic skeleton in Figure 3-38a changes into the skeleton in Figure 3-38b, the associated envelope bends and deforms with it. Modeling an entire human figure like this can result in very effective character models.

A problem may arise with the deforming envelope in the area of a bending joint, however, when the angle of bending becomes too small. In this situation the envelope is liable to bend in undesirable ways as it tries to fit itself into the small area left between the bending elements (Figure 3-39a). In order to address this problem, most systems provide a parameter to control the amount of surface area that deforms at each joint. If the amount of deformable surface area (marked off within the dotted lines in the illustration) is reduced, the unsightly deformation around that joint can be minimized (Figure 3-39b). Some systems also allow you to determine whether the

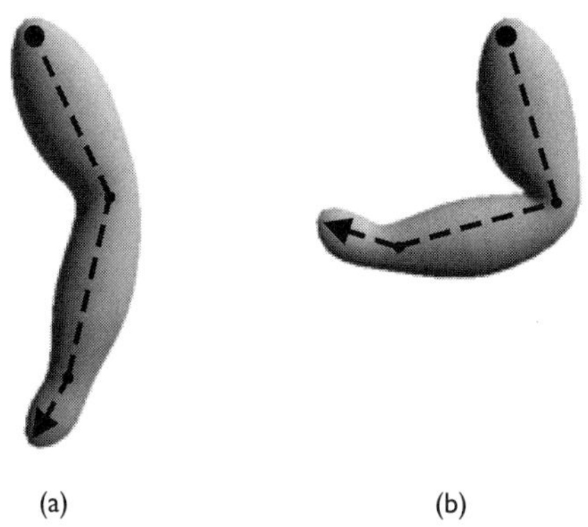

Figure 3-38. As the inverse kinematic skeleton deforms, the envelope associated with it also automatically deforms.

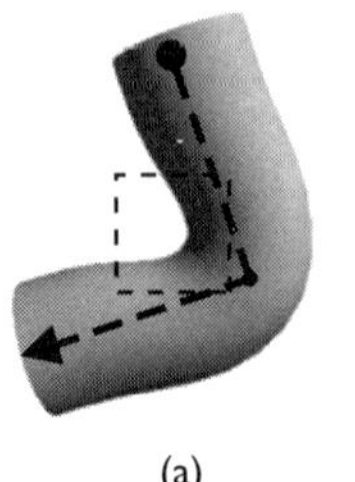

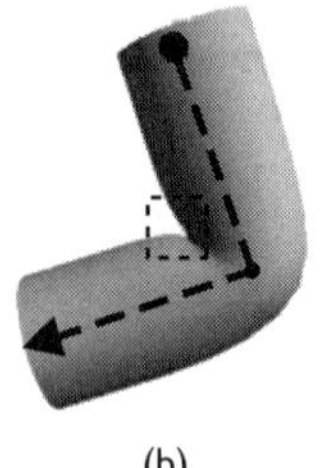

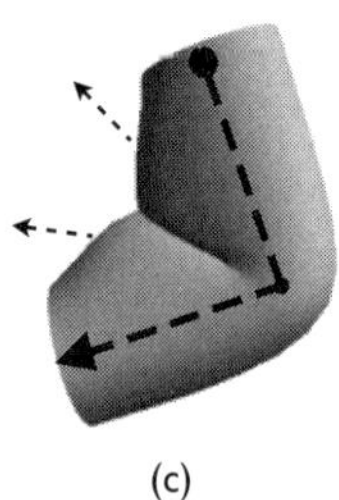

(a) (b) (c)

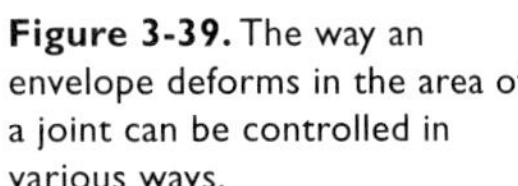

Figure 3-39. The way an envelope deforms in the area of a joint can be controlled in various ways.

deformation at a particular joint pushes the surface inward or outward. When the surface deforms outward, the envelope tends to resemble more closely the expanding muscles of a human limb (Figure 3-39c).

An interesting variation on the envelope technique, often called a **global envelope**, allows you to attach a single surface to an entire hierarchy of inverse kinematic chains. A single blobby ball, for example, can be animated by having a hierarchy of several chains within it (Figure 3-40a). More usefully, perhaps (although not more easily, because of the creasing problems mentioned above), an entire human figure can in principle be "clothed" in a single global envelope, producing a seamless skinlike surface (Figure 3-40b). A very different application of this technique is to group hierarchically several hanging inverse kinematic chains and "dress" them with a single global envelope, to simulate cloth (Figure 3-40c).

Even though the inverse kinematic technique makes the animation of human and animal figures vastly easier than it would be if you were limited to standard hierarchical, or forward kinematic, animation, it is important to realize that inverse kinematics in and of itself does not make good animation. Ultimately, your eye for detail and your appreciation of the complexity of movement determines the quality of an animation. You probably have had the experience of recognizing someone walking along at a distance: even though you cannot see the features of the person, the subtleties of his or her movements tell you who it is. Successful figure animation reflects this sort of refined observation.

To use a different example, think of the complexity and subtlety of the simple act of a human being standing up from a sitting position (Figure 3-41). The upper body leans forward to keep its weight balanced over its feet.

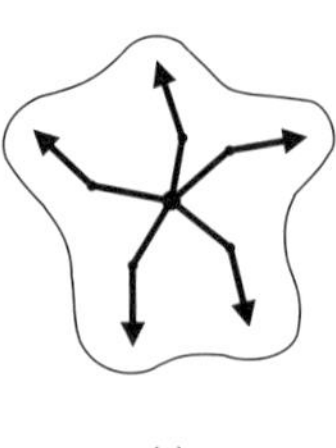

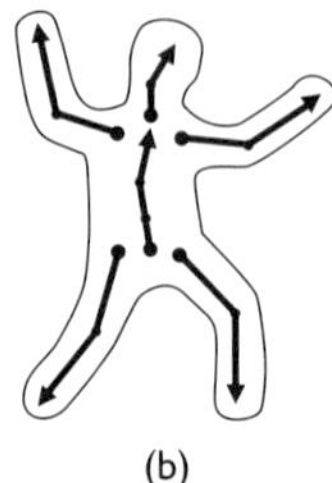

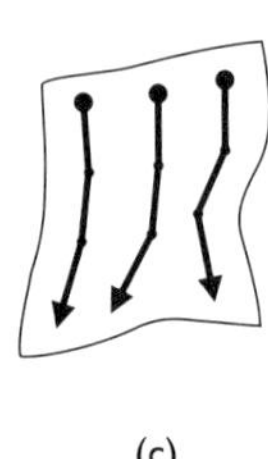

(a) (b) (c)

Figure 3-40. A global envelope covers an entire hierarchy of chains.

As this happens, the head probably tilts backward a bit to allow the eyes to keep looking ahead. As the figure rises, its hands leave the knees where they have been resting. The torso, meanwhile, continues to straighten up, with the head tilting slightly to compensate for the tilt of the torso. Finally, the figure arrives at an upright position.

This sort of subtlety of gesture and movement is the key to good figure animation. Even the simplest of models—even a figure composed of a few rectangular boxes—can look lifelike if it moves properly. Without the right gesture, without the right movement, the figure will never look natural, no matter how realistically it has been modeled.

Figure 3-41. Convincing human movement depends more on the subtlety of the gesture and timing than on the sophistication of the modeling.

Limits and Constraints

With any animation, whether a single object, a hierarchical model, or an inverse kinematic model, it is often useful to restrict the range of the model's motion. One way of doing this is to **limit** its motion. You can define limits for any of a model's three basic transformations—translation, rotation, scale. They are most commonly used, however, for translation and rotation. Let us first consider **rotation limits**.

In some situations you know beforehand that your model should only rotate in certain ways. Consider the rear wheels of a car. They should be able to rotate about the axis of the car's rear axle (call it the X axis), but not about any other axis (unless something breaks)! The front wheels of the vehicle are a little more complicated (Figure 3-42). In addition to rotating about the X axis of the axle, they must also be able to rotate about the Y axis, so that the vehicle can turn. Their rotations about Y, however, will be limited—perhaps to ± 60 degrees. They will not be able to rotate about the Z axis at all. Defining limits for the rotations of your wheel can help you avoid accidentally rotating the wheels in ways you do not want.

Rotational limits become especially important when you animate complex articulated figures, such as humans, other limbed animals, and robots, because our joints have natural, physiological rotational limits. Our knees, for example, can rotate in only one direction. If a leg model is aligned as shown in Figure 3-43a, it will not be able to rotate at all about the Y axis or the Z axis. The only axis about which it can rotate is the X axis. If you define limits for the knee rotations according to these naturally occurring limits, you can force the leg model to behave as a real leg would. Typically, the way you define limits is by selecting the model you want to work on and then selecting a menu for defining rotational limits for it. Within this menu, you select the specific joint you are interested in (in this example, the knee joint), and then, for each axis of that joint, you specify the minimum and maximum

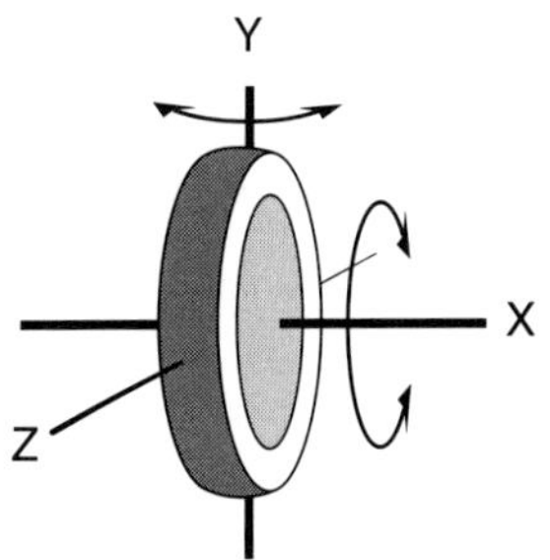

Figure 3-42. The front wheel of a car has rotational limits.

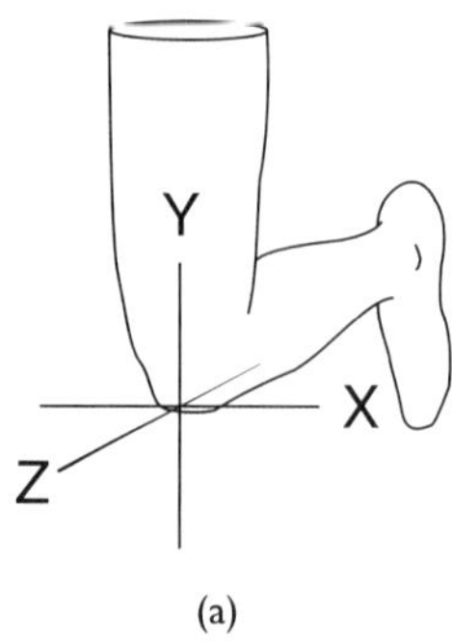

(a)

	MIN	MAX
x	0	130
y	0	0
z	0	0

(b)

Figure 3-43. The joints of animal bodies have naturally occurring rotational limits.

rotations in degrees. Specifying the minimum and maximum rotation values can be done either explicitly by typing them in, or interactively by positioning your model and saving whatever rotation values it has in that position. Typical values for a human knee joint are as shown in Figure 3-43b.

To fully define the rotation limits of a complete human figure, you go through this process for each joint. Many human joints are more complex than the knee joint used as the example. The shoulder joint in Figure 3-44a, for example, might have the indicated rotation limits.

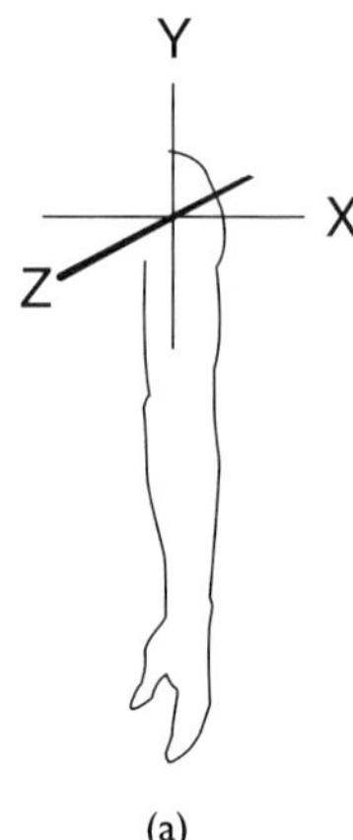

(a)

	MIN	MAX
x	-120	30
y	-20	10
z	-70	25

(b)

Figure 3-44. The rotational limits for a shoulder joint need to be specified around all three axes.

Carefully defining the rotational limits of each joint of a complex model like the human figure can be a time-consuming process, because every joint, both left and right, must be defined for all three axes. Taking the trouble to do this, however, can result in a model that is much more easily animated. Sometimes, in fact, such a model behaves with almost uncanny realism. For example, if the rotational limits have been well defined, lifting the hand straight out to the side and then in an arc across the body will cause the arm to rise and bend in a very natural motion. First, the arm rises up with no bending. When the shoulder joint reaches its rotational limit in Z, it automatically begins to rotate around X, to permit the hand to continue to rise. Next, when the shoulder's X rotation has also reached its limit, the elbow joint begins to rotate. Finally, when the elbow has rotated as far as it can, the wrist rotates.

In addition to limiting the rotations of a model, you can also limit its translations. This is usually referred to as **positional limits**. Imagine, for example, a truck with sliding doors (Figure 3-45). By limiting the translations of each door, you can ensure that the motion of the doors will be accurate and easy to animate. If the doors are oriented as in the illustration, each door should be able to translate a small amount positively in X. The rearmost door should be able to translate a little less than the width of the door in the negative Z direction. The other door should be able to translate the same amount positively in Z. Neither door should be able to translate at all in Y.

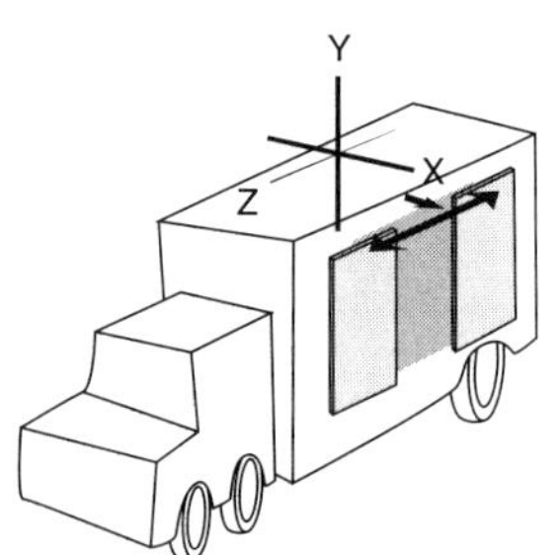

Figure 3-45. Positional limits can be very helpful for some models.

In addition to limiting a model's transformations, you can also **constrain** them. Constraining a model means associating its transformations with the transformations of a second model. There are three common types of constraint: position, rotation, and direction.

A **position constraint** constrains the translation of an object. Figure 3-46a shows two objects, a cone and a cube, in their original positions. The cube is shaded to indicate that it is the controlling, or constraining, object. When the cone's position is constrained to the cube's position, the cone snaps to the location of the cube, as in Figure 3-46b. More specifically, the cone's local origin, indicated by the crosshairs, snaps to the cube's local origin. Now, wherever the cube goes, the cone will also go, as if the two were "joined at the hip"—except that they are joined at the local origin.

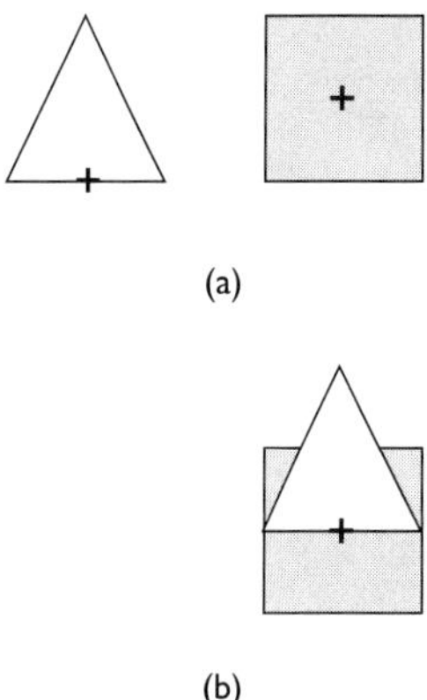

Figure 3-46. A position constraint forces one object to stick to another.

Position constraints can be especially useful with inverse kinematic character animation. By constraining the effector of an inverse kinematic skeleton to some other object, you can produce motion that would otherwise be difficult to animate. For example, consider the problem of preventing a character's feet from sliding or going through the floor as it moves about (Figure 3-47). In Figure 3-47a, you see the hierarchy that has been built for the character, a simple "eggman" fellow with just a ball for a torso, two legs, two feet, and nothing else. Notice that the effector of each leg is constrained to a *Shoe* object, as indicated by the dashed line connecting them, and that the constraining shoes are completely outside of the *Allbody* hierarchy. This structure allows you to move the *Allbody* node and the Leg nodes any way you want without causing the shoes to move. Since the effectors are constrained to the shoes, the effectors also will not move as you move the *Allbody* and *Leg* nodes around.

Now, if you select the *Allbody* node and translate it downward, the character will squat. Moving *Allbody* downward causes the roots of each *Leg* branch to move downward as well, since the roots are children of *Allbody.* However, because the Shoe nodes are outside the *Allbody* hierarchy, they are not affected by *Allbody*'s translation and remain stationary. Since the effectors at the end of each *Leg* are constrained by the *Shoes*, the effectors also do not move. The result is that the legs bend, the feet stay on the ground, and the character squats. This would be a very difficult little animation to produce without position constraints.

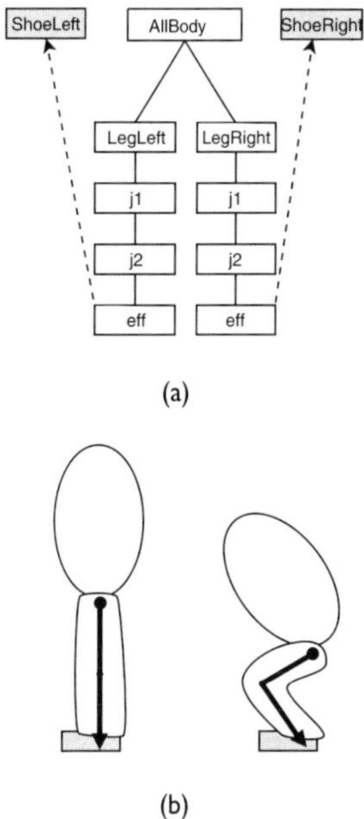

Figure 3-47. Constraining the position of an effector to another object can facilitate complex character animation.

You must be careful, however, in using this technique, because there can be some curious side effects. These occur because the effectors' movements are restricted in two ways: first, by their constraining objects, the *Shoes*, and second by their attachment to the inverse kinematic chain. Recall that an inverse kinematic chain has a root node at the top of its hierarchy that keeps the chain fixed in one spot. Unless you translate this root node, there is a limit to how far the chain's effector can move. If the effector is constrained to an object that moves farther away than the effector can follow, the effector's chain will "reach" towards the constraining object.

You must take this effect into account when constraining effectors. However, it can also be used to good purpose, as illustrated in Figure 3-48. Here

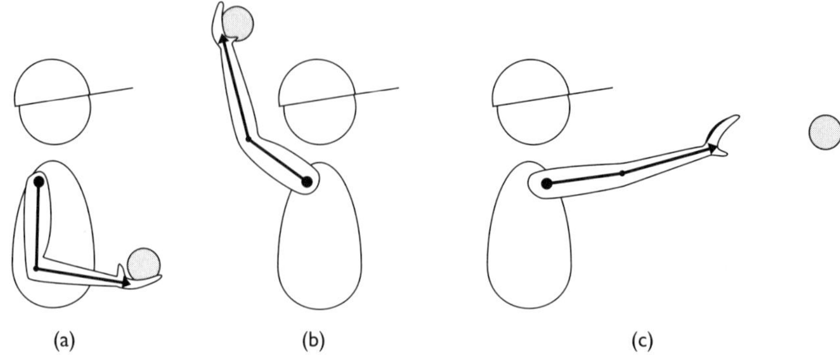

Figure 3-48. Constraining the hand effector to the ball forces the arm to "reach" for the ball.

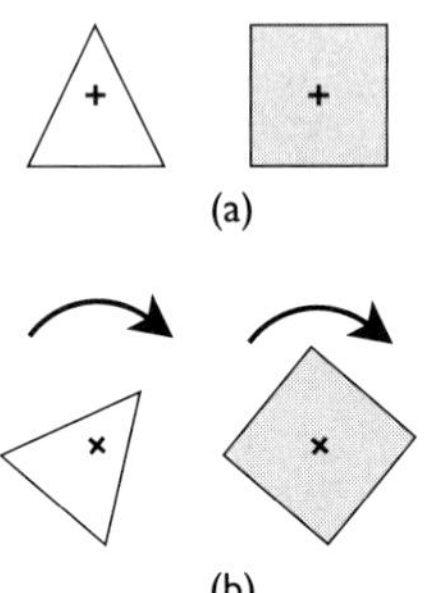

Figure 3-49. A rotation constraint forces one object to follow the rotations of another.

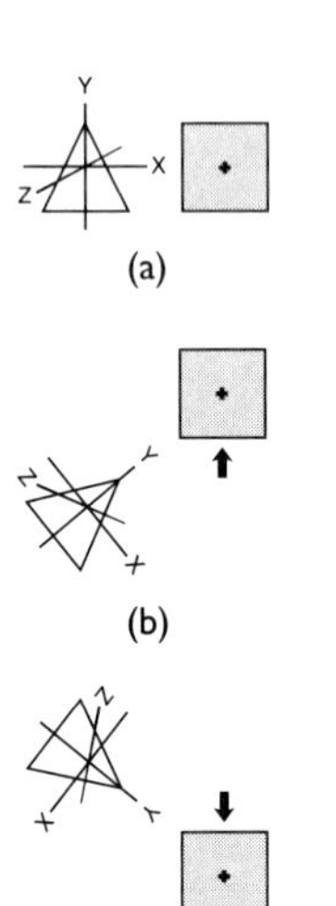

Figure 3-50. A direction constraint forces one object to point toward another.

an inverse kinematic model is animated, with the hand effector of the ballplayer constrained to the ball (so that he will never, *ever* miss). Given the effect just described, it is quite easy to animate a throwing motion for this player. By simply translating the ball, you can cause the player to "throw" the ball. The hand and ball will move together (Figure 3-48a and b), but when the ball has been translated too far to the right, the hand will "reach" towards the ball, simulating a throwing motion (Figure 3-48c).

A **rotation constraint**, also called an **orientation constraint**, constrains the rotation transformations of one object to that of another. In Figure 3-49 the rotation of the cone is constrained to that of the cube, ensuring that however the cube rotates, the cone will rotate exactly the same way.

A **direction constraint** forces an object to point, or aim, toward its controlling object. In Figure 3-50 the cone is constrained in the direction of the cube, with the result that wherever the cube goes, the cone will adjust its rotation; it always points toward the cube.

In setting up a direction constraint, you must pay attention to the local coordinate system of the object to be constrained—the cone, in the example. This is because a directional constraint forces a particular axis of the constrained object (the cone) to point toward the local origin of the constrainer (the cube). In some software packages, you can select which axis of the constrained object's local coordinate system will be used. In others, the axis is fixed, and you must realign the constrained object's local coordinate system as necessary before implementing the constraint.

For all three types of constraint—position, rotation, and direction—the critical point to which the constraint attaches or rotates or points is the local origin of the constrainer. A position constraint snaps to the local origin of the constrainer; a direction constraint points toward the local origin of the constrainer, etc. What do you do if you want to constrain to some other point? One solution is to create a null node (see *Hierarchical Animation* earlier in this chapter) and constrain to that null node. Since a null node has no geometry, it is invisible when your scene is rendered. If necessary, the null node can be made a child of another object. Constraining to a null, therefore, permits you effectively to constrain to any point in space.

Another approach, offered by some software systems, is to define your constraint in relation to some vertex or control point on the surface of your model. For example, perhaps you want to constrain an object to the shoulder of a character's torso. The local origin of the torso, however, has been placed in the area of the pelvis. By constraining to a vertex or control point in the shoulder area, you can solve this problem.

Motion Paths

So far you have seen two broad approaches to animating an object moving through space. The first approach involved visually positioning the object and saving a keyframe for each position. The second approach, a variation on the first, involved editing the parameter curves for the object in order to change either the keyframe values or the interpolation between them. In some situations, however, it is easiest to think about the motion of an object through space in terms of a path that the object follows (Figure 3-51). Most 3D computer animation systems allow you to define motion in this way.

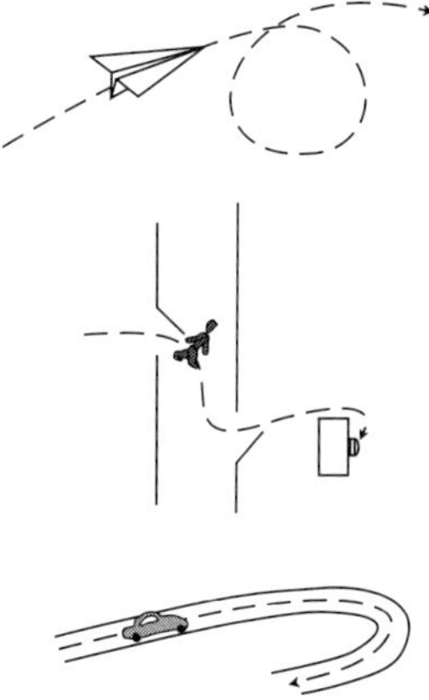

Figure 3-51. The movement of some objects is most easily described in terms of a path that the object follows.

The basic idea is very simple. First you draw a curve in space, using the standard curve-drawing techniques that most systems offer. This curve, usually referred to as the **motion path** of the object, represents the path along which the object will move. You then select the object to be animated and tell the system, through some menu selection, that the motion of this object will be along this motion path and will take place over a certain number of frames. The computer then interpolates the in-between location of the object along that path for each in-between frame of the sequence.

For example, suppose you draw a motion path and assign it to a cube, beginning at frame 1 and ending at frame 400 (Figure 3-52). If you use a standard linear interpolation, then at frame 200, which represents half of the total time, the cube will be located halfway along the path. At frame 100, which is one-fourth of the time, the cube will be located at one-fourth of the distance along the path. And so on.

Even after you have assigned a motion path to an object, many software packages allow you to change the path, using any of the standard curve-editing tools. As soon as the path has been changed, a new interpolation of in-between positions is automatically calculated, resulting in a new animation along the new path.

The basic linear interpolation described above moves the cube along the path at a constant rate of speed throughout the length of the animation. Of

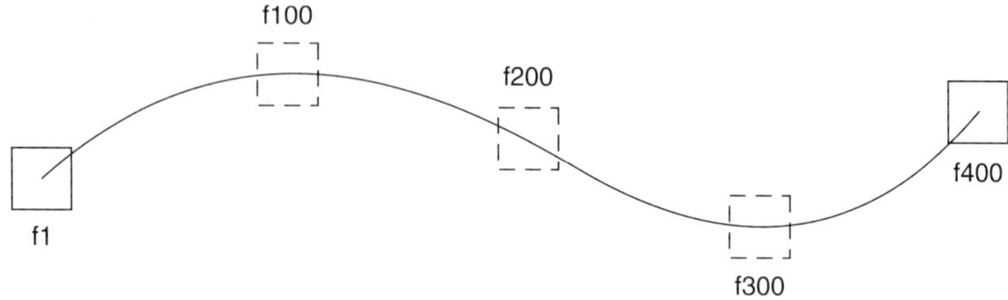

Figure 3-52. The position of an object in space may be interpolated along the length of a motion path.

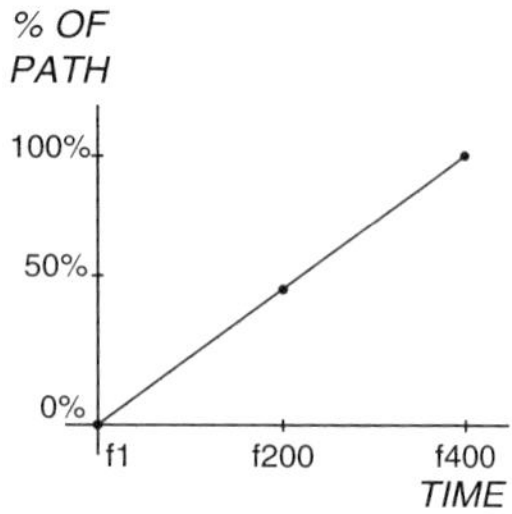

Figure 3-53. A timing curve represents the position of an object along the path for each moment of time. If the interpolation of the timing curve is linear, as here, the object moves at a constant rate along the path.

course, you may not want such a perfectly constant rate of movement along the path, and so most systems provide a technique for controlling the rate of movement by adjusting the interpolation of a second curve, called a **timing curve**, which represents the rate of movement along the path. The timing curve plots time on one axis and the percentage of distance on the path along the other axis (Figure 3-53).

The timing curve is very useful, because you can edit it as you would any other parameter curve. Using the curve-editing tools provided by the software, that is, you can modify the interpolation applied to the position of the cube along the path. This modification might involve changing the type of interpolation, adding a control point, moving a control point, and so on. By changing the timing curve, you change the rate of movement along the path. For example, say you change the linear interpolation of the curve to an ease-in interpolation (Figure 3-54b). The cube still follows exactly the same motion path, but it does so now at a different rate of speed (Figure 3-54a). The cube moves very slowly along the path in the beginning of the animation, covering only a short distance in the first frames, then picks up speed along the path, until it moves very rapidly and covers a great distance in the final frames of the animation.

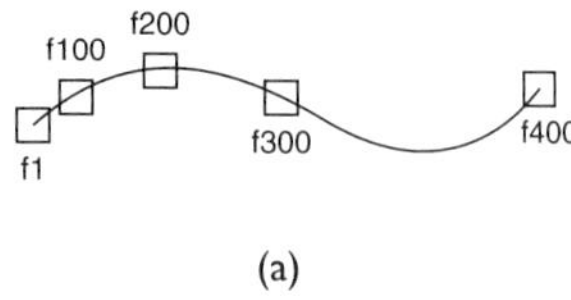

(a)

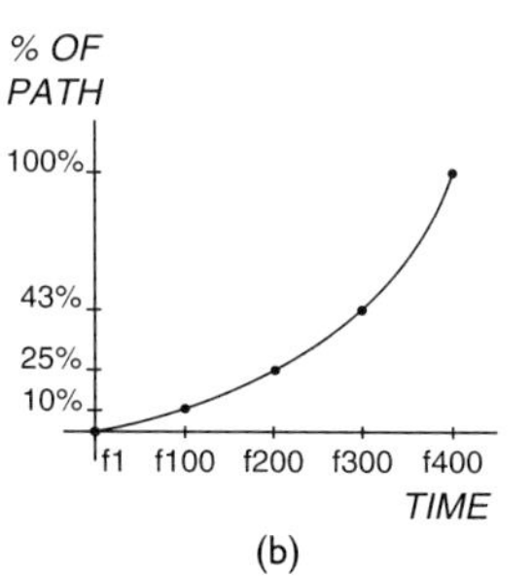

(b)

Figure 3-54. If the interpolation of the timing curve is changed, the rate of movement of the object along the path is changed.

A few interesting, and perhaps surprising, effects can result from the editing of a timing curve. For example, if the timing curve is flattened and made horizontal over a certain range of frames, the object remains at the same location on the path for that range (Figure 3-55a). In other words, the object stops, remaining fixed at a point that is, say, 60 percent of the way along the path, from frame 200 through frame 300. In another situation, if the timing curve slopes downward, the object moves backward: it is located 60 percent of the way along the path at frame 200, but later, at frame 300, it is located only 40 percent of the way along the path (Figure 3-55b).

One final issue that you must consider when animating an object along a motion path is the orientation of the object relative to the path. Suppose you are animating a paper airplane along a motion path (see Figure 3-51). Undoubtedly you want the nose of the airplane to stay on the path (Figure 3-56a). In more technical terms, you want the airplane to remain **tangent** to the curve. Some systems do this by default. Other systems, however, do not adjust the tangency of the object automatically, but by default always keep the object in the original orientation as it moves along the path (Figure 3-56b). In this situation, you must adjust the orientation of the object in a separate operation. Most systems provide a selection that forces the object to remain tangent to the motion path, but less sophisticated systems require you to adjust the orientation by rotating the object and visually keyframing those rotations.

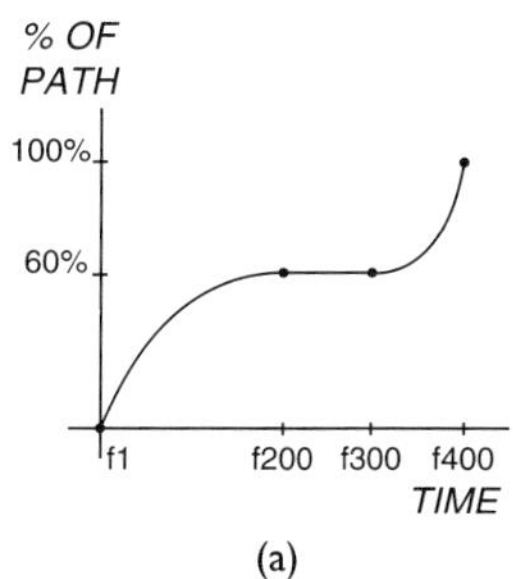

(a)

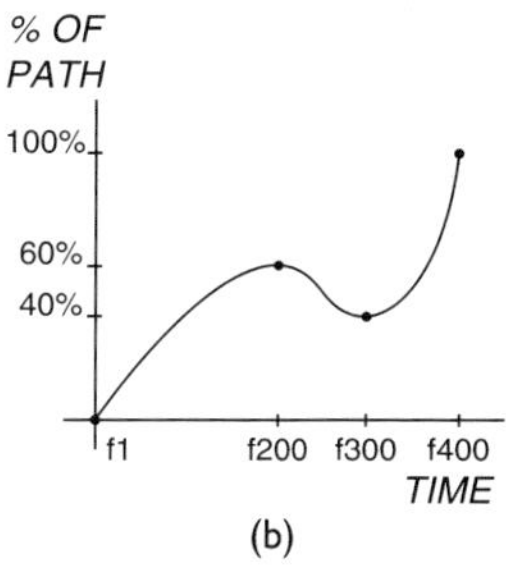

(b)

Figure 3-55. A flat section of timing curve means that the object is not moving during that section. A downward-sloping section of curve means that the object is moving backwards.

Shape Changes

All of the techniques discussed so far have involved the animation of rigid objects. You have transformed objects by translating, rotating, and scaling them, but you have made no attempt to change an actual shape: to reform or deform the shape of the surface of an object. Although you might think that a change of scale is a change of shape, a change of scale does not constitute a change of shape in the sense meant here. Scaling an object makes it uniformly longer or shorter in or more directions, but it does not alter the *configurations* of the surface. It does not alter the "bumps and hollows" (to use Auguste Rodin's phrase) of the surface.

In the real world changes of shape are very common. When a flower is brushed by a breath of air, the stem bends and the petals and leaves may also bend and change shape subtly. When a dog curls up and lies down on a rug, its body bends into a semicircular arc. The expressions of the human face are almost exclusively a matter of the face changing shape. In order to achieve any kind of successful animation of these or similar events, you have to be able to animate changes of an object's shape.

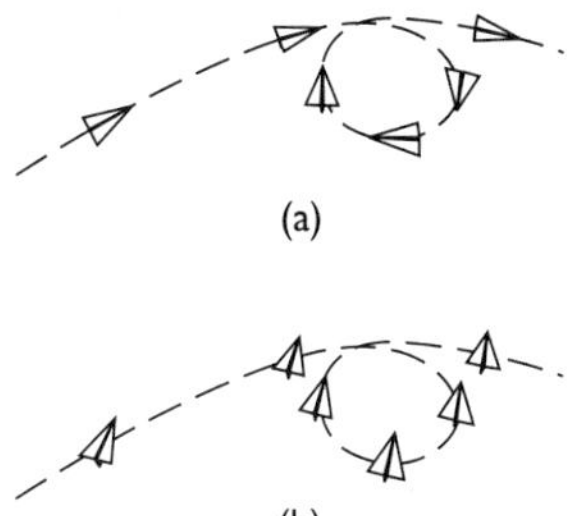

(a)

(b)

Figure 3-56. In most situations, it is important to keep the object moving tangent to the direction of the path.

Shape changes are referred to by a number of phrases, including **flexible surfaces**, **shape metamorphosis**, and **shape deformations**. Most 3D computer animation systems provide some way of implementing these changes, and the basic idea in all these systems is quite simple. Remember that in animating a rigid object, you define the transformations for the object, save these transformations as a keyframe, and then ask the computer to interpolate the transformation values between the two keyframes. The interpolated transformation values yield the in-between positions of the object.

Similarly, in animating a flexible, or changing, surface, you determine the positions of the points that define the surface (the control points or vertices), save the positions of these points as a keyframe, reposition the surface-defining points, save a new keyframe, and then ask the computer to interpolate the values between the two key positions. The interpolated positions of the surface-defining points yield the in-between shapes of the object.

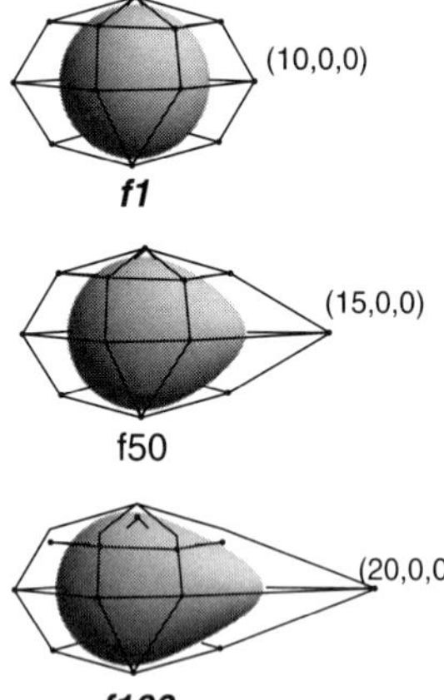

Figure 3-57. Animating a shape change involves animating the positions of the points that define the surface of the object.

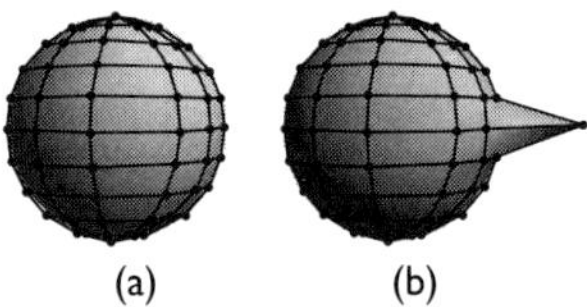

Figure 3-58. In a polygonal model, animating only one point may be insufficient. You may need to animate many points to achieve the desired shape change.

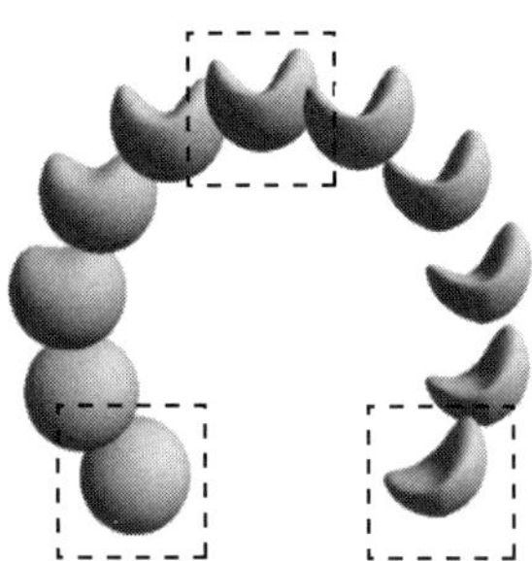
Figure 3-59. The keyshape technique applied to a sphere. Each of the keyshapes is outlined; between these three shapes are the in-between shapes generated by the computer.

Figure 3-57, for example, shows a shape-change animation for a simple spline-based sphere. The sphere in an undeformed state, at the top, serves as keyframe 1. Notice that the coordinates of the control point on the far right of this sphere are (10,0,0). The third or bottom image in the illustration is a second keyframe, keyframe 100. In this keyframe, the same control point, pulled to the right, is now at a location of (20,0,0). Between these two key positions is one of the interpolated in-between frames, frame 50. Notice that the coordinate values of the control point—which has been moved and interpolated in a linear interpolation—are now (15,0,0); that is, the control point is located halfway between the location of that point at the two keyframes. It is the interpolation of the location of the control point in space that has changed the shape of the sphere over time.

Animating the surface of a polygonal model (see chapter 1, *Polygonal Modeling*) is similar to animating the surface of a spline model, except that you have to move more points in order to create a smooth shape change. If you move only a single surface vertex on a polygonally defined sphere (Figure 3-58a), you produce an angular shape change (Figure 3-58b).

A variation on the concept of moving individual control points and saving the positions of those points as keyframes is the technique of defining **keyshapes** (Figure 3-59). Using this approach, you begin by making several duplicates of the model to be animated. You then move control points or polygon vertices on the first copy of the model until you produce the right shape for frame 1. After saving this model as keyshape 1, you manipulate the points of the second copy of the model until you produce the right shape to save as another keyshape, perhaps keyshape 60. Then you alter the next model, save it as a keyshape, and so on. When you have defined all the keyshapes, you instruct the computer to produce the interpolated shapes that come between them.

Notice that the keyshape technique is fundamentally the same technique as saving individual control points or polygon vertices. The only difference is that in the keyshape technique you define and see all the changes that will take place on the model *before* any interpolation is done. With the technique of saving individual control points, the changes are defined at the same time that the interpolation is done.

Both approaches, however, involve repositioning lots of surface-defining points individually, a process that quickly can become tedious. In the case of a polygonally defined sphere, you have to move quite a large number of points in order to make even a relatively simple change. With a spline-based model, simple animations are not difficult, but complex animations might require a great deal of very careful selecting and moving of control points.

For some effects, there is no way around this problem. If you want to create a very specific metamorphosis, you may have to go to the trouble of

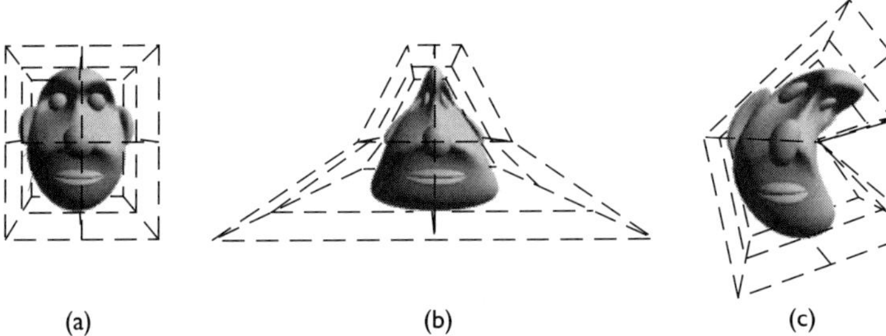

Figure 3-60. Lattice animation allows you to animate the shape of a complex model by operating on the points of a far simpler rectangular lattice structure.

meticulously selecting and moving many control points or surface vertices. Fortunately, however, a number of techniques have been developed to simplify the process of animating the surface-defining points of a model. All of these techniques are based on the concept of associating the many surface-defining points of your original model with a very limited number of controlling points on some other model or curve. By moving the few points of the controlling model, you move the many points of the original model.

In one technique, called **lattice animation** or (more picturesquely) **squishy-box** animation, you define a rectangular box, or lattice, of points to exist around the object you want to animate (Figure 3-60a). Each point of the box/lattice is associated with a cluster of surface-defining points—that is, with a cluster of control points if the model is spline-based, or with a cluster of surface vertices if it is a polygonal model. For example, the upper right, front vertex of the box might be associated with a cluster of control points in the area of the upper right forehead, eyebrow, and eye. Moving a few points on the lattice moves many associated points on the surface of the model and deforms the model (Figure 3-60b and c). Another way of thinking of this deformation process is that the rectangular lattice defines a space inside of which the head model exists. If the "space" of the head is deformed (quite an Einsteinian thing to do!), the head within that space is also deformed.

In order to produce an actual animation with the lattice-animation technique, you animate the points on the lattice structure by positioning them and saving keyframes. When these lattice points animate, the surface points they control also animate; when the surface points animate, the shape of the surface animates.

The great advantage of lattice animation is that the number of points you must deal with in order to produce a complex shape deformation is drastically reduced. In the previous example, only a handful of points on the lattice of the squishy box had to be manipulated in order to make the two very radical, and complex, shape changes. If you had to select and move the individual control points that define the shape of the head, making these same changes would require a great deal more work—even more, of course, if the model were polygonally defined.

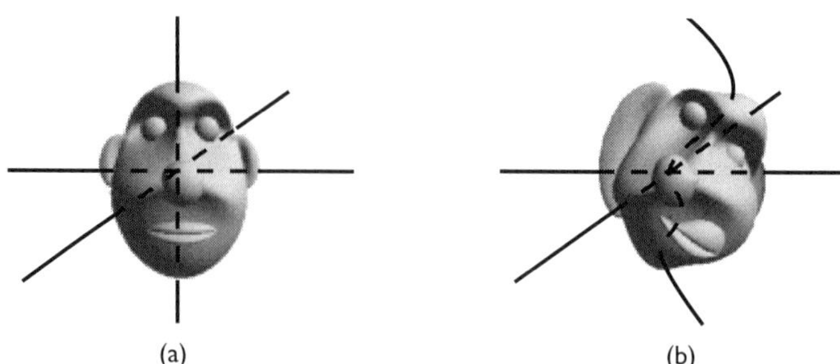

Figure 3-61. The axis-deformation technique defines an axis of the local coordinate system to be curved. Since the space of an object is curved, the surface of that object curves.

A second technique, often referred to as **fitted animation** or **axis deformation**, also can be thought of as defining the space in which your model exists, then deforming that space in order to achieve the deformation of the model. You define and deform the space by substituting a curved line for one or more of the straight axes of the normal Cartesian coordinate system. "Fitting" an animation along an axis has the same basic advantage as lattice animation in that it allows you to make substantial changes to the shape of a complex model without having to push and pull a myriad of control points or polygon vertices. Figure 3-61a, for example, shows the original head within the standard orthogonal Cartesian coordinate system. In Figure 3-61b a wavy line substituted for the normally straight, perpendicular line of the Y axis curves the "space" in which the head exists, and deforms the head accordingly.

Having created a nonstraight axis with which to deform the model, you now can animate the shape of this curved axis by pushing or pulling the control points that define the curve of the axis. As the curved axis changes shape, the model that it controls also changes shape.

A variation on axis deformation, called **spline deformation** or **curve deformation**, allows you to draw a curve through the center of any object, without that curve having to correspond to any of the three axes. This curve is then associated with the model, and you can animate the shape of the curve, and hence the model, in the same way that you might animate the shape of an axis-deforming curve.

In yet another technique, **patch deformation**, you substitute a curved patch for one of the normally flat planes of the Cartesian space of an object. The curved patch (Figure 3-62b) bends the space in which the model exists (Figure 3-62a), bending the model in the process (Figure 3-62c). This technique is especially useful for relatively flat objects that lie approximately in a plane.

A final shape-deformation technique, **path deformation**, is conceptually very similar to the spline-deformation technique. Remember that it is possible to animate an object along a path. A variation on that technique is to also deform the object as it moves along the path. The surfaces of the object (Figure 3-63a) are deformed according to the curvature of the section of path they are on at the moment (Figure 3-63b).

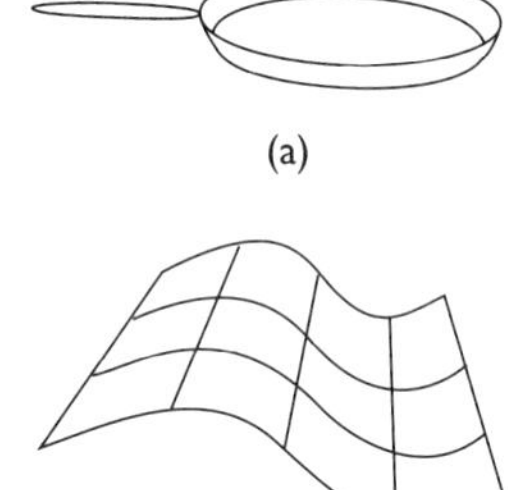

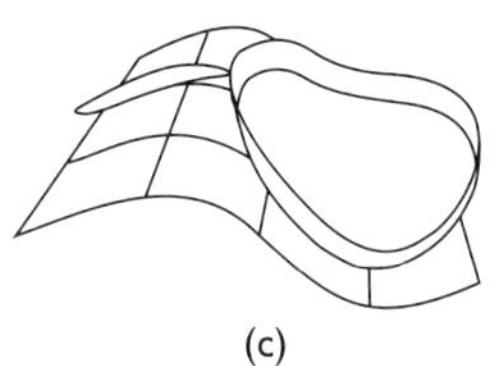

Figure 3-62. The patch-deformation technique also deforms the space in which an object resides. A curved patch is substituted for one of the normally flat planes of the coordinate system of an object.

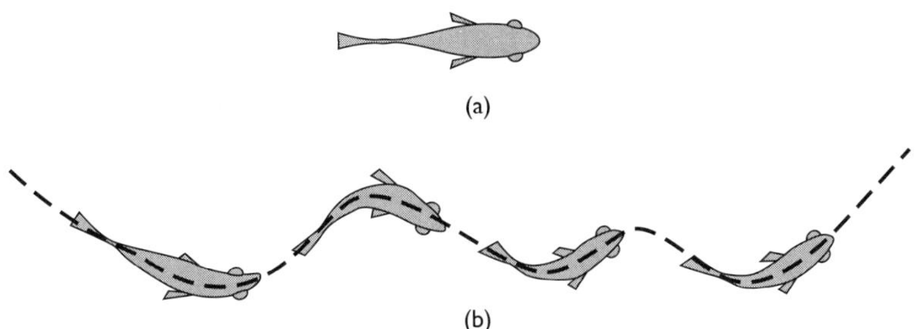

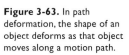

Figure 3-63. In path deformation, the shape of an object deforms as that object moves along a motion path.

At the same time that you animate a shape change for an object, you can transform the object using the standard translation, rotation, and scaling transformations. If you translate and rotate the head model in Figures 3-60 and 3-61, for example, at the same time that you animate the shape, the result is a very odd bobbing and twisting effect.

Bear in mind, however, that animating a shape change is much more computationally expensive than animating a simple transformation of a rigid object. In the animation of a rigid object, at most nine values (three translations, three rotations, and three scales) must be interpolated and recalculated for each frame. In a shape-change animation, on the other hand, the number of values that need to be recalculated for each frame depends on the number of control points or polygon vertices being moved with each frame. If sixteen control points define the surface of a spline-based sphere, and each of these points has an X,Y, and Z value, then 48 values (16 × 3) must be calculated for each frame. If the sphere is polygonally modeled, it easily could have a ten by ten mesh of polygons, with each polygon having four vertices and each vertex three coordinate values. This operation requires the recalculation of 1,200 values (10 × 10 × 4 × 3) per frame! As a result of all this calculation, the feedback time of most computers is slowed down considerably.

This computational overhead, however, goes with the territory, and, as always, the quality of the results can outweigh the inconveniences of the process. Animating the changes in the shape of an object often is critical for the success of an animation. Also keep in mind that computational issues of this sort become less problematic with each new wave of more powerful and less expensive hardware releases.

Camera Animation

In effect, all of the animation techniques discussed so far have involved the remodeling of objects over time, whether by transforming them or by changing their shape. It is also possible, however, to animate rendering parameters, such as the point of view from which a scene is observed, over time.

One of the most critical aspects of an animation may be just such camera animation. In fact, there is no animation in which the movement or lack of movement of the camera is not significant. As examples, think of these scenes from well-known films, both live action and animated. In the famous shower scene in Alfred Hitchcock's *Psycho*, the camera is positioned initially so that the viewer sees someone enter the bathroom well before the victim in the shower is aware of his presence. Once the attacker strikes, the camera cuts repeatedly and rapidly (there are about fifty camera moves in the scene overall) between the attacker, his victim, the shower head, the attacker's knife, the victim, and so on. Almost all of the tension and emotional impact of this powerful scene derives directly from the use of the camera.

By way of contrast, an animated film well known to students of computer animation, *Luxo, Jr.*, employs an absolutely stationary camera throughout the entire animation. In this case, *not* moving the camera becomes extremely effective, as the viewer must try to anticipate what little Luxo is doing each time he moves off screen, out of the range of the camera.

Given the importance of the camera, it is not surprising that 3D computer animation systems provide a number of approaches to animating the camera. The simplest of these approaches is to use a basic keyframing approach for the camera just as for individual objects. In fact, most systems treat the camera as an object, almost (but not quite) as if it were a cube or a sphere, and allow you to manipulate it very much as you would any other object, translating it and rotating it. You select the camera, manipulate it to produce the desired point of view, and then save the settings of the camera as a keyframe. Once you have saved a series of keyframes, the computer interpolates the in-between camera positions for each frame that lies between the keyframes.

Any of the parameters that define a camera in three-dimensional computer graphics—location, direction, field of view, and focal length (see *The Camera*, in chapter 2)—normally can be animated with this basic keyframe approach. Usually you do this by selecting any of the standard camera moves (pan, track, dolly, zoom, etc.) from a menu.

The top row of Figure 3-64, for example, is a storyboard representing an animation. In the first three panels of this storyboard (from left to right), both the camera location and the camera center of interest change. Between the first and second panels, the camera pans right—that is, as it moves to the right, the camera continues to look straight ahead. Between the second and third panels, the camera tumbles, or rotates, though the center of interest, or "gaze," remains fixed on the house. From the third panel to the fourth panel, the camera zooms in—that is, the field of view changes. In the final panel, a change in the focal length of the camera forces the objects in the distance, behind the house, to go out of focus.

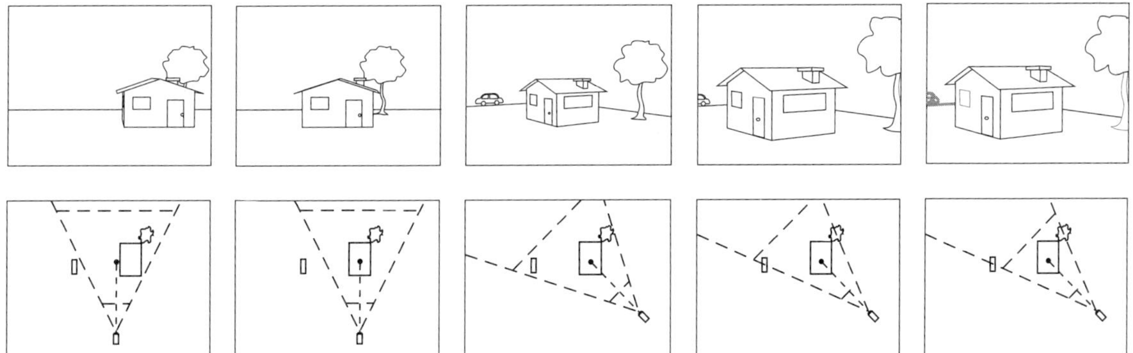

Figure 3-64. All of the standard camera manipulations that might be used when setting up a still image also can be animated with the keyframing approach.

In the bottom row of Figure 3-64 is a diagrammatic illustration of this same sequence. From the first panel to the second panel of this diagram, the location of the eye and the center of interest move as a unit—that is, pan—to the right. In the third panel, the center of interest remains stationary, but the eye rotates about it. In the fourth panel, the field of view, represented by the dotted-line triangle emanating from the eye, changes, indicating a zoom-in. And in the last panel, the farther of the two parallel dotted lines within the field-of-view triangle moves closer, indicating that the maximum distance at which things remain in focus has gotten closer. This last movement represents the shortening of focal length that results in the defocusing of the more distant objects in the last panel of the storyboard.

All four of these camera parameters correspond to what actually happens in the physical world with cameras and with our eyes. Animating these four camera parameters tends, consequently, to be intuitive for most people. Remember, however, that the camera of computer graphics also includes invisible walls, called clipping planes, that define the near and far limits of the visible world (see chapter 2, *The Camera*). Some systems permit you to animate the locations of these near and far clipping planes. Animation of clipping planes, however, may be less intuitive than that of other parameters, since clipping planes do not correspond to any part of the way either real eyes or real cameras function.

The most common application of this technique is to improve the Z-buffer rendering resolution of a scene. Recall that one approach rendering programs use to calculate which objects in a scene are in front of which other objects is to store information about the Z location of each pixel in a separate buffer, called a **Z-buffer** (see chapter 2, *Rendering Algorithms*). The larger the amount of space to be dealt with, however, the less accurate this Z-location information will be, because the algorithm divides the space into a fixed number of subdivisions. (The specific number of subdivisions used is determined by the number of bits of memory devoted to each pixel. For example, eight bits of

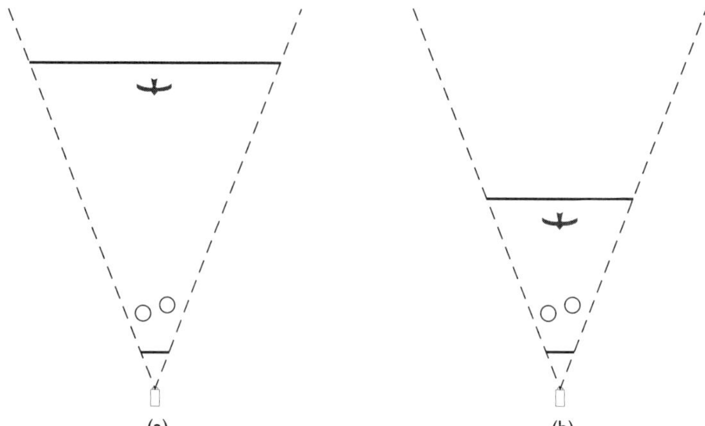

Figure 3-65. The location of the clipping planes can be animated to improve the accuracy of Z-buffer rendering.

memory produce 256 subdivisions.) Moreover, the amount of space to be dealt with is determined by the location of the near and far clipping planes.

If the distances represented within an animated sequence vary significantly over the course of the sequence, it may be worthwhile to animate the near and far clipping planes in order to optimize the Z-buffer resolution during rendering. For example, in Figure 3-65a the viewer (that is, the camera) is watching a bird fly up from the far distance towards it. There are some trees (here drawn simply as circles) in the foreground. At the beginning of the sequence, the clipping planes (the solid parallel lines) must be set very far apart, behind the bird and in front of the trees, to include both the bird in the far distance and the trees in the foreground. In Figure 3-65b, as the bird flies closer to the camera, animating the back clipping plane to stay close to the bird improves the Z-buffer rendering resolution and results in a more accurate rendering.

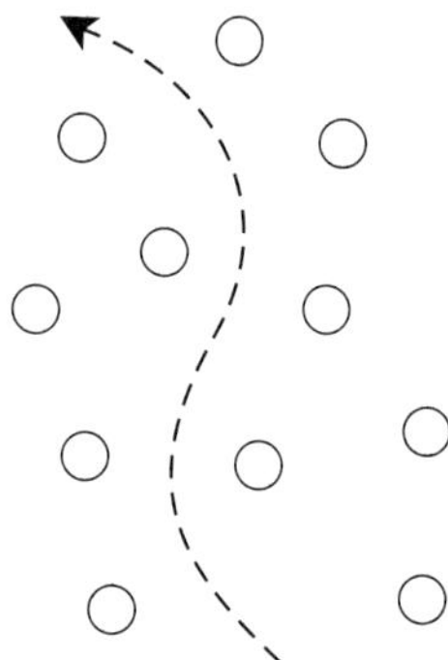

Figure 3-66. Some camera movements are best represented as movement along a path.

Although the discussion of camera animation so far has been in terms of the basic keyframe approach to animation, the same alternate techniques discussed in conjunction with the animation of geometric objects can be applied here. For instance, just as you can edit the animation of the transformations of an object by graphically editing parameter curves, so you can, in most 3D animation systems, edit the graphs of the camera parameters to change the camera animation. More interestingly, however, you can also apply motion-path animation to a camera just as you would to an object. If you were animating the frantic air-bike chase scene from George Lucas's film *Return of the Jedi*, for example, it would be a prime candidate for **camera path animation**. Much of the effectiveness of this scene is the result of the camerawork simulating the hero's ride through a forest at breakneck speed.

A diagram of this scene might look something like Figure 3-66. Here the circles represent tree trunks, and the curving line moving through the forest of circles/trees represents the path of the hero's air-bike. Since the camera is intended to represent the hero's point of view, it should follow this same path.

Clearly, thinking of the movement of the camera in this scene as a path is much more intuitive than thinking of it as a sequence of keyframes. You already have the path of the air-bike, so it makes sense to apply it to your camera. However, some complexities arise when you think of camera animation in terms of motion paths. The camera, remember, is not a simple unary object like a sphere. A camera actually consists of both location and center of interest of the camera, and in setting up a motion path for the camera, you somehow must deal with both components.

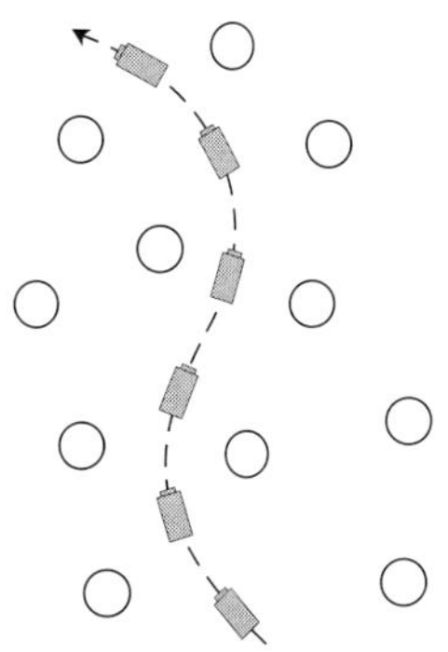

Figure 3-67. If the center of interest stays on the path, the camera always looks down the path.

To return to the example, imagine that you have assigned the motion path to the camera-location component of the camera. You still must determine the direction the camera is looking in as it moves down the path. You probably want the camera—that is, the hero's point of view—to look down the path as the air-bike speeds along through the forest (Figure 3-67.) This is the same issue that you encounter when moving an object along a path. That is, just as you want the paper airplane in Figure 3-56 to remain tangent to the curve, you want the camera—to think of it for the moment as an actual thing—to remain tangent to the curve.)

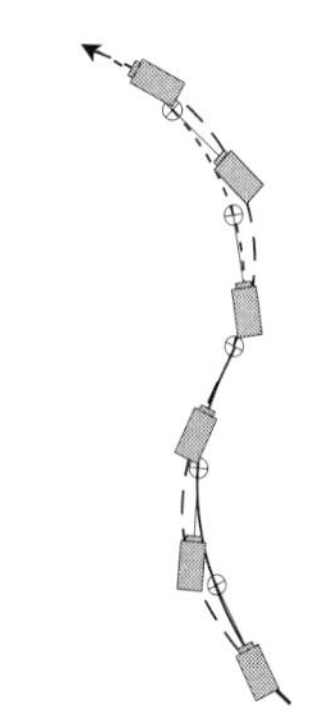

Figure 3-68. The direction in which the camera is looking can be animated along a separate path.

This choice may, however, produce a look that is too mechanical—too perfect. A person sitting on that air-bike would not always be looking exactly down the center of the motion path. Instead, the rider's gaze would slide from one side of the path to the other, now a little to the left, now a little to the right. Some systems allow you to get this effect by specifying a separate path for the center of interest (Figure 3-68). Notice that the path for the center of interest (drawn here as a dotted line) tends to slide away from the location path (the solid line) whenever there is a sharp turn in that path. This tendency simulates a bit more naturally what the (all too human) eye would do as the air-bike speeds around sharp turns.

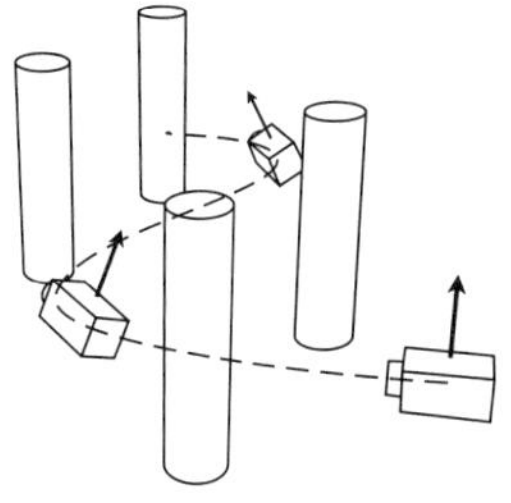

Figure 3-69. The tilt of the camera can also be animated to produce a banking effect.

One last aspect to consider with respect to motion paths is the issue (introduced in chapter 2, *The Camera*, and illustrated here in Figure 3-69), of the tilt, or roll, of the camera around the Z axis. In systems that represent the direction of the camera as a set of rotational values, this tilting of the camera can be created either automatically through a menu selection or by setting specific keyframes for the rotational values of the camera about the Z axis. In systems that represent the direction of the camera in terms of center of interest, the tilt factor can be represented as a point in space that defines the "top" of the camera, and a separate motion path can be defined for that parameter to create the effect of banking around a turn. This method is similar to drawing the extra camera path, as you saw above, for the center of interest of the camera.

Both camera path animation and keyframed camera animation can be very effective tools when used properly. Because it is so easy in most 3D computer animation systems to produce very dramatic camera movements, however, animators often overuse the camera. Keep in mind that camera animation should be used for a purpose, and that sometimes the most effective use of the camera may be to keep it perfectly still.

Animating Lights and Surface Properties

(a)

(b)

(c)

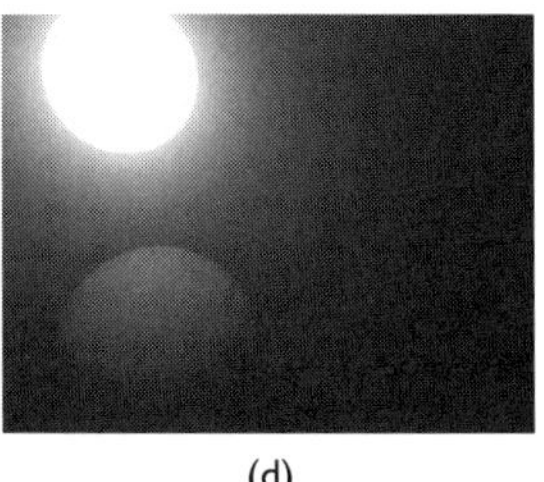

(d)

Figure 3-70. Both the position and characteristics of a light can be animated.

In many 3D computer animation systems, all of the factors that influence the rendering of a scene—lighting, shading, coloring, and so on—can be animated over time. In principle, these animations are no different than the animation of modeling parameters. When you move an object from one place to another over the course of 100 frames, you really are creating an interpolated set of values for the *translation x*, *translation y*, and *translation z* parameters of that object. It is as easy for a computer to create an interpolated set of values for some rendering parameter—for example, the *shininess* parameter—as to create values for the *translation x* parameter.

One of the most significant factors in the rendering of any scene is the lighting. You have seen (in chapter 2, *Lights*) that lights can be defined and placed in the virtual scene just as if they were normal objects. Lights can be transformed in space in all the same ways that, for example, a cube can. It is possible to position a light, save that position as a keyframe, reposition it, save a new keyframe, and then create the interpolated animation of the light moving from the first position to the second. This is, in fact, how the moving "gleams" so common in commercial logo animations are created. As the light moves through space, the highlight it creates on the shiny logo moves about as well, creating a moving "gleam" on the surface of the object.

In addition, you might rotate a spotlight, to create the sort of roving-spotlight effect seen in an "Opening Night at the Movies" animation. Or you might scale some specialized light such as an area light, the definition of which includes a specified size.

In addition to transforming a light, it is also possible in many systems to animate the other parameters that make up the definition of a light. That is, you might animate the brightness of the light over time, or the color of the light, or the spread of the light cone of a spotlight, and so on. You most often animate these parameters by typing frame numbers into a menu window in order to define the range over which the given parameter will animate. You then type in the starting and ending values of that particular parameter. Some systems that offer this approach provide only a default linear interpolation of the parameter values. More powerful systems offer the full range of interpolation types as well as parameter-curve editing capabilities for the animation of these lighting parameters.

Figure 3-70 consists of four panels, *a* through *d*, from an animation. A simple point light provides all the illumination in the scene. Over the course of this animation, the location of the light animates, moving from the lower right of the frame to the upper left. This movement was accomplished by placing the local origin of the light in the center of the large sphere and rotating the light around that origin over time. At the same time that the light moves, several properties of that light also animate. The intensity, or brightness, of the light increases over time. At the same time, the intensity of the glow parameter also increases: the software package used to produce these frames includes an additional parameter associated with the glow parameter that permitted the animator to make the ring effect more pronounced as the glow increased. Finally, notice that in panel *c*, a lens-flare effect results from turning on the lens-flare parameter for this light.

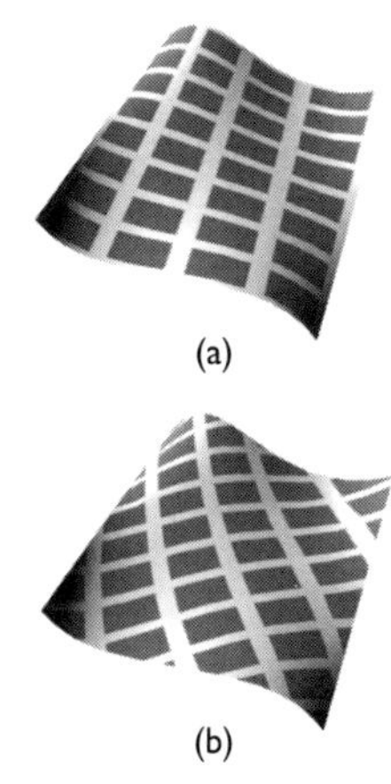

Figure 3-71. Animating the rotation parameter of a two-dimensional texture map.

Just as you can animate various properties of lights over time, you can animate the surface characteristics of objects, such as color, shininess, diffuseness, highlight size, and highlight color (see chapter 2, *Surface Characteristics*, for a discussion of these parameters). And, as with lights, the most common approach for doing this involves a menu window, into which you type values for the surface parameter to be animated.

As you also saw in the sections *Solid Texture Mapping* and *Atmospheric Effects* in chapter 2, a number of mapping techniques are commonly used to create certain surface effects. In applying any of these mapping techniques, you must set certain parameters to define how the mapping will take place—for example, to locate the map on the surface, to scale the effect (that is, the color saturation, the amount of bumpiness, etc.) of the map, and so on. Many 3D computer animation systems allow you to animate these mapping parameters, again usually by typing values into a menu window.

You might, for example, rotate a color texture map on a surface over time (Figure 3-71). Here, the surface geometry and all other properties of the surface remain static. Only the rotation parameter of the texture map is animated.

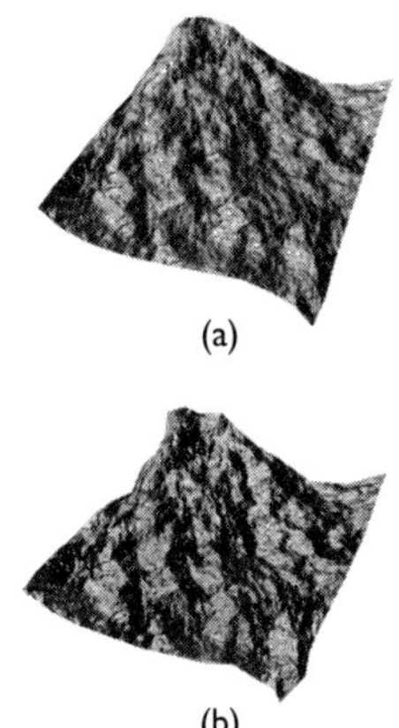

Figure 3-72. Animating the effect parameter of a displacement map in order to increase the cragginess of the surface.

Or you might scale the effect factor of a displacement map over a sequence of frames (Figure 3-72). Here, all parameters are constant except for the scaling parameter on the displacement map. Or you might animate the "noise" parameter in a fractal-based transparency map, producing cloud patterns that swirl about over time (Figure 3-73).

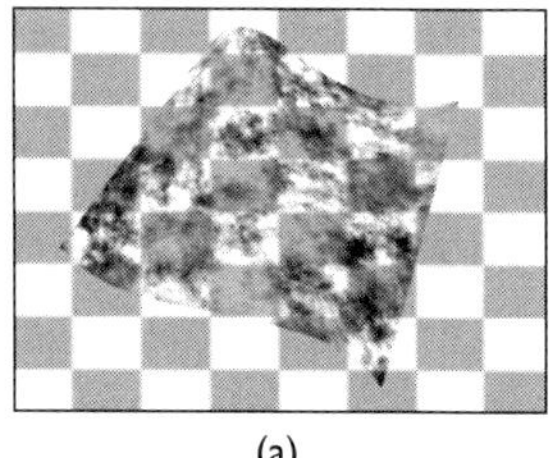

(a)

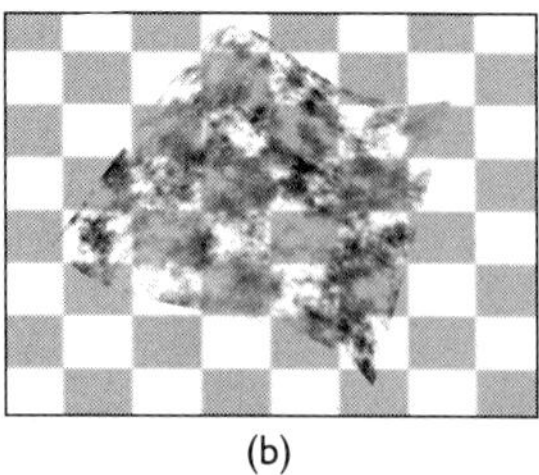

(b)

Figure 3-73. Animating the noise parameter of a fractal-based map causes the patterns to swirl about.

A good example of effective animation of mapping parameters appears in color plate 1. This entire animation was accomplished solely through the animation of texture-map parameters without any animation of geometry at all.

You can animate the same sorts of parameters—color, placement, and so on—in a solid texture as you can in a flat texture. However, it is also possible, because of the nature of solid textures, to produce an unusual sort of mapping animation.

You have seen that the volume of a solid texture is treated like a three-dimensional object and has a transformation matrix associated with it. In most cases, since you want the solid texture to "stick" to the surface, the transformation matrix of the texture volume and the transformation matrix of the surface are linked together so that they both have exactly the same transformation (see chapter 2, *Solid Texture Mapping*).

It is possible, however, to create certain unusual effects by animating the transformation matrix of the texture volume independently of what is happening to the transformation matrix of the surface. For example, if you animate a separate rotation on the texture volume, the texture patterns swirl over the surface: Figure 3-74a shows the object as it receives the solid texture pattern before any transformation of the texture volume. Figure 3-74b and c show the effects on the same object of rotating the texture volume over time.

Another very interesting possibility in the animation of texture maps is that, rather than using a single, static image as the texture for the mapping procedure, you can use an animated sequence of pictures as the source texture images. For example, suppose that you already have produced—either through animation or live-action footage—a sequence of frames, such as the sequence of images from the work of the photographer Eadweard Muybridge (Figure 3-75a). Suppose further that you want to map this sequence of texture images onto the screen of a computer monitor that you have modeled.

(a)

(b)

(c)

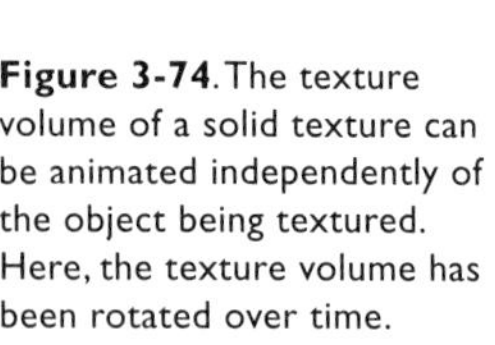

Figure 3-74. The texture volume of a solid texture can be animated independently of the object being textured. Here, the texture volume has been rotated over time.

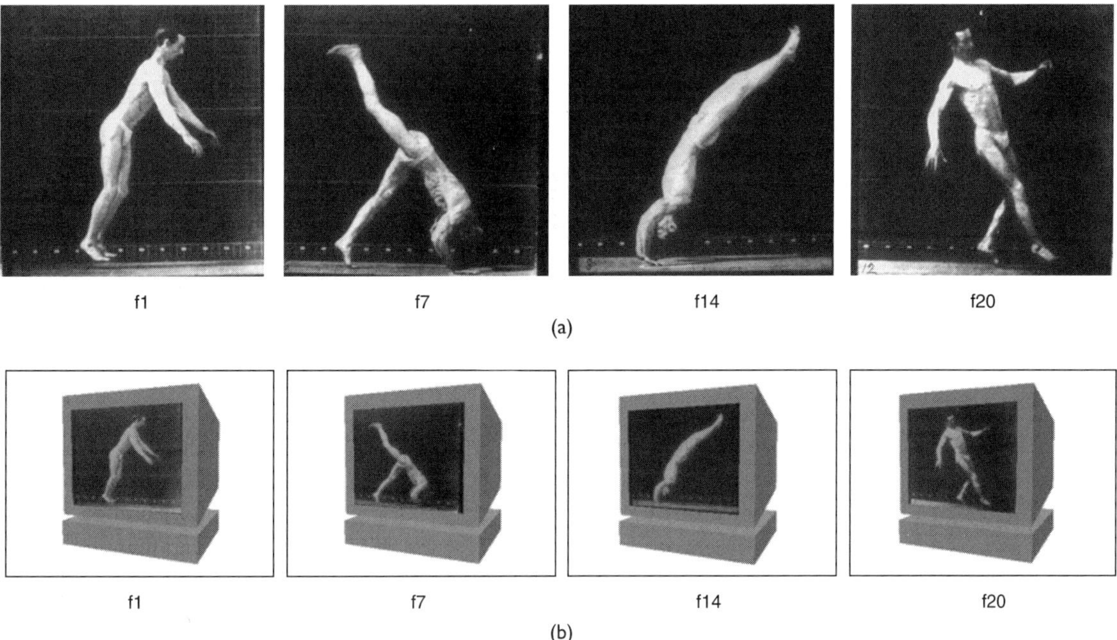

Figure 3-75. A sequence of images can be mapped onto a surface to create an animated image on the rendered surface. (Images from *The Human Figure in Motion* by Eadweard Muybridge, New York: Dover, 1955.)

By specifying that at frame 1 you will use texture image number 1, and at frame 2 you will use texture image number 2, and so on, you can map the animated sequence of images onto the surface (Figure 3-75b).

In most systems, a technique very similar to this also can be applied to the use of background pictures. By specifying that a sequence of background pictures is to be used throughout the animation sequence, you can create an animated background in front of which models complete some series of actions.

CHAPTER 4

Advanced Animation Techniques

Introduction

In the previous chapter you learned about a variety of animation techniques commonly found in three-dimensional animation packages. This chapter is devoted to several advanced techniques.

The word "advanced" here does not mean that these techniques are difficult to understand or use. In fact, depending on how they are implemented in a given software package, they may be quite easy to understand and use. These techniques are deemed "advanced" not because of any inherent difficulty, but simply because they are more recent developments in computer graphics research.

The pattern of research and development in computer graphics is predictable. At a certain time, no one knows how to solve a given problem. Then a handful of researchers begin to develop techniques to deal with this problem. These researchers publish their results in professional journals, and other researchers study the results and refine the solutions. Eventually, the problem is understood well enough that programmers and researchers in commercial software companies begin using the newly developed techniques to write software, which is included in their company's commercially available software package. After being on the market in experimental form for some time, and after the bugs are worked out, the new software becomes one more technique in the standard repertoire of 3D computer graphics.

The techniques included in this chapter are in the last stages of this process. They are all important techniques, and they are all available in many packages, but they are not yet available in all packages. With time, these advanced techniques will become commonplace, will cease to be considered advanced, and will be replaced by a new set of advanced techniques.

Blended Surfaces

In the **blended surface** technique, a new surface is created between, and attached to, two other surfaces. Figure 4-1a shows the two original surfaces,

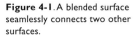

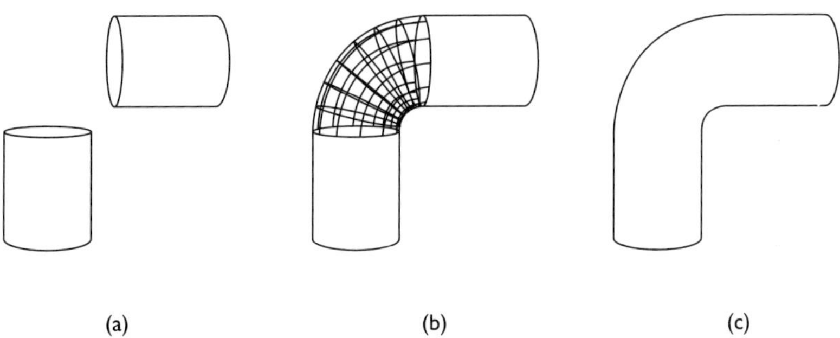

Figure 4-1. A blended surface seamlessly connects two other surfaces.

in this case, two cylinders, and Figure 4-1b shows the new, blended surface, represented here in wireframe, created between them.

An important feature of a blended surface is that it is defined so that it blends smoothly and without any visible seam with the other two objects. In more technical terminology, the blended surface is said to be **continuous** with the two original surfaces. As a result, when rendered as a shaded surface, the three objects—the two originals plus the blended surface—appear as a single, continuous object (Figure 4-1c.)

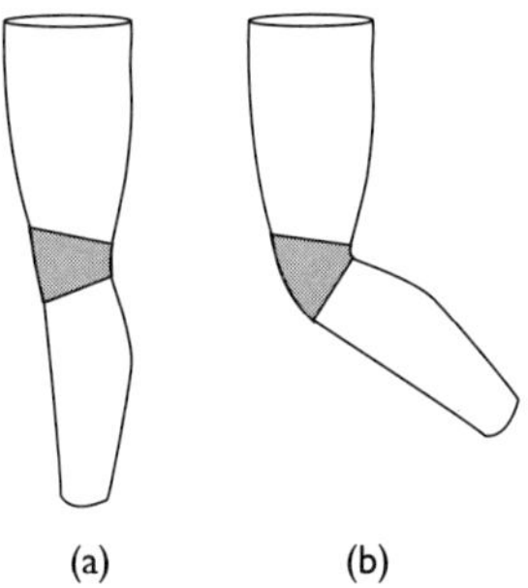

Figure 4-2. A blended surface automatically deforms as its attached objects move about.

Another critical feature of a blended surface—the one that makes it so valuable for animation—is that the shape of the blended surface is automatically recalculated and updated whenever either of the two original objects moves. In other words, if either of the two original objects is animated, the blended surface changes shape appropriately, always remaining, at every frame, continuous with its two end objects. Figure 4-2a shows the static models, an upper and a lower leg, before any animation. Between these, in the area of the knee, is a blended surface. In Figure 4-2b the lower leg rotates backward: the blended surface is automatically recalculated and reshaped, causing the knee to bend. This technique can be extremely effective for human (and other animal) figure models, since it allows the smooth connection of the rigid parts of a body.

In defining a blended surface, you typically begin by selecting the end contours of the two original objects (the bold lines in Figure 4-3a). You then create a default blended surface. This surface may be twisted, as in Figure 4-3b, if the two contours you selected run in opposite directions—for example, one clockwise and the other counterclockwise. The surface may also be twisted if the starting points of the two contours are out of alignment. In either case, this twisting occurs as the blended surface tries to connect the points of one contour to the points of the other contour. To correct this, the software allows you to to "untwist" the blended surface, usually by dragging the mouse cursor in one direction or the other.

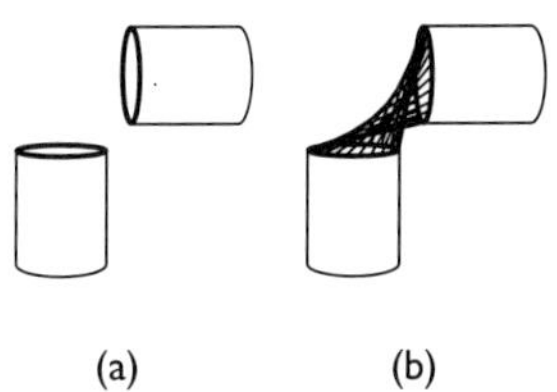

Figure 4-3. To create a blended surface, you select end contours on each object, untwisting the blended surface if necessary.

Blended surfaces very effectively solve the problem of smoothly connecting two animated surfaces. However, recalculating the blended surface at every frame so that it is continuous with each of the other surfaces is mathematically complex and can significantly slow down your program, especially if there are several blended surfaces. You should take this into account in your use of blended surfaces.

Expressions

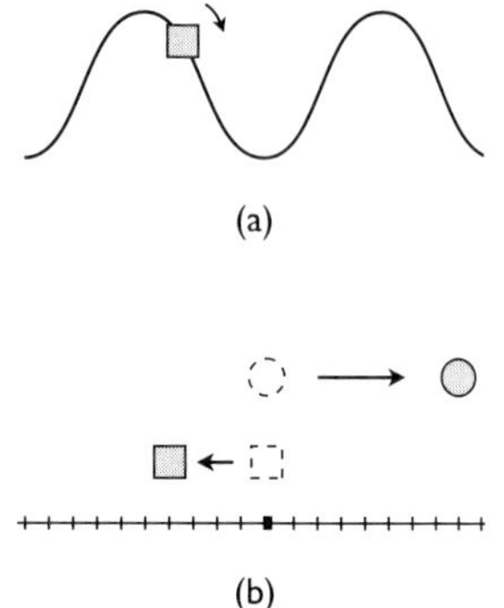

Figure 4-4. The motion of some objects can be easily described by a mathematical expression.

In certain situations it may be best to think of the animation of a specific object in terms of a mathematical formula, or expression, that describes its motion. For example, if you wanted to move an object along a path in the shape of a standard sine curve, as in Figure 4-4a, you could try to draw a path in the exact shape of a sine curve, but a more accurate way of getting this motion would be to tell the animation system to use the mathematical function, Sine.

Another situation in which it might be easier to produce an animation by thinking in terms of mathematical expressions is when the motion of one object depends on the motion of another. Here, the relationship between the two objects can frequently be described most clearly as a mathematical relationship between the two objects. For example, the sphere in Figure 4-4b moves in the opposite direction and twice as fast as the cube.

Defining an object's motion by specifying mathematical formulae or expressions in this way is referred to as using **expressions**. This is a text-based technique—that is, you type in the text of the mathematical expressions. It is very similar in principle to programming, although much simpler in practice. In fact, the software packages that offer this technique go to great lengths to make expressions accessible to and usable by the average animator. Programming experience is not necessary to make good use of expressions.

Nonetheless, some of the basic principles of programming also apply to expressions. Writing expressions, for example, entails using a specific "language." The syntax and vocabulary of that language vary from one 3D software package to another, but they are all language-based. As in programming, it is important that anything you type be exactly in accordance with the rules of your package's expression language. If it is not, you will get an error message.

Whatever package and language you use, you begin by specifying—usually by typing its name—which object you want to control. You next specify, again by typing, which parameter of that object you want to control. Together, the intended object and its intended parameter are considered the **target**. For example, to specify the translation in X of an object called "cube" as the target, you might type something like *cube.TX*. (Here, and in all subsequent ecamples of this section, I use a hypothetical expression syntax.) Similarly, an object called "Head" might have its rotation around Y specified by *Head.RY*, and its scale along the Z axis by *Head.SY*.

Once you have indicated your target object and parameter, you type in the mathematical expression that will control it. The complexity of the expression varies depending on the animation's requirements and your own mathematical skills.

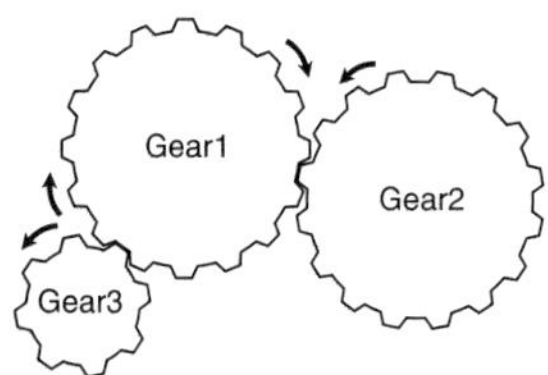

Figure 4-5. The motion of Gear2 and Gear3 can be written as simple mathematical functions of the motion of Gear1.

As a simple example, imagine a set of interlocking gears, as in Figure 4-5, with the central gear, *Gear1*, being animated through standard keyframing techniques. The motion of the other gears—both their speed and direction—will be a function of *Gear1*'s motion. Because the gears all interlock, this is an ideal candidate for the expression technique.

This animation could be produced without expressions, but it is much easier to produce it by taking advantage of the direct mathematical relationships among the gears. (The benefit of using expressions would be even greater if there were dozens or hundreds of interlocking gears!) Consider first the relationship for just one of the dependent gears, *Gear2*. You can see from the illustration that *Gear2* has to rotate in the opposite direction from *Gear1*: if *Gear1* rotates clockwise, *Gear2* must rotate counterclockwise, and vice versa. You can also see that they will have to move at exactly the same speed, since *Gear1* and *Gear2* are the same size (which you can confirm by counting the number of teeth on each gear). In other words, however much *Gear1* rotates, *Gear2* will rotate the same amount, except in the opposite direction. This can be expressed mathematically as:

Gear2.RZ = Gear1.RZ *–1

That is: "The rotation in Z of Gear2 is equal to the rotation in Z of Gear1 times –1". The reason you multiply by –1 is to negate the value of the rotation, thereby making the gear turn in the opposite direction.

Gear3's motion can be written similarly. Again looking at the illustration, you can see that *Gear3* must rotate in the opposite direction from *Gear1*. The speed of *Gear3*, however, will not be the same as that of *Gear1*. Since *Gear3* is only half as big (count the teeth), it will rotate twice as quickly. In short:

Gear3.RZ = Gear1.RZ * –2

The multiplication by –2 doubles the speed and reverses the direction of the Z rotation.

In actual practice most software packages do not require that you write your expressions as equations as we just did. More commonly, you write the

Figure 4-6. Expressions are frequently written in a menu box structure.

TARGET	EXPRESSION
Gear3.RZ	Gear1.RX * –2

left side of the equation—that is, the target object and parameter—in one menu box. You write the right side of the equation—the expression itself—in another. Typically, your menu might look something like Figure 4-6.

In the gear example above, you already made use of one of the **arithmetic operators** that are a standard feature of expressions. These arithmetic operators include the familiar +, –, *, / of programming languages—that is, *add, subtract, multiply, divide.*

All packages that offer expressions also offer a library of standard **mathematical functions** to help you write more complex expressions. These functions are similar to the standard mathematical functions that are part of any programming language. They include sine, cosine, minimum, maximum, square root, absolute value, random number, and others. Usually these functions are referenced, or **called**, by abbreviated names derived from the names of the same functions in the C programming language—for example, *sin(), cos(), min(), max(), sqrt(), abs(), rand().*

In addition to standard math functions, expressions also use the **logical operators** of programming languages, with the syntax of the C programming language again the most common. These operators include:

==	is equal to
!=	is not equal to
>	is greater than
<	is less than
>=	is greater than or equal to
<=	is less than or equal to

And to build more complex expression statements, there are also the standard **boolean operators**:

&&	and
||	or

By using a combination of these syntactical elements, you can write some very powerful expressions.

An additional syntactical element, the **conditional** statement, extends the power of expressions quite a bit (just as it does in programming), by defining the conditions under which an event takes place. This requires some sort of *if . . . then . . . else* statement in your expression. The syntax for such a statement

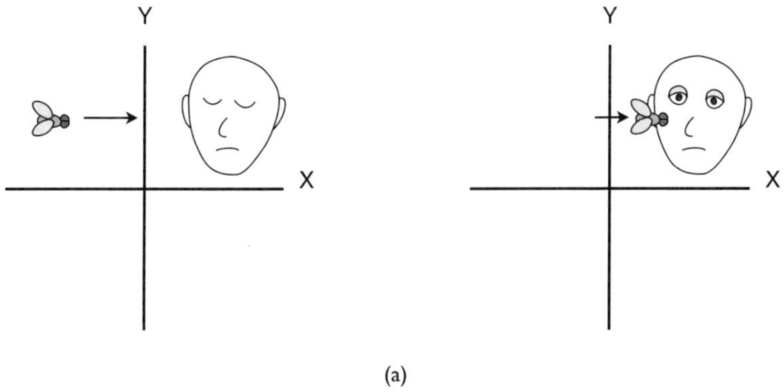

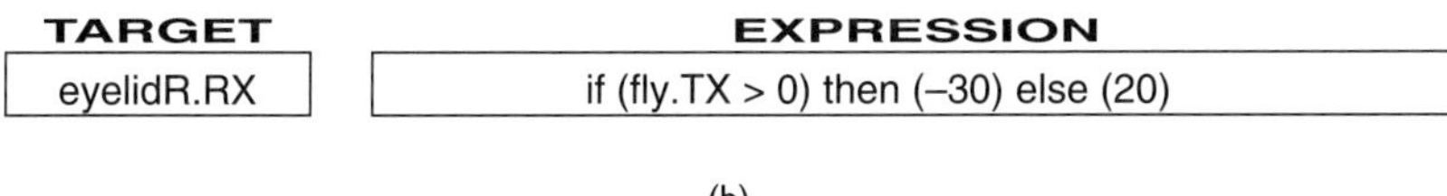

(b)

Figure 4-7. Conditional statements can make an object's motion dependent upon some event.

varies from one software package to the next, but the concept is the same: "If something is true, then do such and such; otherwise, do something else."

For example, suppose you want the eyelids in Figure 4-7a to open—that is, to rotate about X—when the fly gets very close to the face—that is, when the fly crosses into the positive X half of the coordinate system. You could write an expression for each eyelid that uses a conditional: Figure 4-7b shows such an expression for the right eyelid. This expression, translated into English, says: "If the fly's X translation is greater than 0, then the eyelid's X rotation is –30 degrees (that is, open); otherwise, the eyelid's rotation is 20 degrees (that is, closed)."

A more sophisticated test of whether the fly is "very close" to the man would be to measure the distance between the fly and the man's head, rather than simply to test if the fly has crossed into the positive X half of coordinate space. Many software packages include a function that will do just this, calculating the distance between two objects—more specifically, calculating the distance between the local origin of one object and the local origin of another. Because distance is usually calculated from one local origin to another, you normally indicate the name of the two objects, but not any parameters, when you call the function. Modifying the fly example above, you might therefore write a new expression as shown in Figure 4-8b. In English this reads: "If the distance between the fly and the man's head is less than 2, then the eyelid's X rotation is –30 degrees (open); otherwise, the eyelid's rotation is 20 degrees (closed)." With this new, more robust expression, the eyelid will open and close no matter where the man is or where the fly is, so long as they are close enough to each other. With the eyelids controlled in this way by expressions, you can now concentrate on the animation of the fly, knowing that the eyelids will automatically open or close as necessary.

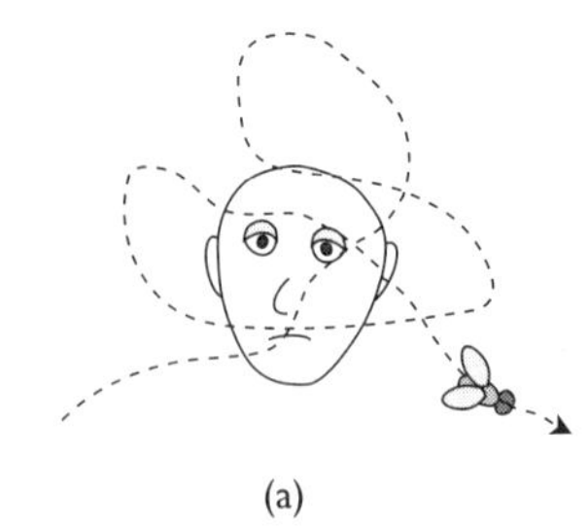

(a)

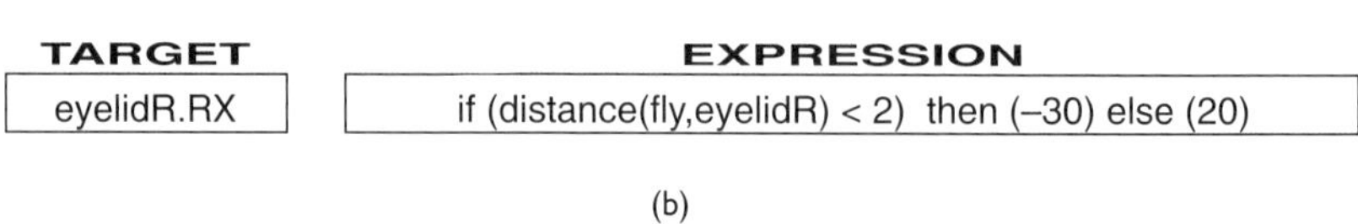

(b)

Figure 4-8. Expression languages allow you to call library functions as you would in programming.

When referencing an object's location in space as in the fly example, you must be careful to pay attention to whether each parameter is in the **global space** of the whole world or in the **local space** of that particular object. This becomes an issue when you are working with hierarchical models.

As you saw in the section on *Hierarchical Animation* in chapter 3, when one object is the child of another in a hierarchy, the child node inherits the transformations of the parent node above it. Thus, in a hierarchical arm model like that shown in Figure 4-9a, if you rotate the whole arm at the shoulder (Figure 4-9b), all the children of the *WholeArm* node will also rotate.

This presents a curious problem when you want to write expressions that reference the location of the children nodes of such a hierarchy. Suppose, for example, that you want to write an expression that uses the location—that is, the translation values—of the hand. In the example illustrated in Figure 4-9, the hand, even though it is clearly in a different location, has not actually translated. The hand has moved because it has inherited the transformations of all the nodes above it in the hierarchy, but within its own local coordinate system it has not translated at all. Consequently, if you reference the hand's translation in your expression by saying, for example, *Hand.TX*, the value of this parameter will be zero. No matter how much you rotate the *WholeArm* and cause the hand visibly to move, *Hand.TX* will always remain zero (unless you specifically translate the hand away from the arm by operating on the *Hand* node directly).

The solution to this problem is that, rather than referencing the hand's translation within its own local coordinate space, you need to reference its translation within the *global* space of the whole world. In global space, the hand has clearly moved. In local space, it has not.

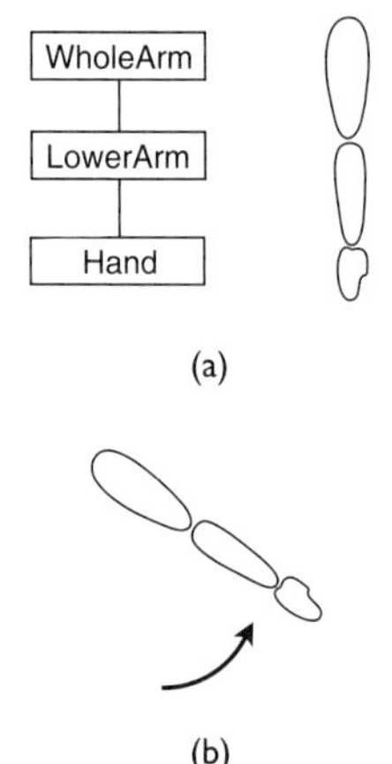

Figure 4-9. Even though a transformation on a parent node may cause a child node to move in global space, the child may not move within its own local space.

Most software packages provide a function to permit you to do this. The name and syntax of the function vary, but the effect is the same—to provide global coordinate readings of an object's transformation. Suppose that you have a function called *global()*. If you simply specify *Hand.TX* in your expression, you will get the local translation of the hand, which in the example is zero. But if instead you type *global(Hand.TX)*, you get the global translation of the hand, which might, for example, be +7.5 in the illustration.

The examples so far have referred only to the nine basic transformation parameters—translation XYZ, rotation XYZ, and scale XYZ. But any parameter of any object can be controlled by an expression. Lighting parameters and shading parameters can also be controlled by expressions. For example, you might want the color of an object to change as the object scales larger. Or you might cause the intensity of a light to dim as the camera recedes from it. You can use expressions to control the location of specific control points and vertices. For example, you could cause the eyeballs of the man in Figure 4-8 to bulge whenever the fly approaches by using expressions to translate some of the eyeballs' control points in an automated fashion.

In addition to all these parameters, there are also certain standard, predefined variables that allow you to reference other parameters of your animation. One of the most basic is the **current frame** number. As your animation plays, the current frame number is constantly rising, or **incrementing**. You can use this number to good effect in expressions. Suppose, for example, that the hand in the previous example is going to reach up and, at frame 100, grab an apple. From that point on, the apple should remain in the hand. By writing an expression that will cause the translation of the apple to attach to the global translation of the hand after frame 100, you can do this very easily (Figure 4-10). Assume, for this example, that before it is picked the apple's X translation is 12.0, its Y translation is 6.0, and its Z translation is 0.0. Also assume that in the software package the current frame number is referenced by a variable called *FrameCurrent*. The expression would be as shown in Figure 4-10b. Notice that more than one expression has been applied to the apple—specifically, one expression for each of the axes of translation. Each of the expressions is similar. The first, for example, translates this way: "If the current frame is less than 100, then the apple's X translation remains at 12.0; otherwise it becomes whatever the global X location of the hand is." By doing this for each of the three translation values, you cause the apple to stick to the hand from frame 100 onward.

Expressions provide a very powerful tool for producing animations that might otherwise be difficult to create. Still, the capabilities of the expression technique are quite simple compared to those of a full-blown programming

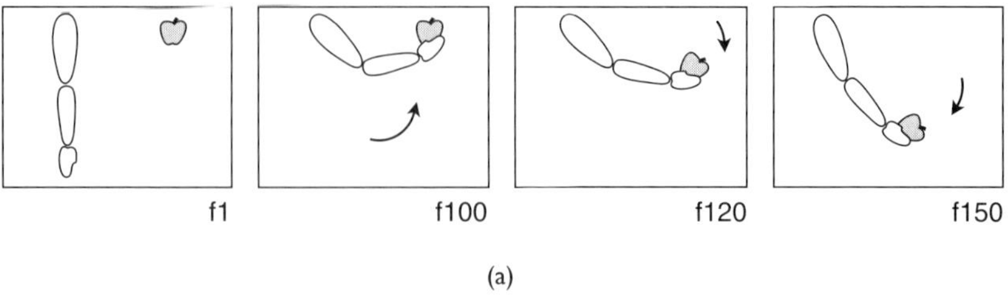

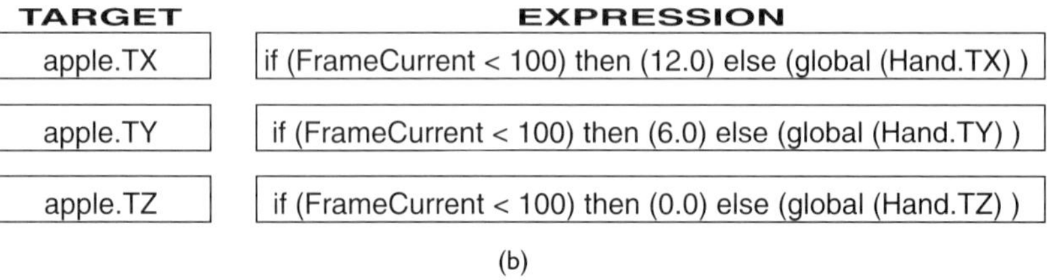

TARGET
EXPRESSION
apple.TX
if (FrameCurrent < 100) then (12.0) else (global (Hand.TX))
apple.TY
if (FrameCurrent < 100) then (6.0) else (global (Hand.TY))
apple.TZ
if (FrameCurrent < 100) then (0.0) else (global (Hand.TZ))
(b)

Figure 4-10. A predefined variable referencing the current frame number can be used to cause events to happen at certain moments.

language. To approach that level of programming power, you must work with a related technique called procedural animation, which is discussed later in this chapter.

Motion Dynamics

In certain situations the movement of an object, such as a ball falling from a height and bouncing on a surface, can be predicted very precisely. Physicists have studied this sort of phenomenon for a long time and have developed very accurate mathematical formulas to describe what happens in this situation. Knowing the effect of gravity and various properties of the ball and of the surface, they can calculate, using the laws of physics, how quickly the ball will fall, as well as how high and how often it will bounce.

This sort of mathematically precise and detailed study of the motion of objects is called **motion dynamics** and can be of great use to animators. The ball dropping straight down and bouncing off a flat surface is not very difficult to animate using standard keyframing techniques, but a more complex situation, such as a box being dropped and bouncing down a stairway (Figure 4-11), is very difficult to animate in a naturalistic way using keyframing. To estimate realistically how far the box bounces with each bounce, how much and in what directions the box rotates as it flies through the air, which edge or corner of the box strikes the surface of the stairs first, and so on, is a *very* complicated piece of animation. The physical laws of motion dynamics, however, are precise enough for you to calculate the motion of the box.

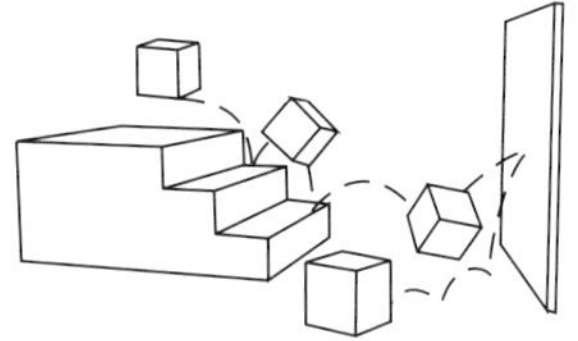

Figure 4-11. The motion of some objects can be calculated precisely according to the laws of physics.

The software of many sophisticated 3D animation packages incorporates this sort of motion-dynamics calculation. The best of these systems provide user interfaces that make the technical complexity of the underlying calculations invisible. Typically, you use a mouse device to open a menu and make several selections. These selections define the various parameters that control the motion of the object to be animated. Once you have defined these parameters, you make a selection that instructs the system to perform the calculations and play back the resulting animation on the screen. This result is called a **simulation**, because it simulates, or mimics, the behavior of objects in a real-world situation behaving under the influence of real-world physical laws.

In setting up a simulation you first define the **physical properties** of the object to be animated. That is, the motion-dynamics system must know certain characteristics of the object in order to calculate the simulated movement of the object. For example, a ball made of solid iron bounces much differently than does a ball made of balsa wood.

In physics—and in motion dynamics—one of the most basic physical properties of an object is **mass**. Mass is related to, but not quite the same as, weight. That is, the weight of an object is the result of gravity pulling down on the massiveness of the object. On Earth, gravity is effectively the same everywhere, so mass and weight have a direct, one-to-one correspondence. However, since weight is linked to gravity, the weight of an object *can* change—for example, if the object were in outer space—although the mass of the object remains the same wherever the object is. An object with a large mass is very difficult to start moving and very difficult to stop once it begins moving, and this property directly affects how the object moves in a motion-dynamic simulation. For example, if you roll a massive ball down a ramp and onto a level surface, the ball tends to keep rolling for a long time because the massiveness overcomes the forces that otherwise would make the object stop (Figure 4-12a). If you roll a less massive ball down the same ramp, it tends to stop much more quickly on the flat surface (Figure 4-12b).

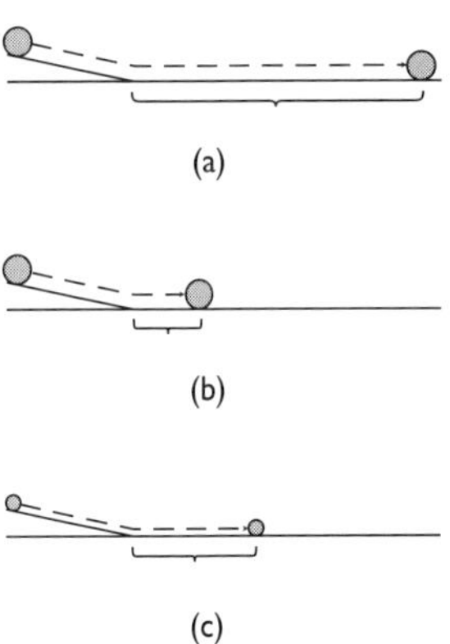

Figure 4-12. The mass of an object plays a key role in how the object behaves as it moves. Mass is a function of both the density of the material and the size of the object.

What makes the one ball more massive than the other is not the size of the objects but the **density** of the materials from which they are made. A balsa-wood ball is less massive than an iron ball because balsa wood is less dense than iron. A solid clay ball of the same size is more dense and more massive than a balsa-wood ball, but less dense and less massive than an iron ball.

Size does play a role, however, in determining mass, which is a function of both the density and the size (more exactly, the volume) of an object. A small iron ball (Figure 4-12c), even though it has the same density as a larger iron ball (Figure 4-12a), has a smaller mass because it has a smaller volume. Consequently, the little, less massive ball does not roll as far as the larger, more massive ball (Figure 4-12b).

Since the mass of an object depends on both volume and density, most people cannot readily estimate it. Consequently, many systems allow you to define mass indirectly by specifying density. By thinking in terms of material (iron, wood, clay, etc.) you can readily give the system a density parameter value—larger numbers for more dense materials, smaller numbers for less dense materials. The software then automatically calculates the volume of the object and then, from the combination of volume and density, the mass.

The density of an object also is important to consider when simulating objects lighter than air. A gas-filled balloon, for example, rises into the air because the gas inside the balloon is of a very, very low density. This causes the total mass of the balloon to be so little that gravity will not even keep it on the ground.

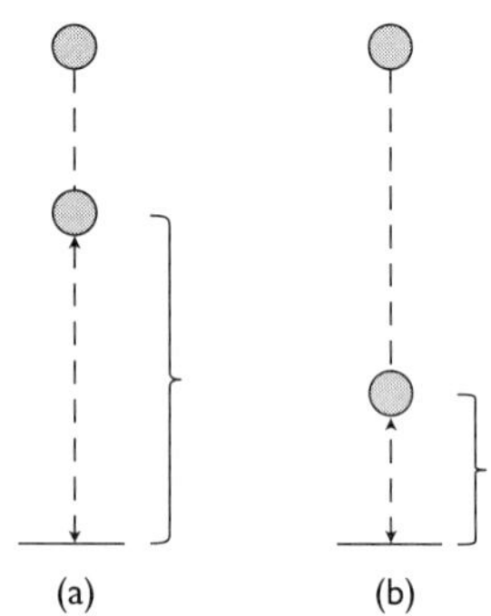

Figure 4-13. The elasticity of an object is a measure of how much the object bounces when it hits a surface.

Another important physical property of objects, called **elasticity**, reflects the way objects bounce. Imagine that two balls have exactly the same mass, but that when you drop these balls, one ball bounces much higher than the other one does (Figure 4-13a and b). A solid rubber ball, for example, tends to bounce much higher than a solid plastic ball—even though, as in this example, the masses of the balls happen to be exactly the same—and a glass marble dropped on a concrete floor bounces much higher than you might expect. Objects that have a high degree of elasticity, such as the solid rubber ball and the marble, tend to bounce a lot. Objects with lower elasticity bounce less.

The term "elasticity" can be a bit misleading, however. In day-to-day usage, the word describes objects easily stretched or deformed. A rubber band and a soft rubber ball that you can squeeze between your fingers are elastic in this sense. As it is used in motion dynamics, however, "elastic" means something different. A glass marble is extremely elastic because it bounces very high, even though it is very hard and does not deform between your fingers at all. In motion dynamics, elasticity refers to the amount of energy lost when an object makes contact with something else. If an object is very elastic, very little energy is lost and the object bounces a lot. If the object is very inelastic, a great deal of energy is lost and the object therefore bounces only slightly.

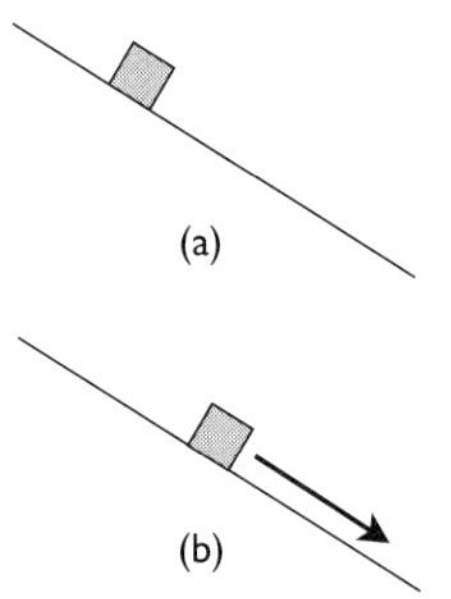

Figure 4-14. The static friction of an object is a measure of how readily the object, when stationary, will start to move after being subjected to some force.

Most systems also require you to define the **friction** created by an object. Since friction is a function of how smooth or rough a surface is, this property is sometimes referred to as **roughness**. The first type of friction, or roughness, is **static friction**, which prevents stationary objects from sliding down inclined planes. It is called "static" because it refers to nonmoving, or static, objects. If the static friction of a box is very great, for instance, the box will not slide at all (Figure 4-14a). If you decrease the static friction, the box will begin to slide (Figure 4-14b).

The second type of friction, **kinetic friction**, causes moving, or kinetic, objects to come to a stop. For instance, suppose you place two boxes identical in mass on two ramps identical in slope. What causes one box to stop sliding after only a short time is the kinetic friction, or roughness, of the surface of the box (Figure 4-15b). If the other box is made of some very slickly polished material and has very low kinetic friction, it will continue sliding for a longer distance (Figure 4-15a).

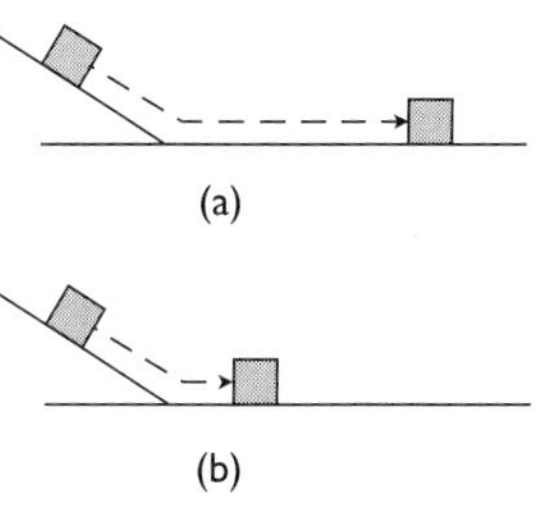

Figure 4-15. The kinetic friction of an object is a measure of how easily the object, when moving, can be stopped by some resisting force.

Static friction and kinetic friction function independently and therefore can be adjusted independently in most systems. For example, if you set the static friction of a ball rolling on a surface to zero, the ball will slide, rather than roll, along the surface. At the same time, you can adjust the kinetic friction of the ball up or down. If you increase the kinetic friction, the ball will slide (because the static friction is set to zero) and stop quickly (because the kinetic friction is high). If you decrease the kinetic friction, the ball will slide (because the static friction is still zero) and come to a stop slowly (because the kinetic friction is low).

So far, we have discussed a number of physical properties important for a motion-dynamics calculation. In order to complete the definition of motion dynamics for an object, however, you also need to describe the **forces** that act upon the object. What causes the object to move in the first place?

Perhaps the most basic force that motion dynamics takes into account is the force of **gravity**. Except in very rare circumstances, gravity affects all objects. Even if no other forces cause an object to move, gravity will keep it on the ground. Technically speaking, gravity is the attraction between two objects, caused by the masses of the objects and the distance between them. A ball falls to Earth because the mass of Earth is so much greater than the mass of the ball that the ball is attracted to Earth. This is why a ball in Antarctica will fall "upward" toward the Earth.

From the point of view of most animation, however, you can think of gravity in simpler terms—as a force pulling all objects downward. Consequently, most motion-dynamics systems define gravity as a simple force that pulls all objects downward at a specific rate in the negative Y direction. This force usually exists by default (just as it does on Earth) and affects all objects equally and automatically. Thus, even if you define no other forces and define no other animation, a ball that starts out suspended in the air at frame 1 of a simulation immediately begins falling in frame 2 because of gravity.

The fact that gravity causes objects to fall at a specific rate affects the dimensions you use when modeling objects in a motion-dynamics system. Because the speed at which an object falls is measured in terms of the distance the object travels per second, the measurements of distance you use in the modeling process must be consistent with the measurements of distance used by the motion-dynamics calculations for gravity. If the software you use measures gravity in feet per second, then the units of measurement for your models must also be feet. If gravity is measured in meters per second, then your models must be modeled in metric units. Normally, a motion-dynamics software package sets up default units of measurement, so that the units are consistent in both the modeling and simulation sections of the software. However, if you change the units of measurement, the gravitational force of the motion-dynamics system will not pull objects downward at a physically accurate rate.

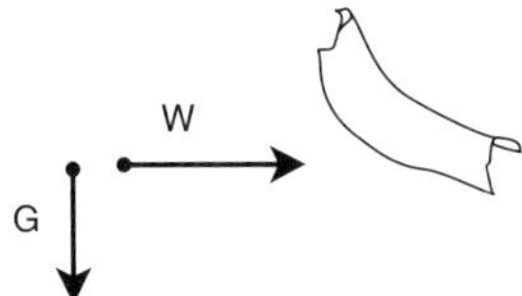

Figure 4-16. Motion-dynamics systems require you to define the forces, such as gravity and wind, that act on objects.

In addition to gravity, another force that many systems allow you to define is **wind**, which can be very useful, for example, in animating a curtain blowing in a breeze, or the branches of a tree bending slightly in the wind. These are subtle kinds of movement, difficult to model convincingly with keyframing techniques. A wind force is usually defined as a vector having a location, a direction, and a strength. In Figure 4-16, the arrow pointing to the right represents the wind force. The arrow pointing downward is the default gravity force. The curtain model has been defined to have a certain mass. When the wind force hits the curtain, it tends to push the curtain to the right. At the same time, however, the gravity force tends to pull the curtain straight down. Both of these tendencies are affected by the mass of the curtain itself. The result of these forces pushing and pulling against each other is that the curtain rises and falls and flaps "in the breeze."

A wind force is defined in most systems to affect an entire scene equally from a given direction. For example, several curtains in a scene, each located some distance from the others, are affected to the same degree by the wind.

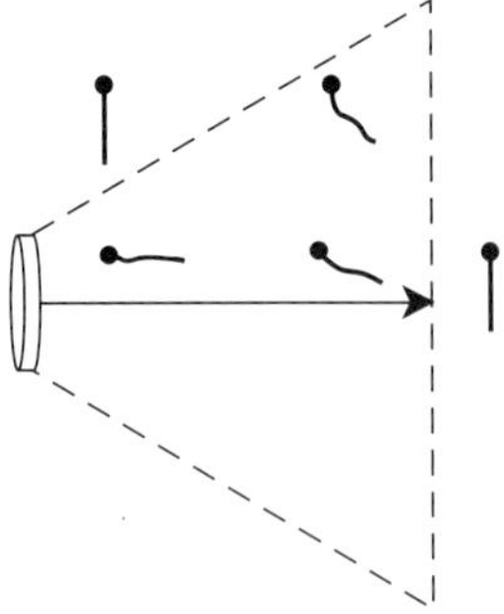

Figure 4-17. Unlike wind, which is omnipresent, a fan force has a limited range.

Some motion-dynamics systems offer a variation on the wind concept, called a **fan** force. Unlike wind, it usually is possible to limit both the distance over which a fan force will carry and the radial area that it will affect. In Figure 4-17, the fan force is represented by the cylindrical form on the far left. The arrow emanating from the center of that form and traveling to the right represents the distance over which the force of the fan will carry. At the base of the arrow—that is, at the cylindrical fan icon itself—the force of the fan is strongest. This is why the string close to the base of the arrow is being blown quite a bit. As the force of the fan travels down the arrow, the strength of that force decreases, which is why the next string is not being blown as much as the first. Beyond the tip of the arrow, the force of the fan dies out completely and the string does not move at all.

The force of the fan not only fades as it travels in the direction of the arrow; it also fades as it moves radially away from the center of the fan. The dotted lines emanating from the fan icon demarcate the radial range of effectiveness. The string at the top left, which is completely outside the radial range of the fan, is not moving at all. The string directly to the right lies just inside the radial limit and therefore is being affected slightly. Notice, however, that this string is not being affected as much as the string directly below it, which, even though it is at the same horizontal distance from the fan, is closer to the radial center of the force field.

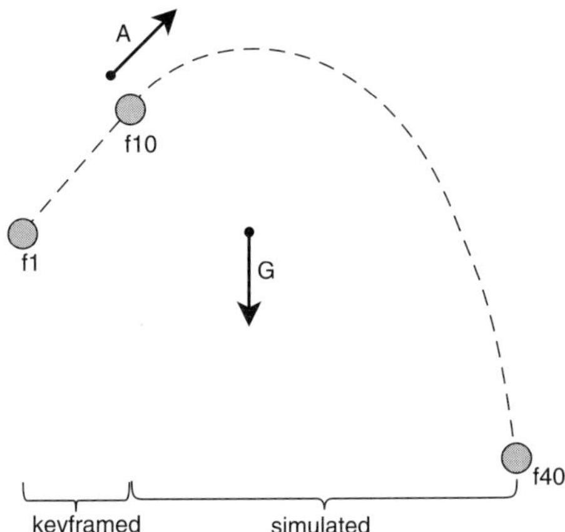

Figure 4-18. Some systems allow you to combine standard keyframed motion with motion-dynamics simulation. Here, the keyframed acceleration of an object is calculated into the motion dynamics.

A final force that can be very important in setting up a motion-dynamics simulation is the acceleration an object has as the result of some keyframed action: **keyframed acceleration**. Acceleration is a measure of how fast the speed of an object changes, and the most basic way of giving an object some sort of speed or movement in a three-dimensional animation system is keyframing (described in chapter 3).

Some software packages allow you to combine keyframed animation movements with motion-dynamic simulation. Thus, you might keyframe an animation of a ball translating from one position to another over ten frames (Figure 4-18). This operation involves the standard keyframing techniques of setting a keyframe for the ball as it appears in frame 1, then setting another keyframe for the ball as it appears in frame 10. Having defined the keyframed animation from frame 1 to frame 10, you then direct the simulation software to take over the calculations from frame 11 through frame 40. When the simulation takes over, two forces are at work: the default gravity force, and the acceleration that the ball has as a result of being translated from the position at frame 1 to the position at frame 10. The combination of this keyframed acceleration and gravity causes the ball to continue rising for a while and then to fall.

One of the areas in which motion dynamics can be most useful is in simulating **collisions**. The reason the animation of a box falling down a flight of steps (see Figure 4-11) is so complex, for example, is that the box collides with the steps and bounces off them when it does. It is the precise calculation of these collisions, called **collision detection**, that makes a simulation of this animation so effective.

The calculation of collisions, however, can be extremely time-consuming for a computer system, and most motion-dynamics systems therefore allow you to elect whether or not to calculate collisions for a given object. If you know that an object, such as an isolated curtain (see Figure 4-16) won't hit

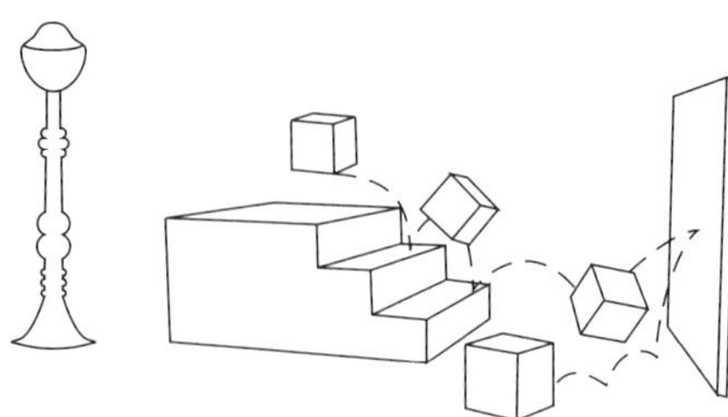

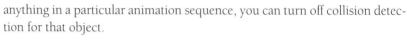

Figure 4-19. Only those objects that the falling box might hit need to be defined as obstacles for that box. This reduces the calculations necessary for collision detection.

anything in a particular animation sequence, you can turn off collision detection for that object.

If you want to calculate collisions for your model, however, most systems offer several options, all intended to minimize the amount of calculation necessary for a successful simulation. The first option is to define which other objects in the scene might be **obstacles**—that is, which objects the animated object might collide with. When the software does the collision-detection calculations, it will consider only these defined obstacles.

For example, suppose you add a lamppost to the scene in which the box falls down the steps (Figure 4-19). Given the position of the lamppost behind the steps, the box will never collide with it, so you can eliminate it from the list of obstacles that the motion-dynamics software needs to consider in collision-detection calculations. Only the steps, floor, and wall need be considered obstacles.

Another area in which most systems offer collision-detection options is in the shape of the objects involved. The collision calculations for a complex shape—a telephone, for example—are more complicated than the calculations for a simple shape, such as a box. Consequently, many systems allow you to use a simpler shape as a stand-in for the purposes of collision calculations. Assuming that a falling telephone is shaped like a simple box, for example, greatly speeds up the collision-detection calculations, although you still see the actual telephone falling. In many animations, the accuracy of the collisions calculations does not need to be exact in order to be visually convincing.

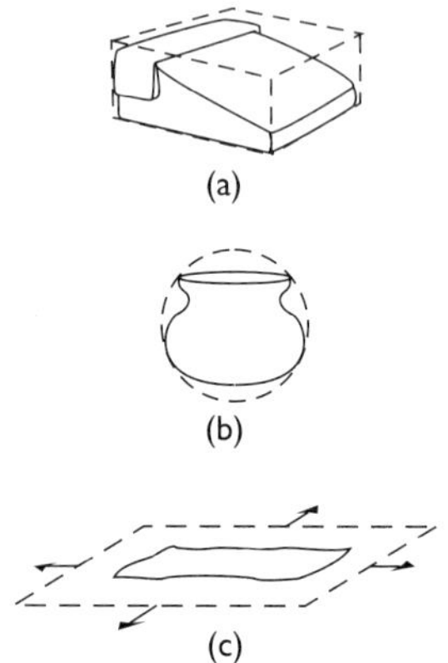

Figure 4-20. Bounding boxes, bounding spheres, and bounding planes—all represented by broken lines in this illustration—can be used to simplify collision-detection calculations.

Among the number of simplifying shapes that motion-dynamics systems permit is the **bounding box**, or the smallest rectangular box into which an object will fit (Figure 4-20a). If you use the bounding box of the telephone for collision-detection calculations, the resulting motion is similar to what it would have been if you had used the actual shape of the telephone, since the shape of the bounding box and the shape of the telephone are similar. Likewise, some objects can be conveniently and fairly accurately approximated with a **bounding sphere**, or the smallest sphere into which they will fit (Figure 4-20b).

Bounding boxes and bounding spheres may be used to simplify either the colliding object itself or the obstacles with which the object will come into contact. Sometimes it is possible to use a **bounding plane** as a simplification technique for obstacles. A flat surface that extends infinitely in all directions, a bounding plane could successfully approximate a bumpy surface, for example (Figure 4-20c).

So far the examples in this section have involved rather simple models, but motion dynamics can be applied to more complex models and scenes as well. Models organized into a hierarchy can be part of a motion-dynamics simulation, as can models defined with inverse kinematics. In fact, some of the most impressive simulations involve precisely this combination of inverse kinematics and motion dynamics. You might model the blowing curtain, for example (see Figure 4-16), as an envelope over an inverse kinematic chain (as described in *Inverse Kinematics*, in chapter 3). When a motion-dynamics force acts on this model, the force affects each of the various links of each inverse kinematic chain (Figure 4-21a). If the bottom portion of a chain is blown by a wind force, for example, then the movement of the bottom portion of the chain causes the upper portions of the chain to move, and so on (Figure 4-21b). Since the envelope surface of the curtain is in turn controlled by the movements of the chains, the curtain animates, blowing in the wind. This combination of motion dynamics and inverse kinematics can be used to create very realistic and complex simulations.

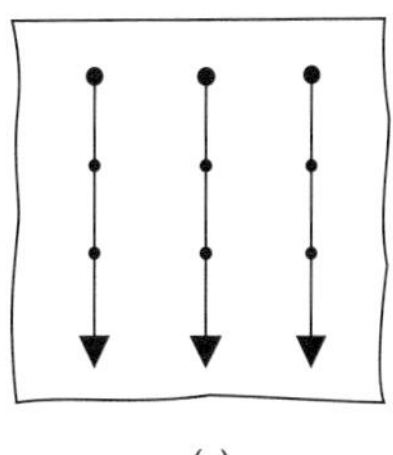

(a)

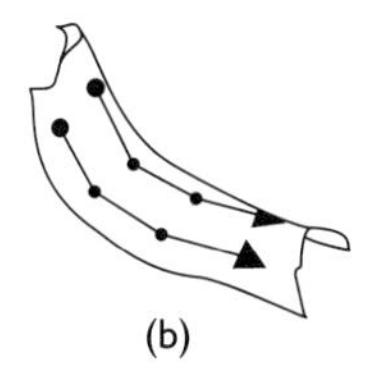

(b)

Figure 4-21. An inverse kinematic model can be effectively animated within a motion dynamics system.

Finally, it is important to understand one aspect of the underlying mathematics of motion dynamics. Whereas in the real world time is continuous, so that there is no break between one instant and another, in motion dynamics time is treated discretely. That is, time is broken up into a fixed number of measurable increments—for example, thirtieths of a second. These increments are called **time steps**. The smaller the time steps, the more closely they approximate the continuous nature of time, and therefore the more accurately they simulate an animated scene. However, smaller time steps also mean more calculations. Consequently, some systems allow you to define the size of the time steps, giving you the option of trading off accuracy of simulation for speed of calculation if necessary.

Because of the mathematics of motion-dynamics calculations, however, two simulations of a given scene that use different time steps will not produce the same motions. The path of an object can differ substantially when calculated under two different time steps. For this reason you may not find it useful to define a larger time step to sketch out a preliminary version of an animation, with the intention of switching to a smaller time step for the final animation.

All these motion-dynamics techniques are very powerful and can yield stunningly realistic simulations of an event. Sometimes, however, the most effective thing you can do is to combine the more standard, keyframe-based animation techniques with these sophisticated motion-dynamics calculations. For example, the human figure in color plate 2 was animated using standard keyframing and hierarchical animation. The bowling balls, on the other hand, were animated using motion dynamics to achieve a high degree of realism as the balls flew through the air and bounced on the ground about the feet of the character.

Motion Capture

Animation typically involves making your characters—whether human, mechanical, vegetable, or animal—behave similarly to the way they behave in the real world. The animation may be deliberately exaggerated or modified to achieve specific effects, but the model for the motion is the real-world behavior of real-world objects and creatures.

In those cases where you may want to mimic these motions extremely accurately, you can replicate them using one of several physically accurate techniques, which collectively are called **motion capture**. The oldest of these, dating from the days of hand-drawn cel animation, is **rotoscoping**. In its cel-animation implementation, rotoscoping consists of taking photographs of real-world motions and using these photographs as templates on top of which the hand-drawn animation frames are traced. Using a series of such photographs, the animator can trace a corresponding series of keyframe drawings.

Applied to 3D computer animation, rotoscoping still involves a series of real-world images, now produced either as photographic still images or as a videotaped sequence. In the latter case, the video sequence is frequently digitized frame-by-frame to produce the necessary still images. These are read into the 3D computer animation program and displayed as background pictures on your computer screen. Using these as templates, you position your three-dimensional model to correspond to the position of the character in the background image (Figure 4-22). Notice how lifelike the model looks, even though it is composed solely of rectangular boxes. Even greater precision can be achieved if photographs or video are shot of the real-world subject from several angles. By carefully aligning your computer model with the pictures in each of several windows—Front, Left, Top, etc.—you can accurately reproduce a fully three-dimensional motion.

Using video as your rotoscoping source has the advantage that it also automatically records the timing of your motion. For example, if your video is the standard NTSC video used in the United States (see chapter 6, *Video*), every thirty frames of video represents exactly one second of motion. Photography can have the same timing accuracy if special steps are taken to shoot at precise and regular time intervals.

Computer technology provides even more accurate and thorough motion capture techniques than rotoscoping, however. The simplest of these,

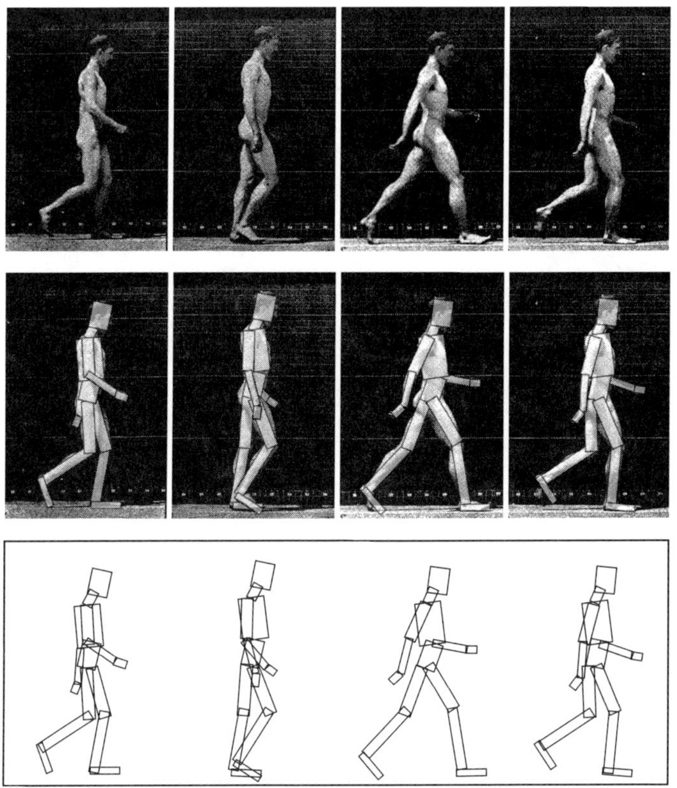

Figure 4-22. In rotoscoping, you align your computer model to the figures in a sequence of real-world images. (Photographs from *The Human Figure in Motion* by Eadweard Muybridge, New York: Dover, 1955.)

channel animation, introduces a radically different and extremely powerful way of defining an animation sequence. With this technique, you generate an animation sequence in real time, without keyframes, by manipulating one or more input devices.

For example, imagine that you want to make a character nod its head repeatedly at irregular intervals, as if the character were listening to a conversation and saying, "Yes. Yes. I understand. Um-hum. Yes." You could do this with keyframing (as you saw in chapter 3) by rotating the character's head around the appropriate axis—say, the X axis. You also have seen, however, that creating this sort of animation with keyframing requires a substantial amount of trial and error in order to get the details of the movement just right. How quickly should the head move with each nod? How far should the head move? How much time is there between each nod? And so on.

If the system you are working with offers channel animation, however, you can produce this same animation very easily and quickly and with very precise control. First, you define a linkage between the X rotation of the character's head and the mouse device. (You will see specifically how this is done in a moment.) Once you have defined this link, any movement of the mouse causes an immediate and equivalent rotation of the character's head. For example, if the mouse moves up a lot, the head will rotate up a lot. If the

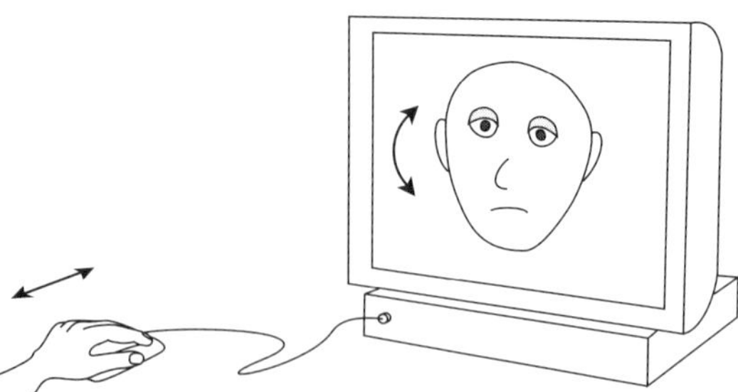

Figure 4-23. Channel animation allows you to create and save animation in real time by manipulating an input device.

mouse moves quickly, the head moves quickly. And so on. With the linkage defined, you then create the actual animation sequence (Figure 4-23).

Suppose the animation is going to be ten seconds long. The system shows a countdown to the start of the animation sequence, and then, for the ten seconds of the running length, the linkage you defined becomes active, and you move the mouse up and down to control the nodding of the character. At the end of the ten seconds, the animation is complete. Whatever head nodding you produced by moving the mouse has been saved and has become the definition of the animation. In other words, you now have a head-nod animation that can be played back and viewed just like any other animation. If you don't like the result, you can either edit the parameter curves of this new animation or completely regenerate the sequence by repeating the channeling process—that is, start a new countdown, move the mouse for ten seconds, and stop.

The link you describe between the input device (in this example, the mouse) and the animation parameter (*rotation x* of the head) is called a **channel**. The first step in making a channel animation is to define any channels you will use. In order to define a channel, you specify (usually through a series of menu selections) several pieces of information. First, you tell the system which input device you will use for this channel. Sometimes you do this indirectly by indicating the name of the **device driver**, which is a program that manages the input and output of a device. The driver for a mouse device, for example, is referred to as the mouse driver.

Next, you specify which information from that device you will use. A mouse device, for example, produces a constant stream of two pieces of information: location of the mouse in X and location of the mouse in Y. Consequently, in the head-nod example, you have to indicate whether you want to use the X or the Y readings—that is, the horizontal or the vertical movement—from the mouse.

Once you have specified the device and the device information, you must indicate which transformation parameter of which object this incoming information will be channeled to. In the head-nod example, which involves a single channel, you channel the incoming information (vertical movement) from the mouse to the *rotation x* parameter of the head.

It is possible to define and use more than one channel for a single animation, but the number of channels you can have at any one time is limited by the input devices you use. A mouse device, as mentioned above, generates two numerical pieces of information: the horizontal, or X, location of the mouse, and the vertical, or Y, location of the mouse. These two values usually are called *mouse_x* and *mouse_y*. You can use either one or both of these two mouse parameters in a channel. In the example used above, the *mouse_y* parameter made the head of a character nod. If you want that character also to shake its head back and forth sometimes as if saying "no," you can define a second channel using the *mouse_x* parameter. This linkage makes it possible for you to create both nods and shakes of the head in one pass, by moving the mouse either vertically (nod) or horizontally (shake).

Normally, in order to produce meaningful numbers for a given transformation parameter, you must **scale** the values that will be coming in from the input device. For example, many mouse devices produce numbers ranging from zero to one. If you use these numbers directly, as is, for the *rotation x* of the character's head, the head rotates anywhere from zero degrees around X to a maximum of one degree around the X axis. In other words, the movement of the head is almost imperceptible. In order to correct this, you specify in the channel definition that the incoming *mouse_y* values be scaled by a factor of, say, forty. Thus, the zero-to-one range of *mouse_y* values that the mouse device produces is changed by this scaling into a more useful zero-to-forty range of rotation values.

Depending on your animation, you may also have to **offset** the values coming out of your input device. In the example just given, the original values output by the mouse range from zero to one. When multiplied by a scale factor of forty, they range from zero to forty, which translates into a motion that ranges from looking straight ahead (*rotation x* equals zero) to looking down a bit (*rotation x* equals forty). But a head nod should also involve a slight rotation of the head upwards—that is, negatively—before its downward rotation. If you specify a negative offset to the values coming out of the mouse device, you can solve this problem. An offset of negative ten, for example, subtracts ten from any value coming out of the mouse. A zero-to-forty range of numbers therefore becomes a negative-ten-to-thirty range of numbers. With these numbers, you can achieve a slight upward (negative) rotation of the head before it rotates downward (positively) a maximum of thirty degrees.

All the information defining an animation channel is usually specified through a menu structure. Figure 4-24 shows how this might look for a head-nod and head-shake channel animation as described above. In addition to a rotation around X to make the head nod up and down, you have also defined a rotation around Z to make it shake left and right, scaling the rotation by sixty and offsetting it by thirty so that its values range from negative thirty to thirty.

Figure 4-24. Each value from the input device is associated with one parameter of the model, scaling and offsetting the value as necessary.

Device	Parameter	Scale	Offset
mouse_x	Head.RZ	60	–30
mouse_y	Head.RX	40	–10

Most systems allow you to save these channel definitions to a file, so that you can use them again in some other animation. In any case, once you define the channel or channels, you can use it or them to create an animation sequence. That is, you start the sequence definition and, for whatever length of time the animation is intended to run, you manipulate the input device. As you do so, the input device sends values to the computer. These values in turn are channeled, in real time, into the transformation values you specified in the channel definition. What is actually happening here is that the software is taking the incoming values from the device driver, scaling and offsetting them according to your instructions, and writing out a parameter curve for that transformation parameter of the object. This means that as soon as the input of channel values is completed, a complete parameter curve exists for the specified transformation parameter. At this point, the parameter curve is like any other parameter curve, in that it can be overwritten or it can be edited with any of the standard parameter-curve editing techniques (see chapter 3, *Parameter-curve Editing*).

The parameter curve written by the channel animation is unusual, however, in one very important respect—it has no interpolated values. Every frame is a key frame. Such a curve is often called a **raw** parameter curve to indicate that there has been no processing or interpolation of the data (Figure 4-25). Here each keyframe is indicated by a dot on the curve. Notice that even in those sections of the curve where there is no change—that is, where the curve is flat—there is still a keyframe at every frame. This overabundance of data can be a problem, and most software systems allow you to **thin** the raw curve, converting it into a spline curve which approximates it. (Thinning is discussed in more detail in *Digitizing Techniques*, chapter 1).

In principle, you can use any device that produces a stream of numbers in digital format as your input device for channel information. The mouse is probably the most common input device on animation workstations, but other devices include joysticks, tablets, and 3D digitizers. If an audio device produces digital output, you can channel that output to the animation in the same way that you channel the output of a mouse. You can make a character jump up and down according to the volume of an audio stream, for example.

Whatever device you use will output a certain number of values, and the number of values a device provides is referred to as the **degrees of freedom**

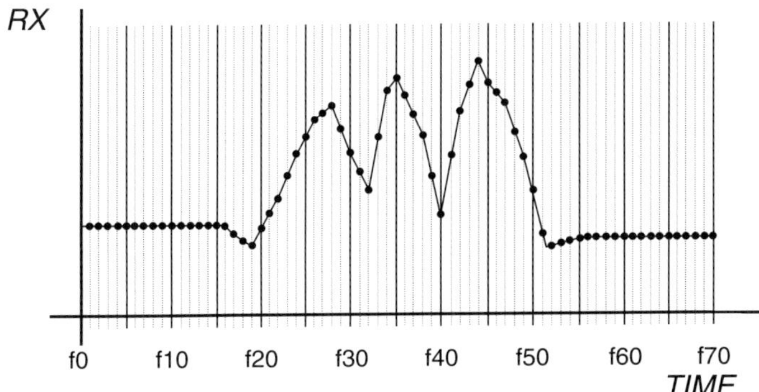

Figure 4-25. The parameter curves produced by channel animation are raw, without interpolated values.

of the device. Thus, a mouse device has two degrees of freedom: movement in the X direction (*mouse_x*) and movement in the Y direction (*mouse_y*). A typical stylus-and-tablet input device also has two degrees of freedom: X and Y directions. If the stylus is pressure sensitive, it has three degrees of freedom: X, Y, and pressure. A 3D digitizing device also has three degrees of freedom: X, Y, and Z directions. The number of degrees of freedom is the maximum number of channels you can define for that device at any one time.

Channel animation can make use of more than one device at a time, however. In the unlikely event that two mouse devices are connected to your computer, for example, you can use them simultaneously in a single channel animation. Using both devices gives you a total of four simultaneous channels of information, allowing you to control four parameters in real time. In addition to making a character nod and shake his head, for example, you also can make him blink and snuffle his nose.

More likely, you have a single input device—perhaps a mouse, perhaps a joystick—with only two or three degrees of freedom. It is still possible in this situation, however, to produce very complex channel animations involving a large number of channels. You do this by creating several channel animations, in sequence, one after another, and adding each one to the previous ones. For example, suppose you want to create that nod-shake-blink-snuffle animation, but you have only one ordinary mouse with two ordinary degrees of freedom. You first define two channels: *mouse_y* = *rotation x* of head (nod), and *mouse_x* = *rotation y* of head (shake). You then create the nod-shake animation sequence using these channels. When you have produced a satisfactory nodding and shaking animation, you delete the channel definitions you have been using and define two new ones. Now you channel *mouse_x* to *rotation x* of the eyelids (blink), and *mouse_y* to *scale y* of the nose (snuffle), then create a second animation of the blinking eyes and the snuffling nose. The nodding and shaking of the head still exist and are not overwritten, because you are creating parameter curves for a different pair of transformation parameters.

When used on an inverse kinematic model, channel animation can be particularly effective. If you have a model of the human body, for example, modeled as a collection of inverse kinematic chains (as described in chapter 3, *Inverse Kinematics*), you can define two channels to control the X and Y locations of the effector at the end of one arm. Since the effector controls the positions and angles of all the joints in the arm, moving the effector under channel control moves the entire arm in real time.

A great advantage of channel animation over standard keyframing, in fact, is the immediacy of channel animation. You look at the screen, move the input device, and generate animation "on the fly," in real time. There is a sense, therefore, in which channel animation is more like puppetry than like traditional frame-by-frame animation. Unlike puppetry, however, channel animation allows you to save, repeat, and even edit the actions you create. If the animation is perfect except for one small detail, you can alter the parameter curves written by the channeling to fine-tune the result.

The rotoscoping and channel animation techniques discussed so far are methods of capturing motion, but the term "motion capture" usually refers to a particular and very powerful extension of channel animation. In channel animation, a single input device produces real-time data to control a few parameters of a model. In **motion capture**, a collection of many input devices, often called **sensors**, is used to simultaneously control a large number of parameters on a model.

Each input device in a motion-capture system has three degrees of freedom, producing either three-dimensional translation data or three-dimensional rotation data. These devices are attached to a **human actor** (Figure 4-26) and the output from them is channeled to the joints of a computer model, or **virtual actor**. As the human actor moves around, the attached sensors send data to the computer model, controlling its movements and generating, in real time, parameter curves for the entire animation. In other words, at the end of a motion-capture session, the computer model of the character will have the exact same motions that the human actor just performed. If the animation doesn't look right when played back, the actor can repeat the scene, in just the same way that an actor on a movie set would do another "take."

In practice, of course, motion-capture systems are much more complex than the brief description here suggests. All the issues that must be addressed for a single input device in channel animation must be addressed for each of the many input devices of motion capture: each device's output values must be linked to a specific parameter of the model, each value must be scaled and offset, and each resulting parameter curve must be thinned. In addition, anomalies, or **noise**, in the stream of input data coming from each device can cause the quality of the captured data to deteriorate, producing erratic and

Figure 4-26. The actor on the stage has been wired with a motion-capture system. Input from each sensor is channeled into the animation system to control the movement of a computer-generated character. (Courtesy R/Greenberg Associates, Inc. Created by R/Greenberg Associates, MTV, and SoftImage; directed by David Lane of Savoy Commercials for MTV's *Enough Is Enough* campaign.)

jerky motions in the virtual actor model. Sophisticated motion-capture software provides procedures for eliminating this noise.

Two broad approaches to motion capture are commonly used. The first approach employs a set of magnetic devices attached to the body of the human actor. Each device emits a magnetic pulse. When the actor moves within a field of sensors, each magnetic device—and by implication, the part of the actor to which it is attached—can be located. The second approach is optical and uses reflective markers, rather than magnetic devices, on the body of the actor. The location of each marker as the actor moves about is determined by a network of cameras that record the light bouncing off the reflectors.

Each of these techniques has advantages and disadvantages. The magnetic approach requires that a series of cables, almost like umbilical cords, be attached to the actor. The optical approach requires no cables, and so permits greater freedom of movement for the actor. Depending on the posture of the actor, however, some of the reflective markers may be hidden from the view of some of the recording cameras, and this blockage can create problems in the acquisition of the original data. In contrast to this, magnetic sensors, no matter what the posture of the actor, continue to emit pulses and to produce recordable data.

Both approaches require that the actor move within a confined arena, because the recording devices, whether magnetic or optical, are set up in a network and have a limited range. This consideration need not be overly constricting, though, since the recordable arena for many systems can be as broad as five or six meters square.

The specific placement of the 3D sensors on the human actor is important. Typically, they are placed at the main joints—elbows, knees, ankles,

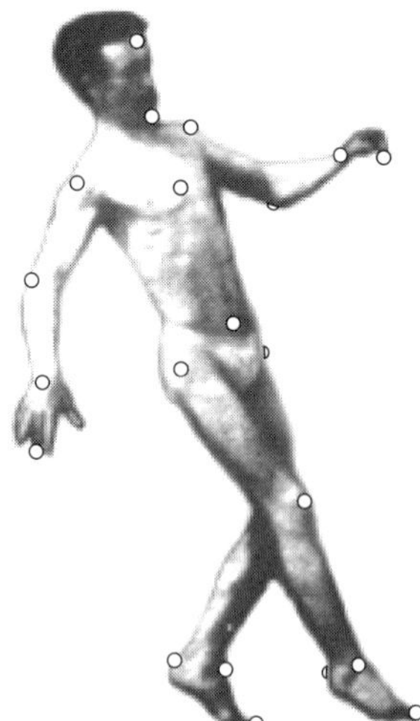

Figure 4-27. Motion-capture sensors must be placed at specific locations on the human actor. (Photograph from *The Human Figure in Motion* by Eadweard Muybridge, New York: Dover, 1955.)

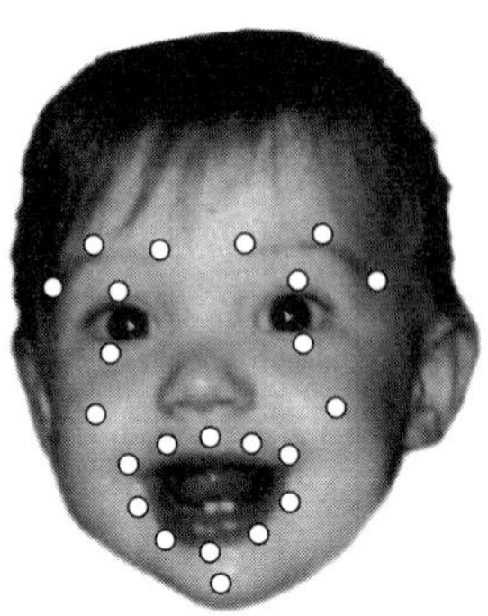

Figure 4-28. An array of sensors can be placed on a speaker's face to record human facial expressions and speech movements.

shoulders, etc. In addition, several are also usually placed at other locations, such as the chest, abdomen, forehead, and chin, to capture the orientation of those parts of the body (Figure 4-27). The more sensors used, the more accurate the captured data, and the more detailed the motion can be. More sensors, however, also produce more data, which may necessitate very powerful computers.

The structure of the model of the virtual actor is also important and must correspond to the structure of the human actor. This usually requires either a detailed hierarchical model or a detailed inverse kinematic model. More than one model may receive the captured motion data, however. The same data generated by a single motion-capture session can be applied to several different models; the data are scaled and offset as necessary to correspond to the proportions of each model.

In any motion-capture situation, the number of sensors necessarily limits which motions can be recorded. With the configuration of sensors in Figure 4-27, for example, the motion of the actor's individual fingers will not be recorded, since there are no input devices there; there is only a single device at the end of each middle finger to give the overall orientation of the hand. The motions of the fingers, in this situation, would have to be animated "by hand," using keyframing or one of the other techniques discussed in this chapter and chapter 3.

A similar issue arises with the facial expressions of the actor in Figure 4-27. Only the general orientation of the head will be recorded by the input devices as they are set up here. For specialized animation situations like **human facial animation**, more detailed configurations of motion sensors can be used to capture the expressions of the human face. Placing a collection of sensors around the lips and mouth, for example, captures the movements of those parts of the body (Figure 4-28). Channeling the data from these sensors to points or controllers on a flexible surface model would permit you to animate a virtual "speaker." For this sort of application, it is also common to record and store a large number of individual facial expressions, associating each with a particular spoken sound and saving each as a pose in a library. By interpolating between these key facial expressions, you can animate a naturalistically speaking computer "talking head." For example, selecting the poses for the "bay" sound and then the "bee" sound would yield a character saying "Baby!"

Any motion-capture system produces large quantities of data. Remember that in a keyframe-based system, only selected frames are defined as keyframes. The rest of the frames are calculated through an interpolation process, which produces data economically. With motion capture, as with channeling, however, *every* frame is a keyframe. There is no interpolation. All of the animation data is raw data. Motion-capture systems produce data from numerous channels simultaneously and consequently can produce huge quantities of data, which only sophisticated systems can handle.

The argument for motion capture, of course, is that it is precisely the lack of interpolated data that makes it so striking. When humans move, their limbs and joints almost constantly change position in very irregular and subtle ways, and the generalization of movement that results from an interpolated-motion curve often does not convey the idiosyncratic "human-ness" of that movement.

On the other hand, it is possible to overuse motion-capture capabilities and to make an animated character too realistic. If an animated character moves *exactly* like a real human, and especially if that character is modeled and rendered very realistically, it may lose all visual and aesthetic interest. Character animation, like any art form, is interesting to the viewer because it is an *interpretation* of the way we behave. If an animation replicates our behavior too exactly, it may lose the appeal of animation and become a dry simulation.

Whether through a single input device such as a mouse or through a complex set of motion-detecting sensors, channel animation and motion capture effectively allow you to use your own body to perform the action of an animation. Instead of creating keyframes visually, you define a physical "dance," even if this dance is limited to the movements of one hand on a mouse device. The physicality of your body itself becomes a tool. Many talented animators think this way anyhow. If you ask an animator to show you the timing or movement of some portion of an animation, he or she may spontaneously mime it for you. "It goes like this," the animator will say, and then move his or her hands or arms to show you the rhythm and shape of the motions. Channel animation and motion capture allow you to take advantage of this kind of intuitive physical representation of action and timing.

Metaballs

One of the most challenging modeling tasks in 3D computer graphics is the naturalistic modeling of human and animal forms, because the variability and subtlety of those forms is extremely difficult to match. Using a hierarchical collection of rigid body parts (see chapter 1, *Hierarchies*) can simulate the skeletal structure of animals very well, but it tends to produce robotic or mechanical-looking creatures. Using an envelope around an inverse kinematic chain (see chapter 3, *Inverse Kinematics*) avoids the robotic look, but it tends to yield overly flexible creatures that have a cartoon quality.

Simulating the muscle masses of an animal and how those muscle masses smoothly flow into one another while still remaining distinct is indeed a difficult modeling problem. The **metaball** technique is particularly effective for this sort of modeling because it creates surfaces that automatically blend together. When you use this technique, models consist entirely of spheres of a special sort. These spheres, which also may be scaled into ellipsoids, are something *beyond* ("meta" means "beyond") normal spheres. Metaball spheres are not defined as having an explicit spherical surface, as would be the case in the standard surface-modeling techniques (described throughout chapter 1). Instead, they are defined to consist of a variable **density field**. Wherever the density is of a certain value, called the **threshold**, a surface exists. What you see, therefore, when you look at a metaball is the implicitly defined surface that follows the contours of the density field, at whatever density value you have defined to be the threshold of visibility. Since the surfaces of a metaball exist wherever the density values are the same as the threshold, these surfaces are referred to in technical literature as **isosurfaces** ("iso" means "same").

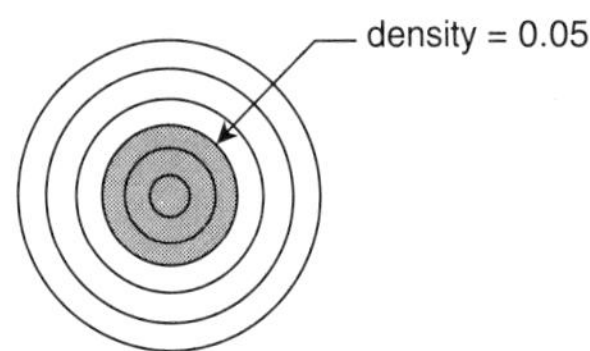

Figure 4-29. The surface of a metaball is defined to exist wherever the density field of the metaball achieves a certain threshold value.

An analogy from the world of physics might make this concept clear. If a tiny metal ball were electrically charged and suspended in the air, the charge from that ball would emanate evenly in all directions, creating a spherically shaped electric field. The electric charge would be greatest at the center of this field and would decrease farther away from the center of the field. The metaball technique is based on a similar idea, except that instead of a decreasing field of electricity, you have a decreasing field of density. The density of a spherical metaball is, like the electric charge, greatest at the center of the metaball and decreases, again like the electrical charge, farther away from the center. When the density of the metaball reaches the threshold value, a surface is drawn implicitly.

In Figure 4-29, the concentric rings represent several different density levels of a single metaball. The small ring at the center is the most dense, and each successive ring, moving outward from the center, is less dense. The visibility threshold for this metaball has been set (more or less arbitrarily) to 0.05. Since the density of the metaball decreases uniformly away from the center, the visibility threshold of 0.05 has a spherical configuration, as if a thin film of 0.05 density surrounded the center of the metaball. Wherever this 0.05 density exists, a surface, represented in the illustration by the shaded circle, is defined implicitly. Notice that the visibility of a metaball is an all-or-nothing issue: the metaball does not become invisible gradually as the density decreases, but becomes invisible abruptly at the 0.05 threshold. This abruptness effectively creates the appearance of a surface defined at that threshold.

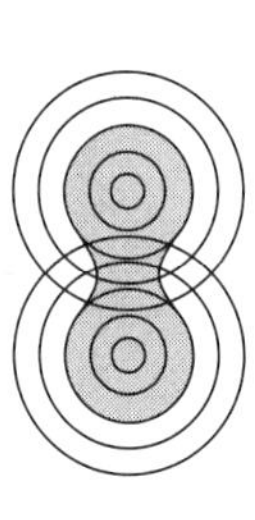

(a)

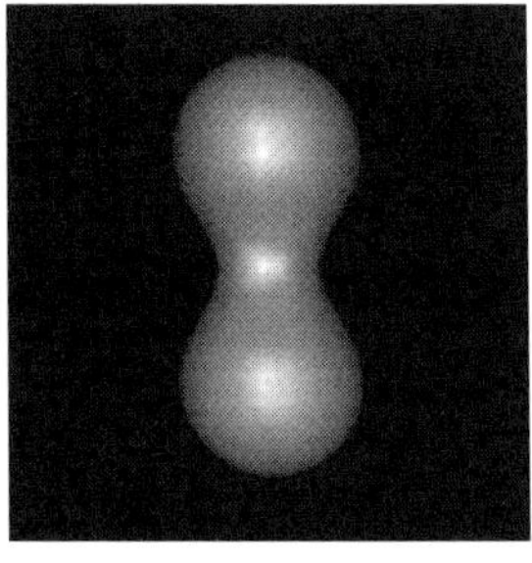

(b)

Figure 4-30. When the density fields of neighboring metaballs overlap, a fusion of density values occurs. The surface that results is a blobby melting of the two spheres into one another.

The power of the metaball-modeling technique is a result of the fact that if two metaballs are placed close enough to each other, the density fields of each will overlap (Figure 4-30a). Wherever the density fields of two metaballs overlap, the density values from the two different balls add up, creating a new density value in a process called **fusion**. If this new density value is greater

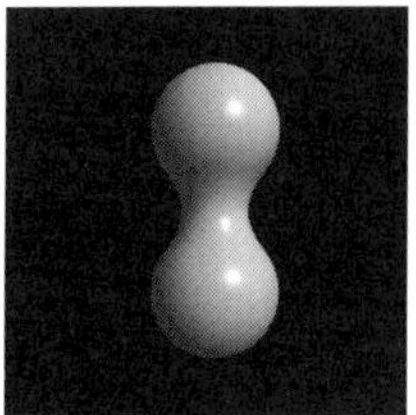

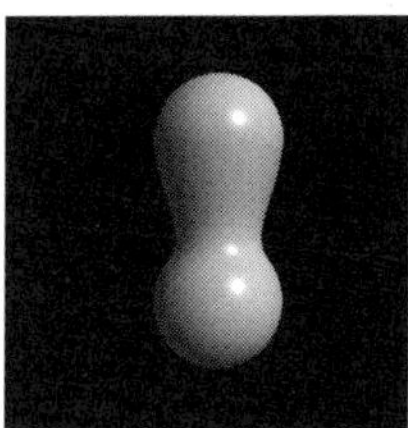

Figure 4-31. Adjusting the parameters that control density and threshold can cause the metaballs to fuse in a wide variety of ways.

than the visibility threshold, the overlapped area between the two metaballs is also visible (Figure 4-30b). This extension of the area of the implicit surface creates a viscous, dripping look which has inspired one of the more whimsical names for metaballs, **blobby molecules**.

In most systems you can control both the density of the field and the visibility threshold of each metaball. Some software packages also allow you to adjust additional, hybrid parameters that control some combination of density and threshold. These parameters may variously be called **weight**, **range**, or **influence**. Whichever parameters a specific package offers, adjusting them allows you to cause the metaballs to fuse in a wide variety of ways. Figure 4-31 shows two metaballs that remain the same size and in the same location in each case. The different configurations were created solely by adjusting the parameters that control some combination of the density field and the visibility threshold.

By carefully positioning a number of metaballs and adjusting the densities and thresholds, you can model some very subtle forms (Figure 4-32). The fusion effect of the metaballs automatically produces a smooth transition between balls, effectively mimicking the way masses of human flesh flow smoothly into one another.

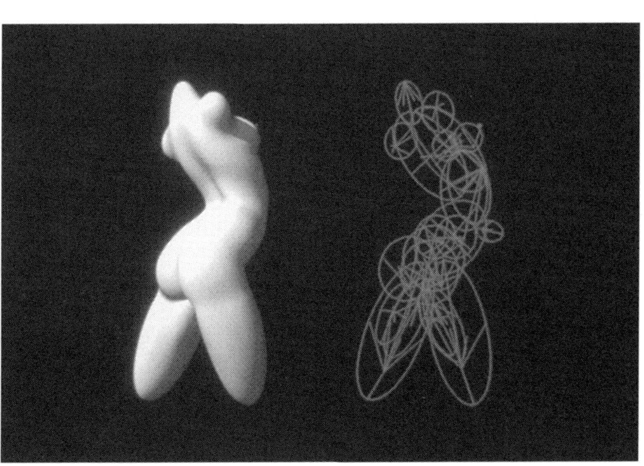

Figure 4-32. This human figure, modeled with the metaball structure seen on the right, exemplifies the subtlety and sophistication possible with this technique. (*Eccentric Dance*, Artist: Eiji Takaoki, © META Corporation Japan.)

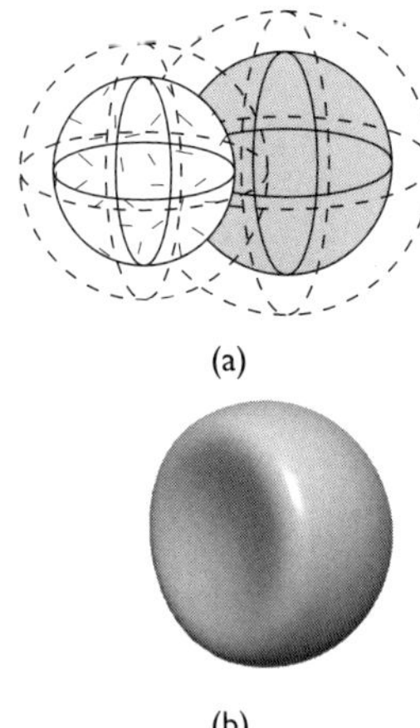

(a)

(b)

Figure 4-33. A metaball can have negative density that subtracts from the density field of its neighbors and produces a concavity.

Many systems also allow you to alter the density field of a metaball in order to create **negative density**. That is, rather than adding to the densities of other metaballs, this field subtracts from them. This approach is very useful when modeling concavities in a surface. Figure 4-33 shows two metaballs. The larger one has a normal positive density; the smaller one has a negative density. Since the density of the smaller metaball is negative, it subtracts from the density field of the larger metaball when the two fields combine, producing the concavity seen in Figure 4-33b.The metaball diagram in Figure 4-32 shows another example of negative density. Here, the ellipsoidal metaball protruding where the navel would be is a negative metaball. The density field of this metaball subtracts density from the metaballs that comprise the belly of the figure, and the result of this subtraction is an abrupt concavity, or navel.

A further refinement of the metaball technique permits you to redistribute the density of a given metaball in a way that is not perfectly spherical. With this approach, known as **eccentric density distribution**, the density of a ball might fade off more quickly on one side of the ball than on another. In Figure 4-34a the density of the metaball drops off normally in a circular pattern to the left of the center, but much more slowly on the right side, producing a bowed look to the rings of the density field. Figure 4-34b shows this metaball as it would look rendered.

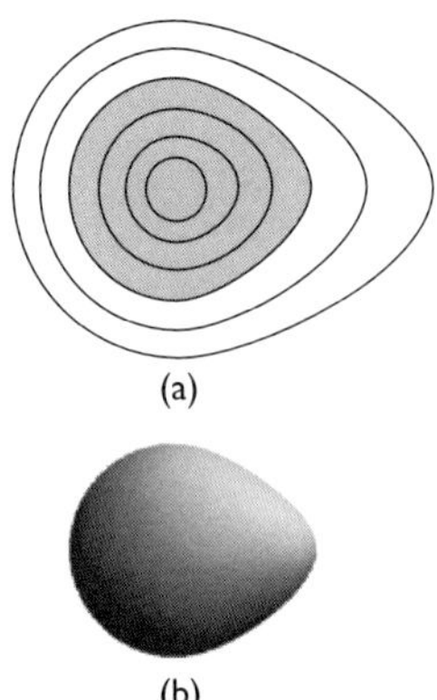

(a)

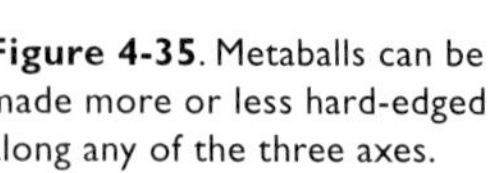

(b)

Figure 4-34. The density field of a metaball can be distorted to produce an eccentric density distribution.

Some software packages provide yet another method of modifying the shape of a metaball away from its standard spherical shape with **hard-edged** metaballs. Using a slider, you can adjust numbers that control how hard-edged, or squared, the metaball will be along each of the three axes. Figure 4-35 shows the original, spherical metaball (a), the metaball made a bit more square along all three axes (b), made more square yet (c), and squared up but only along one axis, producing an approximately cylindrical blob (d).

Some software systems provide a simplified selection of hard-edged metaballs, which they call **metaball primitives**. The metaball in Figure 4-35c, for example, would be a "cube" metaball. A flattened version of that same shape might be available as a "plane" metaball. Figure 4-35d would be the equivalent of a "cylinder" metaball.

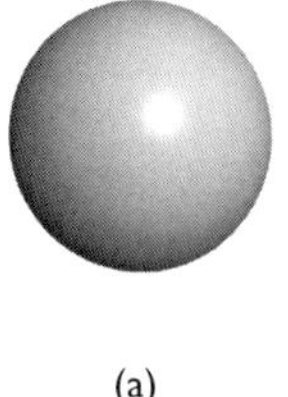

(a)

(b)

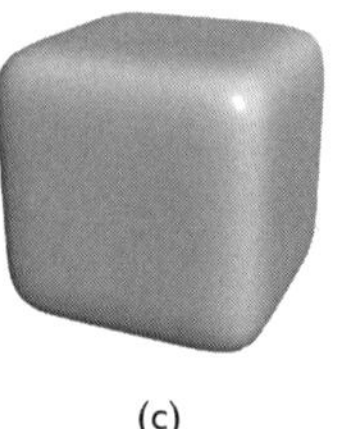

(c)

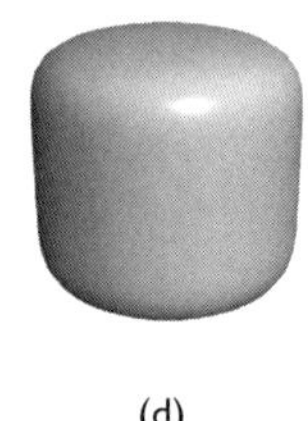

(d)

Figure 4-35. Metaballs can be made more or less hard-edged along any of the three axes.

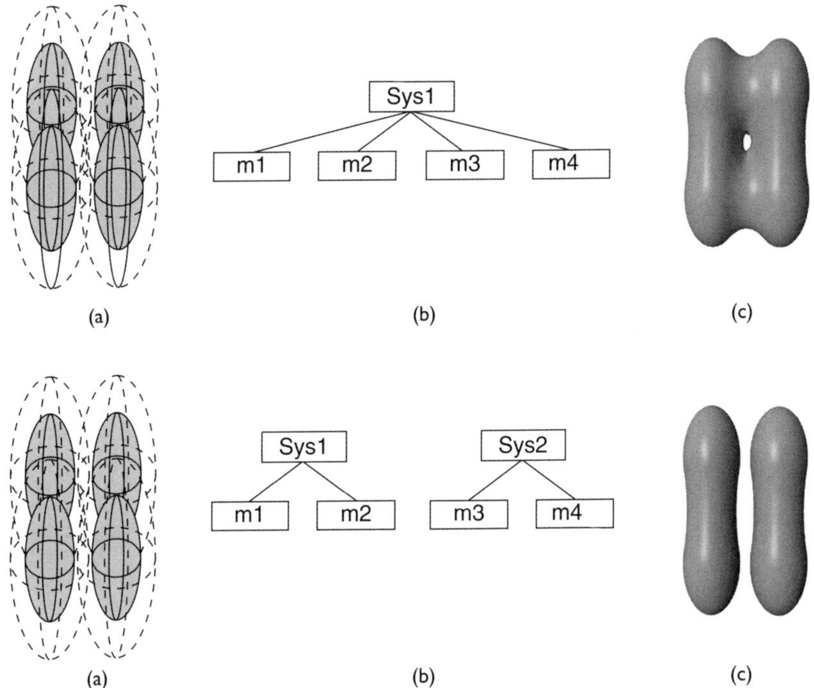

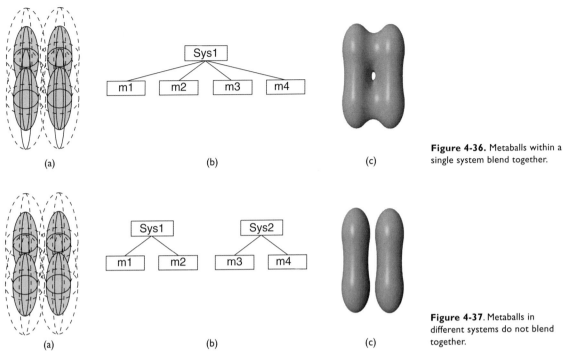

Figure 4-36. Metaballs within a single system blend together.

Figure 4-37. Metaballs in different systems do not blend together.

When modeling with metaballs, you usually organize them into a special hierarchical structure called a **metaball system**. This functions like a normal hierarchy, allowing you to translate, rotate, or scale entire collections of metaballs as a group. In addition, a metaball system structures the way metaballs blend, or fuse, with one another. Typically, all metaballs within a given system blend with each other (assuming, of course, they are close enough for the sum of their densities to exceed the threshold). Figure 4-36a shows a wireframe representation of a metaball system. Notice that in the hierarchical diagram (Figure 4-36b) there is a single metaball system; all four of the metaballs are members of that system. Figure 4-36c shows the rendered result of this system, with all the metaballs fusing together.

When metaballs are in separate systems, by contrast, they typically do not blend with each other (Figure 4-37). The hierarchical diagram (Figure 4-37b) shows that there are two distinct systems, each with two metaballs. The metaballs of *Sys1*, on the left, do not blend with those of *Sys2*, on the right (Figure 4-37c).

In some situations, however, the use of metaball systems will not provide all the control you need over the blending of metaballs. If you are modeling a human hand, for example, all the metaballs need to be in a single system so they can all be transformed—that is, moved, or rotated, or scaled—as a unit. However, if the metaballs are all in a single system, they will blend with each other by default. The fingers will fuse together, creating the sort of webbing shown in Figure 4-36c.

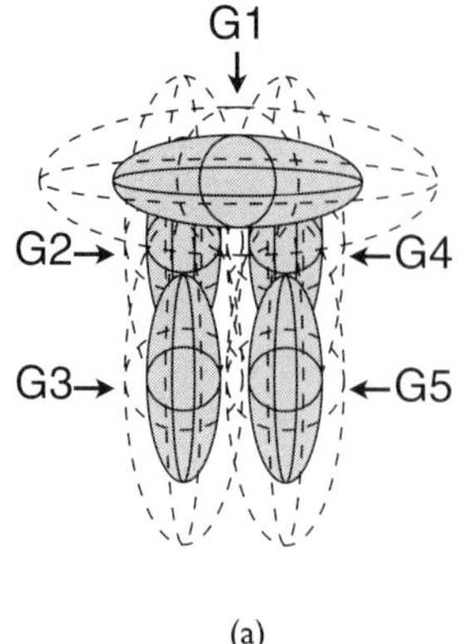

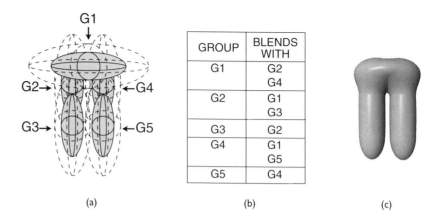

(a)

GROUP	BLENDS WITH
G1	G2 G4
G2	G1 G3
G3	G2
G4	G1 G5
G5	G4

(b)

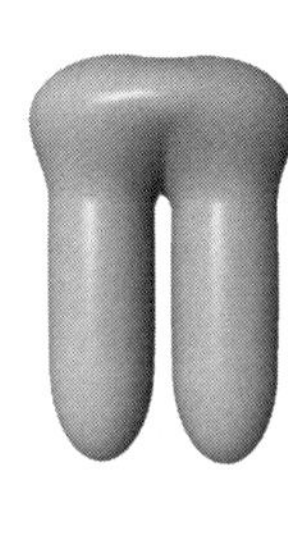

(c)

Figure 4-38. Blending groups define the blending of metaballs within a system or across several systems.

You can solve this problem with **blending groups**, or **fusion groups**, which allow you to define, both within a system and across a system, how metaballs will blend. First you define the members of each group—that is, which metaballs are in the group. Then you specify which other groups each group does or does not blend with.

Figure 4-38a is the wireframe representation of a single metaball system with five blending groups, G1 through G5. In this simple example, each group has been defined to consist of only a single metaball; in a more complex model, there would normally be many metaballs in each group. The chart (Figure 4-38b) lists each group and the names of all the groups it blends with. Notice that group G1, at the top of the model, blends with the top-left and top-right metaballs of the the "arms." Continuing down the list, group G2, the top-left metaball, blends with G1, the top, and also with G3, the lower part of the left arm. Notice that G2 does *not*, however, blend with any of the groups that comprise the right arm. This arrangement keeps the two arms separate and unfused. The metaballs of the right arm are similarly grouped. Figure 4-38c shows the rendered result of this grouping structure.

A blending structure similar to that of Figure 4-38 would be appropriate for many segments of a human or animal character. A hand, for example, would consists of a palm (analogous to the top metaball of Figure 4-38) and several fingers protruding from it. A foot would be structured the same way. An entire body would consist of a central object, the torso, with limbs protruding from it.

Recall from the beginning of this section that when you create metaballs, you are not explicitly defining surfaces, as you are with most other modeling techniques. Instead, metaballs create implicit surfaces at certain density thresholds. Because metaball surfaces are only implicit, they must be converted into explicit surfaces before rendering. When a system of metaballs is about to be rendered, it is automatically converted into polygons, and it is this new polygonal surface that is actually rendered. The number of polygons created determines how accurately the polygonal surface approximates the implicit metaball surface: more polygons yield a better approximation; fewer polygons yield a cruder approximation. Most software packages allow you to control the number of polygons, or **polygon resolution**, created from a metaball system. Figure 4-39a shows a simple metaball system; Figure 4-39b, the polygonal structure and rendering of that system using a low polygon resolution; and Figure 4-39c, the same system with a high polygon resolution.

It is important to understand that once a metaball model has been converted into a polygonal model, it loses all its metaball capabilities. Surfaces no longer blend together, and metaball parameters such as density threshold, weight, and influence no longer exist.

The animation of metaball models involves techniques already familiar to you. For example, you can transform individual metaballs using the keyframing approach. That is, you can translate, rotate, or scale each metaball just as you would any other object in a three-dimensional animation, define a keyframe for these transformations, define another keyframe for another set of transformations, and then generate an interpolated set of frames between the two keyframes. You also can hierarchically group a collection of metaballs and transform the entire group with keyframing. Alternatively, you can create an inverse kinematic skeleton to control your metaball model.

Perhaps even more interestingly, however, you can animate the densities and the density distributions of the metaballs, again using a keyframing approach. This technique provides an easy mechanism for animating shape changes and also permits certain shape changes that would be extremely difficult, if not impossible, to accomplish without the metaball approach. All four of the configurations in Figure 4-40 were modeled with the same three metaballs: two larger balls sitting one on top of another, and a third, smaller ball to the lower right. The differences in these models are a result solely of animating the density fields of each ball.

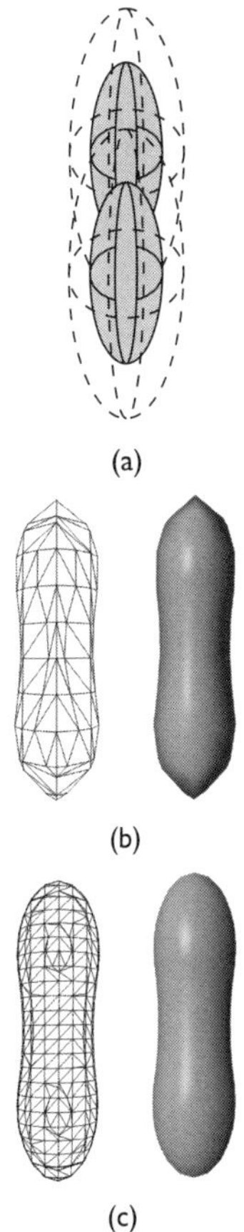

Figure 4-39. A metaball system can be converted into a polygonal surface with a lower or higher polygon resolution.

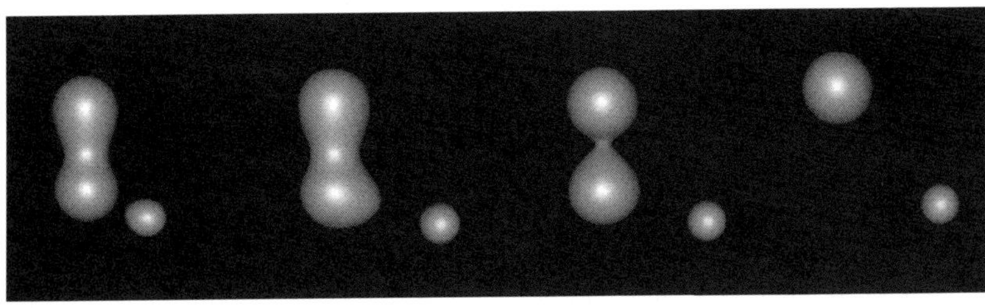

Figure 4-40. The parameters that define a metaball can be animated. Density can be increased or decreased or distorted eccentrically, producing very fluid modeling.

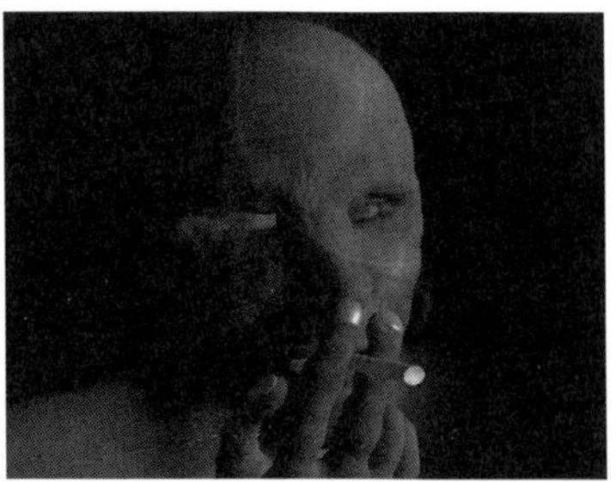

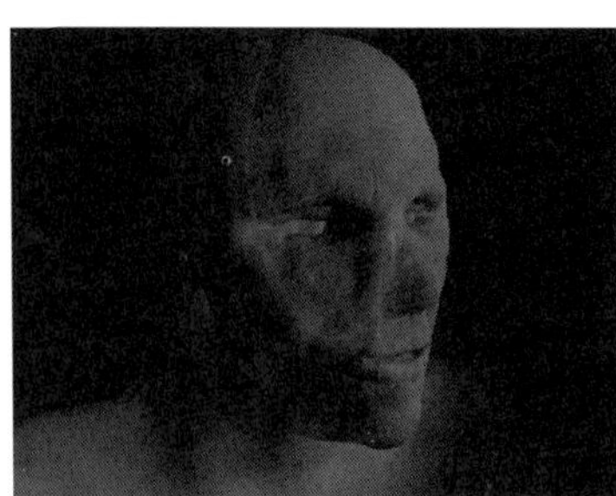

Figure 4-41. Metaballs can produce stunning results, especially in the modeling of human and animal figures. (Courtesy, Jin Wan Park.)

Whichever animation technique you use, complex metaball models can be very slow to work with. The calculations required to fuse the metaballs together and to create their implicit surfaces can slow down the computer considerably. For this reason it is sometimes easier to use metaballs only as a modeling technique. Having created the metaball model, you instruct the computer to create a static polygonal model from it. You then animate the polygonal model with any of the standard surface-deformation techniques. You might, for example, use metaballs to model a human character. Then you could create a polygonal model from that metaball model and apply the deformable envelope technique (see *Inverse Kinematics*, chapter 3). Such an approach takes advantage of the ability of metaballs to model smoothly blending surfaces, but avoids the time-consuming calculation of new implicit metaball surfaces at each frame of your animation.

In Figure 4-41, a striking example of metaball modeling and animation, both the human head and hand were modeled with metaballs. Careful use of blending groups kept the lips and fingers from fusing in unwanted ways. The head was modeled and animated as a metaball model. The hand was modeled with metaballs, then converted to polygons before it was animated with inverse kinematics and envelope deformation.

Particle and Particle-like Systems

Many phenomena, including such ephemeral phenomena as smoke, gas, steam, fire, and clouds, cannot be modeled easily as surfaces. In the case of fire, for example, the "surfaces" of fire (if you even can conceive of them in this way) are really molecule-sized particles, so minuscule and myriad that modeling them is impractical. You can sometimes use transparency mapping to simulate fire and other similar phenomena (see chapter 2, *Surface Texture Mapping*), but this technique has limitations. Fine for modeling the single flame of a candle, transparency mapping is much less successful at modeling the irregular collection of flickering flames in a fireplace. You have also seen that volumetric lights can be very effective for creating certain atmospheric effects (see *Atmospheric Effects,* chapter 2). Volumetric lights, however, also have limitations because they are restricted to geometrically regular volumes such as cubes, cones and spheres.

The **particle system** technique handles ephemeral phenomena such as smoke and fire that consist of masses of molecule-sized particles rather than discernible surfaces. Using this technique, you do not model individual surfaces. Rather, you define the number of "particles" in the system. Defined to exist and move in a three-dimensional space, these particles, which are too small to be seen individually, will, if present in sufficient numbers, become visible. When the rendering program processes the model information for a given frame, it looks at each pixel of screen space and calculates whether enough particles are present at that location to be visible. Because of this approach, such systems are sometimes referred to as **pixel-based** particle systems. If enough particles are found to be present at a given pixel, that pixel is colored appropriately. In this way, even though no surfaces were defined, "something" is rendered.

Particle systems can be tremendously complex, with a myriad of parameters for controlling how the particles move, where they come from, how they are rendered, how they interact with the environment, and so on. Each software package has its unique collection of parameters, but certain key parameters are shared by all packages. One such parameter is the quantity of particles, usually specified as the **emission rate**. Since the particles of a particle system are emitted continuously over time (the flame continues to burn, the rocket exhaust continues to be expelled), the most convenient way to specify how many particles should be in the system is to specify the number of particles emitted per second. This number usually ranges from a few hundred to several thousand. In Figure 4-42a the system represented is emitting relatively few particles per second. In contrast, that of Figure 4-42b is emitting particles at a much higher rate, thereby creating a much denser collection of particles.

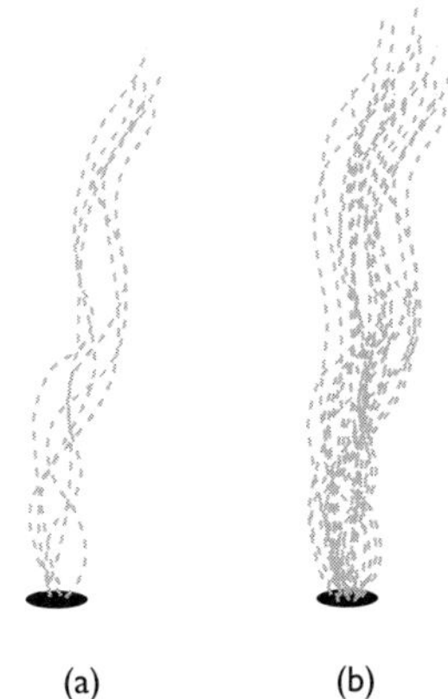

Figure 4-42. The quantity of particles in a system is controlled by the rate at which they are emitted, usually specified as the number of particles per second.

Another parameter you can control is the **speed** of the particles. The blast of exhaust coming out of a rocket emits particles that move through space extremely quickly. The particles of a cloud system, by contrast, drift very slowly.

However many particles there are and however quickly they move, some particles remain visible longer than others before dissipating into the atmosphere. The sparks emitted from a sparkler last only a moment, perhaps half a second. The particles of a slowly rising curl of smoke may be visible for several seconds as they waft upward. The parameter, usually measured in seconds, that controls this phenomenon is the **lifetime** of the particles; we speak of the

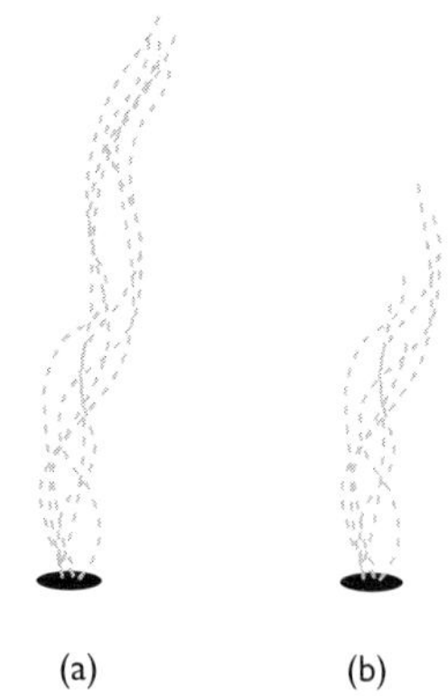

Figure 4-43. The lifetime of particles controls how long they remain visible before dissipating into the atmosphere.

particles "dying" after this amount of time. The two systems in Figure 4-43 are emitting particles at the same rate and at the same speed. The one in Figure 4-43b has a much shorter lifetime than that of Figure 4-42a, however, so its particles dissipate more quickly, resulting in a shorter column of particles.

In defining a particle system you must also specify where the particles are coming from—that is, their **source**. In some systems the source can be defined as an invisible geometric entity that has no actual surface. You might, for example, have an invisible rectangular source hovering above your scene in order to create rain particles, or a spherical source at the tip of a candle to create a candle flame. Some systems also permit you to define a light as a particle source. Thus, you might place a spotlight pointing upward at the base of a water fountain, using it simultaneously to create a spray of water particles and to light them from below.

Frequently, however, you want the source of particles to be a segment of one of the models in your three-dimensional scene. For example, you might want particles to emerge from the spherical tip of a sparkler or the exhaust nozzle at the back of a rocket or a tiny disk at the end of a rifle barrel (Figure 4-44). There are two approaches to achieve this: select a specific surface as the particle source or, as some systems allow, define a shader to be particle-emitting and then assign that shader to the surface in question.

Having defined where the particles are coming from, you must also define where they are going, by specifying the direction in which they are moving. If the source of the particles is an invisible geometric element or a light, the direction is specified by rotating the icon for that element or light. If the particle source is a surface, the direction is frequently defined by the normals of that surface. Recall from *Rendering Algorithms* in chapter 2 that the normal of a surface is effectively a line perpendicular to the surface at a particular point. Figure 4-45 shows two particle-emitting surfaces, with their normals—and therefore the direction of particle emission—indicated by arrows. The normals of the sphere in Figure 4-45a point outward equally

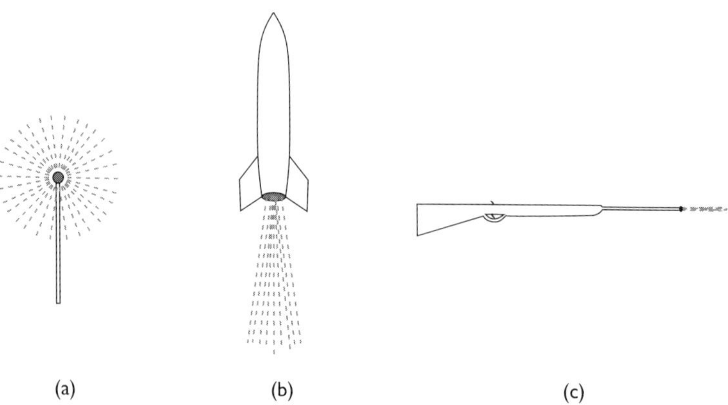

Figure 4-44. The source of particles is frequently associated with a specific surface in your scene.

in all directions; the normals of the flat disk in Figure 4-45b all point upward in the same direction.

Frequently, you want the emission of particles to follow a specific direction, but to fan outward a bit as in the rocket and rifle examples (Figures 4-44b and c). Outward fanning is controlled by a parameter usually called **spread**, specified in degrees. The rocket has a spread angle of about 20 degrees; the burst of particles from the rifle barrel has a narrow spread of only a few degrees.

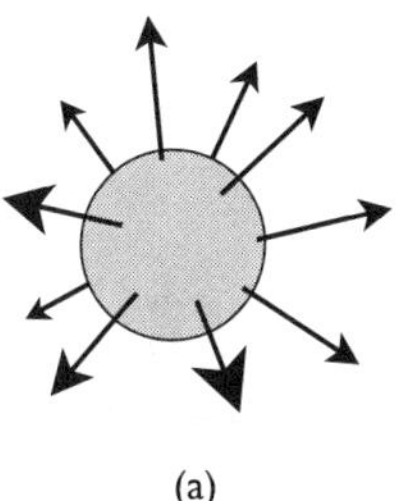

(a)

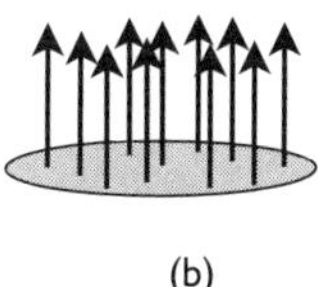

(b)

Figure 4-45. The surface normals of a particle system's source geometry can be used to specify the direction of emission.

Any of the parameters discussed so far may be adjusted additionally by adding **randomness** to them. For example, you may want to vary the direction of particles by spreading them outward, but not all by exactly the same amount. Or you may want the speed of the particles to vary somewhat, to avoid having every particle moving at exactly the same speed. Some packages allow you to control randomness through a **jitter** value, which alters a parameter by plus or minus a certain amount. For example, if the particles' spread is set to 20 degrees, with a jitter of ± 5, the spread of any given individual particle will range from 15 degrees to 25 degrees. Another way of introducing randomness is through a **noise** factor. Larger noise factors mean more randomness applied to that parameter; smaller noise factors mean less. In Figure 4-46, both the spread and the speed of the particles have been randomized.

Figure 4-46. Randomness can be applied to any of a particle system's parameters. Here it is applied to both the speed and the spread of the particles.

A large number of parameters control the rendering of a particle system. One of these is the **color** of the particles, a parameter often animatable as well. For example, you can make the color of a fire particle change as it moves away from the center of the flame. The licking flames of a burning log might be a hot orange color at the source of the flame, change to a darker red at the top of the flame, and finally change to black (no fire) as they move farther away and "cool." Specifying the animation of the particles' color is typically done by selecting a color at the beginning of the particles' lifetime, another at the end of their lifetime and, optionally, intermediate colors at intermediate points.

You can also define and animate the **transparency** of the particles. Some particles—for example, a gentle mist—would be rendered as quite transparent. Others, such as dense smoke belching from a smokestack, would be rendered as more opaque.

Most particle systems also allow you to control how much the particles **blur** when rendered. A system simulating the sparks that flash from an axe when it strikes a stone should have little or no blurring, to keep the sparks distinct. Smoke, on the other hand, is much more amorphous and its particles therefore should be rendered as blurring to the point that none is individually distinguishable.

A particle's **trail life** is related to blurring. As a particle moves through space, it may leave a visible trail behind. The longer the life of such a trail, the

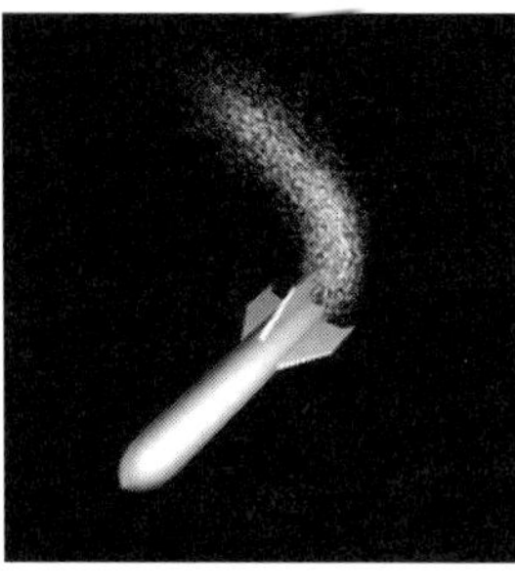

(a)

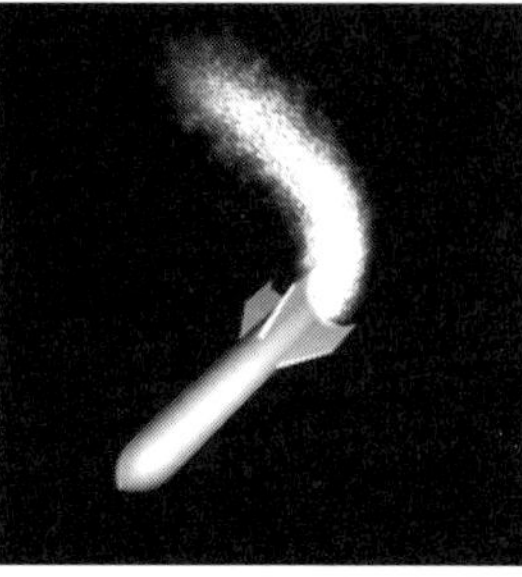

(b)

Figure 4-47. Glow is one of the many parameters that control the rendering of particles.

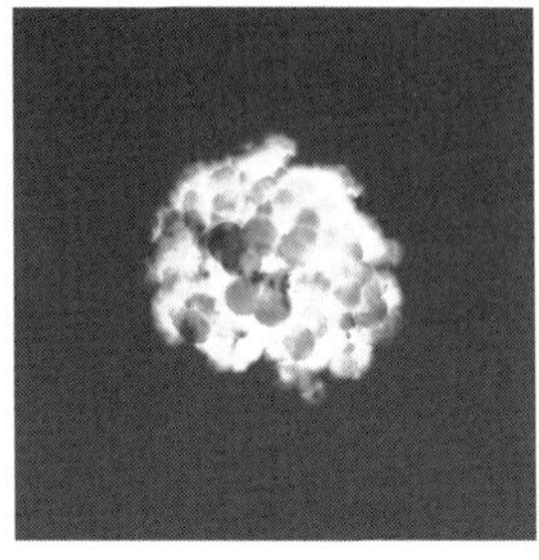

Figure 4-48. Predefined settings to create specific effects may be stored in a particle library, to be retrieved and modified by the user.

longer the trail itself will be and the more visible. Trail life is normally measured in seconds.

Glow makes particles look incandescent by increasing both their brightness and color saturation. Figure 4-47a shows a rendering of rocket exhaust without glow; Figure 4-47b is exactly the same particle system with glow. Glow fuses the particles together, much like blurring, and simultaneously gives them an intense, fiery look.

To help you manage the large number of rendering parameters and all their possibilities, many systems provide predefined collections of parameter settings that yield a particular look. Stored in a particles **library**, these can be retrieved and modified to suit a specific purpose. For example, one library particle system might give you a very wispy, transparent look suitable for smoke. Another might produce clouds. Still another might give you a more opaque, almost blobby look. In Figure 4-48, the particles have been rendered with a very dense, opaque, almost tangible spherical look to simulate the billowing thickness of an explosion's flame and smoke.

As noted at the beginning of this section, particle systems are defined three-dimensionally, and herein lies much of their strength for 3D computer rendering and animation. When you look at a rendering of a particle system, you are seeing only one point of view of a fully three-dimensional "model." Like any other 3D model, it can be turned around, viewed from another angle, moved to another location, and so on. You could, for example, "fly" your camera into the particle-system clouds in Figure 4-49, going through them and coming out the other side.

High-end particle systems also react to light in a fully three-dimensional way. Where there are fewer particles, light passes through more easily, as at the edges of the clouds in Figure 4-49. If there are a great many particles, light does not pass through. Particle systems will also cast shadows onto other objects. A plane flying between the viewer and the clouds in Figure 4-49 would at some point have the shadow of the cloud cast upon it. Some software packages also allow particles to be defined as **self-shadowing**—that is, to cast shadows upon themselves. Both the explosion in Figure 4-48 and the clouds in Figure 4-49 were rendered with this feature.

Another important feature of particle systems is that they incorporate the simulation features of **motion dynamics** (see *Motion Dynamics* earlier in this chapter). Thus, the particles of a particle system can be made to react to gravity or wind. The water of a fountain sprays upward and then is pulled back down by gravity. It may simultaneously be blown to the side by a strong wind, causing some of the particles to spray in that direction.

Since particle systems frequently simulate ephemeral phenomena that are subject to slight shifts in air currents, many software packages contain a parameter called **turbulence**. Rather than defining a number of different wind forces, each of a different strength and each blowing at a different angle, a single turbulence value can be set, creating the desired effect. In Figure 4-50 the smoke is blown to the right by a wind force and shifted in random directions with varying force by turbulence.

In the section on *Motion Dynamics* you saw that collision detection permits objects to collide, bouncing off each other in physically accurate ways. The same is true of particle systems. When defining the parameters of your system, you can elect to turn collision detection on, specifying which models in the scene are to be considered obstacles: whenever a particle encounters one of these obstacles, it reacts appropriately. How it reacts is determined by parameters you set to make the particles bounce off the obstacle, split into several smaller particles, or stop altogether. In addition, you can set parameters to control how fast or how far the particle will bounce. In Figure 4-51 the rocket's exhaust particles, thrust downward, collide with the ground and radiate outward.

Most particle systems also allow you to define how the rendering characteristics of a particle change upon collision. In Figure 4-51 the particles change from a very bright, incandescent, flamelike rendering to a dull, smoky rendering as soon as they hit the ground.

A very powerful and interesting extension of particle systems is their ability to simulate **hair** and **fur**. Recall that one of the parameters of a particle system is its trail life, the amount of time a particle's trail remains visible. If the trail life is set to a sufficiently large number, the trail of the particle will never disappear, effectively creating a solid wirelike column behind it as it "grows" through space. Combining this technique with careful use of transparency, color, self-shadowing, and other parameters, you can effectively model different types of hair. Figure 4-52 shows three examples, all emitted from a spherical source. On the left, parameters have been set to simulate fur; the two other balls use parameter settings that simulate hair. The hair on the ball at right has been "waved" by introducing a limited amount of randomness to the direction of growth of each hair. The hairs of all three balls have different amounts of stiffness: the short, stiff hairs of the furry ball stick straight out, while the more flexible hairs of the other two are pulled down by gravity.

Figure 4-49. Particle systems create fully three-dimensional models that exist in a fully three-dimensional space.

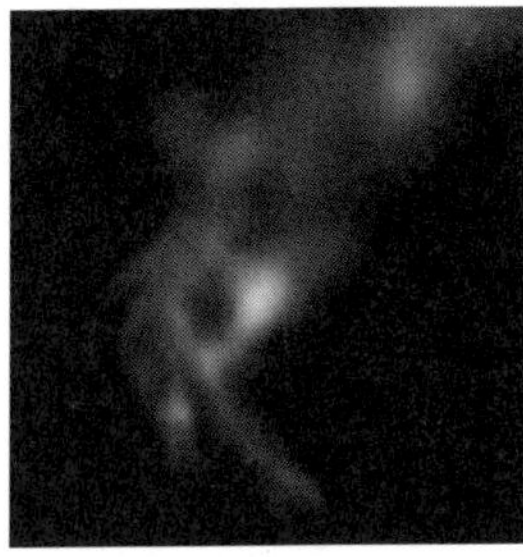

Figure 4-50. Particle systems can be subject to gravity, wind, and turbulence forces.

Figure 4-51. Particles may collide with other objects in the scene, bouncing off them, splitting into smaller particles, and changing color.

Figure 4-52. Hair and fur can be modeled with particles by making each particle leave an opaque trail behind it. (Courtesy, Gevel Marrero.)

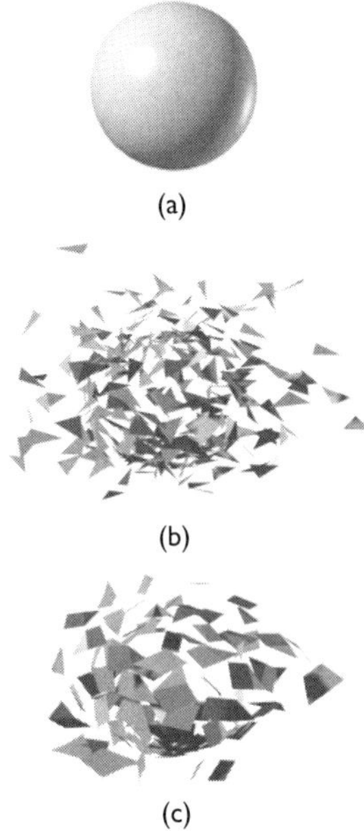

Figure 4-53. Explosion functions manipulate tiny surfaces in a particle-like way.

A more developed example of this technique can be seen in color plate 3. The geometry of the tarantula is quite simple, consisting mostly of ellipsoids. Each of these is a particle-emitting source, from which hair particles grow.

In addition to the true particle systems just described, some advanced 3D packages offer particle-like modeling functions. These functions operate on actual surfaces, but manipulate surfaces in ways that are particle-like. The most common of such functions is an **explosion** function, in which each surface model is broken into many small surfaces (Figure 4-53a), and these small surfaces are made to expand outward in an exploding pattern (Figure 4-53b). This technique is not a true particle system, since it operates on definable and discernible surfaces, usually on polygon models. Remember that any polygonal surface may be broken down into a collection of triangular polygons (see chapter 1, *Polygonal Modeling*). When a polygonal model "explodes," each of the triangles that form the surface is animated outward to create the effect. Since the exploding triangles actually come from the surface of the polygon, the number of exploding pieces is a function of the polygon mesh that defines the original sphere. That is, if the polygon is defined to consist of a 6×6 mesh of polygons, the few triangles exploding outward are quite large. A much denser mesh, say 100×100, produces a great many, and much smaller, triangles.

Some software systems allow you additional control, however, over the size of the exploding pieces. In these software packages, you may decide whether the exploding pieces will be individual triangles or clusters of triangles. If you choose the latter, you also may define how large the largest clusters will be. For example, the largest exploding clusters may consist of ten triangles, and this means that the surface of the sphere will be broken up into pieces the largest of which will comprise ten adjacent triangles (Figure 4-53c).

As with all particle and particle-like techniques, randomness plays a significant role in explosion functions, and you can specify a randomness factor to ensure that not all of the exploding pieces are of a uniform configuration. Other important animation parameters that you can specify include the starting location of the explosion, the strength of the explosion, whether a gravitational force will pull the pieces back down, and how strong this gravitational force is.

A technique related to both particle systems and explosion techniques is known as **flocking**. As the name implies, flocking is designed to simulate the movement of large numbers of creatures in flocking, herding, or schooling patterns. It is most appropriate, for example, for the animation of groups of birds, animals, or fish. In fact, in its most sophisticated implementations, it includes parameters for controlling the behavior of these creatures in realistic ways. One example is **collision avoidance**. Each member of a flock, herd, or school normally moves in such a way as to avoid colliding with its fellows. Sophisticated flocking software incorporates this behavior. Because of the large number of members in a typical flock, however, this can be quite a com-

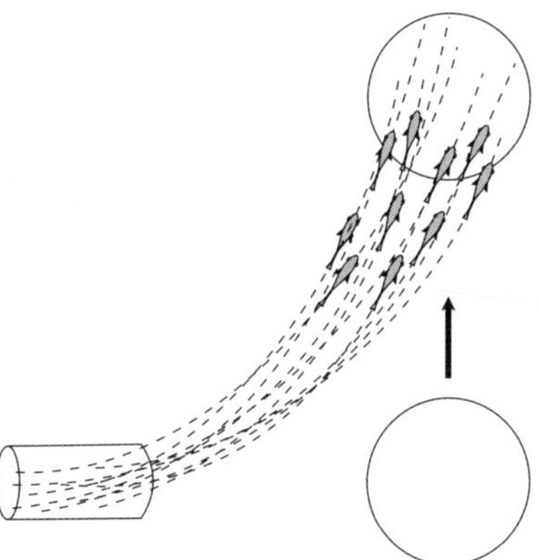

Figure 4-54. Flocking techniques are designed to simulate the movements of birds, animals, and fish. They also can be used to mimic particle and particle-like functions such as explosions or streams.

plicated, and thus slow, calculation. Some advanced flock software also offers controls over species-specific behavior. Pigeons, for example, flock in different patterns than swallows.

Even if the flocking software available to you does not include such sophisticated controls, it can still be extremely useful in simplifying the process of animating large numbers of similar entities. For instance, if you are animating pigeon models, then even a flocking function with limited behavioral controls goes a long way to making your models appear to flock like pigeons.

Flocking software can also be effectively used for other purposes than simulating flocking animals. One such use is to mimic a simple particle system. To do this, you make the basic element to be flocked a simple, very small surface—perhaps a triangle. By animating a "flock" of triangles from a small, inner, starting sphere to a large, outer ending sphere, you produce an explosion effect. Similarly, you can use a lot of triangles to create some of the spray or stream effects that a true particle system produces.

When using the flocking technique, you begin by modeling the element to be flocked, such as a fish (Figure 4-54). The flocking technique will replicate this element as many times as you specify. For example, having modeled a single fish, you might specify that you want a school of fifty fish, and the flocking function will automatically create forty-nine copies.

Having defined the core element, you then indicate how you want the flock to move. Most often you do this by modeling some shape at the location where the flocking animation is to begin and another shape at the location where the flocking is to end. The flocked elements (say, ten fish) are positioned at frame 1 of the animation in such a way as approximately to fill the starting shape. For example, if the starting shape is a cylinder, the fish are arranged to fill a roughly cylindrical shape at frame 1. The words "approximately" and "roughly" are important here, because randomness plays a key role in this sort of function. Fish arranged in a perfectly regular cylindrical pattern are not convincingly flocklike.

Just as you position the flock elements at the start of the animation to fill the starting shape, you position them at the last frame of the animation approximately to fill the ending shape (in Figure 4-54, a sphere). The starting and ending shapes determine the arrangement of the flock elements at the first and last frames, but they do not necessarily indicate how the elements move from the one to the other. By default, the elements of a flock move in an approximately straight line between the starting shape and the ending shape. Once again, the word "approximately" indicates that some degree of randomness is introduced into the path of each element. Usually, you control a randomness parameter, which increases or decreases the amount that each element deviates from the default straight-line path. If you intend the flock to move in some path other than a straight line, you can animate the location of the ending shape. This change causes the flock to "pursue" the ending shape, changing the path of the flock over the course of the animation as the flock tracks the moving target (see Figure 4-54).

Procedural Animation

Another technique offered by some systems involves a very different kind of approach to modeling and animation. In these systems, there is an intermediate step between the interactive work of modeling and animating a sequence and the final rendering of this sequence. In these systems, a text file, usually called a **scene file**, is written out by the interactive package. The scene file is a complete verbal and numerical description of everything in the scene—the models, the lights, the surface characteristics, the camera, as well as any animation that these elements might have.

A 3D software system might use a proprietary language for this scene file, or it might use a standardized language. In either case, the scene file is written in a programmable language. (Since the C programming language is most commonly used by professional graphics programmers, many scene-file languages are adapted from the C language.) By editing the text file with a word processor or text editor, you effectively can write a program to generate models and animation. Since a program is often referred to as a *procedure*, this technique is called **procedural modeling** or, when animation is involved, **procedural animation**.

A simple example of procedural modeling is use of the programmable scene language to create instances of an existing model. (See *Transformations*, in chapter 1, for a discussion of instances.) Suppose you use the standard functions of a software package to interactively model a tree. You then write out a scene file. This text file contains a description of the geometry and the surface characteristics of the tree, and these descriptions constitute the defi-

```
/* define all elements of the scene */

define variables

define image size
define camera for scene
define surface characteristics
define lights

define tree model geometry

/* model a forest by instancing the tree model with
appropriate transformations */

for each tree
    {
    calculate the transformations on the tree
    instance the tree model
    }
```

Figure 4-55. A pseudocode version of a procedure to generate a forest model. The actual code would be written in the scene-file language of the software package.

nition of the tree. You then edit the scene file, adding a loop statement that generates a number of instances of the original tree model. Each time the tree is instanced within this loop, the transformations on the tree (location, rotation, and scale) are recalculated, so that each new tree is in a different location and is of a slightly different size and orientation. Using this procedural approach, you easily can model an entire forest of trees.

Figure 4-55 shows example of the sort of procedural modeling that might accomplish such a task. This program is written in **pseudocode**, which is an informal, Englishlike version of the logic of a program. In actual practice, you write this code in the specific scene language of the software package you use. Notice that in this pseudocode objects and variables can be defined, just as in a normal programming language, and that looping is one of the programming tools available.

Procedural-modeling applications, like particle systems (see the previous section), often make use of randomness. The forest model described above, for example, will not be very convincing if all the trees are positioned at very regular intervals, are all of exactly the same height, and so on. A certain amount of irregularity and unpredictability makes the model feel realistic.

Total randomness, however, is rarely useful. If, for example, the size of the trees is totally random, some of them might be only an inch high and some might be miles high! Clearly, this will not work. More commonly, the randomness programmed into a procedural model is constrained by certain probabilities, such as a relationship between the number of trees in the forest and the height of the forest above sea level. You also probably want the height of the trees to fall within a certain range of reasonable heights, with trees of "average" height being more likely than trees that are very tall or very short. This sort of controlled randomness in a procedure is called **stochastic modeling** and is a very powerful branch of procedural modeling.

Figure 4-56. The components of these two plants were modeled interactively. They were then composed procedurally within a scene file. Both of the plants were generated by the same scene-file program. (© 1992 Sylvain Moreau.)

The forest example as described so far is a very elementary use of procedural modeling, in that each tree is a copy of every other tree, and only the number of trees and the transformations on the trees are produced procedurally. To make the application more interesting, the tree model itself might be produced procedurally.

One way of doing this is to model interactively the components of the tree (trunk, branches, leaves, etc.), and then use the scene-file language to write a program that procedurally constructs a tree from these components. Both of the plant models in Figure 4-56, for instance, were generated from the same scene-file program. The thickness, density, and spacing of the branches and leaves were controlled by a stochastic procedure. Though this application of procedural modeling is clearly more complex than the simple instancing of predefined trees to make a forest, the procedurally modeled trees are conceptually the same as the forest example. That is, a few model elements were modeled interactively using standard modeling techniques, then instanced procedurally within a program loop. Transformations were calculated for each instance of each element within the appropriate loop.

Figure 4-57 shows an example of what the pseudocode for such a procedural model might look like. Notice that the pattern is the same as in the pseudocode for the forest: define model geometry, loop, calculate transformations, and instance. In the more complicated procedure, however, special care must be taken with the placement of the transformations relative to one another. The model being generated by this procedure should be organized hierarchically if it is to function properly. That is, the transformations effected on the whole tree should propagate downward to all the branches of the tree; the transformations on each branch of the tree should propagate downward to all the leaves of that branch; and so on. In order to accomplish this, you use one of the standard textual representations for the hierarchical structuring of transformations (see chapter 1, *Hierarchies*). For example, curly brackets can be used to push and pop the transformations of the hierarchy.

Both of the examples discussed so far involved using procedural modeling to instance and transform preexisting geometry. However, you also can

```
/* define all elements of the scene */
      .
      .
      .
define trunk model geometry
define branch model geometry
define leaf model geometry
      .
      .
      .
/* model a tree by instancing its components with
appropriate transformations */

push /* push trunk transformations */
calculate transformatons for trunk
instance trunk

calculate number of branches
for each branch of the tree
    { /* start branch loop */

    push  /* push branch transformations */
    calculate transformations for branch
    instance branch

    calculate number of leaves
    for each leaf of the branch
        { /* start leaf loop */
        push  /* push leaf transformations */
        calculate transformations for leaf
        instance leaf
        pop  /* pop leaf transformations */
        } /* end leaf loop */

    pop  /* pop branch transformations */
    } /* end branch loop */

pop  /* pop trunk transformations */
```

Figure 4-57. Pseudocode for the plant modeled procedurally in Figure 4-56.

use procedural modeling to generate the geometry of a model. With this approach, you write a section of program code in the scene file to generate actual geometric data. These data might consist of a list of polygon vertices and corresponding coordinates, or perhaps, if the system is a spline modeler, a list of control points and corresponding coordinates. Using this approach you could write code to generate the geometry of the leaf, the branch, or the trunk of the tree in your forest model.

Just as a model can be defined procedurally, so too can the motion of a model be defined procedurally through the process known as **procedural animation**. Anyone familiar with basic trigonometry can program simple geometric patterns, such as circles and parabolas and sine curves. Using a few simple trigonometric functions, you can develop a scene-file program in which objects move about in these patterns. On a somewhat more complex level, you can program the growth of plants procedurally, by controlling the number and size of the branches and leaves over time, or the density of leaf development. You also can define and animate surface characteristics and lighting for any model procedurally.

Effectively, anything that can be defined in terms of some variable or set of variables can be generated and animated in a scene-file program. In an animation of plant growth, for example, you might define the color of the leaves to progress from a lime green when the leaves are young to a deeper, richer green when they have reached maturity. In developing an animation like this, you usually have access to many of the same functions, subroutines, and programming devices that you have available in a normal programming language. Sine and cosine functions, the absolute-value function, remainder functions, various types of ease functions, loop statements, conditional statements, arrays, and so on are standard tools in most programmable scene languages.

Some of the most impressive examples of procedural modeling and animation involve very sophisticated uses of these programming techniques in conjunction with complex mathematics and physics. When scientists develop animations to simulate the orbit of a satellite around a planet, or the growth of a storm front, they use procedural modeling and animation, usually employing data from real-world measurements to produce their simulations.

The film industry produces some of its most stunning special effects through three-dimensional procedural modeling and animation as well. The water creature in *The Abyss* and the stampeding herd of dinosaurs in *Jurassic Park* are two examples. Large special-effects houses normally have both artists and programmers on staff, and when a job comes in that requires a new special effect, the artists and programmers collaborate. Based on what the artists and art directors are looking for, the staff programmers develop code to procedurally generate and animate the models involved. The artists then work with these procedures and make suggestions for changes. This process goes back and forth until the desired effect is achieved.

But what about those animators who do not have a staff of professional programmers to help develop procedural techniques? Sophisticated procedural modeling and animation can require programming skills that many artists and animators do not possess. In addition to the programming skills, these techniques require (depending on the task) a knowledge of physics, biology, meteorology, or other sciences. Clearly, not everyone possesses the scientific skills to develop sophisticated simulations or special effects. However, any animator willing to devote a little time to learning the grammar of a programmable scene language can gain access to some of the power of procedural modeling and animation.

Also bear in mind that many of the interactive techniques discussed in this book began as procedural techniques available only to programmers. It is the nature of the research-and-development process in 3D computer graphics that a technique initially can be accomplished only by those who know how to write the program code that makes it happen. Eventually, however, if the technique has wide appeal, it is written into the interactive portion of commercially available software packages and becomes available to a wider range of users, including artists and animators who may have no particular programming skills.

For example, the flying and bouncing bowling balls mentioned earlier in this chapter (color plate 2) were animated with motion-dynamics techniques. At the time this animation was produced, these techniques did not exist in any interactive software package on the market, and the artist had to write program code in a scene file to produce the motion dynamics of the balls. Today motion-dynamics techniques are a standard part of many commercially available software packages, and tomorrow they will be available in many more.

CHAPTER 5

Compositing and Special Effects

Introduction

While it is often possible to render final, ready-to-record frames of an animation, it is sometimes not possible and frequently not desirable to do so. It is often to your advantage to render each frame in pieces and to assemble the pieces later. For example, you might create a background image and a foreground image separately and then combine these images later to make the final frame. This process of assembling various pieces of an image is called **compositing**.

Why not, you might think, just render the frames in one pass and be done with it? A first answer is that it is almost impossible to "just render the frames in one pass and be done with it." That is, only rarely will you render all the frames perfectly the first time. Even after you have completed all the rendering tests, the chances are that, given the complexity of most animations, somewhere you will have made a mistake and have to rerender some portion of your work. The experienced animator assumes this and considers it part of the process. When it does happen, it is often much easier and faster to correct mistakes and rerender if the frames have been broken down into component images.

Imagine, for example, a sequence of frames in which a three-dimensional character (in Figure 5-1, a robot) walks in front of a complexly modeled three-dimensional cityscape, as the camera pans slowly by. Imagine further that you have rendered these frames and found some rendering error on the character. The rendering of all the buildings is fine, however. In a frame such as the one described, it might take the computer fifteen minutes to render the buildings and one minute to render the character. If you have set up the rendering so that the building models in the background and the character model in the foreground are rendered separately and composited later, you now will be in a position to take advantage of this fact and rerender only the foreground character model. This can save a tremendous amount of time. If this segment of the animation is thirty seconds long and is being recorded at the standard thirty-frames-per-second video rate, in fact, you will have just saved yourself 225 hours of rerendering time (30 seconds × 30 frames = 900

Figure 5-1. It is often advisable to break a rendered frame into component elements—for example, the foreground and background portions of this scene. These components are then composited to form the final frame. (City-scape, courtesy Steve Rittler. Robot, courtesy Steven Lin.)

frames × 15 minutes per frame for background buildings = 13,500 minutes ÷ 60 minutes per hour = 225 hours)! Even calculating in the time needed to do the compositing of all the frames, which might be approximately ten hours, you will have saved about 215 hours. This translates into very nearly nine full days of machine time!

Even if you make no rendering errors, using a compositing approach as part of your rendering process provides flexibility. To continue with the previous example, suppose that upon seeing the rendered frames you decide to change the walk of the character slightly. If you have set up the rendering in the foreground-background composited fashion, you will be able to make this change in about one-fifteenth of the rerendering time it would have taken if you hadn't, since you have to rerender only the figure itself. A difference of this magnitude makes it more likely that you actually will make such an improvement. If you know that you will have to spend nine additional days rerendering the scene, you are more likely to decide that the animation is good enough as is, even though in reality it still could be improved.

This kind of flexibility becomes especially important in production situations where decisions have been made about one portion of the animation but not yet about another. If the rendering is organized appropriately, final rendering of those portions that have been decided upon—say, the background buildings—can proceed even as the details of the other components are being worked out. If the rendering is being done in a noncomposited, all-in-one-pass fashion, all rendering must be postponed until all design decisions have been made. The result of this, of course, is that decisions are often made hastily, and badly.

A final motivation for using a composited approach to produce your final frames is that sometimes there is simply no other way, for example, when 3D computer animation must be combined with live-action footage. Another example would be where some special two-dimensional effect is to be added as a post-process to the rendered frames. In both of these cases, the animation is necessarily in the realm of compositing. The three-dimensionally rendered frame becomes one element, the live-action frame or two-dimensional effect another, and the final frame is the result of compositing the two in some fashion.

All of this is not to say that all animation sequences should be rendered in a composited manner. If there will be no significant advantage to breaking the final frame into component pieces, and if there are no special two-dimensional effects, there may very well be nothing gained by using a composited approach. Very often, however, there is a significant advantage.

Digital Techniques

Some high-end 3D animation packages provide a compositing module within the main body of the software. Others provide a separate compositing program that runs outside the main program. If your software provides neither, or if what is provided is insufficient for your purposes, you can also purchase compositing programs that are completely independent of any individual animation software. Although the full capabilities of sophisticated compositing software are beyond the scope of this book, almost all systems provide certain basic capabilities, which we will discuss here.

Perhaps the most common of these, called **matting**, is the capability of combining a foreground image and a background image, as described in the previous section. The word "matte" here means a mask—something that blocks out, or hides, something else.

Suppose that your foreground picture is a robot, rendered against a plain black background (Figure 5-2a). A matte, or mask, of that image is a black-and-white cutout in the shape of the robot (Figure 5-2b). This matte picture is derived from the original picture. The background color in the original becomes black in the matte picture; everywhere else, the matte picture is white.

In most systems, this matte picture is produced automatically at the same time that the rendered image (the robot, in this example) is calculated. Some software packages store the matte image as a separate picture file. Many packages, however, store the matte image information within the same file that stores the picture's Red, Green, and Blue color information. In this case, the matte information is referred to as the **Alpha channel** of the picture, and the picture itself as RGBA (Red, Green, Blue, and Alpha).

Now suppose that you also have a separately rendered background picture of some buildings (Figure 5-2c) on top of which you want to put the robot. Doing so consists of copying the foreground picture through the matte onto the background picture. If you imagine placing the matte picture over the foreground picture, and if you imagine that the black areas of the matte are opaque and the white areas transparent, then you can understand how this process works. The matte picture blocks out those portions of the robot picture that lie behind the opaque, or black, areas of the matte. Only those portions of the robot picture that lie within the transparent, white areas of the matte go "through" the matte, and the result is a composited picture (Figure 5-2d).

More technically, a matting operation is calculated in terms of pixel values. For a simple matte operation such as the one just described, the computer tests the value of each pixel in the matte picture. If the value at a pixel is 0 (black), the pixel of the foreground picture at the same location is not copied on top of the background picture. If, on the other hand, a pixel value is 255 (white), the color of the corresponding pixel in the foreground picture *is* copied on top of the background image, overwriting the old color of the pixel (that is, the pixel color of the background image) at that location.

A problem can arise, however, when matting is reduced to this sort of all-or-none, black-and-white situation. Recall that most three-dimensional renderings are produced with anti-aliasing, to conceal the staircasing effects that can be so distracting in computer graphics (see chapter 2, *Final-frame Considerations*). Since the edges of an anti-aliased model are a blurred combination of the model's color and the background color, an all-or-none matte will not work. If the white areas of such a black-and-white, or **hard-edged**, matte are large enough to include the anti-aliased pixels, they form a dark halo around the composited model. If the white areas of the matte are small enough to crop off the anti-aliased pixels, it recreates the jagged edges that the anti-aliasing had eliminated.

The answer to this problem, a **soft-edged matte** makes use of intermediate gray values, as well as pure black-and-white values, to determine which portion of a foreground picture will pass through the matte picture onto the background picture. Notice (in Figure 5-3, a blowup of a portion of the matte in Figure 5-2b) that the interior of the robot still translates into white in the matte image, and that the background portion of the original robot image still translates to black in the matte. However, the anti-aliased edges of the robot now translate into shades of gray in the matte, producing a soft edge. When the foreground picture of the robot is copied through this matte, a *percentage* of the color is copied through at these gray pixels. The darker the matte pixel, the less of the original goes through. The lighter the matte pixel, the more of the original goes through. In the center of the robot, for example, the color of the matte is pure white (the pixel value is 255), so 100 percent of the foreground image passes through the matte. Along the edge of the robot, a given matte pixel might have a value of 128. Since 128 divided by 256 equals 0.5, 50 percent of the color of the robot at that pixel will go through the matte. This color is combined with 50 percent of the color of the background image

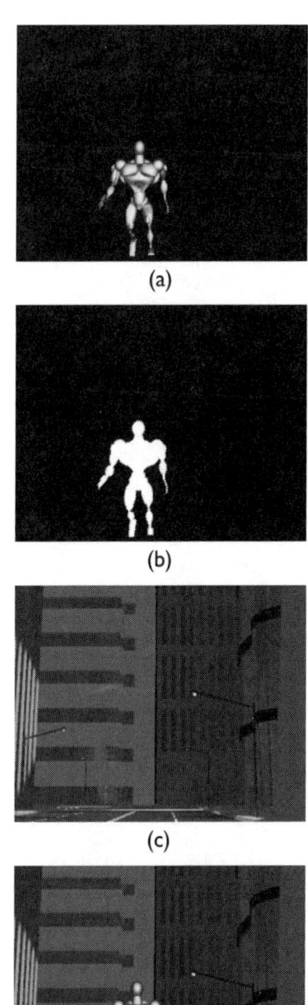

Figure 5-2. A matting operation. The robot (a) is copied through the matte (b) onto the background image (c) to produce the final image (d).

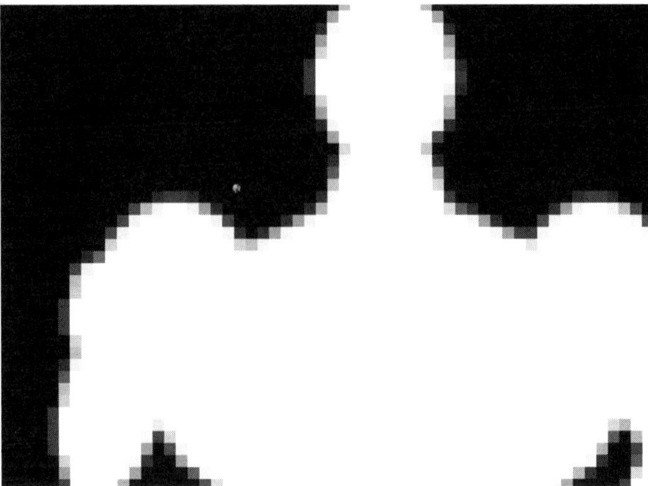

Figure 5-3. A close-up of a soft-edged matte, showing the intermediate values of gray around the edge of the matte.

at the same pixel location. The result is that the robot image blends properly with the background image.

So far we have been discussing a single matte operation for a single still image. When you use a sequence of mattes for a sequence of animation frames, the operation is called a **travelling matte**. One of the most common and powerful uses of such a matte is to combine computer graphics, or **CG**, footage and **live-action** footage. Television advertisements, newscasts, documentaries, and even sitcoms use this technique regularly. But nowhere is it more common than in the production of Hollywood films, where all manner of wondrous CG monsters, ghosts, tornadoes, explosions, and spaceships are seamlessly matted in with live-action footage of our favorite actors.

Combining CG footage and live action has become an enormously sophisticated art unto itself, involving much more than simply the rendering of 3D models and matting them onto film. In order for the effect to be believable, the **lighting** in both the live-action scenes and the computer-generated scenes must match exactly. Color plate 9 is a good example of an industrial-design application of this sort of matching.

Registering your computer model to the live-action scene is another issue that comes up when you combine computer imagery and live-action footage. For animated creatures, this is often done with **stand-in actors**. For example, if a computer-generated monster is to run down a hallway and jump on the back of the fleeing hero, a human actor might play the part of the monster as the scene is being shot. Once shot, the film is digitized frame by frame and the computer-generated monster matted into each frame on top of the human stand-in. The new digital frames are then recorded back to film (see chapter 6, *Recording*).

When dealing with live action, you must also carefully match the camera motion of the computer animation to that of the live footage. This is often accomplished with **motion tracking**, in which the film camera is mounted on a mechanical device whose movements are controlled by a computer program. This enables you to reshoot the scene as many times as you want with exactly the same camera motion, and also to replicate the exact same camera motion in the virtual space of a 3D computer animation program.

Finally, convincing matting of CG over live-action requires careful matching of **reflections**. No matter how carefully a computer model is registered to the scene's action, no matter how well-matched are the lighting and camera motion, if the model does not have the reflections our eyes tell us it should have, something will seem amiss. Here the most useful technique is reflection mapping (see *Environment Procedures and Reflection Mapping* in chapter 2). Special software can analyze the digitized frames of the live-action footage, producing appropriate reflection maps for the computer model.

Another important film application of many of these same matting techniques is the **digital replication** of elements, whether computer generated or live-action. Rather than the "cast of thousands" that was trumpeted by film producers of another era, film producers today often take advantage of the computer's matting capabilities to turn a cast of a few dozen into what seems like a cast of thousands. If a scene calls for a band of horsemen to ride up the hill, it is frequently now much cheaper to hire only a few actors, digitize the footage of them, extract their images from the digitized frames, and replicate those few horseman across the hillside in a cut-and-paste fashion.

Another common compositing function in 3D animation systems is the **cross-dissolve**, in which two images are blended together (Figure 5-4). When performing a digital cross-dissolve, you somehow must indicate how much of each picture is to end up in the final blend. You often do this by specifying a number between zero and one for the first of the two images. Zero means that none of the first image will be used, which in turn implies that all of the second image will be used. A blend value of one means that all of the first image will be used, while none of the second image will be used.

The way in which the percentages are applied is very similar to the procedure for the soft-edged matte. Suppose that 20 percent of the first image and 80 percent of the second are to be used. For each pixel of the final image, the three RGB pixel values of the first image are multiplied by 0.2. Then the three RGB values of the same pixel in the second image are multiplied by 0.8. The two results are added together to produce the final color for the new, blended image at that pixel. This process is repeated for every pixel of the image.

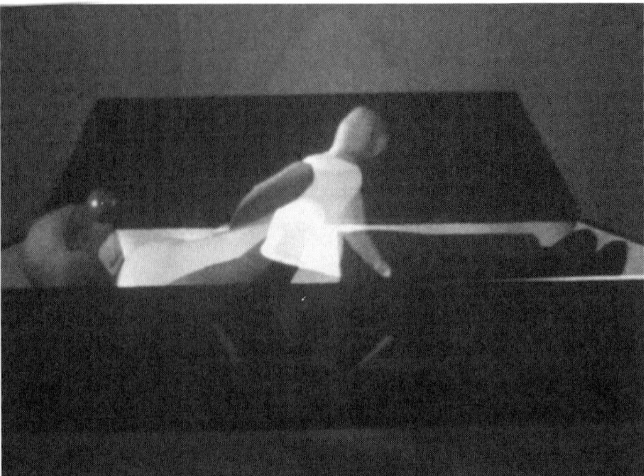

Figure 5-4. A cross-dissolve blends together two images (one the person walking, the other the clown in a coffin). (*Iggy's Dream* #74, © Michael O'Rourke)

With both of these operations—matting and cross-dissolving—you normally can specify that the operation be performed either on a single frame or on a whole sequence of frames. For example, in the matting example involving the robot, there might be a sequence of 200 frames as the robot walks down the street in front of the buildings. The matting operation might be repeated automatically for each of the 200 frames in the sequence.

Compositing an entire sequence normally requires that all the component pieces of each frame be calculated in advance and accessible to the compositing program. For a sequence of 200 frames you have to precalculate 200 background images, 200 foreground images, and, if your system does not automatically store each picture's matte information within an alpha channel, 200 matte images. You have to name all of these files in some way that will make them understandable later, then store them on disk or tape until you are ready to composite them. This sort of file management is a drawback of the compositing process, but the result of compositing is usually well worth the effort.

In addition to letting you perform isolated compositing operations on frames, most systems allow you to perform a sequence of compositing operations on each frame. For example, you might first matte a foreground picture onto a background picture; then matte another picture on top of that. Finally, when these two operations have been completed, you might cross-dissolve the result with yet another picture in order to produce the final frame.

In addition to operations such as mattes and cross-dissolves that involve combining two or more pictures to produce one final frame, most systems provide **image-processing** functions that operate on a single image at a time. Some of the different image-processing functions you might find in a good 3D animation system include changing the **brightness** of an image, changing the

contrast of an image, increasing or decreasing the **color saturation** of an image (for example, by pulling down all the red values, or pulling up all the blue values), **blurring** an image, **rotating** an image, and **magnifying** an image. The list also includes the myriad image-processing filters you find in image-retouching software packages.

As with matting and cross-dissolving, higher-end software systems allow you to perform any of these functions either on a single frame or on an entire sequence of frames. In many systems, these operations are controlled through a series of menus. You typically select the operation to be performed, indicate the name of the animation sequence (or sequences), and then indicate the range of frames to be affected.

As mentioned above, however, the management, including the naming, of animation files, becomes an important issue when you composite or process sequences of frames. Though they vary from one software package to another, file-naming conventions tend to be similar and must be followed. Commonly, the name of a given frame is composed of the **root name** plus the **frame number extension**. The root name is the name of the entire sequence—for example, *testwalk*. The frame number extension indicates which frame of that sequence the picture represents. Some systems specify this simply as *.1, .2, .3,* and so on. Others require a fixed number of digits, making the extensions *.0001, .0002, .0003,* and so on. Thus, the complete filenames in the example would be either *testwalk.1, testwalk.2,* and so on, or *testwalk.0001, testwalk.0002,* and so on. This naming convention makes it possible for the software to find and operate on all the frames of a given sequence in order.

Frequently you must also specify a **file format** extension (see *Final Frame Considerations* in chapter 2). This is usually a three- or four-letter extension added to the end of a filename to indicate which of the many standard picture formats has been used for this file. For example, if the *testwalk* pictures we described above were being saved in PICT format, whose extension is typically *.pict,* their full filenames might be *testwalk.1.pict, testwalk.2.pict,* and so on. As mentioned, many 3D software packages use standard menu selections within the main program to control compositing and special-effects operations. Those 3D systems that provide more extensive image-processing and compositing capabilities, however, often do so through a program that runs entirely outside the main animation program. Even more powerfully, complete digital editing, compositing, and image-processing software programs can be purchased independent of specific 3D animation packages, as discussed in the next section, *Video Editing*.

Yet another approach to compositing and processing animation frames is through a collection of stand-alone programs in an **image-processing library**. Each of these programs performs a specific operation—for example, a matte,

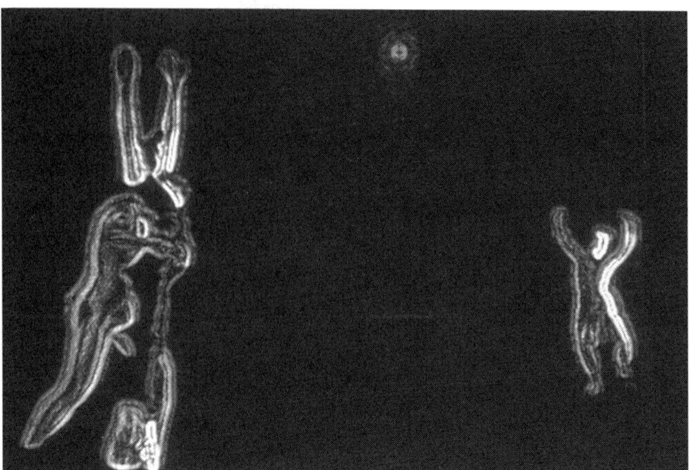

Figure 5-5. Scripts can be used to run a series of stand-alone programs on an image. Here, a complex sequence of compositing and image-processing programs was run to produce the final frame. (*The Weary Ghost Questions His Mother*, © Michael O'Rourke)

a cross-dissolve, or a blur—and can run independently of the others. This approach is often used in large production houses where a staff of professional graphics programmers continually updates and adds to the library of programs, frequently in reaction to the needs of a specific client on a specific job.

Typically, you run each of these stand-alone programs by typing a text command at the screen, specifying which program to run, which pictures to operate on, what to call the new files it produces, how many frames to process, and any other parameters necessary. If a number of programs must be run on a given sequence of frames, you usually write some sort of **script**, or **command file**, to control the compositing. Sometimes you use a special-purpose language provided by the software package, but more often you use the standard command-processing language of the operating system for the computer. Many high-end 3D computer animation packages run on machines that function under the UNIX operating system. In this operating system, the standard command-processing language is called the *Shell* (the *C-Shell* is a variant), and scripts written in this language are known as **Shell files** or sometimes **Shell scripts**. On machines that run under the Windows operating systems, a **batch file** serves the same purpose. Whichever language they may be written in, compositing scripts usually consist of a loop that instructs the computer to step through each of the frames of the sequence, and a series of compositing commands within the loop.

An example of the potential of scripts when used in conjunction with a powerful library of image-compositing and processing functions is Figure 5-5. The raw material for this sequence was an animated sequence and a live-action sequence. The animated sequence consisted of a simple sphere moving through space along a three-dimensional path. The live-action footage was of three dancers. Within a Shell script, a number of steps were performed: the rendered sphere was subjected to a variety of image-processing operations to yield a swirling, circular area of white color; a matte was generated for the live-action imagery; the live-action was matted on top of the processed sphere imagery; and finally, the dancers-plus-processed-sphere imagery was subjected to another series of image-processing operations to achieve the final frame.

Still another approach to compositing and processing your frames is to create a **history** file within a standard 2D paint program or 2D image-retouching program. You begin by activating the history function through some menu selection. You then work normally with mouse or stylus, painting, erasing, changing colors or contrast, cutting and pasting, and so on. As you work, the program automatically keeps a record of every brushstroke you make or operation you perform. When you have achieved the effect you want, you instruct the program to perform the entire history of operations you just created on any number of frames, effectively saying, "Whatever I just did to this picture, do the same thing to all those other pictures." Notice that this is very similar to the scripting or batch-file approach described above in that it applies a sequence of operations to a range of pictures. In fact, a history file *is* a text script, which you can look at and read if you wish. An advantage of the history file is that its script is created for you completely automatically. Rather than thinking verbally and typing text commands, you can think visually, letting the software translate your visual operations into a sequence of text commands, which can then be reexecuted as often as you like.

A final special-effect technique that is very effective but often overlooked by computer animators is the hand-painting of individual frames. In certain situations, if the number of frames is not too great, the best way to get an unusual effect (such as a flash of lightning, a puff of smoke, or an explosion of light) on your already rendered three-dimensional frames is to retouch the images by hand, frame by frame. Once the frames have been rendered, like any other picture, they can be read into a digital paint program, retouched or added to, and then resaved.

Computer animators, especially those who are less experienced, tend to take a rather purist approach to the production of their animation frames. The feeling is that if it is not done in 3D, it is "cheating." In fact, however, the final criterion in animation is not how was it done, but how it looks. Whether your frames were produced entirely through three-dimensional rendering, or through some combination of hand-painted special effects and script-based compositing is ultimately insignificant. If it looks good, it looks good. There is no such thing as "cheating."

A good example of this principle is the frame from *The Absolute Contingency*, color plate 7. In this animation, the ring, the mapped image within it and the fire around it were all rendered three-dimensionally. The school of fish was produced in a two-dimensional image-processing program and then matted on top of this rendered image. Finally, the lightning was hand-drawn frame by frame on top of the composited image to produce the final frame.

Video Editing

Although it is outside the scope of this book to discuss video editing in any detail, it is worthwhile to look into the compositing and special-effects capabilities of video, because these capabilities are substantial, easy to implement, and used very commonly. These capabilities are used so commonly, in fact, that they usually—and rightly—are treated as an integral part of the process of producing computer animation. Often an animation project consists of a **production** phase, during which the animation frames are produced, and a **video post-production** phase, during which the rendered frames are composited and manipulated in various ways using video. Experienced animators plan their animation projects in the knowledge that certain effects possible in the video post-production stage are either not possible at all or much more difficult to achieve in the digital frame-production stage.

Video exists in two broad categories: digital and analog. Until several years ago, all video was **analog video**. Analog information runs in a continuous stream, without discrete subdivisions. Examples of such information include the sounds you hear and the light you see. There is, for example, no dichotomy between the shade of yellow light entering a window and the slightly whiter shade of yellow a bit to one side of that light. These colors progress smoothly and continuously from one to another. Physically, analog information of this sort is created by light waves and sound waves, and usually is represented as smoothly curving waveforms, to capture the continuous nature of the information. Analog video records visual information as a sequence of continuous analog signals onto a magnetically charged videotape. When played back through the proper equipment, these continuous analog signals appear as moving imagery.

Digital video handles imagery in the same way that the computer graphics techniques you have seen throughout this book handle imagery. The smooth, continuous information of the visual world is broken down into tiny, discrete elements. Since each of these pieces of information can be represented as an individual number, the information is referred to as "digital." Instead of representing visual information as a series of analog waveforms, digital video represents information as collections of discrete, digital "bits" of information, which can be stored either on disks or on tapes.

Digital information has the advantage over analog information of being completely unambiguous. In the digital world, a particular element either does or does not have a certain numerical value—it either is or is not a certain color, for example. With analog information, things are never this clear-cut. A particular analog color is always "this color plus or minus a little."

When working with digital video, you normally begin by recording animation frames onto a special digital disk with a very large storage capacity. This disk might be either a standard **magnetic disk** (in principle, the same as a floppy disk, but much larger and much faster), or an **optical disk**, from which information is retrieved by means of a laser beam, much like the audio CDs used at home. The point of both of these disk-storage techniques is that a great deal of information can be stored, retrieved very quickly, and retrieved in any order.

The last point is especially significant. Using standard analog video, if you want to view a segment that is twenty minutes into the animation, you must advance the videotape sequentially through the entire animation until you reach the sequence you are seeking. For this reason, analog videotape is known as a **sequential access** storage medium. The need to access all imagery sequentially in analog video can become cumbersome in complex and involved video-editing sessions.

Digital video, on the other hand, does not require a sequential search: you can just "jump" to the animation segment you are looking for. This process is similar to what happens when you "jump" to a new track on an audio CD, without having to progress sequentially through the entire music selection. Digital video disks are **random access** storage media. Because of this, the time spent accessing imagery during a video-editing session can be greatly reduced.

A current disadvantage of the disks used to store digital video is that the amount of imagery these disks can store is more limited than the amount stored on a sequential piece of videotape. For this reason, digital video is frequently transferred to digital videotapes for permanent storage once the information has been edited together and is final. Like analog videotapes, these videotapes are sequential devices. However, since the information on a digital videotape is stored digitally, accuracy of reproduction is preserved.

D1 and **D2** are the two formats in which digital video is commonly stored on videotape. Of the two, D1 is of somewhat lower quality, but more affordable.

Editing with the random-access capabilities of digital imagery is frequently called **non-linear editing**, to distinguish it from the sequential, linear approach required by analog video. Non-linear digital editing is more flexible and faster than the older, analog editing and has replaced it as the professional standard. It also preserves image quality in ways that analog video cannot do. All video editing involves making copies of your footage. When copies are made in analog video, each copy, or **generation**, suffers a slight loss of color information because the continuous, analog information cannot by its nature be replicated with 100 percent accuracy. Digital imagery, however, has no such generational problem because its discrete, numerical information can be copied repeatedly with no loss of color information.

The process of editing video with a digital, non-linear system combines approaches from digital image compositing, discussed in the previous section, with approaches from traditional analog video editing, discussed below. Digital editing programs, however, vary in complexity significantly depending on whether you are working on a low-end system suitable for small production environments or on a full-scale, high-end system suitable for feature-length films. Some of the most salient features of all digital video editing systems are summarized here.

When you work with a digital video-editing system, the visual material is organized into **clips**, segments of either computer-generated or live-action imagery that may range in length from a few frames to several minutes. Segments of sound are also referred to as clips. Clips of imagery are **video clips**; clips of sound are **audio clips**.

You begin by reading into your editing system the clips you will be using. Within the system are **tracks**, usually represented graphically as horizontal bars, the horizontal direction of the track representing time. Using a cut-and-paste approach, you define the sequence in which clips should occur by selecting a clip and dragging it to a particular track. By sliding it horizontally left or right, you define where in time the clip should occur. You then select the next clip and position it in one of the tracks, either the same track or one of the other tracks.

Figure 5-6 shows a typical interface of such a system, with two video clips inserted on the first video track, V1, and a third video clip inserted on a second video track, V2. Below them are two audio tracks, with a single, long audio clip in audio track A1, and two short clips in audio track A2. Audio clips are normally represented as waveforms, the graphs seen in tracks A1 and A2. At the top of the screen is a timeline, in seconds, indicating that the total running time of this example is twenty-five seconds.

It is not necessary to use the entire length of a clip. You may elect, for example, to use only seven seconds of a ten-second clip, cropping off one second from the beginning of the clip and two seconds from the end. In this example, the starting point, or **in-point**, of the clip would be one second into the clip; the ending point, or **out-point**, would be two seconds from the end. The in-point and out-point are collectively known as **edit points**. Adjusting the edit points can usually be done either visually, by dragging a marker along

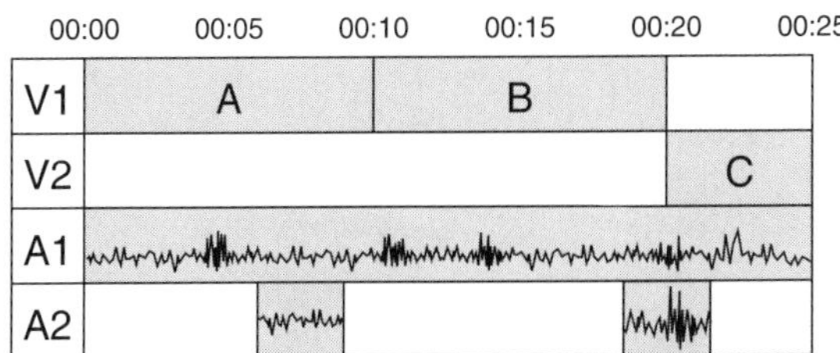

Figure 5-6. Digital editing systems allow you to define the sequence of events by visually positioning both video and audio clips in tracks.

the length of the clip, or numerically, by typing in the exact frame number at which you want the clip to begin or end.

Once you have specified the sequence in which clips will occur, you specify the **transition** between the clips, or how the end of one clip interacts with the beginning of the clip that follows. In the simplest transition, a **cut**, one clip abruptly begins just as another abruptly ends. The clips in Figure 5-6 all have cut transitions between them: as soon as clip A ends, clip B begins; as soon as B ends, C begins.

Because there are many types of transitions, video editing moves beyond the mere sequencing of imagery and becomes a form of image compositing. One of the most common transitions is the **cross-dissolve**, discussed in the previous section (see Figure 5-4).

Closely related to the cross-dissolve are the **fade-in** and **fade-out** edits (Figure 5-7). A fade-in is a cross-dissolve from a blank black screen to the sequence to be viewed. A fade-out goes in the opposite direction, cross-dissolving from the animation sequence to a black screen.

Another common technique for making the transition between two sequences is the **wipe** (Figure 5-8). In this kind of edit, one sequence slides or "wipes" across the screen, revealing a second sequence behind it as it goes. Depending on the style of wipe, the new sequence can come in horizontally, vertically, or diagonally. Some systems also allow you to bring in the new sequence through an expanding circular pattern, or an expanding square pattern.

The **matting** possible in video operates in much the same way that the soft-edged matting technique, described in the previous section, operates (see Figure 5-2). In video, this form of matting is often called **alpha channel matting** to distinguish it from the several other types of matting common in video applications. One of these is **chroma keying**, which is similar to a hard-edged mask in that it is an all-or-nothing operation. Certain color ranges are defined to be transparent, or "keyed," out of an image, and any colors in this range are invisible, allowing the imagery from a second source to show through. The range of colors defined to be the "key"—that is, to be invisible—is controllable by the editor. The most common colors used for this process are specific hues of blue and green, and the process of keying these out from a video image is referred to as **blue screening** or **green screening**.

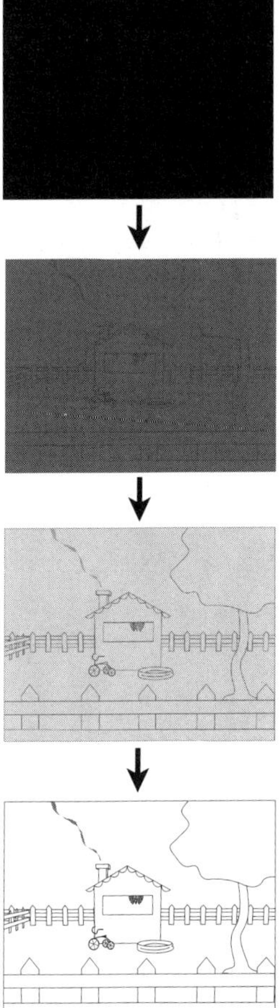

Figure 5-7. A fade-in dissolves from black to picture. A fade-out dissolves from picture to black.

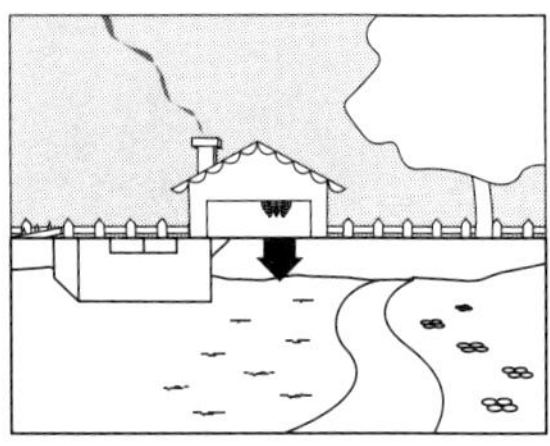

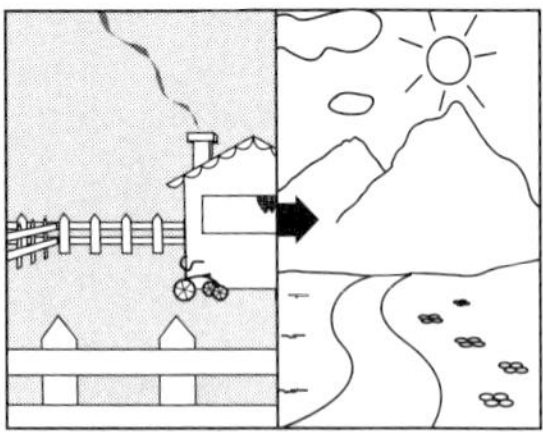

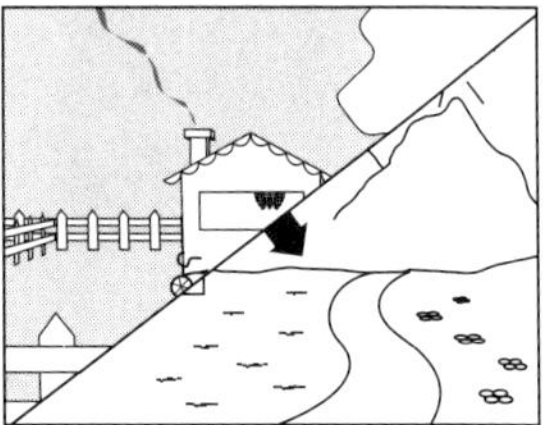

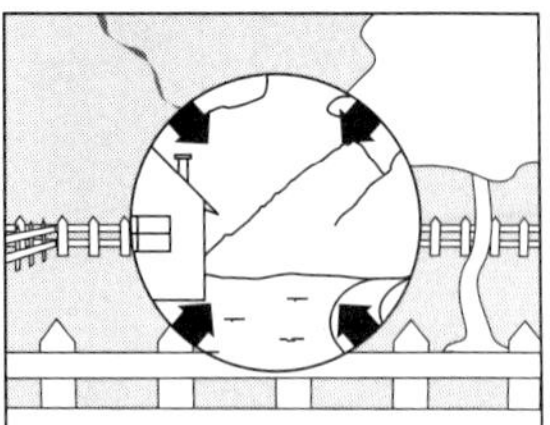

Figure 5-8. A wipe replaces a scene with a new scene. The new scene slides in horizontally, vertically, diagonally, or through a circular window.

You operate on transitions in the same way as clips. First you select a transition, for example a cross-dissolve, and drag its icon to a transition track. Then you position the transition in time by sliding it horizontally along the track. As with a clip, you can adjust the length of the transition by sliding markers at its beginning or end to the left or right. By placing the transition between two video clips (Figure 5-9), you indicate how you want those two clips to interact and for how long.

One of the great advantages of digital video editing is that you can use transitions to composite any number of video tracks without any deterioration in the quality of color information. (This is true of digital audio as well.) In Figure 5-10, video clip B cross-dissolves with clip A at the same time that clip C fades in and at the same time that clip D mattes in. Because all the information for these clips is purely numerical, there is no loss of image quality as the various images are composited together.

Although the same is not true of the older analog video technology, analog video editing is still extremely powerful and may be of great use to the animator. The generational image loss that is a necessary part of analog video can be negligible when you use good video equipment. After all, analog video was the professional standard of the industry for decades!

In the recording of an animation sequence to analog video, animation frames are recorded (as discussed in some detail in the next chapter) to magnetic analog videotape, which is effectively the same sort of videotape used in the home VCR. Standard home-use videotapes are half an inch in width. Higher quality, professional analog videotapes used in animation are either half-inch or three-quarters of an inch in width. Some of the standard video tape sizes and formats in use today are half-inch VHS (the standard home-video tape), three-quarter-inch U-matic, and half-inch Betacam.

When preparing to work with analog video, you must be aware of a few factors in order to make proper use of the analog video-editing technology. First, any analog videotape onto which you intend to record frames must have **timecode**, a special signal, recorded onto it. Timecode (discussed further in chapter 6, *Video*) permits the videotape player to locate specific frames. Without proper timecode, an analog video-editing system will not be able to locate the recorded footage accurately, or to start or stop precisely on the frame you choose. Without timecode, in other words, you cannot have **frame accuracy**, and without frame accuracy any video edit you attempt will happen only at approximately the frame you have in mind.

The second factor you must be conscious of when working with analog video is the need to record onto separate videotapes any scenes that are to be composited. In video editing, original footage is called **source** footage. Many video-editing operations, such as mattes and cross-dissolves, require two

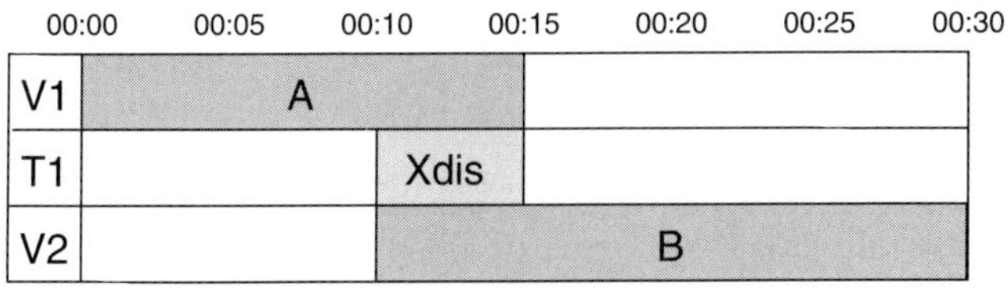

	00:00	00:05	00:10	00:15	00:20	00:25	00:30
V1		A					
T1			Xdis				
V2					B		

Figure 5-9. Between any two segments of video you can define a transition, adjusting its type and length.

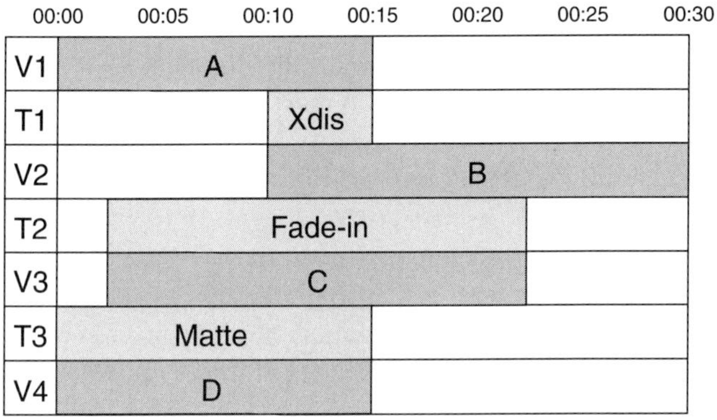

	00:00	00:05	00:10	00:15	00:20	00:25	00:30
V1		A					
T1			Xdis				
V2					B		
T2			Fade-in				
V3			C				
T3		Matte					
V4		D					

Figure 5-10. In digital video, any number of tracks of imagery can be composited together without loss of image quality.

pieces of source footage. When an edit is done, each source is put into a separate videodeck. This process requires that the pieces be recorded onto separate videotapes, called **source A** and **source B**. If you have not foreseen this requirement and have mistakenly recorded both source segments onto the same videotape, you will have to copy one of the sources onto a separate tape before editing can proceed. This copying introduces an extra **generation** of image loss. A final cross-dissolve (see the previous section), for example, loses two generations of image quality rather than one in this situation: one generation to make the copy of the source footage, and then a second generation to make the cross-dissolve itself.

In addition to the several basic video-editing functions listed here, high-end video-editing systems, such as those found in commercial production houses, often offer a tremendously wide array of other compositing and effects capabilities. This is especially true of high-end digital video-editing systems, in which a full range of digital-image processing operations normally is available in addition to the all of the standard video-editing techniques.

Even if you are restricted to the basic video functions described here, and even if you are working on an older analog system, video editing offers compositing capabilities that you would be foolish to ignore. The seasoned animator knows this and considers editing, whether on an analog video system or on a digital video system, an integral part of the process of making animation.

CHAPTER 6

Recording

Video

Much of computer animation is recorded onto videotape, as opposed to film, because recording animation to video is much faster and less expensive than recording it to film.

Video technology is tremendously complex and could easily be (and has been) the subject of entire books. Nonetheless, and without striving to become an expert, you can learn enough about video to enable you to produce, record, and display your animation to the best advantage.

One of the first issues you need to think about in relation to the recording of animation frames is the playback rate of the technology you use. The playback rate of video in the United States is thirty frames per second. This standard has been set by the National Television Systems Committee (NTSC) of the video industry, so video that complies with this standard is referred to as **NTSC video**.

Elsewhere in the world, other standards are used. Two of these standards that you might encounter are **PAL** (Phase Alternation Line) and **SECAM** (French for Sequential Color with Memory), both of which require a playback rate of twenty-five frames per second. Each of these standards is incompatible with the others, so video recorded in one format must be translated into the host format of the machine used to view it.

Throughout the remainder of this chapter, assume that the rate being used is the thirty-frame-per-second rate of NTSC video. The principles discussed here, however, apply equally to any of the other standard video formats.

In planning an animation, you must keep this thirty-frames-per-second rate in mind, both while developing the animation and while recording it. An animation sequence that runs for twenty seconds, for example, requires 600 frames of video (20 seconds × 30 frames per second = 600 frames). With experience, you will develop a very refined sense of timing as it is measured in frames. Watching or planning a movement, you might feel intuitively that the sequence is "about twenty frames" long. Very skilled animators become capable of seeing the difference between an image held for one frame and an image held for two frames!

Several techniques are available for recording the frames of an animation—some of which are used for digital video and some of which are used for analog video (for differences between digital video and analog video, see chapter 5, *Video Editing*). If you are going to record the animation frames to a digital video storage disk, the process is straightforward: you merely copy the frames to the digital disk in the same way that you copy any digital file from one disk to another. If you are going to record the frames directly to a digital videotape, the process is similar to the procedures described below for recording to analog videotape.

The recording of animation frames to analog video involves several approaches. The most common technique is **real-time synced recording**, which requires special hardware and special software, both usually residing on a separate workstation cabled to the video recording machine. To create your recording, first you copy your animation frames from the animation workstation to the recording workstation. Next, you use the recording software to translate the frames into its own special format. This usually produces a single file containing the entire range of frames you wish to record. The new file is stored on the system's special-purpose hardware, usually a separate disk, which can play the animation extremely quickly. You then specify the rate at which you want the animation to play—for example, thirty frames per second for video. Because of the hardware, the system can play all the animation frames at exactly the rate you specify—that is, at a **frame-accurate rate**. Next, using a menu with the standard "Forward," "Reverse," and "Stop" video playback buttons, you begin to play back your animation. As it plays back on your monitor at the correct rate it is simultaneously converted from digital to analog and recorded to the videotape.

The conversion from digital to video format is a critical part of any recording of computer animation frames to analog video. Recall from chapter 5 that computer images are digital—that is, made up of discrete pieces of information (bits)—while analog video is made up of continuous, nondiscrete information (waveforms). Before being stored on a standard videotape, a computer image must be translated from the original digital form into analog form. This translation process is called **encoding** and is accomplished by a hardware device called a **video encoder**. Because this process is extremely fast, real-time recording is possible.

Some real-time synced recording systems also allow you to do simple editing as you record. (See *Video Editing* in chapter 5 for a more complete discussion of this topic.) By selecting several animation files and cutting from one to the next, you can play back and record the entire sequence of files at once. Butting one segment up against another like this is called a **cuts-only** edit and the cuts are sometimes called **butt cuts**. You can also change the order of an animation sequence. For example, you might begin by recording the sequence of animation files *scene1, scene2, scene3*. Upon seeing the recorded result, however, you might rerecord your scenes in a different order, this time using the sequence *scene2, scene1, scene3,* to see if the new sequence gives a better effect.

Some more sophisticated recording systems also allow you to perform a handful of other video transitions, such as a cross-dissolve or a fade-in or fade-out. For some animations, these transitions suffice. Even if they do not, this sort of preliminary edit can help you imagine what your animation will look like when it is fully edited.

An additional advantage of real-time synced recording devices is that, since the real-time, frame-accurate playback of the animation shows up on your monitor as it is recorded, it is frequently not even necessary to record. If you are still at the testing stage, you may use the recording system simply to preview your rendered frames at the correct frame rate, without making any attempt to record them yet. When you have more nearly final versions of your frames, you can use the same system actually to record them.

A disadvantage of real-time synced recording devices is that the amount of animation they can play back in real time is limited by the amount of fast-playback memory they have. Today's systems typically are limited to anywhere from one to four minutes of animation.

An older technology for recording animation frames to videotape records each frame individually and one by one to the videotape and is called **single-frame recording** or, sometimes, **frame-by-frame recording**. In single-frame recording, a single frame of the animation is displayed on the screen and encoded into an analog video signal. The videotape then rewinds a few seconds and begins rolling forward again until it is rolling at the correct thirty-frame speed. This process is called the **preroll**. Just when the videotape reaches exactly the right location on the tape for the next frame, the displayed image is recorded. The next frame in the animation sequence is displayed on the screen and the process repeats itself.

When frames are recorded in single-frame recording, each individual frame of the animation is recorded for exactly one-thirtieth of a second onto the videotape. This produces the correct playback rate, since thirty frames each at one-thirtieth of a second yield the correct one second of animation for every thirty frames. All of the actions of the animation will play back at the exact rate at which they were intended to play back.

A final approach to recording animation frames is sometimes used in non-professional situations where a frame-accurate recording device, whether real-time or frame-by-frame, is not available. Many workstations have built-in video-encoding capabilities and have a **video-out** plug on the back of the workstation. Connecting a video cable from the video-out plug to the **video-in** plug of a video recording machine, you can record, in real time, whatever happens on the monitor of your workstation. You can now use your animation software to create a sequence of rendered frames, often called a **flipbook**, and to play them on the screen of your workstation. Since the video-out of the workstation is cabled to the video-in of the videotape machine, the frames of your flipbook will be recorded to video at the same time that they play on your monitor.

The problem with this approach is that the frames are not necessarily synced to the correct video rate—thirty frames per second. Instead, the frames play back as quickly or slowly as the hardware allows: more complex or larger frames play back more slowly; simpler or smaller frames play back more quickly. To address this, many animation packages allow you to define the intended frame rate for a flipbook playback, but without special-purpose hardware the playback will be jerky because the software will discard some of the frames during playback in order to keep up the pace. If only one or two frames are discarded, this may not be noticeable. But if the software discards substantial numbers of frames, the result can be very unsatisfactory.

With a frame-accurate synced approach, whether real-time or frame-by-frame, you typically record each and every frame of the animation–that is, all thirty frames of every second of animation. This is called recording **on ones**. Sometimes, however, it is possible to render and record fewer than the full thirty frames per second for each second of animation. For example, every other frame could be rendered and then held for twice as long when it is recorded. This process is known as recording **on twos**, and works as follows.

In the interest of saving rendering time, you render only every other frame: frame 1, frame 3, frame 5, and so on. That is, you render fifteen distinct frames for each second of animation, instead of the normal thirty frames. The video equipment onto which the animation is going to be recorded operates at a thirty-frame-per-second rate, however, so you must do something to stretch out the fifteen frames you have rendered to a full one second of time. When recording the animation, therefore, you hold each frame for twice as long as normal: each frame is recorded for one-fifteenth of a second instead of the normal thirtieth of a second. Another way of saying this is that each frame is held for a count of two frames. The frames of animation recorded onto the videotape effectively end up as frame 1, frame 1; frame 3, frame 3; frame 5, frame 5; and so forth.

In other words, using NTSC video, you need 600 frames in order to make an animation play back in twenty seconds. If you are going to animate on twos, however, you need to render only 300 of those frames (frame 1, frame 3, etc.). When you record them, you hold each of these frames for twice as long as normal, stretching 300 frames of animation into 600 frames of video.

The point of all this, as noted, is to save rendering time. Since only half as many frames are rendered, only half as much time is spent rendering. This can be significant. If each of 300 frames takes twenty minutes to render, you

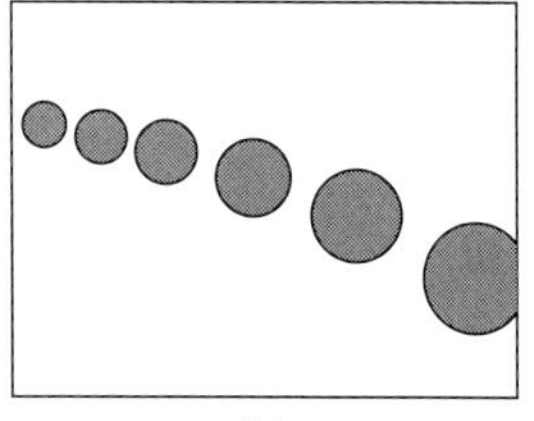

(a)

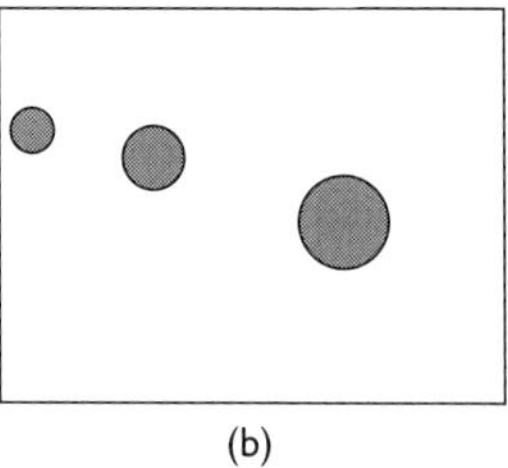

(b)

Figure 6-1. Rendering on ones, as in (a), produces smaller spatial increments between frames. Rendering on twos, as in (b), produces larger increments. For a quickly moving object, rendering on twos can result in jerky animation.

save 100 hours of rendering time by rendering on twos (20 minutes × 300 frames = 6,000 minutes ÷ 60 minutes per hour = 100 hours). In a longer animation, the savings are even more dramatic.

There is a serious potential drawback, however, to animating on twos. For many kinds of motion, the animation may not look as smooth on twos as on ones. This lack of smoothness is most noticeable when there are very fast-moving objects in the animation sequence. Imagine, for example, a ball flying across the screen very quickly. Perhaps it takes only six frames for the ball to cover the distance from screen left to screen right (Figure 6-1a, in which each of the six frames is superimposed on one screen to show the relative placement of the ball from frame to frame). If you render and record this sequence on twos, you render only three frames: frame 1, frame 3, and frame 5 (Figure 6-1b). The distance covered by the ball between each two of these frames probably is large enough for the eye to notice when the animation plays back, and the result is that the motion of the ball appears jerky. Animating this sequence on twos, therefore, noticeably diminishes the quality of the animation.

In an animation in which the objects move very slowly, on the other hand, animating on twos may produce no visible deterioration of the image quality. Imagine the same ball drifting very slowly across the screen, over perhaps five seconds, or 150 frames. When rendered on ones, the distance covered by the ball between successive frames is almost imperceptible (Figure 6-2a). When rendered on twos, it still is barely perceptible (Figure 6-2b).

The two examples just given are extremes. In actual practice, most animations are neither so fast moving nor so slow moving, and a great many animations can be done on twos without any noticeable loss of quality. In order to find out whether recording on twos will cause an image to deteriorate, you must make a test recording.

Even when animating a sequence on twos will detract from the quality of the final animation, an animator often will produce test recordings on twos—or even on threes (rendering only every third frame) or fours (rendering every fourth frame). Only after the sequence has been developed and refined to the point that the final frames are ready to be rendered does the animator switch to working on ones.

In some situations an object moves so fast that even animating on ones does not produce a smooth look. A useful rendering technique in this situation is motion blur (see chapter 2, *Final-frame Considerations*). Another approach to solving this problem is offered by some high-end systems, which allow you to render and record animation frames at twice the temporal resolution of the standard video rate—that is, at one-sixtieth of a second instead of the normal thirtieth of a second. This approach is possible because of a peculiarity in the way a frame of video is generated.

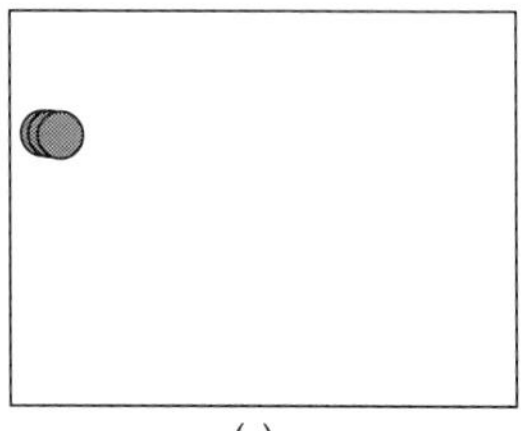

(a)

(b)

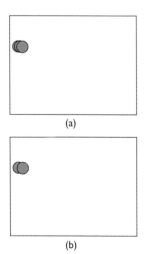

Figure 6-2. For a very slow-moving object, the spatial increment is very small whether the scene is rendered on ones or on twos.

You have seen that every frame of animation is composed of pixels and that these pixels are arranged into horizontal rows and vertical columns (chapter 2). A video image is also composed of rows and columns (as you can see if you examine a television monitor through a magnifying glass). When a frame of video is displayed, an electronic beam passes, or scans, over each row of the image, turning on the video equivalent of pixels—actually a tight cluster of three tiny vertical bars: one red, one green, and one blue—as it does so. This scanning across the rows is done in two passes, each of which is called a **field**. In the first pass, the beam displays the information of the odd-numbered lines of the frame, starting at the top of the image and progressing to the bottom. This information constitutes the **odd field**. As soon as the odd field has been displayed, the beam turns on the information for the even-numbered lines of the frame, again from top to bottom. This information constitutes the **even field**. Each of these fields takes one-sixtieth of a second to record. The two fields are said to be **interlaced** together—the odd field for one-sixtieth of a second, then the even field for one-sixtieth of a second, then the odd field again, and so on. The interlacing of an odd field and an even field, each taking one-sixtieth of a second, produces the thirtieth of a second that is the duration of the standard video frame.

Some systems take advantage of this fact and allow you to render and record by fields, rather than by frames. Doing this produces twice as many images as the normal rendering on ones produces. For each frame, an odd field is rendered and then, for a moment one-sixtieth of a second later, an even field is rendered. Effectively, this produces two "half-images" for each thirtieth of a second.

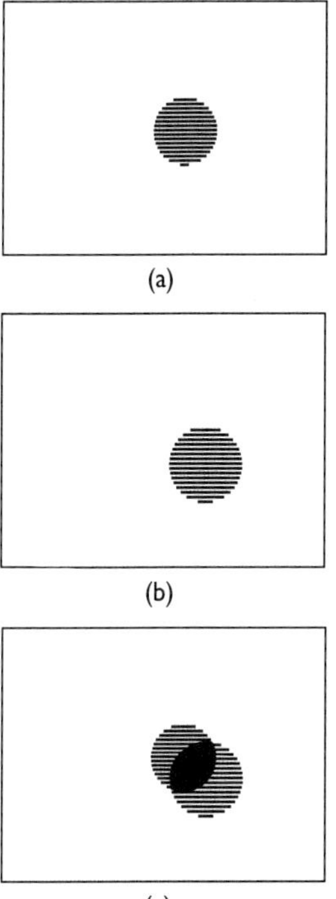

Figure 6-3. Rendering on fields renders only half the lines of each image, but does so twice as frequently.

Figure 6-3a shows the odd-field rendering of a fast-moving ball at some moment in time. Notice that the ball appears in slices, because only the odd lines of the image have been rendered. (The slicing of the ball in this illustration is very exaggerated; it consists of only about 15 slices. It actually would consist of many more than that.) Figure 6-3b shows the even-field rendering of the same ball, rendered one-sixtieth of a second later than the first version. Again only alternate slices of the ball have been rendered—in this case, only the even-numbered lines of the image.

Since the two field renderings illustrated here are recorded only one-sixtieth of a second apart, the eye fuses the two images together seamlessly and sees them as one (Figure 6-3c). Notice, though, that because the two images represent the ball at slightly different moments, the two renderings are displaced horizontally from one another.

To see more clearly how rendering on fields can produce a smoother-looking animation than can rendering on ones, compare the six superimposed frames of a fast-moving ball rendered on ones (Figure 6-4a) with the twelve superimposed renderings of the same animation rendered on fields

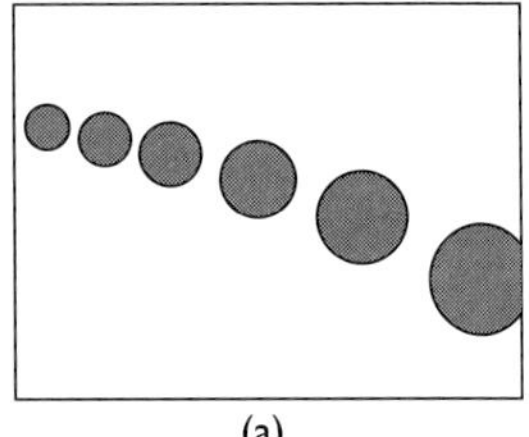

(a)

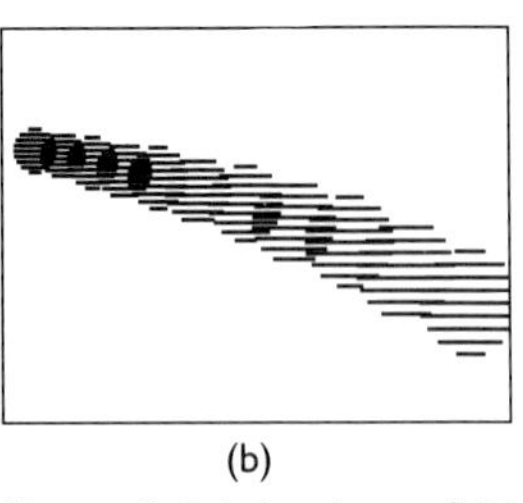

(b)

Figure 6-4. Animating on fields reduces the spatial increment between frames, which can result in smoother movement for quickly moving objects.

(Figure 6-4b). Notice how much shorter the distance between each ball is when the image is rendered on fields: it is this reduction of the distance between objects from frame to frame that makes a recording done on fields appear smoother than a recording done on ones.

The preceding variations on the frame-by-frame recording technique require the video-recording system to function with great deal of accuracy. Whether by ones, by twos, or by fields, that is, each frame of animation is recorded individually onto the videotape, and if the recording process is off by even a fraction of a second, the error will be noticeable to the eye.

In order for a video system to be capable of this kind of frame-accurate recording, some system is needed to mark exactly which locations on the tape are to receive which frames of the animation. The system that does this (mentioned in chapter 5, *Video Editing*) is called timecode.

The basic idea behind timecode is that a sequence of very fast pulses, called a **timecode signal**, is recorded onto the videotape before the recording of any animation frames. Once recorded onto a videotape, the timecode signal can be read by a video device as a sequence of numbers. These numbers tell the device the exact current location of the videotape—whether it is at frame 1, or at frame 2, and so on.

One type of timecode, called **longitudinal timecode**, is stored within one of the audio tracks on the videotape. It is called "longitudinal" because the soundtrack unwinds in a horizontal fashion as the tape plays. Many animation recording systems, however, use a different kind of timecode, called **vertical-interval timecode**, that is based upon the concept of video fields.

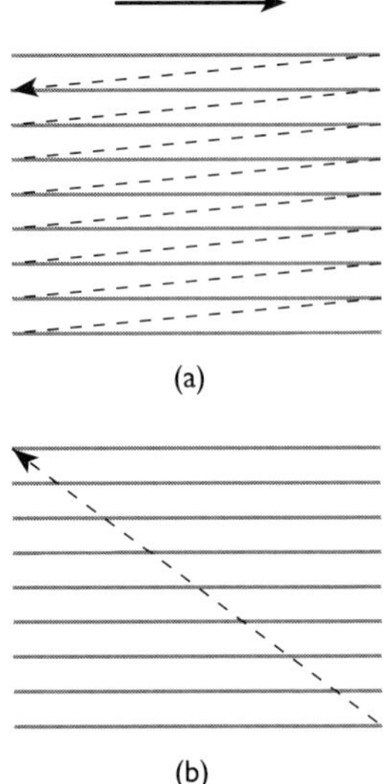

(a)

(b)

Figure 6-5. The beam that produces a video image traces through the image row by row. At the end of each field of rows, there is a vertical retrace of the beam.

Figure 6-5a shows the pattern traced by an electronic beam as it scans the rows of a video image. Notice that the beam traces from left to right along each horizontal row of the image, and that at the end of each row the beam jumps back and down to the beginning of the next row. Figure 6-5b shows what happens when the beam reaches the far-right end of the bottom row—that is, when it reaches the end of the current field. At this point, the beam retraces the path back up to the top-left corner of the image so that it can begin the next field. This movement of the beam from the bottom of one field to the top of the next field is called the **vertical retrace**, and the time required to perform it is called the **vertical interval**. A vertical-interval timecode signal is recorded during the vertical interval in the video area of the tape between the odd-field information and the even-field information.

Both longitudinal timecode and vertical timecode provide frame-accurate control of the video, and both can be recorded onto a single tape. Since longitudinal and vertical timecodes are stored on physically different parts of the videotape—one in the audio signal and one in the picture signal—it is possible to have both types of timecode on a single tape. This may be necessary, for example, if your recording equipment uses vertical timecode but your editing equipment uses longitudinal timecode. In order to be able to do single-frame recording on your recording equipment in this case, you need vertical-interval timecode on your videotape. In order to frame-accurately edit your tape on your editing equipment, you need to have longitudinal timecode on your tape.

Whether your system requires longitudinal timecode or vertical-interval timecode or both, you must record timecode onto your videotape before attempting to record animation frames. You do this with the same video equipment you use for recording the animation.

Another important consideration in recording computer animation onto analog videotape arises from the fact that, as you have seen, the digital computer imagery must be translated, or encoded, into an analog form for videotape. This process of translation, or encoding, is not 100 percent exact, however. The range of colors that can be accommodated in the digital format is greater than the range of colors that can be accommodated in the video format, and some loss of color may result. This loss usually is visible as a decrease in the saturation, or "punch," of the colors. If you want to see what the true, final recorded colors will be, therefore, you must look at them on actual video. What you see on the digital RGB monitor is *not* what you will get on the encoded video recording. Some specialized monitors address this problem by providing a switch that allows you to toggle back and forth between RGB-display mode and encoded video-display mode. In this way, you can preview the video-encoded colors before actually recording them.

Another limitation on the colors recorded onto video derives from the standards of the television broadcast industry—again, in the United States, the NTSC standards. Certain very saturated colors exceed the capabilities of video reproduction as defined by the NTSC, and because they cannot be properly represented by the NTSC color system these colors tend to spill over, or **bleed**, into neighboring areas of color. A very saturated red, for example, often does this, creating a blurry look around the edges of the red areas of the image. In extreme cases, very saturated colors produce a black area in the video image. These colors may look wonderful on a digital RGB monitor, but they are considered "illegal" video colors and cannot be broadcast as televised video. If you intend to have your work shown on television, then, you must desaturate certain colors before recording them to video, so that they will be within the legal range of colors.

Another factor that you must take into account when recording to video is the **bandwidth** of the videotape. In general, "bandwidth" refers to the amount of information that can be processed in a given time. In the world of video, the higher the bandwidth of a videotape, the more visual information

(a)

(b)

Figure 6-6. When a computer-generated frame is played on a television monitor, some portion of the image is cut off.

can be recorded per frame. And the more information per frame, the higher the quality of the image. This corresponds to the issue of image resolution in a digital image and affects the quality of the video image in a similar way. The higher the bandwidth of a videotape, the better the quality of the video image. Today's three-quarter-inch U-matic and half-inch Betacam, both used professionally, are of higher image quality than the half-inch VHS standard in home video systems.

A final issue, independent of whether the video is analog or digital, has to do with the final viewing of the recorded video on television screens and monitors. That is, when the rectangular image of an animation frame is displayed on a television screen, the outer edges of the image are obscured both by the plastic housing of the screen and by the slightly rounded shape of the screen itself. This effect, called **TV cutoff**, is always present but varies from one television set to another, depending on the shape of the plastic housing.

In the case of a digital image in which a character standing at the far left of the frame watches a bird flying at the very top of the frame (Figure 6-6a), the edges of the image on all four sides will be cut off on a typical television screen (Figure 6-6b). In this frame of animation, the TV cutoff is disastrous. Since part of the main character and all of what he is looking at are concealed, a viewer cannot understand the action of the animation at all.

Thus, you must be aware of the effects of TV cutoff and plan the composition of your frames accordingly. Many software systems facilitate doing this by the inclusion of a **field guide**, which can be displayed temporarily on top of the animation frame (Figure 6-7). The guide consists of a rectangular grid of lines, called "fields." (These fields have nothing to do with the odd and even fields of a video frame.) Animators speak of placing their imagery within certain fields of the guide—that is, within certain grid lines. For example, an image might be kept "within ten field."

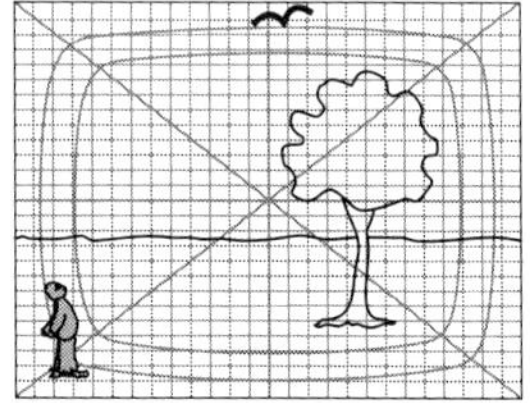

Figure 6-7. A field guide is used to determine whether the action of the animation frame is "TV safe."

With the field guide in place, you can see which parts of the image are likely to be obscured by TV cutoff, and adjust your composition accordingly. The area of the frame that will not be affected by TV cutoff is called **TV safe**. Sometimes, the TV safe area is further subdivided into two areas. The inner area, represented by an oval in the shape of a television screen, is known as **title safe**, meaning that titles and text should be kept within this area. A larger area, represented by a second, larger oval, is known as **action safe**.

Film

As noted in the previous section, most computer animation is recorded to video. Traditionally, however, noncomputer animation has been recorded to either 16mm film or 35mm film, and several good reasons remain for recording 3D computer animation to film.

In the United States, the NTSC standard for video requires an image resolution of approximately 645 × 486 pixels. The resolution of film, by contrast, tends to be several thousand by several thousand. This does not mean that your animation frames must be rendered at such an extremely high resolution, but it means that they can be. Rendering animation frames for film at approximately twice the normal video resolution, for example, can result in a very noticeable improvement in the sharpness of the image.

Another advantage of using film as your recording medium is the accuracy of the color transferral. As you saw in the previous section, the range of colors that video can accommodate is not as great as the range of colors that digital imagery can accommodate. Consequently, there usually is some loss of color—especially among the more vibrant, saturated colors—when digital imagery is recorded to video. With film, this loss does not occur.

Rendering and recording to film is more time-consuming than rendering and recording to video, however. In order to take advantage of the very high image resolution of film, you must render frames at a higher resolution, and higher resolutions mean longer rendering times. Moreover, the actual process of recording frames to film is slower than the process of recording the same frames to video.

A second disadvantage of recording to film is cost. The cost of purchasing film stock and processing (that is, developing and printing) the film far exceeds the cost of a videotape. For example, a ten-minute, professional-quality three-quarter-inch videotape costs approximately $10 as of this writing. This is the total cost of the recording materials involved, since a videotape doesn't need to be developed. The same ten minutes of 35mm film stock, on the other hand, costs approximately $450. To develop and print this film costs an additional $400.

Film is inconvenient, too, because developing and printing a reel of film is normally an overnight process. Video, on the other hand, requires no processing at all. As soon as video footage is recorded, it is viewable.

A final disadvantage of film recording is simply that, for all of the reasons cited above, video recording of computer animation is much more common than film recording. While almost all 3D computer animation packages come equipped with software to permit video recording, it is much rarer to find film-recording capabilities in the same software.

Still, because of the advantages in image quality, the recording of computer animation to film does occur. Most commonly, it is used in the commercial film industry, where the large projection size of the final image demands the highest possible image quality, and where the substantial funding behind big-budget films permits the expenditure. This has become true especially in

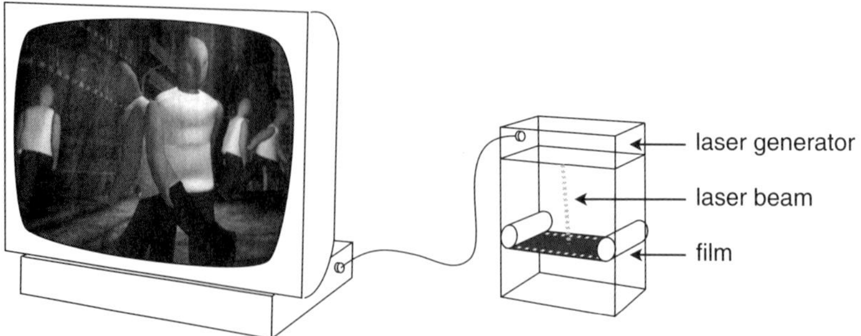

Figure 6-8. Some digital film recorders use a laser beam to expose the flim negative pixel by pixel. (Iggy's Dream #123, © Michael O'Rourke.)

recent years as more and more live-action films incorporate computer animation and special effects, all of which must eventually be composited with and recorded onto the same film stock used for the live-action footage.

As with video recording (see the previous section), you must pay attention to the playback rate of the equipment you work with. In film, the standard playback rate for both 16mm film and 35mm film is twenty-four frames per second. As with video, it is possible to render and record frames either on ones (in this case, twenty-four distinct images per second) or on twos (twelve images, each of which is held for two frames). Note, however, that it is not possible to record to film on fields, which are unique to video technology and do not occur in film.

Since the frame rates of video and film differ, animation developed for one medium must undergo special processing before in can be recorded on the other. Thirty frames of video, if recorded directly to film, will yield more than the intended one second of animation. Because of this, animation houses that record to film use special software to alter video animation frames before recording them to film.

The actual process of recording to film involves either of two types of a **digital film recorder**. The first uses a **laser** beam to expose the film stock (Figure 6-8). In this case the recording device consists of a laser generator capable of emitting laser beams of varying intensities and colors, and a film-advance device that holds and advances the negative film stock. Digital RGB information for each frame of animation is sent to the recording device, where it is used to modulate, pixel by pixel, both the color and intensity of the laser beam. With each modulation, the beam exposes one pixel-sized area of the film negative. Scanning across the film negative pixel by pixel and line by line, the beam exposes the negative for that frame with the correct amount and color of light. The entire process takes place relatively quickly; sophisticated recorders require only a few seconds to expose and advance each frame.

An older film-recorder technology is based on the use of **color filters** (Figure 6-9). Within film-recording devices of this type is a very high-quality

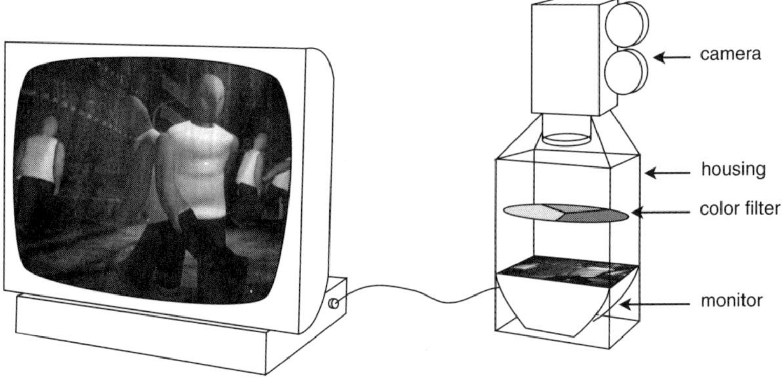

Figure 6-9. Some digital film recorders shoot each frame, displayed on the screen of a high-quality black-and-white monitor, through color filters. Each frame is exposed three times: once for each of the red, green, and blue components of an image. (*Iggy's Dream* #123, © Michael O'Rourke.)

black-and-white monitor, the screen of which is unusual in that it is flat. The monitors of normal televisions and computers are curved, and even though you may not be aware of it, the image you see on a normal monitor is distorted slightly because of the curvature of the screen. The screen of the monitor within a digital film recorder is flat in order to avoid this distortion of the screen image.

Above the monitor is a housing for the film camera. Within it the camera shoots, frame by frame, the images that come up on the special-purpose monitor. The housing around the monitor keeps light out, so that only light from the screen is exposed onto the film.

The recording of each frame is actually a three-step process. In the first step, the red component of the digital image is displayed on the black-and-white monitor as a gray-scale image. Suspended between the monitor and the camera lens is a wheel that holds red, green, and blue filters. When the red component of the image is displayed on the black-and-white monitor, the color wheel automatically rotates so that the red filter is in place over the image. At this point, the software controlling the camera causes the camera to take an exposure. Since the camera sees the black-and-white image on the monitor filtered through the red filter, what is exposed onto the film is the red component of the image, with all the proper shades of red.

Once the red component is finished, the green component of the same image is sent to the small monitor and displayed as a gray-scale image. The color wheel automatically rotates so that the green filter is in place above the monitor, and the camera takes a second exposure. Notice that the film has not advanced. The camera has taken two exposures—a double exposure—onto the same frame of film.

This process is repeated for the blue component of the image. Finally, when all three exposures have been shot to the one frame of film, the frame is fully exposed. At this point, the film is automatically advanced to the next frame, and the whole three-step process, which can take as much as half a minute, begins again for the next image.

Both laser and color-filter film recorders are often designed to accept any of the standard film formats—16mm, 35mm or 70mm. And both require that you carefully set all of the standard photographic parameters. That is, you must decide upon the **shutter speed**, the **f/stop**, and the **color balance**.

The mechanics of digital film recorders, both laser-based and filter-based, makes them much slower than video recorders, which can record digital frames in real time. Another, less obvious factor also makes film recording times longer. In video, if you want to record a still frame for a hold of, say, fifteen seconds, the actual recording takes exactly as long as the length of the hold—in this case, fifteen seconds. This real-time recording occurs not only in real-time synched recording but also in single-frame recording, where it is possible to hold a frame for an arbitrary length of time. In digital film recording, by contrast, a hold of fifteen seconds requires that the held image be recorded separately onto each of the twenty-four frames required for each second of animation. In other words, the held image has to be recorded 360 times (24 frames per second × 15 seconds).

In spite of these disadvantages, film is still used for direct recording of computer animation when the highest possible image quality is demanded and when the animator's budget permits. The higher resolution of film will be less important, however, as **high-definition television** (HDTV) becomes more commonly available. Since the resolution of HDTV is approximately 2,000 × 1,000, the difference between video resolution and film resolution will be far less significant.

CHAPTER 7

Production Planning

Introduction

Producing even a simple 3D computer animation can be a complex process in many respects. In addition to the technical issues on which this book has focused, other important issues must be carefully considered, including the story of the animation, the visual style of the animation, the availability of resources, and the timetable for the production.

Because of the number and variety of issues that must be considered, careful planning of a production is very important, especially when a project is large and involves many people and expensive facilities. Even for a small, personal animation, however, planning is critical. Even if you are working alone, have your own equipment, and are not working against a deadline, there still remain important issues of story development and technical requirements that demand careful planning. The details of production planning vary depending on many factors, including size of the project, output, purpose, resources and so on. But certain issues common to all animation productions are the focus of this chapter.

Storyboarding

Before you begin working on the production of an animation, you must deal with a number of issues that comprise the preproduction phase of the project. One of the most critical parts of this phase is the development of a storyboard.

A **storyboard** is a sequence of images and verbal descriptions describing the intended animation. The "board" part of the term refers to the fact that the images are often mounted on a rigid board for presentation purposes. The "story" part of the term refers to the flow of events in the animation. The concept of **story** is more general than simply "narrative." For example, you need not have characters to have a story. A short station-identification animation or an abstract animation of forms swirling about can have a story in the sense that the events progress in a carefully and effectively developed way, with a clear progression of events.

In order to successfully communicate what will happen in an animation, typically a storyboard consists of several components, each of which is designed to convey certain information. The first critical component of a storyboard is the sequence of images, called **panels**, describing the animation. These are arranged in temporal sequence, from the beginning of the animation to its end, and may be produced with a variety of techniques and media, including drawing, painting, or computer graphics. The level of detail and finish in the panels and the actual size of the panels vary depending on the purpose of the storyboard. A **preliminary storyboard** intended to capture a first, fleeting idea may be sketched quickly as a series of small, black-and-white pencil line drawings. At this stage it is preferable not to be too elaborate or detailed. The purpose of a preliminary storyboard is to help generate ideas. Spending too much time creating each panel only serves to slow down the idea-generating process. It is also useful in these preliminary stages to draw each panel on a separate piece of paper. This allows you to physically move them about, altering their sequence and that of the animation's events. This is sometimes called a **paper edit**.

At a later stage you may develop a much more elaborate **presentation storyboard**. Here, the intended audience is usually a client and the purpose is less the generation of ideas than the exposition of a well-developed idea. Contract decisions frequently are based on a presentation storyboard, which is therefore carefully painted or drawn in full color, frequently by a professional storyboard artist. Color plate 17 is a segment of a final presentation storyboard. Its panels were meticulously and beautifully painted in watercolor, each panel measuring about 4 by 5 inches.

The first purpose of storyboard panels is to show the story, or progression of events. You should have enough panels to do this effectively, without leaving gaps in the story's progression, but you do not need to illustrate every movement as if you were making keyframe drawings. In the early stages of a preliminary storyboard, fewer panels may be needed to sketch out the overall progression of events; more are added for presentation purposes. A **production storyboard**, used to guide animators in the actual production of the animation, has even more panels, so that details of each scene will be understood clearly by all working on the production.

In addition to telling the basic story, storyboard panels illustrate the **framing** of each scene—that is, what the camera sees. Framing and camera movement have a tremendous impact on the viewer. Is the camera set low and looking up at the towering monster to convey a sense of its power? Has the camera cut to a close shot of the knife to focus our attention on it? Is the camera dollying into the apartment very slowly to create a sense of ominous foreboding? All these camera issues, which affect both what the viewer knows and how the viewer feels, should be conveyed in the storyboard panels. For this reason, it is also important that panels be drawn at the correct aspect ratio of the final medium. For example, if you will be recording to NTSC video, your panels should have the 4×3 ratio of that format's frames. If your panels are not drawn at the correct aspect ratio, they cannot properly convey the intended framing.

Another aspect of the animation conveyed through the storyboard panels is the **visual style**, or **look**, of the animation. These terms refer to the visual design elements of the animation, which are in turn determined by the goals of the animation. Is it a light cartoon for children? A ribald short for adults? A disturbing emotional treatment of political suppression? The answers to these questions affect the look of each animation's environments, characters, and lighting and should be conveyed through the panels of a well-developed storyboard.

The visual panels of a storyboard, however, are not enough to convey all the information that is needed. A brief **verbal description** of what is happening at that moment in the animation usually adjoins each panel. The text describes the action represented in the panel, paying special attention to aspects of the action that cannot be gleaned from the picture alone. For example, if a panel shows that a character stands up and the accompanying description says, "She slowly stands up," it tells us something we did not know from the static drawing alone.

Verbal descriptions also are critical to describe the animation of the camera. If one panel shows a long shot of a scene and the next shows a close shot of the same scene, we cannot tell what the camera did to get from the first panel to the second panel. Did the camera cut, or did it dolly into the close shot? Or was there a cross-dissolve between the two cameras? Occasionally, graphic icons are used to help convey this information—for example, an arrow to indicate that the camera pans right. Icons can be ambiguous, however, and concise wording, such as "Cut to close shot," clarifies the situation. Notice in color plate 17 that the verbal description under each panel includes a clear description of the camera transition.

The storyboard's verbal descriptions also must address the **soundtrack**, the collection of sounds, music, and dialogue that accompany the animation. The soundtrack has a profound effect on the viewer's reaction. Imagine a simple scene in which a character walks in from screen left, walks across the empty screen, and continues walking off screen right. Now imagine the same animation with three different soundtracks. In the first, there is silence except for the light clicking of the character's shoes as he walks across an invisible marble floor. In the second version of this same animation, the character walks to the accompaniment of blaring rock and roll music. In the third version, the character walks as a heavy, ominous wind blows through invisible trees. Each of these three soundtracks radically changes how viewers respond to the animation. Describing the soundtrack verbally—for example, "Silence except for clicking of his shoes on marble floor"—clarifies the feel and intention of the animation. Refer once again to color plate 17 and notice that each panel description includes notations on the soundtrack.

A final, critical component of a good storyboard is **timing**. How quickly or slowly do things happen? How long does a scene last? How long is that close-up? Timing is best indicated in seconds and, if the animation is long enough, minutes. For example, one standard representation of time is *02:40*, to indicate "two minutes, forty seconds." Animations of scenes less than a minute long typically represent only seconds, either *:05* or *5 sec.* to indicate "five seconds."

For two reasons it is rare for the timing of a storyboard to be indicated in frames. First, the timing indications of most storyboards are approximations. We probably do not know whether an action will require twenty-two frames or twenty-six frames. (An exception to this would be a final, detailed production storyboard in which frame-accurate timing has been developed for each scene. This might be the case if a dialogue soundtrack has already been recorded and the animators are matching to the existing, and precisely timed, soundtrack.) A second reason not to use frames as timing units is that most people have difficulty translating large frame counts into comprehensible time. Just how long is 1,429 frames, anyhow?

Finally, indicating both the timing in seconds for each panel and the cumulative running time of the animation so far makes it much easier for someone looking at the storyboard to understand quickly how long the animation is. If only the timing for each panel is indicated, a reader of the storyboard has to add up the seconds of each panel to understand the running time of a scene or of the whole animation. There are many ways of showing the individual panel and cumulative running time. In color plate 17, the timing of each panel is indicated above the upper left corner of the panel and the cumulative running time is indicated above the upper right.

Sound Design

As suggested in the previous section, the soundtrack of an animation can have a significant impact on the overall effect of the animation. The design of the soundtrack, therefore, is important and should be considered an integral part of the planning of an animation. The full complexity of this process is beyond the scope of this book, but some of the most significant issues are discussed here.

A soundtrack can be thought of as consisting of several possible components, any or all of which may be present in a given animation. **Sound effects** are such sounds as the closing of a door, the rustling of leaves, the barking of a dog, the shattering of glass, and so on. Recall the simple animation of a character walking across the screen described in the previous section. The sound of shoes clicking on a marble floor will create a very different effect than if each footstep is accompanied by the rustle of leaves, and yet another effect if the sound is the clanging of pots and pans. Shoes clicking create a subdued, elegant mood. Leaves rustling create a quiet mood, but suggest a very different physical environment. Pots and pans clanging create a sense of harsh surreality. In planning your animation, you should consider the sound effects of your piece just as seriously and in as much detail as you do the visual actions of the animation. For some animators, in fact, the first ideas for an animation often come in the form of sounds, with the imagery developing out of them. In professional animations, sound effects are considered so important that professional sound designers and sound-effects artists are hired to design and produce them.

The job of one artist, the **foley artist**, is to use various props and gadgets to produce synchronized sound effects in real time while watching the finished animation. For example, if the sound to accompany a character's walk is rustling leaves, the foley artist, will push a hand into a small pile of leaves with each of the character's footsteps. A microphone placed near the leaves records the sounds either onto a separate audio tape or directly onto the soundtrack areas of the animation's videotape. If the animation shows a character opening a door and walking down some steps into the backyard, the foley artist would open and close a door and make the sound of footsteps on wood, perhaps by knocking a shoe against a plank of wood. Since each of these sound effects is done in time with the action of the animation, they are both created and synced in one session.

Dialogue may be another major component of an animation's soundtrack. Like sound effects, human dialogue can be critical and requires careful planning. If dialogue is to be part of an animation, a detailed script is usually written in the storyboard phases of development. **Voice actors** are then hired to record the dialogue before any work on the animation proper begins. It is much easier for an animator to adjust the timing of an animation to match prerecorded dialogue than it is for an actor to adjust the timing of dialogue delivery to match preexisting animation, especially when the spoken dialogue needs to be synchronized with the animated characters' mouth movements, a process called **lip syncing**.

Finally, **music** may be a component of an animation's soundtrack. As with the other soundtrack components, music, if it is to be used at all, should be part of the early planning . Recall the example of the character walking across the screen to the sound of rock and roll music described in the *Storyboarding* section. Now imagine that the music is a very gentle, peaceful classical piece—for example, the beautiful violins of Pachelbel's Canon in D Major. This radically alters the mood of the animation; it may even change the audience's interpretation of the action. If the music is perceived as what is going on inside the head of the character, the two soundtracks portray quite different internal "actions."

Even before specific music is composed or chosen, it is extremely helpful to include notes in the storyboard describing the type and mood of the music. Whether you call for "soft, gentle violins" or "blaring rock and roll" suggests a great deal about the mood of the piece.

Technical Tests

Given their technical complexity, almost all 3D computer animations require testing of the technical feasibility of different aspects of the animation. If something is to move in a certain way, how should it be modeled? Should a character be modeled with rigid body parts and animated with inverse kinematics, or with flexible body parts, animated as a deformable envelope? These sorts of questions must be answered before you begin production to avoid major problems later on.

Sometimes the answers to these questions are obvious, and the more experience you have, the more frequently this is the case. But if you want to know whether something will work, or the best way to make it work, it is important to test *before* you begin production so you do not spend weeks or months on a project only to discover that something will not work technically and you must throw away the work done. This is a frustration and a waste of time; in a commercial production, it can also be a financial disaster.

Even if you do not have to discard your work entirely, belatedly discovered technical problems may oblige you to modify the animation. Reasonable changes are a normal part of the animation process. One of the most valuable skills of the experienced animator is the ability to find "workarounds"—other approaches that convey the original idea but avoid technical problems. But technically motivated changes are only feasible to the extent that they do not alter the look of the animation. Because of this, it is important to test for technical problems early.

In order to be able to do intelligent technical testing, you must first have a clear idea of what the animation will be—that is, you must have a well-developed storyboard. If you have only a vague idea of the animation, you will be unable to do meaningful technical tests. The more specifically you have storyboarded the animation, the better you will be able to foresee areas that present potential technical difficulties.

You should consider all aspects of an animation—modeling, motion, textures, lighting, final rendering issues, and so on—for potential problems. For example, if a model's shape is to be deformed and that model is also to receive a texture map, how will the texture behave as the model's surface undergoes its shape deformation? Will the texture stretch in undesirable ways? Will it appear to slide across the surface? Different texture mapping methods give different results; testing these mapping techniques early can avoid major problems later.

To take another example: imagine the animation of a snakelike creature. Several techniques might be appropriate, including motion path animation, spline deformation, and inverse kinematics. Which one will give the best results? And depending on which you elect to use, what does that require of your model? It is better to know before you build your model than after.

Anti-aliasing is another example that might merit technical testing . Many narrow parallel lines or objects in a scene may present a severe aliasing problem that can only be solved by using an anti-aliasing algorithm that doubles or triples rendering time. If you know this in advance and test for it, you can decide whether to keep the original design and accept the additional rendering time it requires, or to modify the design and avoid the problem and the long rendering time per frame.

You do not have to wait until your final models, animation, or textures are developed before you can do effective testing. If you know, for example, that thin parallel lines cause aliasing problems, you do not need to model an entire brick building with louvered windows to find out if it is going to present aliasing problems. You can do a simulation—perhaps model a sample window using simplified geometry such as scaled cubes to approximate the final geometry of the intended model. You also do not have to have the final brick texture available to approximate its aliasing problems; you can make a simple texture consisting of repeating rectangles and apply that to a flat surface to simulate the wall. Proceeding in this way, you can very quickly—in perhaps half an hour—build a model that simulates the suspect features of your planned animation and discover early in your planning process any areas of potential difficulty.

The more you know about the technical aspects of 3D computer animation, the more effective the testing can be. If you do not know beforehand that thin parallel lines are problematic, you will not know to test for that. One of the advantages of experience is that your technical testing becomes increasingly effective, allowing you more regularly to avoid significant technical problems.

Production Estimates and Schedules

Any animation project benefits from careful production estimating and scheduling. In a commercial environment, these are critical and may spell the difference between profit or loss, between a company's survival or bankruptcy.

When a client approaches a company with a possible project, the company must bid on the job, specifying what it will do, for how much money, in what timeframe. In order to do this, the company must know specifically what the job entails–what the components are, how long each component will take, who will work on it, and so on. The more specific the estimates, the more accurate the bid. And the more accurate the bid, the better the chance the company will make a profit. This is so crucial in the commercial world that many large companies have a permanent full-time staff member whose sole job is to make **production estimates**.

Good planning and scheduling are important even in a personal animation not being done for profit or against a deadline. By realistically estimating what a project will entail in terms of hardware requirements, the animator's time, additional personnel, and so on, you can determine whether the animation is feasible. If production estimates suggest that it will not be feasible as storyboarded, you can modify the storyboard to make the animation realizable.

As a simple example, imagine a story that takes place in a city. If your production estimates reveal that it will take you three hundred hours to model all the buildings, you might elect to model simple boxes and texture-map pictures of buildings onto them, reducing your modeling time drastically. In order to take advantage of the texture-mapping approach, you might also modify the storyboard to eliminate extreme close-ups of the buildings, or limit the close-ups, and therefore your modeling, to only a few buildings.

It should be clear that any effective production estimates or scheduling require a detailed storyboard. You cannot make intelligent estimates about how long something will take unless you know what it is. The more carefully developed your storyboard, the more accurate your production estimates can be.

The first phase of developing production estimates usually is to develop a **list of tasks**. You can organize it in any number of ways, but the goal is to list what needs to be done for the entire animation: modeling, motion tests, texture painting, lighting, rendering tests, final rendering, credits, sound effects, working with a composer to develop original music, and so on. The list of specific tasks varies. One animation may involve a great deal of complex character animation but only very simple modeling for the environment. Another may require sophisticated lighting and subtle camera animation, but no character animation at all.

The list of tasks frequently is broken down by scene. Imagine that Scene 1 involves the camera flying through the city; Scene 2 cuts to a close shot of one of the buildings, with a character who peers through a louvered window and turns to leave, long hair swinging behind. The tasks for Scene 1 are quite different than those for Scene 2. For Scene 1, you will model the buildings as simple boxes and develop—perhaps by photographing actual buildings—detailed texture maps for each building. You will do a motion-path animation for the camera. You will collect the sound for Scene 1 from a sound-effects CD and modify it to produce the whooshing sound of flying.

Scene 2's tasks are quite different. Because the camera is very close to the building, you will model the actual geometry of the building, including a detailed model of the louvered window. You also will model the character. There is no camera animation, but there is a complex bit of character animation. You will use particle systems to model and animate the character's hair and work with a foley artist to create the sound effects of the character moving away from the window and crossing the room. Both Scene 1 and Scene 2 will require time to set up the lighting, do motion and rendering tests, and render final frames.

Proceeding in this way for each scene as well as for any credits or titles, you develop a detailed list of what needs to be done to produce the entire animation.

Next you assign **time estimates** to each task. How long do you expect it to take to model this building, to photograph those buildings, to select and edit the sound effects? Making realistic time estimates requires experience, and even the most experienced professionals must resist the normal human tendency to underestimate the amount of work a task will require. But estimating time is important even when you are just a beginner. One of the most common problems of inexperienced animators is undertaking an animation project that is more ambitious than they can actually realize and being faced with the unpleasant choice of either not finishing the animation or cutting back on it so much that it no longer has the original spirit. You can avoid disappointment if you develop realistic time estimates in the early planning stages. If your estimates indicate that the project is too ambitious, you can modify the storyboard to reduce the demands of the animation, while still retaining its core idea and spirit. Frequently this editing results in a *better* storyboard. By forcing yourself to economize, you often find more concise and effective ways to tell the same story.

In a commercial environment, good time estimates are, of course, essential: time translates directly into money. The time an animator spends on a given scene, the time a machine is devoted to rendering frames, the time the director spends consulting with the composer—all must be calculated into the budget and paid for if the production company is to survive.

Once a thorough list of tasks and time estimates has been developed, the next step is to develop a **production schedule**. The organization and level of detail in a schedule varies depending on the type of animation and the size of the company (if one is involved), but the purpose of a schedule is always to help you organize your project in such a way that it can be successfully completed. A weekly schedule shows what should be accomplished by whom within each week of the production. A daily schedule is common in some commercial situations; with an extremely short timetable, companies sometimes actually develop hourly schedules specifying that, for example, by 11 A.M. Tuesday the lighting for Scene 4 should be set up.

In a personal animation, schedules normally need not be nearly so rigid. Still, some schedule is extremely useful because it allows you to plan the work flow of your project. This may not be obvious. For example, it is rarely best to proceed through a production in strict sequence from Scene 1 to Scene 2 to Scene 3 and so on. On the contrary, it is frequently more effective to work nonsequentially. To use the example of the city and the character at the window again, imagine that Scene 3 consists of a slow pan of the camera up the length of one building. In this case, you might plan to work on Scene 3 first. Since the camera animation of the scene is very simple, you could quickly get to the point where it is ready for final rendering, so you could have one machine rendering final frames for that scene while you are working on the more time-consuming Scene 1 and Scene 2.

It is also not advisable to work through the production of an animation in the seemingly logical order suggested by "modeling, rendering, animation" (or, if your logic so dictates, "modeling, animation, rendering"). In fact, following this progression is one of most common mistakes of inexperienced animators, and can be disastrous. Modeling, rendering, and animation are interdependent. The way an object is to be rendered may affect the way it should be animated; the way it will be animated may affect the way it should be modeled, and so on.

In scheduling, also keep in mind the undeniable facts of human psychology. Sometimes it is most productive to change tasks deliberately, just to avoid boredom and reinvigorate yourself. Spending a month on textures may actually decrease efficiency. The natural need for variety applies in both small-scale and large production environments. Although large companies commonly hire people to do specific tasks—for example, modeling or lighting—most companies make an effort to give each employee a variety of tasks, even if that variety is within the individual's area of specialization. Small companies often deliberately avoid the categorization of assignments, giving each artist on staff a chance to work on all aspects of an animation—for example, to be responsible for an entire scene.

However it is implemented, a good production schedule is invaluable both for the individual animator working on a small personal animation and for the large production company with scores of employees working on big-budget projects.

Top-down Animation

As you begin work on each scene of an animation, consider which of two broad approaches to the animation process you might take. In traditional **straight-ahead animation**, you define keyframes in order, from first to last, defining each keyframe in full detail as you go. For example, if the animation consists of a character walking across a room, looking about and scratching himself as he walks, you would begin by fully defining keyframe 1, positioning the legs, feet, arms, head, etc. Once the pose for keyframe 1 is satisfactory, you would move on to the next keyframe, which might occur at frame 12. At this second keyframe, you again completely define the pose, incorporating into it any walking, looking about, or scratching actions. When the second keyframe is complete, you move on to the next keyframe, and then the next, and so on.

Straight-ahead animation can be very effective and is not uncommon in traditional, hand-drawn animation. Among its drawbacks, however, is that the animator requires a great deal of skill and experience to set up each keyframe pose exactly as it should look in its final form, and must also have an extremely good sense of timing to know just when each keyframe should occur.

In **top-down animation**, in contrast, the animator does not work strictly sequentially, but begins by roughing out the animation's major actions, filling in progressively more detailed actions with successive revisions of the animation. Using this approach for the same animation described above, you might develop a walk cycle for the character—that is, a repeating walking-in-place stride. Then you might translate the character across the room; as a result, the character's feet slide over the floor. Next you might adjust the walk cycle of the character to ensure that the feet do not slide over the floor or go through it. With the character's walking now reasonably good, you might begin working on the secondary actions, starting with the looking-around motion and then adding the scratching motions. Once all these are animated, you might go back and fine-tune the walk animation, which now needs slight adjustment to take into account the scratching motions of the character's arm.

Notice that you are working from the grosser, more major motions to the finer, more detailed motions. Hence the name "top-down": you begin at the top and you work your way down to the details.

The advantages of top-down animation can be significant. Permitting you to gradually construct the animation, it avoids the necessity of getting it just right the first time. Top-down animation also takes advantage of the technology of computer animation. With traditional animation techniques such as cel animation or puppet animation, you cannot "construct" an animation as just described. You cannot gradually build up the animation of a wooden or clay puppet; you must pose it and shoot your frame straight-ahead. With hand-drawn animation you can approximate the top-down approach by doing preliminary drawings, or **pencil tests**, but you cannot add more and more layers of refinement to the drawing gradually; at some point you have to do your final drawing.

Computer animation is quite different. Because all the information you are building up can overwrite previous information, and because all of it can also be saved for later retrieval if necessary, you can add more and more layers of detail to your animation gradually. If something you do does not look right, you can delete it, or retrieve the previous version. If it does look right, you save it, adding to the definition of the keyframes, and moving on to the next level of detail. Top-down animation gives you a great deal of flexibility and is much more commonly used in 3D computer animation than straight-ahead animation.

Conclusion

In the course of this book you have learned the basic principles and techniques of 3D computer animation. To begin with, since in any 3D animation there must be objects to animate, you saw all the major approaches to "building"—that is, modeling the shape of—an object. You also examined the issues involved in making a picture, or rendering, of a three-dimensional scene: the definition of the surface properties of an object, the lighting, the use of the camera. You then investigated at length the major principles and techniques involved in actually making an object move—that is, animating it—within the computer, including techniques commonly found in all 3D computer animation software packages and more advanced techniques currently found only in the more sophisticated software packages. Finally, you considered the compositing techniques that yield special effects and the issues involved in recording animation to both film and video.

You now should be prepared to apply the knowledge you have gained, perhaps pursuing animation as a form of entertainment or as a branch of the fine arts, or perhaps employing it in any one of a multitude of fields, such as television-commercial graphics or the feature-film market. Industrial designers, architects, interior designers, and sculptors are among those professionals who have greatly enhanced their work through the simulation capabilities of three-dimensional computer animation . Biologists, chemists, and medical professionals have found 3D computer animation useful as a means of previewing a situation or of visualizing a scientific model.

You can expect that the applications, and with them the power of computer animation will continue to expand very rapidly. The capabilities of 3D computer graphics are vastly more sophisticated today than they were even as short a time as five years ago. This evolution is partly due to the tremendous growth in the speed and memory capacities of computer hardware, and partly to a delightful dragon-biting-its-tail phenomenon involving the capabilities of the technology and money. As the technology has become more useful to more professionals, they and the institutions they are part of have become more willing to invest in the hardware and software of 3D computer animation. As more money has been invested, more research has been possible. With increased research have come more improvements in the capabilities, and these in turn have attracted more investment, and so on.

Techniques, for example, that at this writing are described in chapter 4, "Advanced Animation Techniques," will become standard. As they do, new techniques currently only incubating in research laboratories and hardly conceivable now will replace them. At the same time, the hardware that underlies all of this technology will continue to develop—faster than you can imagine, if the past is any guide. Approaches and techniques that researchers cannot even dream of attempting to implement now, simply because they are physically impossible given the current hardware, will be possible within a few years. And all of this development will, as it has in the past, sift down and (sooner rather than later) become part of the standard, off-the-shelf 3D computer animation packages that you or I or your company or my company can buy.

It is a truly exciting time to be involved in three-dimensional computer animation.

Index